Contemporary Rhetorical Criticism

Contemporary Rhetorical Criticism

Sarah Kornfield
Hope College

Strata Publishing, Inc.
State College, Pennsylvania

9 8 7 6 5 4 3 2 1

Contemporary Rhetorical Criticism

Published by:
Strata Publishing, Inc.
P.O. Box 1303
State College, PA 16804
USA
1-814-234-8545
http://www.stratapub.com

Photo on front cover and on pages iii, 1, 43, 133, 189, and 261: Cracked concrete vintage brick wall background by iStock.com/Modify260.

Credits and acknowledgments appear on pages 283–284 and on this page by reference.

ISBN (13): 978-1-891136-44-3

To Matt Roberts,

my partner in all ways, always

with

my parents, sister,

and sons

Brief Contents

Contents

Preface

Contemporary Rhetorical Criticism invites students into the art of rhetorical criticism by showcasing its social and practical value. For my own courses in rhetorical analysis, I wanted a book that would not only show students *how* to use critical methods and approaches, but also *why* they would want to use rhetorical criticism—a book that demonstrates how rhetorical criticism helps students understand, navigate, and improve social and public life. Moreover, I wanted a book that would help them choose their critical methods and approaches, guide them in their use, and help them resist cookie-cutter analyses. Through my conversations with colleagues, I discovered that other people teaching rhetorical criticism had similar needs.

The book is organized around major critical methods and approaches, both traditional and contemporary, and encourages students to choose and combine them, as needed, according to their research questions and their texts. After the introductory chapters, which provide a framework for engaging in rhetorical criticism, each chapter includes a section on "Choosing This Method," followed by a section on the "Strengths and Weaknesses" of that approach. These sections guide students in selecting approaches that are appropriate for particular texts.

To illustrate how rhetorical criticism can help students understand their own lives and the rhetoric they encounter, *Contemporary Rhetorical Criticism* incorporates a wide array of examples drawn from politics, popular culture, and media. Longer research examples—summaries of published scholarship from a diverse array of scholars—show how critics use and combine rhetorical approaches in order to explicate their texts and explore a vast array of political and social concerns.

Contemporary Rhetorical Criticism is intended for courses that lead students into the critical analysis of public discourse. I use it in a rhetorical criticism course titled "Rhetoric & Public Culture." Colleagues who reviewed the manuscript in progress also said they would find the book useful in courses that study rhetorical analysis, or that analyze public and popular culture. To meet my own and others' teaching needs for such courses, the book attempts to (1) introduce students to the theoretical underpinnings of rhetorical criticism; (2) enable students to craft their own rhetorical analyses; and (3) help students grasp the social and practical utility of rhetorical criticism.

Ultimately, *Contemporary Rhetorical Criticism* is designed to show students that rhetorical criticism is fascinating, refreshing, and intellectually stimulating. Accordingly, I have attempted to write in a clear and lively prose and to choose examples that would resonate with students' own interests and lived experiences. It is my hope that this book will be a valuable resource for students and teachers of rhetorical analysis.

FEATURES OF THE BOOK

- *Organized around critical methods and approaches,* the book explores the principles and uses of traditional methods as well as very recent critical concepts.
- *Sections on "choosing this method" and "strengths and weaknesses of this approach"* help students understand the distinctions among critical approaches, select, and, as appropriate, interweave methods in order to best explicate their texts.
- *Guidelines for approaching critical analysis* (Chapters 1 and 2) and *writing a critical essay* (Appendices A and B) guide students in exploring their texts and writing their own essays. Using examples from significant scholarship, the book shows students how to build strong rhetorical arguments.
- *Research examples* explore selected works from the literature, translating them so they are accessible for undergraduate students and pointing out how scholars have used (and sometimes combined) methods to reveal the workings of their texts.
- *Examples from a wide range of scholarship, contexts, and topics,* from historical to very current rhetoric, were chosen for their clarity and their ability to connect with students' own lives. I have also attempted to showcase a diverse array of scholars and scholarship, reflecting critical engagement with numerous public issues and controversies.
- *Discussion questions* at the end of each chapter invite students into thoughtful explorations of key concepts.

ORGANIZATION

Contemporary Rhetorical Criticism consists of eleven chapters organized into four parts, plus two appendices. The first two chapters introduce rhetorical concepts and criticism. Each subsequent chapter begins with a theoretical framework, moves into a "how-to" section, provides two or three research examples, explains the strengths and weaknesses of that critical approach, and concludes with a discussion of how a student can discern whether to use that method for a particular rhetorical analysis.

Part I, "Introduction," provides a framework for understanding the goals and practices of rhetorical criticism.

Chapter 1, "Introduction to Rhetorical Criticism," provides foundational perspectives on what rhetoric is and why critics analyze it. Defining rhetoric as the arts of address, this chapter explains the concepts of symbols, meaning, and social construction, and ultimately argues that rhetorical criticism is fundamentally concerned with insight, judgment, and ethics.

Chapter 2, "Rhetorical Analysis and Critical Essays," explains how students can practice rhetorical criticism. This chapter introduces the key tenets of close textual analysis and Lloyd Bitzer's rhetorical situation. It then provides detailed explanations of how students can organize and craft their own critical essays.

Part II, "Orienting Methods," includes four chapters, each focusing on a traditional rhetorical method that elevates a single aspect of a text's symbolic form as the entry point for assessing the entirety of that text. These chapters provide a framework for students as they learn these foundational methods of rhetorical criticism and see the connections and fault lines that run among them.

Chapter 3, "Narrative Criticism," is grounded in Walter Fisher's theory of narrative reasoning. It explores the concepts of narrative probability, narrative fidelity, cultural archetypes, myths, and narrative transportation. It also demonstrates how to identify and analyze a narrative's story and discourse and assess their role in storytelling.

Chapter 4, "Dramatistic Criticism," introduces Kenneth Burke's theory of dramatism, exploring the concepts of terministic screens, worldviews, symbolic action, and motives. The main focus is on pentadic analysis, but the chapter also introduces the guilt, purification, and redemption cycle.

Chapter 5, "Genre Criticism," builds on Carolyn Miller's definition of genres as fusions of formal and substantive elements that accomplish specific symbolic actions, then helps students understand that genres are constructed through textual features, audience practices, and industry norms. It guides students through the process of choosing generically representative texts, analyzing the genre of a text in relation to its context(s), and assessing the symbolic action.

Chapter 6, "Metaphor Criticism," is grounded in I. A. Richards's conceptualization of tenors and vehicles. It goes on to explore "dead," "entrenched," and "novel" metaphors, and, through a sequence of principles and interpretive questions, explains how to use metaphor criticism.

Part III, "Ideological Critique," contains two chapters that demonstrate how all rhetorical criticism is ideologically engaged, and yet how ideological criticism is distinct from more traditional methods.

Chapter 7, "Ideological Criticism," is grounded in Gramsci's theory of hegemony and explores the concepts of dominant ideologies, the second persona, and ideographs. This chapter explains how to engage in ideological criticism through an exploration of the stylistic features, power hierarchies, and ideographs of a text.

Chapter 8, "Feminist Criticism," provides a specific example of ideological critique. It introduces students to feminist theories, demonstrates how students can participate in feminist ideological critique, and discusses the types of questions feminist critics typically ask.

Part IV, "Rethinking Rhetorical Texts," contains three chapters on recent approaches to criticism. It is intended to help students rethink what counts as a rhetorical text and how critics might analyze that text.

Chapter 9, "Audience Rhetoric," explores audience-generated rhetoric as a text and the unique aspects of analyzing it. Drawing on media and cultural theory, this chapter discusses ways to gather audience rhetoric—including rhetorical fieldwork—and to analyze audience rhetoric within its context.

Chapter 10, "Visual Rhetoric," connects visuality to its ancient conceptualizations and then draws students into a present-day understanding—including visual metaphors, visual narratives, and visual ideographs. The chapter frames interpretive questions that help students explore how visual rhetoric functions in its interaction with the audience and the cultural context.

Chapter 11, "Material Rhetoric," explores how materiality itself can function rhetorically—for instance, through the rhetoric of architecture, memorials, works of art, and corporeality. This chapter helps students make sense of spaces, places, and the things within them. It concludes with a set of interpretive questions that help students assess material rhetoric.

Two Appendices take students through the process of writing a rhetorical essay. Appendix A, "Writing a Critical Essay," focuses on articulating the argument. It outlines the structure of a critical essay, including the requirements of evidence, thesis statements, and the literature review. Appendix B, "Analyzing a Single Text or Multiple Texts," guides students in understanding the differences between analyzing a single (seemingly) discrete text and analyzing multiple texts. The second part of the appendix is intended to help students avoid cherry-picking evidence in analyses of single or multiple texts.

ACKNOWLEDGMENTS

This book has been brewing for some time; as such, many people have played a role in bringing it to fruition. I am grateful for their advice and support and would like to take this opportunity to acknowledge their help and thank them.

I teach a course in rhetorical criticism almost every semester. This has provided me with the opportunity to test examples and explanations, and solicit the reactions of students on a continuous basis. I would like to thank the students of Rhetoric & Public Culture at Hope College, whose partnership in learning has improved the quality of this book.

As this book took shape, it did so within a rhetorical community and has benefited in every way from the thoughtful recommendations made by colleagues from a number of colleges and universities across the country. While I received their advice anonymously, I am extremely grateful for the time, effort, and wisdom they contributed to this project and would like to express that gratitude. My thanks to Meredith M. Bagley, University of Alabama; Jeffrey A. Bennett, Vanderbilt University; Lawrance Bernabo, University of Minnesota Duluth; Jason Edward Black, University of North Carolina at Charlotte; Kathryn Cady, Northern Illinois University; Dana L. Cloud, independent scholar; Pamela Conners, Gustavus Adolphus College; Jason Del Gandio, Temple University; George Dionisopolous, School of Communication, San Diego State University; John Dowd, Bowling Green State University; Tasha N. Dubriwny, Texas A&M University; Daniel Grano, University of North Carolina at Charlotte; Andrew Hansen, Trinity University; Stephanie L. Hartzell, California State University, Long Beach; Rebecca A. Kuehl, South Dakota State University; Ron Lee, University of Nebraska–Lincoln; Nancy J. Legge, Idaho State University; Peter Marston, California State University, Northridge; Joan Faber McAlister, Drake University; Angela M. McGowan-Kirsch, The State University of New York Fredonia; Martin J. Medhurst, Baylor University; Charles E. Morris III, Syracuse University; Hillary Palmer, University of Georgia; Jay Self, Truman State University; and Anne Marie Todd, San José State University. Additionally, early in this project, I sought the advice of Rosa A. Eberly (Pennsylvania State University), Stephen H. Browne (Pennsylvania State University), Theon Hill (Wheaton College), and Mark Hlavacik (University of

North Texas); thank you for your advice, support and friendship. And an endless thank you to Kristin Mathe Coletta (Pennsylvania State University), whose friendship has shaped my life, research, and pedagogy in countless ways.

The Hope College Communication Department has fully supported this project, providing material support in addition to my colleagues' boundless collegiality. Moreover, the Division of Social Sciences at Hope College supported this work, as did Hope College's Jacob E. Nyenhuis Faculty Development grant program. I would like to express my gratitude to my colleagues, Scott VanderStoep; Isolde Anderson; Dawn DeWitt-Brinks; Jayson Dibble; Marissa Doshi; Choonghee Han; Lauren Hearit; Deirdre Johnston; Rob Pocock; and Linda Koetje.

A special thanks goes to my retired colleague Jim Herrick (Guy Vander Jagt Professor of Communication, Hope College), who first recommended that I write this book—and then recommended it again after I dismissed the idea the first time. Moreover, it was Jim Herrick who recommended I work with Strata Publishing; this was extraordinarily good advice. Which brings me to my thanks for Kathleen Domenig of Strata Publishing. Kathleen Domenig's thoughtful attention to this project has been instrumental in its development, and her coaching and literary jokes have made my work all the more possible and enjoyable.

Finally, my thanks to my beloved spouse, Matt Roberts—a software engineer who believes in the importance of rhetorical criticism enough to (1) listen while I work through examples and distill theories, (2) gamefully rearrange schedules when I'm in the zone, and (3) prioritize this work so it met its deadlines. Likewise, my thanks to my sons, Jacob and Geoffrey whose boundless enthusiasm that I was writing a book has meant the world to me.

PART I
Introduction

Chapter 1

Introduction to Rhetorical Criticism

Silent women stand outside the Capitol Building in Washington, DC. They wear crimson robes and white bonnets. With bowed heads, they carry signs protesting "gender discrimination and the infringement of reproductive and civil rights."[1] These protesters are part of a "handmaids' protest": their outfits, posture, and silence were inspired by Margaret Atwood's 1985 novel *The Handmaid's Tale,* which Hulu released as a streaming series in 2017. *The Handmaid's Tale* is set in a dystopian future in which a religious, authoritarian government has stripped most women of their rights, treating them as reproductive slaves who are forced, among other things, to wear red robes and white bonnets. In the wake of Hulu's retelling of the story, women's rights activists across the United States used this imagery (the red robes and white bonnets) in their protests. "Handmaids' protests" have occurred outside the United States Capitol Building and in several states, including Ohio, New Hampshire, Texas, Missouri, and New York.[2] Heather Busby, an activist who helped organize a protest in Texas, said the robes were "very eye-catching" and drew attention to the ways the reproductive policies that the Texas State Legislature was considering affected women's rights.[3]

Indeed, "handmaids' protests" are often highly visible yet eerily silent. In the story, the handmaids are slaves who cannot voice their own rights, but are required to listen to government officials. Explaining how protesters understood their own silence, Elena Lipsiea (who protested in Washington, DC) stated that it represents the way the government fails to listen to their concerns when they speak or protest in other ways.[4] Moreover, by protesting silently, these activists can remain present during legislative proceedings from which more vocal protesters might be ejected for being disruptive.

Their silence, however, allows state and federal legislators to ignore them. Elaina Ramsey (who protested during a hearing at the Statehouse in Columbus, Ohio) noted that the protesters "were not challenged or asked to leave," and that she felt invisible to the legislators, who continued with the proceedings as if the protest was not occurring.[5] Reminiscent of the ways government officials made decisions about handmaids' silent bodies in *The Handmaid's Tale,* these protesters experienced their own government making decisions regarding their bodies.

Margaret Atwood's dystopian novel, Hulu's rendition of it, the reproductive policies under debate in state and federal legislatures, and the protesters' visually striking but silent demonstrations are all examples of rhetoric. There are many ways to define rhetoric. Indeed, ever since ancient Athenians such as Isocrates, Plato, and Aristotle began keeping records of the ways they thought about rhetoric, scholars have differed in their specific definitions of rhetoric. For our purposes, however, let us think about **rhetoric** as rhetorical critic Stephen Howard Browne described it: as *the "arts of address."*[6] The utility of this definition hinges on our understanding of "arts" and "address."

Defining rhetoric as the *arts* of address draws attention to the multiple ways rhetoric is crafted—to the techniques and sometimes even genius demonstrated in a rhetorical act. Margaret Atwood's novel is indisputably crafted, or artful: it is meticulously organized, its words well chosen, its style compelling. Similarly—but in an entirely different form—the protesters' appearance is artful: their visually striking robes and staged demonstrations conceptually link current legislation to a dystopian fictional government that sexually enslaves women.

Defining rhetoric as the arts of *address* draws attention to the way rhetoric functions in society. Rhetoric is active; it engages or addresses an audience. The word "address" is often used in sentences such as "We need to address that problem" or "I addressed the audience, saying . . . ." When we address a problem, we try to change the situation for the better. When we address an audience, we try to change the audience as well—sometimes simply by stating information that audience members need, at other times by persuading them to a new idea.

Moreover, rhetoric creates or calls its audience into being by addressing people. For instance, before Hulu released its streaming version of *The Handmaid's Tale,* there was no audience for this series. No one had seen it. If *The Handmaid's Tale* had not streamed on Hulu, there would be no community of people who had been addressed by this series. Ultimately, describing rhetoric as the art of address focuses our attention not only on the techniques of how a message is constructed and presented, but also on how that message acts in society—especially as it draws an audience into being.

Rhetoric is created by a **rhetor,** *the person, group of people, or organization that creates and presents a rhetorical address.* For example, the person who wrote and delivered a speech would be the rhetor of that speech. A television episode usually has a group of people who form the rhetor for that episode: the creator, executive producer, writers, directors, and actors. An organization or institution can be understood as the rhetor of its official website. Rhetors create rhetoric. **Rhetoricians,** meanwhile, are *people who study the theories of rhetoric, working to understand the effectiveness and ethics of how humans communicate.*

Rhetoric is commonplace. We are artfully addressed all day long by newspapers, politicians, films, advertisements, sermons, music, television series, billboards, tweets, and so on. This book is about learning to make sense of the rhetoric that surrounds us and calls us into being as part of one audience community after another. This process of *making sense of rhetoric* is formally known as **rhetorical criticism.** This first chapter will present some foundational ideas about rhetoric, key ways in which rhetorical critics think about rhetorical criticism, and explanations about why rhetorical criticism is useful and important in society. It closes with an explanation about how this book is written and organized. The chapters that follow offer guidelines for how you might work to understand the artful techniques of rhetoric, its active role in society, and the ethics involved in how it calls its audience into being and how it seeks to change that audience.

UNDERSTANDING RHETORIC

When thinking about rhetoric as the arts of address, rhetorical theorists point out that these arts are often symbolic. A **symbol** is *something (such as a word, sound, or image) that represents another thing, idea, or action.* For example, the word "tree" is a symbol that represents a real tree. Similarly, the handmaid protesters' crimson robes are symbols that represent a draconian relationship between the government and women's bodies.

The relationship between a symbol and the thing it represents is arbitrary. There is nothing natural or necessary about the letters "t-r-e-e" that connect it to an actual tree. There is nothing natural or necessary about the color red or the design of the robes that connects the handmaids' outfits to the idea of a government that enslaves women. Rather, a symbol is connected to the meaning it represents through people's repeated usage: by repeatedly using the letters "t-r-e-e" to refer to an actual tree (or red robes and a white bonnet to refer to an authoritarian government that does not respect women's sovereignty over their own bodies), a culture constructs the connections between symbols and their designated meanings.

Many symbols represent tangible things (such as trees, cows, tables, and teacups). Other symbols, however, represent constructed realities. **Constructed realities** are *the ways of life that humans take for granted as the natural order, even though humans originally constructed them through symbols.* For example, nation states (such as the United States of America, Ghana, Germany, and Thailand) are real. These countries exist, and their rules, regulations, and borders fundamentally affect the lives of their citizens and other residents. Yet these nation states are also constructed from symbols. They were invented by humans. Their borders, citizens' rights, and immigration policies change regularly. There is nothing inherently different about the soil one inch south of the border between the United States and Canada and the soil one inch north of the border. But on the basis of which inch of soil one is born on, one is subject to entirely different sets of rights, responsibilities, taxes, and benefits. The difference lies not in the soil itself, but in the symbolic understanding of that soil: everyone agrees that the southern inch is part of the United States and the northern inch is part of Canada.

To some extent, constructed realities are fairly similar to actual buildings: both are constructed by humans; both have histories to their constructions; both serve specific purposes; and both can be changed through human effort. The difference is that constructed realities are built out of symbols, not bricks and mortar. Humans use symbols such as maps, birth certificates, social security numbers, the bald eagle, the flag, the words "America" and "United States of America," the Statue of Liberty, Uncle Sam, the national anthem, the White House, and US passports to construct and represent the country of the United States and its citizens.

Ultimately, rhetoric is far more than any single speech, protest, film, novel, or political policy. Because rhetoric is the arts of address (and because the arts are symbolic and the address is active), it is about **symbolic action,** *the way symbols act in our world.* Rhetorical theorist Jeremy Engels offers two analogies that help clarify this concept.

First, Engels describes rhetoric as "the scaffolding of our social world."[7] He likens rhetoric—symbols in action—to the inner support beams of a building. It is rhetoric that constructs our realities, that creates the support systems through which we find firm foundations to go blithely about our lives with the confidence that the floors will hold our weight. We go to school, go to work, make friends, relate to family members, fall in love, relax with entertainment, vote in democratic countries, and so on, yet all of this is constructed through rhetoric.

Take the family, for example. In the United States, the family is symbolically represented (through entertainment and through legal policies) as a unit consisting only of adult parents and their biological or adopted children. For instance, a person cannot take a child to see a pediatrician unless the child is legally defined as her/his child or the person has a legal waiver—even if s/he alone houses, raises, loves, feeds, clothes, and parents that child. Similarly, children expect to move out of their parents' houses and form their own parent/child families away from their parents and siblings.

There are other ways to experience family relationships, however. We could define "family" on the basis of how people interact with each other rather than who was born to whom. We could gather large extended families under one roof rather than multiplying the roofs and separating adult siblings from each other and grandparents from grandchildren. To say that rhetoric is the "scaffolding of our social world" is to point out that it is the symbolic understanding of families (legal definitions, representations in entertainment, and so on) in the United States that leads to houses with floor plans designed for two adults and two children, rather than for extended family units. Floor plans could easily change (a builder could simply build a different type of house) but as long as people in the United States symbolically represent families as nuclear units, they will keep building "single-dwelling" homes.

Engels's second analogy likens rhetoric to grammar and the social world to language. He writes that rhetoric is "nothing less than the grammar of social life."[8] Grammar is a set of rules for how words are arranged in a sentence. For example, in English, nouns typically go before verbs. The English sentence "Sarah runs to the store" follows grammatical norms, but the sentence "Runs to the store, Sarah did" does not. Every language and dialect has its own grammar, but grammar—as a system—suggests that there are correct ways to use a language, and thus there are also incorrect ways. Although one can use words out of order (as Yoda famously does in the *Star Wars* franchise), such usage is noted as unusual at best and, at worst, wrong, ignorant, uneducated, uncouth, or uncivilized. Engels's analogy focuses our attention on the way rhetoric (the arts of address) shape the way humans interact with each other. Just as grammar tells us which words go in which order, so too rhetoric tells humans how to relate to one another.

For example, during a political campaign season in the United States, advertisements for state legislators and governors flood TV screens and social media. These advertisements often describe a candidate's values or character. In doing so, they invite the audience to imagine themselves as a specific type of person—the type of person who supports those values. Rhetorical theorist Kenneth Burke focuses on this function of rhetoric, writing about how "communication makes us a part" of a community as we identify with certain groups and how our identification with those groups then shapes our actions.[9] Just as grammar tells us how to arrange words into a sentence, rhetoric tells us how to arrange ourselves into communities—and tells us what those communities stand for and what type of actions they engage in. Ultimately, as rhetoric calls audiences into being, it unites some people and divides others. Engels concludes that it is through the arts of address that we "draw close" to some people, "others we ignore" or "push far away." Some we refuse to even "recognize as human."[10]

RHETORICAL TEXTS

Rhetorical critics use the word **text** to refer to *a symbolic form that a critic is studying.*[11] Defining texts as symbolic forms emphasizes that texts are made up of symbols. Every text, whether it is a film, music video, website, newspaper article, or political speech, is composed of symbols. Critics can study one text at a time or several related texts together. For example, a critic might take, as a text, a president's inaugural speech, an award-winning film, a graphic novel, an episode of a television series, a whole television series, or the top five best-selling political memoirs.

Although the word "rhetoric" is commonly associated with words and the word "text" is quite closely associated with words in everyday speech in the United States, rhetoricians understand "rhetoric" and "texts" to be far more inclusive categories. For rhetoricians, "rhetoric" and "texts" are not limited to words or language use. Indeed, rhetorical critics study a wide variety of symbolic forms—whether or not they feature words.

Rhetorical critics Martin J. Medhurst and Thomas W. Benson explain that a text is a symbolic form whose "structure and context lead the audience to think, feel, believe, understand or act in an arguably predictable way."[12] Consider a television sitcom. Sitcoms have a symbolic form: they have a particular style of lighting and cinematography; they often use familiar studio layouts for their main locations (such as living room configurations); they often use laugh tracks and thus sound the same; usually, each episode tells one central story and then mixes in two other minor plotlines; and they feature familiar storylines of family drama, friendship, or humorous workplace problems. In addition, sitcoms exist in particular contexts. Whether they air on television, stream online, or play on DVDs or Blu-ray players, they are housed within the context of entertainment. The combination of the symbolic form and the entertainment context creates predictable results: audience members relax, laugh, and (however briefly) ignore the pressing concerns or boredom of their current circumstances. In studying a particular text, a rhetorical critic investigates how its structure and context lead to predictable audience responses.

Rhetorical critics usually choose their texts from **public discourse,** such as speeches, laws, policies, judicial rulings and dissents, news editorial cartoons, tweets, museums, historical monuments, films, television series, and music. **Public** means *widely accessible within a culture.* **Discourse** is *communication that is symbolic or uses symbols.* Public discourse tends to be **political,** or *pertaining to the way power is achieved and used in society.*[13] Although people often think of "politics" as synonymous with "voters, parties, elections, public policy, and the processes of contestation and representation," it encompasses far more.[14] Indeed, government is only one of many ways in which power is achieved and used in society.

Some types of public discourse are overt in their political ramifications. When analyzing such a text, it is fairly clear how it intersects with issues that matter to people in a community. For instance, investigative news reportage can uncover misuses of tax dollars, affecting not only how future funds are spent but also which politicians and administrators are removed from office. In so doing, it clearly engages in politics as it addresses the use (and abuse) of power.

Other types of public discourse are less overt in their politics. Consider, for example, a comedy special on Netflix. At first glance, jokes might appear to have little to do with politics, but many jokes are fundamentally concerned with politics. Because comedians and audiences must share values and assumptions to find a joke funny, jokes make apparent and reinforce a culture's assumptions of what (or who) is right, good, trivial, and so on. For example, when Louis C. K. returned to the stage after his #MeToo hiatus, following his admission to "sexually harassing five women," he included "a joke about the phrase 'clean as a whistle,' which built up to a joke about how rape whistles are not clean."[15] To joke about rape whistles—or laugh at a rape joke—is to consider the idea of sexual violence funny. This idea represents a political assumption: it offers sexual predators a free pass by reimagining their violence as humor and further delegitimates victims' experiences by reimagining their trauma as funny.

Many types of public discourse are not only political in their own right, they are embedded in industries that are also political. For example, cultural theorists Stuart Hall and Paddy Whannel discuss the political nature of teenage pop music, such as Taylor Swift's "Lovers" and Harry Styles' "Sign of the Times." This music is "part of a culture of leisure"; teenagers generally engage with pop music as a leisure or entertainment activity, rather than for work, school, or civic activism.[16] Yet Hall and Whannel argue that the music is nonetheless engaged in relations of power. For instance, they note that the lyrics relentlessly deal with love (falling in love, being in love, and falling out of love) and angsty feelings of isolation. They argue that this music mirrors teenagers' "attitudes and sentiments," thereby providing an expressive field and set of symbols through which these attitudes can be projected."[17] That is, teenagers experience feelings of love and isolation, and the music offers them not only a reflection of themselves but also a way to express themselves. It offers not just lyrics, but whole styles—ways to dress and talk, as well as repeated metaphors through which to describe life experiences—for expressing various emotions and identities. Thus, "the authentic and the manufactured" become intertwined.[18] To express love or isolation in a way that makes sense and seems authentic to other teenagers, a teenager must use a manufactured, commodified style.[19]

We can see the political connections. Pop music is embedded in the music industry and thrives through the commercialization of particular styles and the commodification of pop stars themselves. This manufactured, commercialized pop music can achieve power over how teenagers "authentically" express themselves—shaping how they think of themselves and others, how they interact with others, and how they spend their money (for example, by purchasing items to complete a particular look). Moreover, teenagers who master a particular style can rise to power within a social group if others see them as authentic embodiments of that social group's way of life. Just as teenagers often regard pop stars as role models—as idealized, successful, glamorized versions of themselves—teens who fully embody a particular style can function as role models within their social groups.

Critics analyze a wide variety of texts. One critic might analyze the news reportage of a natural disaster, noting how it framed the disaster and influenced public understandings of and attitudes toward the disaster—which in turn affect how tax dollars are allocated to rescue and rebuilding efforts, whether relief concerts and fundraising events are organized, whether service trips are planned, whether funds are donated, and how relocated people are received into their new communities. Another critic might analyze *Nanette,* the Netflix comedy special by Hannah Gadsby, noting how it invites audiences to understand sexism, pain, and human dignity. Still others might analyze a campaign speech, a documentary film, a public protest, a museum exhibition, the portraits in the Smithsonian's National Portrait Gallery, a horror film, a novel, or an advertisement.

RHETORIC: MEANING AND DOING

Rhetorical texts are symbolic forms within particular contexts that result in predictable responses, yet they themselves are without meaning. Discussing one type of symbol—words—rhetorical theorist I. A. Richards typically argued that "words work because people actively supply prior experience and construct meaning from linguistic context; in short, people, rather than words, mean."[20] Essentially, Richards was pointing out the arbitrary nature of words and symbols: symbols have no inherent meaning. Texts—symbolic forms—also have no inherent meaning. Rather, people interact with the symbols and, by supplying their prior knowledge and assessing the context, derive meaning.

Here, currency serves as a useful analogy. The paper rectangles and metal discs in our wallets are without meaning. Meaning resides in the minds of people who agree that particular paper rectangles and metal discs will have particular amounts of purchasing power. Or consider how you might swipe a smartwatch at a register to buy a drink: bits of data are sent through the ether, changing the total that appears on a screen in a banking app; then someone hands you a drink. The paper bills and metal coins, like the ones and zeros on a screen (the symbols), are meaningless, but people make meaning out of them. The federal government certifies that paper money is legal tender and insures the banks. Indeed, one way we know that each dollar (whether paper or digital) is meaningless is the way its meaning constantly changes: each day, a dollar is worth a different amount, depending on whether the dollar is "strong" or "weak" compared to international currencies. Similarly, birth certificates, marriage certificates, and so on are all meaningless in themselves—simply pieces of fancy paper—except that society (including the government) agrees upon the meanings these symbols represent. Meaning resides in people's minds, not in the symbols themselves.

Understanding that meaning resides in people and that people use symbols to act in the world fundamentally shapes the project of rhetorical criticism. A rhetorical critic is not interested in what the text *means* (because the text has no meaning), but in what the text *does* in society—the meanings it forms within audience members as they interact with the text, and the things they believe and do as a result of those meanings.

Ultimately, rhetorical criticism is primarily concerned with audiences. In 1925, rhetorical theorist Herbert Wichelns, who helped establish the modern field of rhetoric in US colleges and universities, said that rhetorical criticism "is not concerned with permanence, nor yet with beauty. It is concerned with effect."[21] The idea here is that rhetorical critics do not study texts (such as *Moby Dick* or the Declaration of Independence) to understand why they have permanence—why generations of Americans return to them. Similarly, rhetorical critics do not study texts (such as the film *Life of Pi,* which won Oscars for Best Director, Visual Effects, and Cinematography) to understand what makes them beautiful. Instead, rhetorical critics study texts to understand their effects—the way these texts act in the world.

DOING RHETORICAL CRITICISM

Rhetorical criticism is the process of making sense of rhetoric. As rhetorical critic Stephen Howard Browne put it, rhetorical criticism attempts to explain "the ways in which the arts of address are employed to make a difference."[22] The arts of address are employed all around us, and they are making a difference: shaping how we vote, what we value, the professions we consider admirable, the news sources we deem credible, the facts we are aware of, our assumptions for how our lives will unfold, and so on. Rhetorical criticism is a process through which we come to understand and explain how a text functions in society—what the text does and the difference it makes.

Broadly speaking, rhetorical criticism is a practice of drawing close to a text to study its symbolic form and its interaction with its contexts. Critics study the symbolic form of texts because those symbols are active—they do things in the world. They study the contexts of texts because it is within those contexts that the texts act. (Chapter 2 provides an overview of how a critic goes about studying a text's symbolic form and its context.)

Texts have a wide variety of symbolic forms. Some texts, including many films, are narratives: they tell stories. Some, such as presidential inaugural speeches, participate in larger **genres,** or *fluid categories of discourse.* Others, such as many music lyrics, rely on metaphors. Still others, such as photos, rely primarily on visual rather than verbal symbols. Some, such as monuments, use physical materials to communicate. A text might invite the audience into an **ideology**—*a particular way to see the world.* For example, a monument invites each passerby to consider the person or event being memorialized as worthy of esteem, honor, and remembrance.

There are many ways to do rhetorical criticism. Different types of rhetorical analysis focus the critic's attention in different ways and, thus, emphasize different aspects of how a text functions in society and how its symbolic form accomplishes that function. Metaphorically speaking, some types of rhetorical analysis are like binoculars; some are like telescopes; some are like reading glasses; some are like microscopes; and some are like X-ray vision. Using different rhetorical approaches to study the same text will reveal different aspects of that text. To some extent, then, critics can use their own research goals—the concern or curiosity that motivates them to analyze their texts—to help them determine how to analyze their texts. Yet, at another level, some types of rhetorical analysis are better suited for some texts. A biologist would not use a telescope to study a bacterium in a petri dish—it simply would not render useful information. Similarly, rhetorical critics must select critical approaches that are well suited to the symbolic forms of their texts.

Almost any text has more than one form or type of symbol fused together in its symbolic form. A critic might also have more than one motivating research goal or question in approaching a text. Accordingly, a critic may need multiple types of rhetorical analysis in order to assess any given text. For instance, a film might use visual symbols, verbal symbols, and audio symbols (such as background music); it might be structured as a narrative; and it might participate in a larger genre. Similarly, a political speech might use metaphors, express an ideology, and rely heavily on the speaker's delivery—how the speaker looks and sounds while presenting the speech—to act symbolically. Although this book explains one approach to rhetorical analysis at a time, these approaches work best in collaboration with each other, according to the critic's motivating research concern or question, as well as the symbolic form(s) of the text.

Chapter 2 explains close textual analysis. This traditional version of analysis provides a starting place for new critics to learn how to do rhetorical criticism. It also explains how critics draft critical essays—how they organize and present their analyses of their texts in essay form—and provides a framework for newcomers to begin practicing rhetorical criticism.

Chapters 3 through 6 comprise Part II, "Orienting Methods." The methods presented in these chapters (narrative criticism, dramatistic criticism, genre criticism, and metaphor criticism) elevate a single aspect of the symbolic form of a text as a critic's central approach to that text. Nonetheless, a critic should assess the entirety of a text, not just that single aspect of its symbolic form. For example, a critic using metaphor criticism would address the entirety of a text, not just its metaphors, even though metaphor criticism orients the critic in such a way that the entry point to the whole critical analysis is through the metaphors of that text.

Part III, "Ideological Critique," is comprised of Chapter 7, on ideological criticism, and Chapter 8, on feminist criticism. Unlike those in the previous section, these chapters introduce an approach to rhetorical analysis that does not focus on just one aspect of the symbolic form of a text. Instead, ideological critiques focus more broadly on the assumptions and beliefs a text activates in its audience and the ways in which audiences respond to this activation. To some extent, most rhetorical criticism participates in ideological critique, because critics are usually concerned with the meanings (assumptions and beliefs) audience members derive from texts and their ensuing actions.

Ideological critiques, however, are known not only for focusing on the ideology a text activates, but for judging that ideology (the set of assumptions and beliefs symbolically represented in a text) relative to the critic's own ideology. In other words, critics who routinely engage in ideological critique tend to analyze texts toward which they are morally and politically favorable, and to demonstrate how those texts act in positive ways. The inverse is also true: ideological critics routinely analyze texts toward which they are morally and politically unfavorable, and demonstrate how these texts act in society in negative ways.

Feminist criticism, one type of ideological critique, provides a clear example. Feminism is a political movement that aims to end sexism. Critics using feminist criticism often analyze texts they consider sexist and demonstrate how these texts act in harmful ways; or, alternatively, feminist critics analyze pro-equity texts and demonstrate how they act in beneficial ways. Many other types of ideological critique—for example, queer criticism, Marxist criticism, and antiracist criticism—are featured in examples throughout the book, as critics infuse an ideologically based approach with other critical methods.

Part IV, "Rethinking Rhetorical Texts," is comprised of Chapters 9, 10, and 11. These chapters explore ways to approach texts that include aspects for which the methods and approaches discussed previously are not entirely equipped. Chapter 9, on audience rhetoric, explores ways to analyze texts that are comprised of audience responses rather than the film, speech, television series, and so on to which the audience is responding. Chapter 10, on visual rhetoric, explores ways to analyze texts that are primarily visual in nature, such as photographs or other images, or that contain visual elements. Chapter 11, on material rhetoric, explores ways to analyze texts that are fundamentally material (physical) in nature, such as buildings, memorials, or landscapes.

Although each approach to criticism explained in these chapters can function as a critic's only methodology, sometimes critics combine these approaches to assess how texts function in society. For example, a critic might use narrative criticism to orient an analysis of the nightly news, focusing on the ways in which the news anchors', reporters', and witnesses' statements are organized into a story. Adding visual analysis, however, allows the critic to address how the news anchors, reporters, and witnesses appeared on the screen, as well as the use of other graphics, props, and settings. Similarly, a critic might use genre criticism to orient an analysis of superhero films, focusing on the way these films conform to genre-based expectations. Adding an analysis of audience texts allows the critic to demonstrate how the audience responded to the elements of that genre (such as action sequences and origin stories), and how impactful (or not) these elements were to audience members' responses to these films.

Finally, there are two appendixes that conclude this book. They contain advice for writing a rhetorical analysis and offer examples of various elements of a research essay. These appendices are designed to help you craft your own rhetorical analyses.

RHETORICAL CRITICISM AS PURPOSEFUL ART

Rhetorical criticism is an art. Just as sculptors apply theoretical knowledge, methodological skill, and their own artistic sense to material entities (such as marble or metal) to create works of art, so too rhetorical critics apply theoretical knowledge, methodological skills, and their own critical sense to create works of art—their criticism.[23] Critics create art as they make sense of rhetoric.

This art is socially useful. As rhetorical theorist Lisa Flores states, "the art of rhetorical criticism is concerned with politics and publics, with cultural discourses and social meanings, with rhetors and audiences."[24] She explains that the "art of rhetorical criticism" is fundamentally concerned with "insight and judgment."[25] That is, the art that rhetorical critics produce provides insights by helping us understand how our world came to be and what types of communicative strategies are likely to persuade particular types of audiences. Simultaneously, the art of rhetorical criticism renders judgment, ethically evaluating the quality of the rhetorical text. Indeed, rhetorical theorist Karlyn Kohrs Campbell argues that critics must make an "ethical assessment" of the rhetorical texts they study.[26]

Rhetorical critics Kent Ono and John Sloop recognize that in creating insight and judgment through rhetorical criticism, critics are engaged in something purposeful. They describe rhetorical criticism as a "moment when a person's pen is put to paper purposively, when ideas become words and when will becomes action."[27] In other words, rhetorical criticism is an art with purpose: an art we practice on purpose in order to accomplish specific purposes.

Rhetorical critics are animated by many purposes. One recurring purpose is to create new knowledge regarding what makes communication effective. Rhetorical critics are often concerned with understanding why and how a particular text was successful or unsuccessful in activating particular meanings, beliefs, and actions in its audience. A second recurring purpose is to assess the quality of communal life into which a text invites its audience. Given the ways in which rhetoric invites audiences to "draw close" to some people, ignore or push away others, and even perhaps refuse to recognize them as human, rhetoric fundamentally shapes our communal lives.

Consequently, rhetorical critics are often animated by the goal or purpose of assessing how a rhetorical text affects our communal lives—how it sets the boundaries for "humanity," for "us" and "them," for "important" and "unimportant," and for "real" and "imagined."[28] Within the context of the United States, rhetorical critics are often drawn to texts that address our communal life in terms of democracy, sexism, and racism. The purposes guiding these critics are largely to generate insight (understanding how texts represent democracy, sex, and race), but also to render judgment—to assess the quality of communal life that these texts activate.

This book features rhetorical critics' research, offering synopses of prominent critics' research projects. Each chapter, towards its conclusion, summarizes two or three critical essays that exemplify the type of criticism that chapter explores. The research exemplars are chosen for their ability to showcase the type of analysis under consideration, for their ability to demonstrate how methods can be combined, and for the ways in which they reflect central concerns regarding democracy, sexism, and racism within the context of the United States.

Ultimately, rhetoric is no less than the "scaffolding of our social world" and the "grammar of social life."[29] Rhetorical criticism—the art of understanding how texts function in society—is fundamentally concerned with how humans address one another as we construct our social world through symbols. As you progress through this book, learning how to practice rhetorical criticism, you will learn how to analyze the world you live in. Rhetorical criticism is immensely practical. It can help you gain insights and render judgment on the texts that matter in your communities.

ABOUT THE AUTHOR

My name is Dr. Sarah Kornfield and I am the author of this book. I have taught rhetorical criticism for more than a decade. I earned my BA in communication and literature from Wheaton College in Illinois, my MA in communication from Texas A&M University, and my PhD in rhetoric with a graduate minor in women's studies from the Pennsylvania State University. I currently teach at Hope College in Michigan. I am married to a beautiful spouse and we have two children. I run half-marathons and play violin. I am phenomenal at Tetris and lousy at Scrabble. I am a real person. I say this by way of introduction. After all, although this book is shaped by the contours of the field of rhetoric and features the work of rhetorical theorists and critics, it is also shaped by my own hand.

Throughout this book, the vast majority of examples are drawn from public discourse, so you will be familiar with many of the events and texts. Most chapters also contain an anecdote drawn from my own experiences, which I offer to ground this heady academic study in real life. Rhetorical criticism is useful because it unpacks the arts of address—and we are artfully addressed throughout our lives. In other words, rhetorical criticism helps us make sense of our lives.

DISCUSSION QUESTIONS

1. Describe an instance where you were addressed by rhetoric. What type of art form was used? How artful was the address? How did you respond as an audience member?
2. Describe an instance in which you used rhetoric to address a group of people. What type of art form did you use? How artfully did you compose your rhetoric? How did your audience respond?
3. This book offered nationality as an example of constructed realities to show how humans use symbols to create the everyday structures we take for granted. Develop and explain a different example of how humans use symbols to construct reality.
4. In your own words, explain what rhetorical theorist Jeremy Engels meant when he described rhetoric as "the scaffolding of our social world" and as "nothing less than the grammar of social life."[30]

5. Name three texts that you might want to use rhetorical criticism to make sense of. What types of symbolic forms do these texts use? Who are their audiences? Why are you interested in studying these texts?
6. Reflect on rhetorical theorist I. A. Richards's claim that "people, rather than words" have meaning. How does this idea shape rhetorical critics' study of texts, symbols, and audiences?
7. Reflect on the dual goals of rhetorical criticism: to provide insight and render judgment regarding a text. Offer a concrete example of how such insight and judgment could be beneficial to society.

NOTES

1. Christine Hauser, "A Handmaid's Tale of Protest," NYTimes.com, June 30, 2017, https://nyti.ms/2us9ZSe.
2. Hauser, "A Handmaid's Tale."
3. Quoted in Hauser, "A Handmaid's Tale."
4. Quoted in Hauser, "A Handmaid's Tale."
5. Quoted in Hauser, "A Handmaid's Tale."
6. Stephen Howard Browne, *The Ides of War: George Washington and the Newburgh Crisis* (Columbia, SC: University of South Carolina Press, 2016), xi.
7. Jeremy Engels, *Politics of Resentment: A Genealogy* (University Park: Pennsylvania State University Press, 2015), 152.
8. Engels, *Politics of Resentment,* 160.
9. See Monica Brown, "Woman as Mysterious Machine: Metaphor, Rhetoric and Female Sexual Dysfunction," *At the Interface/Probing the Boundaries* 55 (2009): 127.
10. Engels, *Politics of Resentment,* 14.
11. Martin J. Medhurst and Thomas W. Benson, eds., *Rhetorical Dimensions in Media: A Critical Casebook* (Dubuque, IA: Kendall/Hunt, 1984), xx.
12. Medhurst and Benson, *Rhetorical Dimensions in Media,* xx.
13. Natalie Fixmer and Julia T. Wood, "The Personal is *Still* Political: Embodied Politics in Third Wave Feminism," *Women's Studies in Communication* 28, no. 2 (2005): 235–236.
14. Melissa Harris-Perry, *Sister Citizen: Shame, Stereotypes, and Black Women in America* (New Haven, CT: Yale University Press, 2011), 4.
15. Quoted in Hunter Harris, "Two Women Describe Louis C. K.'s 'Uncomfortable' Comedy Cellar Set," Vulture.com, August 29, 2018, http://www.vulture.com/2018/08/louis-ck-comedy-cellar-women-describe-rape-whistle-joke.html.
16. Stuart Hall and Paddy Whannel, "The Young Audience," in *Cultural Theory and Popular Culture: A Reader,* 3rd ed., ed. John Storey (Harlow, England: Pearson Education, 2006), 50.
17. Hall and Whannel, "The Young Audience," 47.
18. Hall and Whannel, "The Young Audience," 47.
19. Hall and Whannel, "The Young Audience," 47.
20. See David Douglass, "Issues in the Use of I. A. Richards' Tenor-Vehicle Model of Metaphor," *Western Journal of Communication* 64, no. 4 (2000): 407.
21. Herbert Wichelns, "The Literary Criticism of Oratory," in *Studies in Rhetoric and Public Speaking in Honor of James Albert Winans,* ed. A. M. Drummond (New York:

Century, 1925). Reprinted in *Readings in Rhetorical Criticism,* 5th ed., eds. Carl R. Burgchardt and Hillary A. Jones (State College, PA: Strata, 2017), 22.

22. Browne, *The Ides of War,* xi.
23. Lisa Flores, "Between Abundance and Marginalization: The Imperative of Racial Rhetorical Criticism," *Review of Communication* 16, no. 1 (2016): 6.
24. Flores, "Abundance and Marginalization," 6.
25. Flores, "Abundance and Marginalization," 6.
26. Karlyn Kohrs Campbell, "'Conventional Wisdom—Traditional Form': A Rejoinder," *Quarterly Journal of Speech* 58, no. 4 (1972): 452.
27. Kent Ono and John Sloop, "Commitment to *Telos*—A Sustained Critical Rhetoric," *Communication Monographs* 59, no. 1 (1992): 48.
28. Engels, *Politics of Resentment,* 14.
29. Engels, *Politics of Resentment,* 152, 160.
30. Engels, *Politics of Resentment,* 152, 160.

Chapter 2

Rhetorical Analysis and Critical Essays

While watching TV, I saw a laundry detergent advertisement that puzzled me. In it, a girl in a sports uniform—likely soccer—enters a house and sits down with her mother. The mother, clearly disturbed by the girl's smell, asks her to put her clothes in the laundry, as five large male athletes who wear pigtail wigs and sports uniforms that match the girl's outfit surround the mother and a male voiceover asks, "Do your athletes bring home big odors?" The scene cuts to the mother adding laundry detergent to the wash, while still surrounded by the five male athletes. The advertisement ends by recommending that viewers buy a specific brand of laundry detergent. As I thought about the ad, I understood that the girl's apparently shocking stench was being represented visually by the crowd of male athletes—as if to say that the girl's sweaty clothes smelled like five adult, male athletes.

The choice of symbols puzzled me. I wondered why the advertisement featured an array of male athletes—including the professional football player, Rob Gronkowski—to indicate the girl's stench. I considered and rejected two options. First, I considered that the male athletes might be there because they participate in the same sport as the girl. But the athletic uniforms appear to be soccer uniforms, not football jerseys, as one would expect for Rob Gronkowski. There did not seem to be a direct connection between the male athletes' reputations and the girl's sport. Second, I considered that the commercial might be capitalizing on television's traditional use of cross-dressing as comedy; however, the male athletes are not played for laughs in this commercial. Indeed, other than their pigtails and the lavender color of their sports shirts, their outfits are not particularly cross-dressed: several of the men have visible facial hair (short beards and/or mustaches) and none are wearing bras. It seems, then, that neither the sport nor the comedic effect drove the choice to use male athletes to symbolize athletic stench. Having ruled out these possibilities, I considered a third option: given the taboos surrounding female sweat in US culture, even an advertisement that is pointing out how smelly girls can be chose to use men to represent sweat. Here, I wondered—despite US culture's propensity to pretend girls "glisten" rather than sweat—whether the advertisement might have met its target demographic (mothers of athletic girls) better by replacing the male athletes with players from the United States Women's National Soccer Team.

As I attempted to make sense of the commercial, I engaged—in a general sense—in rhetorical criticism, a process in which we consider how others "chose what to say in a given situation," decided to "arrange or order their thoughts," selected "the specific terminology" they used, and chose how to "deliver their message."[1] People often engage in this general level of rhetorical criticism while making sense of advertisements, films, speeches, news, music, and so on. Yet we typically go about the process in a rather haphazard way—leaping from one association to another and rejecting interpretations without necessarily knowing why.

By studying rhetorical criticism, however, one can learn how to systematically draw close to a text, studying its symbolic form and its interaction with its context, in order to discern how the text acts in society. Through rhetorical criticism, critics can discern and explain "the ways in which the arts of address are employed to make a difference."[2] This book is designed to invite you into this practice of rhetorical criticism—to offer you the resources, skills, theories, methods, orientations, and critical approaches through which you can study the symbolic forms of texts and their interactions with their contexts.

The approach laid out in this chapter, **close textual analysis,** is *a traditional version of rhetorical criticism that focuses on drawing close to a text, carefully observing its details, considering how those details combine as a whole, considering how the text fits in its context, and then offering an interpretation of the text that accounts for how it functions in society.* Some rhetorical critics rely almost exclusively on close textual analysis. Others might start their research projects by using elements of close textual analysis and then layering in other methods. Close textual analysis is not only a useful place to begin learning the practices of rhetorical criticism, it is also a useful place to begin almost any research project in rhetorical criticism.

The previous chapter laid out the foundational perspectives upon which close textual analysis is built: the ideas of (1) rhetoric as the arts of address, (2) rhetoric as symbolic action, (3) texts as symbolic forms, (4) meaning as residing in people, and (5) rhetorical criticism as the process of making sense of rhetoric by understanding how symbolic forms interact within their contexts. This chapter demonstrates how critics apply these foundational perspectives in order to analyze texts. It also explains how critics organize and present their analyses in essay form.

DOING RHETORICAL CRITICISM: CLOSE TEXTUAL ANALYSIS

A critic typically begins with a text from public discourse to analyze—a film, speech, newspaper editorial, campaign advertisement, novel, music album, and so on. Critics frequently choose texts that catch their attention: they are drawn to the texts, curious about them, and often feel strongly about them. Rhetorical criticism is often a lengthy process as critics patiently engage in a disciplined study of the text and its contexts.[3] Consequently, rhetorical criticism is a much more joyous research experience when the critic feels genuine passion regarding the chosen texts.

Because critics begin with texts they are curious about—texts whose symbolic action they want to understand better—they also begin with fledgling questions. One of a critic's first tasks is to take that fledgling curiosity and craft it into a **research question,** *an overarching question a critic is trying to answer.* Asking research questions helps critics focus their research. By answering their research questions, critics generate new or newly useful information in the world.

Rhetorical critics typically derive their research questions from the theoretical understanding of symbolic action. An overarching research question typically has two components: (1) what does the text do in society? (In other words, what does it invite people to assume or believe and, therefore, do?) and (2) how does the text accomplish this symbolic action through its form and content?

Depending on the text, its context, and the critic's larger research goals, the specific phrasing of a research question may take many shapes. For example, critics Kathleen Battles and Wendy Hilton-Morrow chose their text (the sitcom *Will & Grace*) and developed their research question as they considered the broader cultural context surrounding homosexuality in the late 1990s and early 2000s.[4] For instance, in 1996 the United States Congress passed the Defense of Marriage Act, which defined marriage at the federal level as being the union of one woman and one man. Similarly, thirty-four states enacted laws denying the recognition of same-sex marriages performed in other states. Moreover, in *Boy Scouts of America et al. v. Dale,* the Supreme Court ruled that the Boy Scouts could exclude gay and lesbian people from scout leadership positions on the basis of their sexuality. In addition, the 1990s saw considerable violence against LGBTQ+ individuals and communities. In one high-profile case, two men murdered Matthew Shepard, a student at the University of Wyoming, because of their hatred for his sexuality.

In 1998, in the midst of this widespread resistance and violence toward nonstraight sexualities, the sitcom *Will & Grace* (which prominently features two gay characters) not only premiered on NBC but found a large, mainstream US audience, as well as wide critical acclaim. Intrigued by the success of this series, Battles and Hilton-Morrow asked a version of the broad research question, "what does this text do in society?" Their research was framed around the central question, "does *Will & Grace* make homosexuality more acceptable in society? And if so, how?" In other words, Battles and Hilton-Morrow were specifically interested in what *Will & Grace* did and how it did that.

To answer a research question, a critic analyzes a text and its context, which are ultimately interwoven. During analysis, the critic is likely to move fluidly between text and context, working to understand how text and context inform and shape one another. To illustrate this process, the steps laid out in the following pages move from the text to the context, and then back again. This toggling between text and context is an ongoing project, not a once-and-done checklist. Critics often repeat these steps, observing their texts and then considering the contexts—and learning about their texts by studying the contexts. Indeed, because texts and contexts are interwoven, a critic might not seem to be so much "toggling" between the two as hovering over a multifaceted entity.

Becoming Familiar with Your Text

To study the symbolic form of a text, critics using close textual analysis often begin by familiarizing themselves with their texts. At this stage, critics often immerse themselves in their texts: repeatedly rereading, rewatching, relistening to, and reexperiencing them. Many critics create verbatim transcripts of their texts—especially speeches, films, television shows, music lyrics, and other longer texts for which no script is already available or complete.

One of the longstanding ways through which rhetorical critics have familiarized themselves with their texts is to begin with the **rhetorical canon,** *a set of principles, codified by the ancient Roman rhetorician, Cicero, that identifies five aspects of oratory: invention, arrangement (or organization), style (or expression), memory, and delivery.* The canon can provide a general checklist for critics to start familiarizing themselves with their texts. Because it was designed with oratory (speeches) in mind, however, the canon may be a more useful analytical tool for some texts than for others.[5]

Invention refers to *the arguments and the main ideas of a text, as well as the evidence (if any) it presents to support them.* To become familiar with the invention of a text, a critic might ask the following interpretive question: What is the main point of this text, and what claims or evidence does it present to support that point? Then, the critic would review the text, focusing on its content. A critic may consider whether or how a text bases its claims on logical arguments, on emotional appeals, and on the rhetor's authority or credibility.

Arrangement refers to *the organizational structure or pattern of a text.* To become familiar with the arrangement of a text, a critic might ask the following interpretive questions: How is this text organized? What comes first, second, third, and so on? How are transitions between sections marked in the text? By studying the arrangement, a critic becomes familiar with the overarching pattern of the text and the way it subdivides its content.

Style is *the expression of a text—its word choices and how it looks, sounds, and/or feels.* To become familiar with the style of a text, a critic might ask the following interpretive question: What style or tone is produced through the symbols deployed in this text? Here, the critic evaluates the word choices, color schemes, stylistic devices, and so on.

Memory refers to *how a text is produced and delivered.* This aspect of the canon is most applicable to speeches that are delivered—in part or in whole—from memory; yet it can be reimagined to reflect other types of texts. To become familiar with the memory of a text, a critic might ask the following interpretive question: How does this text depend on the rhetor and/or the audience's memory? For instance, the critic might note when a speaker, news anchor, or comedian deviated from a teleprompter or prepared remarks, and consider what prompted the rhetor to do that—and how those impromptu remarks operate within the text. Alternatively, a critic might consider how a long-running television series asks audiences to remember plot twists, or how an episode in the series attempts to refresh audience's memories with an introductory segment that shows snippets of previous episodes. Here, a critic attempts to understand the role of memory in constructing and interpreting the text.

Delivery refers to *the presentation of a text.* Although delivery was originally conceptualized in terms of a speaker's body language and vocal qualities, this canon can have wide-ranging applications as a critic considers the medium, platform, technological presentations, layouts, material embodiment, and so on of a text. To become familiar with the delivery of a text, a critic might ask the following interpretive questions: How does this text look, sound, feel, and/or move? What is most noticeable about its presentation? How is its delivery shaped by its technological production, industry traditions, and/or media platform?

When familiarizing themselves with their texts, critics begin with a "severely empirical orientation."[6] This means cataloguing a text's different features and how those features interact—for example, how a story mentioned at the beginning of a speech is tied back into a later point or how a dream sequence in a film affects the storytelling throughout the film. This initial cataloguing of the text's features is an important step, but it is likely to be incomplete.

As critics continue working with their texts, they notice new aspects—especially as they come to understand the contexts of those texts better. For example, I grew up attending Christian Sunday School programs and other church services, where I often heard a gospel story of how Jesus visits a man possessed by demons (the demons name themselves "Legion") and exorcizes them, sending them into a herd of pigs (Mark 5:1–20). Yet it was only very recently, while reading Pádraig Ó Tuama's book *In the Shelter,* that I learned that the Roman legion occupying the territory in the story used a boar "as their standard on their banners."[7] This new contextual information now informs how I understand the story and its connections—even political connections—suggesting that the demons name themselves and act in ways that align them with or connect them to an oppressive occupying military force. As this example demonstrates, text and context are interwoven; texts cannot be fully understood without understanding their contexts. Although a critic usually begins by becoming familiar with the text itself, this process is only part of the whole project. To analyze a text, a critic must also attend to its context.

Becoming Familiar with the Context: The Rhetorical Situation

One reason that rhetorical critics tend to understand text and context as interwoven is that rhetoric itself has often been theorized that way. In 1968, rhetorical theorist Lloyd Bitzer persuasively argued that rhetoric responds to its context, observing that we have a commonsense understanding of dangerous situations as those in which events, persons, or objects threaten someone or something.[8] Further, he noted, it is the situation itself—the constellation of things, events, people, and motives—that poses the danger. Building on this commonsense understanding, he proposed a similar understanding of rhetoric: that there are **rhetorical situations**—*constellations of situational elements that call rhetorical texts "into existence."*[9] Bitzer claimed that rhetorical situations have three components, which critics can use as a starting place to consider different aspects of the contexts of their texts.

The first component, Bitzer said, is an **exigence,** *(1) a "defect, an obstacle, something waiting to be done, [or] a thing which is other than it should be," that* *if (2) addressed in a timely manner could (3) be moderated, improved, or resolved through discourse.*[10] As this three-part definition suggests, exigences are complex. For example, some problems—such as natural disasters—cannot be improved through discourse: no amount of talking to or about the Earth's tectonic plates will prevent or undo an earthquake. An earthquake itself is not a rhetorical exigence, but a city's expansion plans—in relation to earthquakes—may be. If a city situated near a tectonic fault line planned a development project without requiring earthquake-resistant building designs, this situation would qualify as a rhetorical exigence because (1) there is a clear problem (once built, the buildings will likely collapse in the next earthquake); (2) the problem is time sensitive (the city must revise its requirements before awarding a contract to a development group and the building project begins); and (3) speaking to the city legislators, planners, mayor, and residents could indeed result in beneficial changes to the city's plans. When considering the exigence of a text, a critic asks interpretive questions such as: To what event or events does the text respond? What problem is the text trying to solve? What need or expectation does this text fulfill?

Second, a rhetorical situation has an audience. Although we generally think of an audience as all those who see, hear, or otherwise experience a text, Bitzer focuses more narrowly on what he calls **rhetorical audience,** which includes only *"those persons who are capable of being influenced by discourse and of being mediators of change."*[11] Essentially, by theorizing rhetoric as an address—a calling out to, an orienting toward, and active engagement with—he stipulates that the audience must also be active in the situation. If rhetoric engages with someone, then that someone—the audience—must also be actively engaging with the rhetoric. This is not to say the audience is always happy with, persuaded by, or receptive to the address. Indeed, the audience need not be influenced by discourse, but must be open to being influenced by it.[12] By describing audiences as capable of "being mediators of change,"[13] Bitzer stipulates that audiences in rhetorical situations are capable of doing something, such as changing their attitudes, behaviors, ideology, or lifestyles.

For Bitzer, then, rhetorical audiences are not merely "hearers or readers," but rather those who engage with a text and who are capable of change as a result of that engagement.[14] When considering the audience for a text, a critic asks interpretive questions such as: Who is the audience for this text? Who was intended as the audience for this text? Who could respond to this text in the ways it would prefer?

The third aspect of a rhetorical situation is that it has **constraints,** *elements (such as persons, identities, events, objects, physical locations, time limits, technologies, facts, histories, or values) that "have the power to constrain [the] decision and action needed to modify the exigence."*[15] Put another way, in addition to immediate factors such as the physical setting and time limitations, broader elements (such as beliefs, attitudes, historical facts, and cultural traditions) influence how an exigence can be resolved and how an audience can be persuaded.

For example, after the 2019 mosque shootings in Christchurch, New Zealand, killed fifty people, the New Zealand government quickly enacted legislation that banned all semiautomatic firearms, magazines, and parts for those weapons.[16] This legislation included an amnesty and buyback policy for the now-prohibited weapons. Comparing the US government response after a mass shooting to that of New Zealand, many pundits lament the US inability to follow New Zealand's example. Essentially, they argue that the United States and New Zealand are similar countries, and that in the wake of a mass shooting the United States ought to be able to accomplish what New Zealand did.

This argument, however, fails to take into account that, although the United States faces a similar exigence, the two countries face different constraints—different historical facts and different cultural traditions. Throughout its history, New Zealand has had a patchwork of different gun laws, but it was not until the 1983 Arms Act that New Zealand consolidated and amended its prior laws, creating its national statute regarding firearms.[17] Essentially, the law that was revised after the 2019 Christchurch mosque shootings was only thirty-five years old—and it had already been amended in 1990 after a massacre that killed thirteen people.[18] In contrast, the Second Amendment to the United States Constitution—ratified in 1791—declares that "the right of the people to keep and bear Arms, shall not be infringed."[19] Because New Zealand was not constrained by a two-hundred-year-old Constitutional Amendment, radically different options were available to that country that are not available to the United States as it responds to its onslaught of mass shootings. Consequently, although pundits routinely recommend that the United States follow New Zealand's example, any argument regarding gun control in the United States will have to deal with the constraints imposed by its historical laws and cultural reverence toward the Constitution.

Bitzer further explains that some constraints originate with the rhetor. For example, in ancient Athens, the rhetorician Isocrates repeatedly excused himself from public oratory by describing his voice as a *mikrōphonia*—a small or quiet voice.[20] Instead of speaking in public, Isocrates wrote down his persuasive ideas and then had his writings publicly circulated.[21] Isocrates seems to have recognized a constraint—the quietness of his voice—that originated with himself, and, taking this constraint into consideration, found an alternative way to promote his ideas. Historical scholar Yun Lee Too, however, suggests that this example could be understood in another way: perhaps Isocrates was dealing with a situational constraint that he navigated by claiming his voice was too quiet for public oratory. Lee suggests that in Isocrates's culture, public speaking was increasingly associated with demagogues and manipulative politicians. Isocrates therefore faced a constraint: if he spoke his ideas aloud in a public speech, his audience would lump him in with the people and ideas from which he wanted to distance himself. In that case, we might understand Isocrates's "quiet voice" excuse and use of writings as a clever—and successful—negotiation of his rhetorical situation.

When considering rhetorical constraints, a critic asks interpretive questions such as: How do the physical and/or technological aspects of this text constrain or shape it? What cultural values, identities, traditions, histories, facts, or precedents constrain or shape this text? How does the rhetor's strengths, weaknesses, or reputation as a rhetor constrain or shape this text?

When critics familiarize themselves with the contexts of their texts, Bitzer's rhetorical situation can be a fruitful starting place: they can look at exigences, audiences, and constraints to understand those contexts. Additionally, a critic ought to look at responses to the text—such as critical reviews, box-office numbers for films, ratings for television series, audience feedback (such as fan message boards), newspaper editorials, and so on—to help understand how audience members interacted with the text. Because critics argue that their texts accomplish something in society, they should have a fairly comprehensive understanding of the society in question.

Sometimes, when researching context, critics can become uncertain of whether they know enough of the context. A critic can even feel lost in what seems like a never-ending web of possible contextual connections. Close textual analysis can help the critic discover the most relevant aspects of the context, because it maintains that "text informs context, and vice versa."[22] That is, texts themselves reveal their relevant contexts, including but not limited to their exigences, audiences, and constraints. The idea is to look at the text itself and see what it states as the problem(s) it attempts to solve or the event(s) to which it refers, and thus find its exigences; to see what types—if any—of persuasive appeals it makes (and whom it names or ignores) and thus infer its audience; to see what sources it cites and therein find its inspiration; to see what technologies it uses and thus understand one aspect of its constraints; and so on.

For example, during the height of the midterm election season in 2018, a gunman entered a Pittsburgh synagogue, Tree of Life, and murdered eleven people in a mass shooting. In the following days, while campaigning at rallies on behalf of gubernatorial and congressional candidates, President Trump stated that "the hearts of all Americans are filled with grief."[23] The *New York Times* reported that "Mr. Trump said "the nation's gun laws had 'little to do' with the shooting" and that if the synagogue had had armed guards "the results would have been far better."[24] Listening to these speeches, one might question why a US president was lauding the idea of religious institutions having armed guards. After all, the founding premise of "freedom of religion" seems to imply that religious sanctuaries would not need the protection of armed guards.

Yet in recognizing that "text informs context, and vice versa" a critic using close textual analysis would see these statements as indicators of the relevant contexts of these speeches: the mass shooting, the Second Amendment, and progun arguments during a campaign season.[25] In addition, a close textual analysis perspective suggests that Trump's speeches act upon the world. The speeches selected their relevant contexts and solidified them for audiences, so that audience members remember this synagogue shooting in connection to wondering whether a good person with a gun could have prevented this hate crime, instead of wondering whether the United States has religious freedom when religious sanctuaries are under violent attack. Ultimately, close textual analysis recommends that critics use the text itself as a guide when familiarizing themselves with the context, even as they use Bitzer's rhetorical situation as a guiding framework.

Reviewing the Literature

Rhetorical critics are concerned with what texts do in society, not simply because they find texts fascinating and want to understand their activity, but because they want to understand communication, community, civics, persuasion, influence, meaning-making, art, eloquence, judgment, decision-making, expression, and so on. That is, rhetorical critics' interest goes beyond particular texts and their contexts. They are interested in learning how texts accomplish their activity so that they might understand more generally how symbolic acts are accomplished.

Because rhetorical critics' interest extends beyond their texts, so too must their research. Having begun to be familiar with a text and its context, a critic might begin to hypothesize the key aspects of the text and the contexts that might be instrumental in the activity of the text. For example, having familiarized themselves with *Will & Grace* and its multiple contexts, Kathleen Battles and Wendy Hilton-Morrow began to hypothesize that its genre—a sitcom—constrained what this text could accomplish.

At this point, critics begin to research the **scholarly literature,** *the published books and essays in which scholars present their arguments (claims and evidence) and theories on a given topic,* such as the sitcom genre, or inaugural speeches, advertising campaigns, satirical news programs, and so on. By reviewing a scholarly literature, a critic learns what other scholars have already learned about texts in that genre.

A critic reviews a scholarly literature by using library resources. Many communication scholars begin with keyword searches in the database Communication & Mass Media Complete, which is hosted through EBSCO and likely accessible through the website for your college or university library. For example, we might imagine Battles and Hilton-Morrow searching this database for research articles containing the keywords "genre" and "sitcom." This search would bring up a number of articles regarding the sitcom genre that were written by other critics. By reading these essays, Battles and Hilton-Morrow could establish a strong understanding of what those critics have already learned about the that genre.

In reviewing the scholarly literature, critics are often focused on accomplishing two tasks regarding their own analyses. First, while reviewing a scholarly literature, a critic tries to become familiar with the types of terms, concepts, theories, and approaches that other scholars have found useful in their analyses. The idea is that if these terms, concepts, theories, and approaches were useful to others, they may be useful analytical tools for the critic's own analysis. Returning to Battles and Hilton-Morrow's work, for example, we can see that through their review of the literature, they found that sitcoms typically feature opposite-sex dyads, diffuse tension with comedy, and feature interpersonal relationships—whether they are set in the home or office. These three classic components of the sitcom genre then became useful as Battles and Hilton-Morrow analyzed *Will & Grace,* working to identify if, when, and how *Will & Grace* featured these components.

Second, a critic researches the scholarly literature in order to make a new contribution to communication scholarship. Critics do not want to reinvent the wheel, reaching a conclusion that has already been established. Instead, they want their analyses to create new knowledge—knowledge that contributes to the broader understanding of a specific culture or community, technology, symbolic form, the effectiveness of a specific rhetorical technique, and so on.

Communication theorist Kenneth Burke describes scholarship as a conversation, saying, "Imagine that you enter a parlor. You come late. When you arrive, others have long preceded you, and they are engaged in a heated discussion, a discussion too heated for them to pause and tell you exactly what it is about."[26]

After you listen quietly for a while, he says, you manage to catch on—to understand the debate and the key arguments. Then you speak up, adding your own argument. In response, someone counters you and another rushes to your defense. Eventually, however, "the hour grows late and you must depart. And you do depart, with the discussion still vigorously in progress."[27] Essentially, critics must "listen" for awhile to the ongoing conversation before they can join in with their own research. By reviewing the scholarly literature, critics listen to prior scholars, catching onto what has already been established, what remains debatable, and what the main arguments are. Only then are critics ready to join the conversation by closely analyzing their own texts and ultimately proposing their own arguments in their critical works.

Analyzing the Text: The Fusion of Form and Content

Having become familiar with a text, contexts, and relevant literatures, a critic is ready to analyze the rhetorical address of the text. When using close textual analysis, a critic recognizes that form and content are fused. Although distinct from one another, they belong together—they are a meaning-making team. **Form** is *the embodiment of a text: its organization, tone, syntax, and style.* **Content** is *the ideas expressed through the form.* Rhetorical critic Stephen Howard Browne offers this metaphor: "form is to content as the dancer is to the dance."[28] A dance is only expressed through a dancer, yet the two are distinct entities. A dancer is a person and a dance is a sequence of choreographed movements, but they become one in the performance. Similarly, form and content become one in a rhetorical address—and together, they artfully address an audience.

Rhetorical theorists Michael Leff and Andrew Sachs offer the following example. If you were to describe someone's height by saying, "he is very, very, very tall" you would mean something slightly different than if you merely said, "he is very tall."[29] Although the two sentences contain the same content (the words denote the same interpretations), their form is different. The "very, very, very" in the first sentence creates emphasis and lengthens the sentence in a way that mirrors the person being described. Because the forms of the two sentences are different, the meanings they express are different too.[30]

At this stage in the analysis, a critic is essentially asking the following interpretive question: how do the formal elements sponsor (or stymie) the content? Critics review their prior work (in which they familiarized themselves with their texts, making observations regarding their various elements) and look for instances in which form and content work together, as well as instances in which form and content might not be paired effectively. Essentially, critics assess whether the formal elements effectively enhance the content of their texts, and vice versa.

For example, when analyzing a 2008 campaign speech by Hillary Clinton, rhetorical critic John Murphy noticed that the organization of her speech ultimately undermined her intended content.[31] Clinton laid out her argument in the first four paragraphs of her speech, but then the rest of the speech rambles through a repetition of her previous arguments.[32] Murphy observed that the formal elements of the speech (its organization) did not effectively sponsor the content (an explanation of the economic collapse of 2008). Instead, the organization functionally stymied the content, making the speech boring and uninspiring.[33] He noted that Clinton's chosen metaphors (she described the economy as running, freezing, falling, and dropping) further stymied her content.[34] Murphy identified Clinton's central argument: the problem with the economy was a "crisis of confidence" in US leadership[35]—a perfectly reasonable central argument for a presidential campaign speech. Yet, he noted, this argument was not sponsored by the metaphors, which describe the economy in natural and physical terms: like the weather, the economy is freezing. The disparity between the argument and the metaphors poses a problem because US citizens rarely think of placing their confidence in the weather or other natural phenomena, and very rarely believe their political leaders can affect the weather. By using these metaphors, Murphy pointed out, Clinton used formal elements that conflicted with her content.[36]

Depending on the text, critics go about analyzing the fusion of form and content in different ways. For instance, when analyzing a film, TV episode, or television advertisements, a critic might pay attention to elements such as the background audio (including music), the cinematography, the staging and costuming, and the shot sequences, and consider how these formal elements sponsor (or stymie) the content. When analyzing a novel, a critic might pay attention to elements such as the narrative voice (if there is one), the plot structure, and the characterization, and consider how these formal elements sponsor (or stymie) the content of the novel. When analyzing a statue, a critic might pay attention to elements such as the material from which the statue is built, its physical design, and the way people interact with it, and consider how these formal elements sponsor (or stymie) the content of the statue as a text.

Different texts have different formal elements and different content, so a critic using close textual analysis must work closely with the text to understand the intricacies of its symbolic form and the ways in which form sponsors the content. For many new students of rhetorical criticism, this task can seem herculean. Rest assured, the following chapters will provide you with the means to better understandings of forms (such as narrative, metaphor, and genre) and content (the ideology of a text and its interactions with context), as well as a sense of how to combine and interweave different methods to assess the form and content of a text.

Articulating Your Argument

The beginning stages of close textual analysis are largely observational.[37] The critic chooses a text, drafts a research question, becomes familiar with the text and its context, reviews the literature, and then observes the fusion of form and content in the text. Moving into the final stage of close textual analysis, however, a critic offers an interpretation of the symbolic action of the text—thus answering the research question. In other words, having studied a text closely, a critic is ready to offer an interpretation of how it invites audiences to understand it, to feel in response to it, to think as a result of it, and ultimately, to act because of it. This, a critic claims, is the **preferred interpretation**—*the interpretation into which the text invites its audience, regardless of the stated purposes of the text or the rhetor.* The preferred interpretation is the critic's account of the symbolic action of the text—how the text functions in society.

Returning to Murphy's analysis of Hillary Clinton's 2008 campaign speech, we can see that the speech itself has a stated purpose: to explain the causes of and remedies for the economic collapse. We might imagine that Clinton (the rhetor) would tell us that, indeed, the speech was intended to educate audiences regarding the financial collapse, but that it was also meant to support her candidacy for the Democratic presidential nomination. Murphy's analysis, however, argues that the particular combination of form and content invites audiences, first, into a state of boredom, and second, into an understanding of the economy as a largely natural, and therefore uncontrollable, phenomenon—like the weather.[38]

For critics to convince others that their interpretations of their texts are correct—that this is indeed how their texts function in society—critics must be able to provide evidence from the texts themselves. That is, critics use their empirical observations of their texts as the evidence for their interpretations. For example, while discussing my research on the television series *The Mentalist* with a colleague, I mentioned that this crime series featured a slow-burn romance between two of its lead characters, Teresa Lisbon and Patrick Jane. My colleague disagreed, stating that Lisbon and Jane were not a couple: they had never kissed, did not flirt with each other, and had no chemistry. It's true that Lisbon and Jane were not a couple and had not kissed; and depending on one's definition of "flirting" and "chemistry," my colleague might have been right on those accounts too. Having observed the minute details of this series, however, I was able to present convincing evidence that the series was designing a romance between Lisbon and Jane. For example, Jane's gaze often lingered on Lisbon; Lisbon acted jealous whenever Jane flirted with other women; and the narrative paired the two together for undercover missions. My ability to convince my colleague that *The Mentalist* was constructing a slow-burn romance rested on my ability to point to concrete evidence in the text and to match that evidence to well-established trends for what counts as romance within a television series: "Look here, and here, and here, and here—all of that adds up to a slow-burn romance."

Because rhetorical critics justify their interpretations of how texts function by pointing to concrete evidence (see Appendix A), a critic's account of a text is neither a subjective opinion (such as "this film is the best!") nor an objective description (such as "this film features a murder mystery"). Rather, a rhetorical critic presents an argument: an interpretation of how the text functions in society, backed by substantial evidence from the text itself.

RESEARCH EXAMPLES

The following two examples demonstrate how rhetorical critics analyze texts closely and present well-supported arguments regarding how a text functions in society. In the first research example, Thomas W. Benson analyzes a documentary film, demonstrating how form and content merge as a meaning-making team. He presents his preferred interpretation of the text, explaining how the text itself invites this interpretation. In the second example, Karlyn Kohrs Campbell analyzes suffragist Elizabeth Cady Stanton's famous speech, "The Solitude of Self." This analysis showcases Campbell's mastery of rhetorical forms as she illuminates how the text functions in society.

Thomas W. Benson
"The Rhetorical Structure of Frederick Wiseman's *High School*" (1980)*

Frederick Wiseman is a documentary filmmaker who chronicles US cultural institutions. His latest film, *Monrovia, Indiana* (2018), produced when Wiseman was eighty-eight, focuses on the idea of small-town USA. Similarly, his films *National Gallery* (2014), *Hospital* (1970), *Public Housing* (1997), *Juvenile Court* (1973), and *High School* (1960), all focus on these classic US institutions.

Rhetorical critic Thomas W. Benson analyzed *High School,* drawn to it in part by its lack of narration. Instead of using a disembodied voiceover to explain things to the audience, *High School* thrusts audiences directly into the experience of high school. The cameras show viewers the teachers, administrators, students, and buildings. The audio captures their speech and background sounds. Without narration, *High School* has no explicitly stated purpose, no clearly stated idea that audiences are supposed to learn by watching it. Benson observes, however, that the documentary clearly communicates that high schools are places of "conformity, boredom, apathy, and empty gestures of rebellion," which churn out graduates who are "very confused, oddly loyal, and self-sacrificial human victims, ready to take their places as the next generation of housewives, beauticians, astronauts, soldiers, secretaries, and high school teachers."[39]

Benson begins his analysis with a research question, "How does [this film] draw upon the skills and contexts of [the] viewers to invite them to experience a particular complex of meanings?"[40] This question directly focuses on what the text does. Specifically, it focuses Benson's analysis on how the text targets specific "skills" and "contexts" it assumes the audience has and, thereby, invites the audience to experience a "complex of meanings" while they watch the film.

At first glance, the idea that a text can target audience members' skills, contexts, and experiences in order to generate a "complex of meanings" may seem far-fetched, but texts accomplish this on a daily basis.[41] Virtually all advertising rests on the premise that texts can target audiences, activate their prior skills, contexts, and experiences, and thereby invite particular responses. For example, this chapter opened with an example of an advertisement that targets mothers' experiences doing laundry, and attempts to convey that their experiences will be improved through a particular brand of detergent.

Benson argues that *High School* offers audiences two discrete invitations. The first invites audiences to think consciously that high schools wield power inappropriately, suffocating students' personalities. At the same time, it invites audiences to feel subconsciously the emotional tensions and discomfort of adolescence. This subconscious feeling then magnifies the audience's conscious thought (that high schools inappropriately wield power to suffocate students' personalities) because the audience members themselves are feeling suffocated and tyrannized by high school as they relive the emotional turbulence of high school and adolescence. This two-part argument is Benson's answer to his research question: What does the text

---

*This essay may be found in *Communication Monographs* 47, no. 4 (1980) 233–261.

do to audiences? It invites them to think that high schools suffocate students' individuality and reinforces this meaning by inviting viewers to feel that suffocation.

Benson supports his arguments with evidence from the film itself. Specifically, he demonstrates that it is through the relationship of form and content that these "particular meanings emerge."[42] The form (the selection of scenes and shots), the framing (what the camera work shows viewers), and the editing (the sequencing that establishes the order and flow of the audiovisual content) combine with the content (footage of teachers lecturing, students studying, football teams practicing, administrators filing paperwork, and so on) to communicate clearly how high schools use power to dominate students instead of educating them.[43]

Benson offers evidence from his text that features this fusion of form and content. He describes scene after scene, telling readers how the shot sequences work, what the camera frames on screen (for example, a heavyset administrator behind a desk with a picture of the American flag visible behind him), and what the people say to one another. He offers example after example of teachers and administrators wielding power unfairly, confusing students and then punishing them for being confused, refusing to explain what seem to be arbitrary grades, and using tone and body language in threatening ways. Benson presents convincing evidence that *High School* invites audiences to think consciously that high schools inappropriately subjugate, confuse, and tyrannize students.

Benson's second argument—that *High School* invites audiences to subconsciously feel the emotional turbulence of adolescence, which then magnifies their conscious, intellectual condemnation of US public high schools—is much harder to prove, but it is convincing. For evidence, Benson points to multiple examples of vaguely sexual imagery that has been framed, edited, and sequenced in a way that suffuses the whole documentary with an underlying, unspoken sexual tension. For example, in addition to showing a sex-ed class, the camera pans by a jersey on a laundry line bearing the number 69, teachers and students licking and stroking their lips, female students sucking on the ends of their pens, and a woman vertically stroking a cylindrical wooden post while the men around her talk about being judged based on "performance." The editing cuts scenes together in a way that makes it appear that a male teacher who is monitoring the hallway is watching a female student walk away from him and then peering through a classroom window at girls' bottoms as they exercise. During a scene in which students play softball, the camera plays a visual joke on "ball breakers" by repeatedly showing the ball being whacked, then focusing in such a way that the ball is framed by the batter's crotch. This "ball breaker" joke is then escalated during a home economics class in which students chop nuts. The examples go on and on. Throughout the film, teachers and administrators criticize the students' clothing (skirts are too short, and so on) and offer them confusing and contradicting advice about gender and romance. While none of these examples alone would support Benson's claim, the sheer number of examples is convincing. Vaguely sexual content suffuses this film. Whenever it rises to the level of consciousness (for example, when teachers criticize girls' skirt lengths), the students are punished and suppressed.

Ultimately, Benson argues convincingly that *High School* does something in society: it stirs its audience to a conscious and intensely felt conviction that US public high schools wrongly repress their students' autonomy. In Benson's words, the film makes audiences "bitterly alert to the uses of power and repression" in high schools.[44] By presenting evidence from his text and interpreting that evidence to show the interplay of form and content, Benson successfully argues that the film accomplishes its goal by inviting audiences to think and feel in particular ways.

Karlyn Kohrs Campbell "Stanton's 'The Solitude of Self': A Rationale for Feminism" (1980)*

In 1892, Elizabeth Cady Stanton's speech "The Solitude of Self" was delivered to the House Committee on the Judiciary as part of a lobbying effort to persuade Congress to let women vote in federal elections. The speech was extremely well received. Stanton's close friend and fellow suffragist, Susan B. Anthony, declared that it was "the speech of [Stanton's] life." House Committee members were so impressed they had ten thousand copies of the speech printed and distributed around the country.[45]

Rhetorical critic Karlyn Kohrs Campbell begins her analysis of this extraordinary speech by pointing out that the speech defies conventions: "It makes no arguments; it provides no evidence. . . . it has no logical structure. It refers briefly at the outset to some shared values but makes no appeal to them. It has no proper introduction, and it ends abruptly."[46] Moreover, reflecting on its immediate effects, one might conclude that the speech was a failure despite its initial warm reception: Congress continued to vote against women's suffrage for approximately the next twenty-five years—until the Nineteenth Amendment passed the House by a two-thirds majority in 1918, passed the Senate in 1919, and was ratified by the states in 1920. Yet the speech haunts US history, retaining its "power to speak" as a "strange and moving" tribute to women's rights.[47]

Campbell begins her analysis with a research question, asking, "how and why [does this speech] still [have] the power to speak to and move today's audience"?[48] Working to answer this question, Campbell carefully observes the text, familiarizing herself with its various elements and noting how they coalesce into a whole. Stanton's speech centers on the idea that every human is utterly alone—the "solitude of self." Campbell notes that the speech enumerates "human solitude in all its dimensions" and moves associatively from one aspect of solitude to the next.[49] The tone of the speech is intimate. The language choices are sensory, figurative, and image based. The speech features repeated phrases, ideas, and parallel sentence structures. Drawing on her vast understanding of rhetorical forms, Campbell recognizes these elements as part of the lyric mode. Lyrics are a type of poetry known for their enumeration; associative structure; intimate tone; sensory, figurative, and image-based language; repetition; and parallelism. Although the speech is prose, not poetry, it speaks in the lyric mode and Campbell assesses the speech as a lyric triumph.

However, the lyric mode does not account for all the elements in this speech. While analyzing the speech closely, Campbell finds significant elements that do

*This essay may be found in *Quarterly Journal of Speech* 66, no. 3 (1980): 304–312.

not fit within the lyric mode. Thus, to complete her analysis, Campbell needed to account for them.

Campbell observes that the speech often emphasizes the role of destiny or fate, and that it focuses on beginnings and endings as it illustrates each human's fundamental solitude. Observing these elements and drawing on her understanding of rhetorical forms, Campbell recognizes that this content embodies the tragic perspective. Literary forms are often divided into the categories of comedy and tragedy. The vast majority of policy speeches utilize comedic perspectives—not that policy speeches are funny, but they imagine a world that can and will get better: a happy ending, if you will. But Stanton's "The Solitude of Self" is different. Campbell conclusively demonstrates that it uses a tragic perspective that focuses on the individual (not a community) and shows how we are fated to move inexorably toward suffering and death.

It is curious that such a tragic perspective could win the approval of congressmen and more broadly support women's suffrage. Yet Campbell demonstrates how this tragic content blends with the lyric form, coalescing into a whole that acts powerfully upon its audience, creating an irrefutable case for suffrage. Campbell highlights the "interrelationship between form and substance," arguing that the lyric form with its emphasis on subjective experiences and sensory-based language modifies the tragic perspective.[50] Essentially, the lyric mode keeps the substance of the speech from veering into stark individualism, which would render each woman responsible for her oppression (as Oedipus and King Lear bear sole responsibility for their downfalls), and thus unfit for the vote. Instead, the lyric mode guides the speech's consideration of the individual into an existential contemplation of how each of us experiences solitude throughout our lives.

Just as Elizabeth Barrett Browning's lyric poem, Sonnet 43, famously lists all of the ways in which she loves her beloved, so too Stanton's lyric tragedy lists all the ways humans are alone, through sensory-based, image-laden language to which audience members can relate and that they can recognize in their own life experiences. The lyric form makes tragic solitude poignant, relatable, and recognizable as each of our own life stories. For example, Stanton likens life to a "solitary voyage that each makes alone" and to a "soldier who requires provisions from society but bears the burdens of fighting alone."[51] She imagines the human condition as akin to Jesus's solitude in Gethsemane, and explains that in both our "greatest triumphs" and "darkest tragedies" we "walk alone."[52] Although most of the speech addresses conditions that apply to both men and women, Stanton specifically notes that women experience this fundamental solitude. "Whatever the theories may be of women's dependence on man, in the supreme moments of her life, he cannot bear her burdens. Alone she goes to the gates of death to give life to every man that is born into the world; no one can share her fears . . . and if her sorrow is greater than she can bear, alone she passes beyond the gates into the vast unknown."[53]

Rather unexpectedly, by causing the audience to cognitively and emotionally recognize how each human is fundamentally alone, this speech irrefutably promotes women's suffrage (and other rights). If we accept that each person is a unique entity who is responsible for her/himself, then one cannot endorse legal, educational, or economic systems that presume men will take responsibility for women.[54]

Campbell concludes by stating, "Stanton's argument, lyric and tragic though it is, attains its full power" as its enumerative, resonant, personal examples demonstrate that "Men cannot take responsibility for women . . . . men can take responsibility only for themselves, and, of course, women are the only ones who can be responsible for themselves."[55] Stanton drives home this point and its political implications in the jarringly pointed question that concludes the speech, "Who, I ask you, can take, dare take on himself, the rights, the duties, the responsibilities of another human soul?"[56] Ultimately, Campbell argues convincingly that Stanton's speech, "The Solitude of Self," does something in society: the combination of its lyric form and tragic content irrefutably demonstrates women's and men's shared ontology (aloneness) and therefore the necessity of equal rights.

CRAFTING A CRITICAL ESSAY

As these research examples demonstrate, critics begin by choosing texts they find to be interesting and relevant—texts they believe do something in society. Then, focusing attention on the text, a critic asks rhetorical research questions: nuanced versions of "what does this text do in society and how does it accomplish this?" Next, the critic becomes familiar with the text, its context, and the relevant literature. Then, the critic analyzes the interplay of form and content, probably using additional rhetorical approaches that relate specifically to the research question and the form of the text. For example, Campbell uses lyric criticism to understand Stanton's speech. (The following chapters will introduce several of these approaches to criticism.) Through analysis, the critic answers the research question, developing an argument—with substantial textual evidence—for what the text does in society, how it accomplishes this symbolic action, and why all this matters.

Finally, critics write, revise, and publish their arguments as critical essays. These essays tend to follow a specific structure or layout: introduction, literature review, context and/or textual overview (if needed), analysis, and conclusion. Most critical essays use creatively worded headings and subheadings to indicate the transition from the introduction to the literature review and so on. There is an established (but modifiable) pattern for critical essays. Following this pattern often helps new critics ensure that all the necessary parts of their arguments are well developed and clearly articulated in their essays.

Introducing the Critical Essay

There are many possible ways to approach an introduction. Most introductions, however, feature the following five elements, and thus provide a firm foundation for the essay's argument. An introduction typically includes: (1) a description of the text, so readers know what text the critic analyzes; (2) a justification for selecting this text for analysis, in which the critic explains why the text (and, therefore, the critic's argument) matters and is worth reading about; (3) a research question and/or thesis statement; (4) the relevance of the research to readers; and (5) a preview of the essay's organization, so readers understand the logical structure of the argument. (See Appendix A for more information on preview statements.) There are many ways to accomplish these five elements. The following paragraphs explain the function of a thesis statement and outline three popular approaches to crafting the introduction to a critical essay.

A **thesis statement** is *a concise articulation (typically one or two sentences) of the critic's central claim about how a text functions in society: what the text does and how it accomplishes this symbolic action.* Most critical essays state their thesis statements in their introductions. Sometimes an introduction presents both a research question and a thesis statement; in this case, the thesis statement is presented as an answer to the research question. (See Appendix A for more information on thesis statements.)

Approach 1: Begin with the Text. A critic might use the opening sentences and ensuing paragraphs to offer a short, dramatic glimpse of the text. For example, in his essay about *High School,* Thomas Benson begins with a compelling description of watching the documentary in a theater. This approach works particularly well with dramatic, famous, or compelling texts—texts that showcase their artistry. A critic might then explain why the text warrants rhetorical analysis. Benson's article makes this move quite explicitly in the third paragraph: after the brief account of watching the film, Benson explains who Frederick Wiseman is, describing him as "one of the most productive and consistently successful documentary filmmakers in the history of the medium," then lists many of Wiseman's famous films.[57] He does not have to work particularly hard to justify his textual selection to his readers. He largely assumes that his readers know of Wiseman and respect his films, and that he only needs to announce that the text is one of Wiseman's documentaries to justify selecting it for rhetorical analysis.

Benson transitions into his research question by discussing how Wiseman himself speaks about the artistry and the form or structure of a documentary film. Then Benson poses his research question, "How does Wiseman draw upon the skills and contexts of his viewers to invite them to experience a particular complex of meanings as they view *High School?*"[58] He then answers in a preliminary way—providing a thesis statement—as he writes, "I will try to show that *High School* is about power . . . ."[59] Next, he previews his organization, stating, "In order to answer the [research] question of how *High School* means, I will present a detailed analysis . . . ."[60] Both his thesis and his preview statement are self-conscious: Benson draws attention to his argument by using "I-statements." Not all critics are so overt, but this approach is fairly common for thesis and preview statements. (See Appendix A.) Benson finishes his introduction by discussing the relevance of his argument—why his text and argument matter. Written in 1980, when the analysis of film was fairly new to rhetorical studies, Benson's essay makes its scholarly contribution by identifying how details in film "relate to one another to form a structure" and then how this filmic structure "may invite a rhetorical response" from the audience.[61] In other words, his essay shows how the details of a film coalesce into structures and how those structures act in society.

Approach 2: Begin with the Context. For critics working with fairly ordinary, everyday sorts of texts, opening with a scene or lines from the text may not generate the type of poignancy desired for the opening paragraphs—which brings us to a second option. A critic may begin by setting the cultural or historical stage so that readers can understand the relevance of the text. Kathleen Battles and Wendy Hilton-Morrow used this approach in their analysis of *Will & Grace*. Their introductory paragraphs recount the origins of the series, its critical acclaim, its singularity as a sitcom starring gay characters, and the legal, political, and violent cultural contexts that surrounded homosexuality when the series premiered.

This approach works well with mundane texts (such as sitcoms), but can also be a useful way to introduce a pivotal text—a text that creates a turning point, marking a before and an after. For example, Karlyn Kohrs Campbell's analysis also begins with the context: Elizabeth Cady Stanton delivered this speech at the end of her life; the House Committee on the Judiciary heard it first; the speech was part of the ongoing efforts for suffrage; and the speech was recognized as a masterpiece—as a pivotal speech—by its original audiences. By opening with context, a critic can show the before and after, thus indicating how a text influenced its context. By beginning with context, critics can indicate why they selected their texts and then transition into their research questions and/or thesis statements, signal the relevance of their research for other critics, and preview the organization of their essays.

Approach 3: Begin with the Research Question. Sometimes a critic begins the introduction with a research question—not that the opening sentence is the research question, but that the critic begins by revealing an inconsistency or shortcoming, or by pointing out an underdeveloped premise, and so on, in communication theories. In other words, the critic calls readers' attention to a curiosity in how rhetoricians understand rhetoric, and then poses that curiosity as a research question.

Murphy's analysis of Hillary Clinton's 2008 campaign speech on the economic crisis provides an excellent example of this type of introduction. Murphy begins by discussing how a rhetorical theorist, Thomas B. Farrell, defines rhetoric as the art of "making things matter."[62] He then teases out some possible meanings of this unusual definition, before reframing it as the basis of his research question, "How does rhetoric make things matter? What facets of argument make matters subject to public dispute, reflection and, if we are granted good luck, solution?"[63] By starting with a theory-based research question, an introduction also signals its relevance to other critics. A critic who answers the research question well contributes to all critics' understanding of how rhetoric makes things matter in society, and thus improves the ways in which we understand rhetoric.

Having begun with a research question and the relevance to other critics, the introduction is likely to present the text as a case study, through which the critic will attempt to answer the research question. Murphy makes this precise move: he describes the economic collapse (and politicians' responses to that collapse) as a recent controversy with significant consequences for people in the United States and, thus, provides an excellent case study of how a politician made the economy "matter" to the US public. In other words, Murphy identified his text and justified its selection as a meaningful controversy. He then previewed the organization of his essay, explaining how he would analyze the text in order to answer his research question.

Joining Scholarly Conversations

A critical essay typically features a section (or sections) known as a **literature review,** defined earlier in this chapter as *a section in a critical essay that succinctly outlines the relevant concepts and key arguments from the scholarly literature.* Following Kenneth Burke's conversation metaphor, critics imagine their critical essays as joining a scholarly conversation, and the authors of the research cited in their literature review (and other scholars who are interested in this body of research) as the audiences for their own critical essays. Thus, a literature review section demonstrates that the critic has "listened" well to the prior conversation and is making an original contribution that builds on, clarifies, nuances, or even overturns part of the established scholarly literature.

Depending on the text and its contexts, a critic may need to review multiple scholarly literatures. For example, Campbell needed to review the literature on both the lyric mode and the tragic perspective to analyze Stanton's speech "Solitude of Self." When a critic has only one literature to review, it is very common to transition directly from the introduction into a literature review and then into a context/overview section (if needed), and then into the analysis. But with multiple literature reviews, a critic tends to have—and need—more organizational options.

For instance, a critic with two literature reviews could put both literature reviews in a single section but divide them into two subsections, such as lyric modes and tragic perspectives. Alternatively, a critic could have one section that reviews one literature (such as lyric modes), and then immediately follow it with a second literature review section that reviews a second literature (such as tragic perspectives). Still another alternative is to eliminate a stand-alone literature review section and incorporate the two literature reviews into different parts of the analysis. This is Campbell's approach. She moves from her introduction into a section with the heading "The Lyric Mode," in which she first reviews the literature on lyric modes and then analyzes the portions of Stanton's speech that are lyrical. Then, she moves into a section titled "The Tragic Perspective," in which she reviews the literature on the tragic perspective and then analyzes the portions of Stanton's speech that are tragic. How many literatures need to be reviewed and the best place to incorporate those reviews in the essay is determined by the critic's understanding of the text, the argument to be crafted regarding that text, and the constraints of what the critic's scholarly readers will find persuasive.

Overview of Text and Context

At some point in the essay, a critic typically needs to provide an overview of the text—a sort of bird's eye view, so that readers understand the whole before diving into the details in the analysis section. Depending on the text, this can be done quite succinctly. For example, Murphy provides an overview of Clinton's 2008 campaign speech, describing it as a "policy address" and then explaining that "four paragraphs at the beginning state her argument; the remainder of the address, the long remainder, turns back and recapitulates the points made in the opening paragraphs."[64] Other texts, however, require more description in order to fully orient readers. For example, when providing an overview of *Will & Grace,* Battles and

Hilton-Morrow take a full paragraph to introduce the series' central characters and recurring themes.

Similarly, at some point in the essay, a critic typically needs to establish the relevant context of the text. Here, the critic describes the key elements of the context with which the text interacts. Murphy did this quite succinctly in his analysis of Clinton's 2008 campaign speech. In a few sentences, he recounts the history of US economic crises, pointing out a gap (a period without crises) from 1929 to 1987, and noting that during this gap, the United States had its strongest market regulation.[65] Murphy establishes this history and the 2008 collapse as the relevant contexts for Clinton's speech, which proposes new (and renewed) market regulations as the solution to the collapse.

Although critics need to provide overviews of their texts and contexts, there are many options for how to include this information in the critical essay. A critic might create a short section between the literature review and the analysis that contains this information. Alternatively, some or all of this information could be contained in the introduction, as the text is presented or in the course of providing a justification for studying the text. Another approach would be to put the overview of the text in the introduction and the context information in the beginning of the analysis section, or vice versa. Occasionally, a critic might even include the contextual information in the literature review section. For instance, a critic who is analyzing President Trump's inaugural address might open the literature review section with an overview of the crowd attending the inauguration, the weather, the gathered dignitaries, the gruesome partisanship of the 2016 campaign season, and Trump's preferred speaking style. This contextual information could fit as the opening to a literature review section, because that section would go on to establish how communication scholars understand the interplay between setting, audience, ceremony, campaign history, presidential styles, and inaugural addresses.

Crafting the Analysis

The analysis typically forms the bulk of the critical essay. In this section, the critic presents the specific claims about the text and presents evidence to support those claims; then, through argumentation, demonstrates the preferred interpretation and the symbolic action of the text. Each critic will have to make a judgment about how to organize this section, determining which claims and corresponding evidence to present first, second, and so on, in order to build the most persuasive argument.

Depending on the text and the argument, a critic might subdivide the analysis into two or more subsections. For example, Benson divides his analysis of *High School* into three subsections: first, he provides evidence to prove his claim that power is a recurring theme in *High School;* second, he provides evidence that the film features miscommunications and misunderstandings in ways that invite viewers to understand how power is misused in high schools; and third, he provides evidence that the film invites viewers to feel sexually confused and frustrated—thus amplifying viewers' understandings of high schools as oppressive places that misuse their power.

How a critic organizes the analysis section and uses subheadings is largely a matter of the critic's own judgment. A critic might organize the analysis section by working chronologically through the text. This approach often works with texts such as speeches, advertisements, and narratives (such as novels, films, and television series); however, this chronological approach is not usually a good fit with texts such as statues or photographs. Another critic might organize the analysis section topically, presenting the argument surrounding one topic and gathering evidence from the entirety of the text to support that one argument, then moving on to the next topic. This was Benson's approach: each of his subsections (power, miscommunication, and frustrated sexuality) features a different topical argument and gathers evidence from the film to prove that argument.

Concluding the Critical Essay

When concluding a critical essay, a critic will usually summarize the argument and then focus on why the symbolic action of the text—and thus, the argument—matters. In fact, a critic will typically spend the bulk of the conclusion making the relevance of the argument plain.

How, exactly, a critic approaches the conclusion typically depends on the nature of the text and the argument. For example, a critic might focus on the relevance of the argument in light of a cultural context, arguing that by understanding a text's symbolic action, we understand a cultural context and can then engage in cultural reasoning and action on the basis of this new knowledge. In another instance, the major contribution of an argument might be related to communication theory: the critic's analysis reveals something previously unknown, misunderstood, or undertheorized about the way communication works. In that case, the conclusion emphasizes how this new knowledge affects our understanding of communication itself.

Ultimately, the whole critical essay works together to form a persuasive argument regarding what a text does in society, how it accomplishes that symbolic action, and why all this matters. The introduction presents the argument (thesis statement) and signals its relevance to readers; the literature review joins a scholarly conversation and demonstrates how the argument advances that conversation; the analysis presents the specific claims and evidence through which the critic proves the argument; and the conclusion focuses on the relevance of the argument to its readers, many of whom are intended to be participants in the scholarly conversation cited in the literature review. As a whole, the essay functions as a prolonged argument intended for a specific audience.

CONDUCTING YOUR RESEARCH

The following chapters and the appendixes provide more specific and nuanced advice for how to develop a rhetorical research project: how to pick a text, interpret its symbolic action, articulate your argument, and organize a critical essay. The principles laid out in this chapter should provide a firm foundation as you hone your analytic skills and develop your own arguments. Ultimately, close textual analysis guides critics to focus on the text itself (both its minute details and its overarching patterns), understand its interplay of text and context as well as its fusion of form and content, and, finally, offer an interpretation of the whole text that accounts for its symbolic action.

DISCUSSION QUESTIONS

1. Consider the last time you analyzed why someone had said or written something way they did: why they chose those words, why they organized their message in that particular way, and why they chose to deliver the message in the way they did. How did you reason through these questions? What conclusions, if any, did you reach?
2. Pick a text with which you are familiar and draft a rhetorical research question regarding that text. Your question should be a more specific version of "what does this text do in society?" Use what you know about the features and the context of the text to develop your question.
3. Building on your research question, draft a thesis statement—an answer to your research question. That is, based on what you know about the text, what do you hypothesize could be the answer to your question?
4. Consider the Declaration of Independence and identify its rhetorical situation. What was its exigence (or exigences)? Who was (or is) its audience? What were (or are) its constraints? To what extent do you think the Declaration of Independence is a fitting response to this rhetorical situation? That is, how well does this rhetorical text respond to its situational components (exigence, audience, and constraints)?
5. In your own words, define "form" and "content." Explain how these are different but always fused aspects of rhetoric.
6. Consider the claim that through close textual analysis, a critic identifies the preferred interpretation of the text. Have you ever rightly identified a preferred interpretation of a text (as I did with *The Mentalist*'s romantic storyline) and struggled to convince others that your interpretation was correct? How did you attempt to convince them? Were you successful?

NOTES

1. Martin J. Medhurst and Thomas W. Benson, *Rhetorical Dimensions in Media: A Critical Casebook* (Dubuque, IA; Kendall/Hunt, 1984), vii.
2. Stephen Howard Browne, *The Ides of War: George Washington and the Newburgh Crisis* (Columbia: University of South Carolina Press, 2016), xi.
3. Browne, *Ides of War,* viii; Stephen Howard Browne, "Close Textual Analysis: Approaches and Applications," in *Rhetorical Criticism: Perspectives in Action,* ed. Jim A. Kuypers (Lanham, MD: Rowman & Littlefield, 2009), 63.
4. Kathleen Battles and Wendy Hilton-Morrow, "Gay Characters in Conventional Spaces: *Will and Grace* and the Situation Comedy Genre," *Critical Studies in Media Communication* 19, no. 1 (2002): 88.
5. James A. Herrick, *The History and Theory of Rhetoric: An Introduction,* 6th ed. (New York: Routledge, 2017), 110–111.
6. Michael Leff, "Textual Criticism: The Legacy of G. P. Mohrmann," *Quarterly Journal of Speech* 72, no. 4 (1986), 378.

7. Pádraig Ó Tuama, *In the Shelter: Finding a Home in the World* (London: Hodder & Stoughton, 2015), Kindle.
8. Lloyd Bitzer, "The Rhetorical Situation," *Philosophy & Rhetoric* 1, no. 1 (1968): 1.
9. Bitzer, "The Rhetorical Situation," 2.
10. Bitzer, "The Rhetorical Situation," 6–7.
11. Bitzer, "The Rhetorical Situation," 8.
12. Bitzer, "The Rhetorical Situation," 8.
13. Bitzer, "The Rhetorical Situation," 8.
14. Bitzer, "The Rhetorical Situation," 8.
15. Bitzer, "The Rhetorical Situation," 8.
16. "New Zealand Gun Laws Pass 119-1 after Christchurch Mosque Shootings," ABCNews.au, April 10, 2019, https://www.abc.net.au/news/2019-04-10/new-zealand-gun-laws-pass-119-1-after-christchurch-mass-shooting/10990632.
17. Collette Devlin, "First New Gun Law since the Christchurch Mosque Attacks Passes First Reading," *Stuff*, April 2, 2019, https://www.stuff.co.nz/national/christchurch-shooting/111735092/first-new-gun-law-since-the-christchurch-mosque-attacks-passes-first-reading.
18. Devlin, "First New Gun Law"; Lea Jones, "Return to Aramoana," NZHerald.co.nz, November 5, 2005, https://www.nzherald.co.nz/nz/news/article.cfm?c_id=1&objectid=10353715.
19. "The Second Amendment," *Constitution Center*, accessed December 31, 2018, https://constitutioncenter.org/interactive-constitution/amendments/amendment-ii.
20. Yun Lee Too, *The Rhetoric of Identity in Isocrates: Text, Power, Pedagogy* (Cambridge, NY: Cambridge University Press, 1995), 85.
21. Too, *Rhetoric of Identity*, 74–75.
22. Browne, "Close Textual Analysis," 65.
23. Katie Rogers and Jeffrey Mays, "Trump Calls for Unity after Synagogue Shooting, Then Swiftly Denounces Democrats," *The New York Times*, October 27, 2018, https://nyti.ms/2Jm695V.
24. Rogers and Mays, "Trump Calls for Unity."
25. Browne, "Close Textual Analysis," 65.
26. Kenneth Burke, *The Philosophy of Literary Form* (Berkeley: University of California Press, 1941), 110–111.
27. Burke, *Philosophy of Literary Form*, 110–111.
28. Browne, "Close Textual Analysis," 65.
29. Michael Leff and Andrew Sachs, "Words the Most Like Things: Iconicity and the Rhetorical Text," *Western Journal of Speech Communication* 54, no. 3 (1990): 258.
30. Leff and Sachs, "Words Most Like Things," 258.
31. John Murphy, "Political Economy and Rhetorical Matter," *Rhetoric & Public Affairs* 12, no. 2 (2009): 303–316.
32. Murphy, "Political Economy," 308–309.
33. Murphy, "Political Economy," 308.
34. Murphy, "Political Economy," 309.
35. Murphy, "Political Economy," 308.
36. Murphy, "Political Economy," 309.

37. Leff, "Textual Criticism," 378.
38. Murphy, "Political Economy," 308–309.
39. Thomas Benson, "The Rhetorical Structure of Frederick Wiseman's *High School*," *Communication Monographs* 47, no. 4 (1980): 233, 238.
40. Benson, "*High School*," 234.
41. Benson, "*High School*," 234.
42. Benson, "*High School*," 234.
43. Benson, "*High School*," 236.
44. Benson, "*High School*," 260–261.
45. Karlyn Kohrs Campbell, "Stanton's 'The Solitude of Self': A Rationale for Feminism," *Quarterly Journal of Speech* 66, no. 3 (1980): 303–305.
46. Campbell, "'The Solitude of Self,'" 305.
47. Campbell, "'The Solitude of Self,'" 305.
48. Campbell, "'The Solitude of Self,'" 304.
49. Campbell, "'The Solitude of Self,'" 306.
50. Campbell, "'The Solitude of Self,'" 309.
51. Campbell, "'The Solitude of Self,'" 306.
52. Campbell, "'The Solitude of Self,'" 306.
53. Campbell, "'The Solitude of Self,'" 307.
54. Campbell, "The Solitude of Self,'" 310, 312.
55. Campbell, "'The Solitude of Self,'" 312.
56. Campbell, "'The Solitude of Self,'" 307.
57. Benson, "*High School*," 233.
58. Benson, "*High School*," 234.
59. Benson, "*High School*," 234.
60. Benson, "*High School*," 234.
61. Benson, "*High School*," 235.
62. Murphy, "Political Economy," 303, 314.
63. Murphy, "Political Economy," 303.
64. Murphy, "Political Economy," 308.
65. Murphy, "Political Economy," 308.

PART II
Orienting Methods

Chapter 3

Narrative Criticism

President George H. W. Bush nominated Clarence Thomas for the Supreme Court in 1991. During the confirmation hearings, the report of an FBI interview with Dr. Anita Hill was leaked to the press. Dr. Hill was then called to testify in televised Senate hearings regarding her statements that Clarence Thomas had sexually harassed her when they worked together at the Department of Education and the Equal Employment Opportunity Commission (EEOC).

In 2016, HBO released a gripping film, *Confirmation,* that narrativizes those hearings. Starring Kerry Washington as Dr. Hill, this film depicts events leading up to the hearings, events occurring in backrooms during the hearings, and some of the fallout as a result of the hearings. At the center of the film stands a recreation of the verbatim testimonies of Dr. Hill and Clarence Thomas, who is now a Supreme Court Justice.

When I watched this film, I found it compelling—at times chilling. The narrative was a political thriller, even though I knew the outcome. Before sitting down to watch, I knew that the senators (both Democrats and Republicans) who questioned Dr. Hill would treat her in outrageously rude ways. I knew that other witnesses who were willing (some under subpoena) to testify to similar experiences of sexual harassment would be dismissed by the senators without their testimony being heard. I knew that Thomas would be confirmed by the Senate and take a seat on the Supreme Court—where he remains as of this writing. And having watched the 2018 Senate hearings for Brett Kavanaugh's confirmation to the Supreme Court, I knew that the same accusations made against Dr. Hill—for example, that at times she was too emotional or not emotional enough—would be repeated against Dr. Blasey Ford.

What makes *Confirmation* a thriller is not mystery but exceptional storytelling. The narrative powerfully depicts a process that inexorably grinds toward confirmation—hence the title of the film. *Confirmation* tells the story of these Senate hearings in a way that reveals the political machinations behind Thomas's nomination, the timing and nature of the hearings, and the careful political handling of both Thomas and Hill throughout the processes. Without claiming to know which testimony upholds the truth, the film depicts how an entire political institution—the US Senate—was brought to bear against Dr. Hill.

Broadly speaking, a **narrative** is *an account (real or fictional) of related events.* **Narrative criticism,** then, is *a method for analyzing narratives, evaluating their quality, and demonstrating how narratives influence particular audiences and larger cultures.* This method helps orient a critic by focusing attention on one aspect of a text's symbolic form—its narrative—as the critic's central approach.

Narrative critics work to understand the symbolic action of narratives—what they do in society—by evaluating narratives and assessing their ethics and effectiveness. Critics address how narratives influence their audiences and how some narratives—myths—can provide the reasoning through which a whole culture thinks. To understand how to use this method, we first need to explore what narratives are and how humans use them.

A THEORY OF NARRATIVES

Communication scholars identify four narrative criteria a discourse must possess to qualify as a narrative. First, there must be events that are linked together.[1] That is, more than one thing must happen, and the things that happen must be connected to each other in some way.

Second, as theorist Gérard Genette pointed out, events must be situated in time, but "need not be told chronologically."[2] In other words, for something to qualify as a narrative, there must be events that are not only related to one another but that have a chronology so that audiences can ultimately understand (or attempt to understand) which event happened first, which events happened simultaneously, and so on. But the narrative itself can use flashbacks and flashforwards, or begin in the middle of the story. It can also use other techniques that intrigue audiences as they make sense of the chronology of events.

Third, a narrative has a "central subject."[3] Essentially, after hearing, seeing, or reading a narrative, one can answer the question, "What was it about?" For example, *Confirmation* is about the Senate confirmation of Justice Clarence Thomas, despite multiple allegations of lurid sexual harassment.

Finally, a narrative is told.[4] Narratives are "fundamentally communicative"; or as narrative critic Caren Deming put it, "notions of a 'teller' and a 'told to' are immanent to narrative."[5] Events happen all the time—a tree falls in a forest, dislodging a boulder that rolls into a riverbed and shifts the course of river, causing a town's wells to run dry—but these events only become a narrative when people tell the story, even if they only tell it to themselves.

On the basis of these broad criteria, many discourses qualify as narratives. For instance, the vast majority of novels, biographies, historical accounts, films, documentaries, sitcoms, television dramas, and theater productions qualify as narratives. Similarly, most news reportage, as well as some songs, poems, ballets, comic strips, speeches, conversations, advertisements, and music videos, are or contain narratives.

Humans as Story-Telling Animals

Communication theorist Walter Fisher argued that narration was "the foundation of human communication."[6] Following the philosopher Alasdair MacIntyre, he described humans as "homo narrans" or "*story-telling animals.*"[7] The idea here is that humans think in narratives, speak in narratives, interpret events through narratives, and assume our world will conform to expectations established through narratives.

For example, analyzing candidates' statements and news stories from the 2016 Republican primaries, rhetorical critic David Cisneros identified two repeating narratives, which he termed the "Latino vote" and the "Latino threat."[8] The first narrative characterizes Latinx citizens as a prized voting bloc, to whom Republican candidates desperately needed to appeal. Thinking within this narrative, Marco Rubio and Ted Cruz squared off—occasionally speaking in Spanish during live debates and duking it out verbally in a competition to demonstrate which was the more authentically Latinx and thus had the greater appeal to Latinx voters. The "Latino vote" narrative led these Republican candidates (and many news sources and US voters) to interpret Latinx citizens as a homogeneous group and as valued voters, and to assume that without their electoral support a Republican candidate could not win the presidency.

The second narrative, "Latino threat," characterizes "Latinxs as a group that needs to be policed and removed . . . as interlopers, criminals, threats, and dangers."[9] Donald Trump often gave voice to this narrative as he referred to Mexican and Latin American immigrants as "criminals and rapists" during the primary election campaign and promised a "border wall paid for by Mexico."[10] This narrative led many Republican candidates, news outlets, and voters to interpret Latinxs as criminals, and to assume that without policing, border walls, tent cities, and mass deportations, the United States would be overrun by Latinx criminals.

In this example, we can see humans using stories to interpret events and people. (Latinxs are either a valued resource or an imminent threat, depending on the story being told.) We think in narratives, imagining a future based on the story (either a Republican electoral failure without the Latinx vote, or a nation destroyed through Latinx criminality, depending on the story being told). And we speak in stories: journalists and Republican candidates, as well as US citizens generally, rehearsed these stories as they discussed the 2016 campaign and the future of the nation. Considering how we think in stories, interpret events through stories, tell stories, and expect reality to conform to our storylines, we can see why Walter Fisher calls us *homo narrans.*

Narrative Reasoning

Theorizing narratives as the foundational aspect of our humanity, Walter Fisher specifically described what he called a "narrative paradigm" to explain how narratives provide the basis for human reasoning and decision-making.[11] Typically, logic is understood as inductive and deductive reasoning. **Inductive reasoning** is *a two-step process that moves from evidence to conclusion.* Consider, for example, this logically flawed inductive argument:

1. Inductive Evidence: This Latinx individual speaks Spanish.
2. Flawed Inductive Conclusion: Therefore, all Latinx individuals must speak Spanish.

In contrast, **deductive reasoning** is *a three-step process that moves from a widely recognized belief or assumption (known as the major premise) to a specific piece of evidence (known as the minor premise), to the conclusion.* Consider, for example, this logically flawed deductive argument:

1. Deductive Major Premise: All Latinxs speak Spanish.
2. Deductive Minor Premise: This person speaks Spanish.
3. Flawed Deductive Conclusion: Therefore, this person must be Latinx.

Both inductive and deductive logic present evidence and claims in an almost formulaic sense. We can work through their causal relationships and test the strength of the evidence and the structure of the arguments. Indeed, when inductive and deductive arguments are boiled down to the simple presentation of premises (as above) it can be quite clear whether, how, and why these arguments are flawed. We can recognize that the inductive argument above makes a mistake in generalizing about millions of people on the basis of the evidence of one individual.

Meanwhile, the deductive argument begins with an untrue major premise, which invalidates the whole argument. A second reason why this argument is flawed is that it has a faulty structure. At no point did it stipulate that *only* Latinx individuals speak Spanish. Even if the major premise were true, the evidence presented in the minor premise (that a particular person speaks Spanish) is inadequate evidence for concluding that the person is Latinx.

Here, we begin to see the complicated rules governing the articulation of and analysis of formal logic. Indeed, this type of logic has to be taught—many colleges and universities have courses in argumentation and logic. Thus, while allowing for the utility of formal logic, Walter Fischer rejected it as the basis of human reasoning, demonstrating that few humans have the formal training for it, and, more important, that narrative reasoning provides humans with the skills to reason effectively.

Narrative reasoning is *the process of making "decisions based on 'good reasons' that are derived" from cultural narratives.*[12] The stories we hear growing up, the histories taught in school, the religious stories preached to us, and the narrative entertainment we immerse ourselves in become a bank of narrative elements. This bank stores all the emotions (such as greed, jealousy, love, and honor) that we expect to function as motives; all the plotlines we consider reasonable (such as causal relationships, red herrings, and plot twists); all the characters we expect to meet (such as mean girls, evil geniuses, selfish brutes, white knights, the girl next door, a gay best friend, and greedy bosses); and the endings we consider satisfactory (happily ever after, learning from a mistake, revenge, and so on). When we make decisions, we draw on the narrative elements in our banks to construct a reasonable narrative that accounts for motives and causation, and that points the way toward a satisfying conclusion.

Returning, for example, to David Cisneros's analysis of news narratives and Republican talking points of Latinxs during the 2016 campaign, we can see how the two narratives offer *reasons*—embodying logic in characters, motives, and plotlines. On the surface, these narratives appear quite different: in the Latino vote narrative, Latinxs are a valued resource that—if handled appropriately—will lead to Republican success; in the Latino threat narrative, Latinxs are a criminal threat that—unless handled appropriately—will destroy the United States. However, Cisneros argues that the two narratives operate on the same logic: in both, Latinxs are seen as a homogeneous demographic (either good or criminal); in both, Latinxs are seen as easily handled (either speaking Spanish is seen as sufficient to appeal to Latinxs or a bigger wall is seen as sufficient to terminate migration and criminal trafficking); in both, Latinxs are portrayed as a "'sleeping giant,' awakening to a singular purpose, whether for good or for ill"; and in both, Latinxs' foundational and longstanding roles within and contributions to this nation are ignored and erased.[13] The two different stories use the same logic: an easily manipulated, homogeneous group of people has just arrived on the scene, and is about to upend life as we know it—unless we act.

Distilling these narratives to their logical core, Cisneros demonstrates that they implicitly frame White Americans as the "we" and present White Americans' forthcoming actions as the point of these narratives. Moreover, by revealing how the same logic undergirds both narratives, Cisneros is able to explain these narratives as "two sides of the same coin," thus explaining how "Donald Trump was able to slip between them" as his rhetoric careened from accusing Mexicans of being rapists to attempting to woo Latinx voters by tweeting Cinco de Mayo pictures of himself eating a taco bowl.[14]

For humans to accept a narrative's reasoning, it must pass two tests. **Narrative probability,** *the first test of narrative reasoning, tests the likelihood or probability that a story is coherent, that its plotlines and characters' actions make sense.*[15] Here, we ask: (1) Would those actions probably lead to those consequences? (2) Would those characters probably act that way? and (3) Are the outcomes probable in this narrative's world? For example, I once read a story about a world where a woman could make magical potions using herbs—but each herb exacted a magical price. Throughout the entire narrative, each herb exacts its expected price every time. Then, in the conclusion, the herbalist used an herb that would cost her life in order to defeat the evil one—but the magic chose not to claim her life and she lived happily ever after with her true love. Despite the happy ending, I was deeply dissatisfied with this conclusion: it broke narrative probability. The happy ending was entirely improbable within this narrative: the narrative refused to play by its own internal rules of cause and effect, thus losing its own coherence and deeply frustrating me.

Narrative fidelity, *the second test for narrative reasoning, tests whether a story "rings true" with the stories one "knows to be true."*[16] Both the Latino vote and Latino threat narratives would fail this fidelity test for audiences who are familiar with the variety of cultures, language use, religious backgrounds, and ethnic identities within Latinx communities. For such audiences, neither the Latino vote nor the Latino threat characterizations of a homogeneous Latinx demographic would ring true.

Unlike formal logic (inductive and deductive reasoning), where validity tests must be carefully taught and memorized, humans rather intuitively use narrative probability and narrative fidelity to test narrative reasoning. Narratives either seem plausible to us, or they don't; they ring true for us, or they don't. We consistently reject narratives that seem either internally implausible or unfaithful representations of reality—with a few exceptions. Science fiction and fantasy narratives routinely feature monsters, impossible technology, magic herbalists, futuristic settings, and so on. None of these things "ring true" with our known reality. Yet as long as a narrative states up front that its world is unlike our own and as long as the human characters within the narrative act in ways that ring true to human lives and motives, audience members tend not to mind these infidelities.

Cultural Narratives

When people base their decisions primarily on narrative reasoning (as opposed to inductive and deductive reasoning), their cultural backgrounds play extremely important parts in their decision-making. Our narrative banks are filled during our childhoods and adolescence with the story elements we repeatedly hear. **Culturally told narratives** are *the narratives that recur within a given culture, told repeatedly with different character names and setting locations but the same motives, plotlines, casts of characters, and conclusions.* For example, children in the United States often hear "rags to riches" narratives, "ugly-duckling" narratives, and "underdog" narratives. "The Tortoise and the Hare," "David and Goliath," and "The Little Engine That Could" are all underdog stories popular with young children; underdog film franchises such as the *Karate Kid* and *Star Wars* usher children into adolescence (and beyond). These narratives train children to dream big, try hard, and expect perseverance to pay off.

Later in life, we will judge the probability and fidelity of other people's stories, as they explain their motivations and actions, on the basis of the plotlines and types of motives that feature in our cultural narratives. We will assess other people's personalities on the basis of the types of characters that feature in those narratives. On the basis of the motives, plotlines, and characters of those narratives, we will make decisions and chart out futures for ourselves. And on the basis of the types of satisfying endings of our culturally told narratives, we will risk health, wealth, relationships, and safety while pursuing what we see as the only acceptable outcomes.

Some concepts repeat so regularly in the narratives of a culture that they represent cultural **archetypes,** which psychologist Carl Jung theorized as *a community's collective (subconscious) understanding and symbolism of concepts central to the culture of that community.*[17] For example, traditional US culture has two basic understandings of adult women—the good mother and the evil, selfish woman—that surface as archetypes throughout narratives. The good mother is symbolized through archetypes such as the fairy godmother and the self-sacrificing mother; the evil, selfish woman is symbolized through archetypes such as the evil stepmother and the seductress. Typically, archetypes appear in narratives as discrete elements, for instance, as a particular character (an evil stepmother), as a plotline (a quest), or as a setting (the forest). The details (what these archetypes look like or specific details of their backstories) can vary immensely without "losing their basic pattern."[18] As a result, archetypes can appear in a wide variety of narratives and are typically identified by repetition of a general pattern rather than a single defining characteristic.

Some cultural narratives function as **myths,** *narratives that address a community's "ultimate questions," express a community's "spiritual meaning," and speak to "the meaning of life" as conceptualized by that community.*[19] Essentially, myths express a culture's most deeply felt "that's the way it is" values, truths, assumptions, and expectations, and offer encompassing explanations for that culture's reality. For example, the narrative of the United States as founded as a City on a Hill is a foundational myth: it tells an origin story of how the nation was founded to be a place unlike any other on Earth—uniquely successful and uniquely blessed by God. This myth lays out the values and logics of US exceptionalism and the Protestant work ethic.

Myths typically feature archetypes and, as theorized by cultural critic Richard Slotkin, always depict the universe, a protagonist, and a moralistic plot.[20] As a result, a myth reveals what a culture thinks the world is like (the universe); how that culture thinks humans (the protagonist) should act; and how that culture conceptualizes "laws of cause and effect," natural processes, and what constitutes good and bad behavior (the moralistic plot).[21] For narrative critics, the word "myth" does not imply that a story is necessarily untrue. Indeed, many myths narrativize historical events, thus grounding the values and meaning of a community in an interpretation of its history.

Enjoyment and Transportation

People love narratives. We read books, watch movies, stream Netflix, and listen to our friends recount their days. Most narratives are fiction—yet we happily spend our time thinking about people and events that do not exist. Although these fictions represent and communicate cultural norms, grounding and reinforcing our decision-making processes, media scholars suggest that the reason people derive so much pleasure from narratives is that they are "transported" into the story world, losing "awareness of the actual world" as they enter a "state of flow" during the narrative.[22] In other words, they are entirely absorbed by an activity. Making sense of the narrative requires one's full concentration but is not overly taxing.

When people are **transported into a narrative,** *their attention is fully consumed by the narrative, which determines both their sense of imagery and their feelings.*[23] My sister is regularly transported or "lost in a book." When she is reading, she neither sees nor hears the real world around her. Media scholars suggest that when audience members are transported into the narrative they are more likely to be persuaded by it.

The argument here is that just as a traveler returns home a changed person, so too do those who are transported into a narrative. For example, astrophysicist Neil deGrasse Tyson starts his book, *Astrophysics for People in a Hurry,* with a chapter titled "The Greatest Story Ever Told." This chapter tells a narrative of the universe, which starts in "one ten-million-trillion-trillion-trillionths of a second" time increments.[24] When I read this narrative, I was transported—wholly engrossed in thought and imagining energy, gravity, strong nuclear forces, radioactive decay, atomic nuclei, and electromagnetism.[25] I'm not an astrophysicist. I never wanted to be one and I still don't. But being transported by this narrative gave me a new appreciation for our cosmos, the scientists who study it, and the research they produce. In practical terms, I am much more likely to attend a campus lecture by an astrophysicist now than I was before reading the opening narrative of *Astrophysics for People in a Hurry.*

Ultimately, narratives are essential building blocks of social and political life.[26] Not only do mythic narratives establish morality (good and bad behavior), but culturally told narratives establish what a community believes is normal, probable, and reasonable. Because people regularly rely on narrative reasoning, culturally told narratives also determine our decision-making, informing what we do and why we do it. Critics generally use narrative criticism when they (1) attempt to understand why a narrative is popular, (2) study what a culture—at a particular point in time—deemed "reasonable," and (3) evaluate how a narrative might influence audience members' decisions.

DOING NARRATIVE CRITICISM

Narrative criticism has several phases: a critic analyzes what happens in the narrative, how the narrative is told, and finally, the narrative's medium and context, working to understand how the mode of dissemination affects the narrative itself. These phases are not exactly a linear progression—one doesn't complete the first phase and then move on to the next without ever looking back. Rather, each phase helps inform the others as a critic revisits prior phases throughout the research process to understand a narrative's symbolic action.

Analyzing the Story

When conducting narrative criticism, a critic is likely to start by examining the **story,** *the combination of the plot, characters, and settings, or "the* what *in the narrative."*[27] In this phase, the critic asks interpretive questions such as: What happened? Who did it? Where did it happen? And what happened next? To begin evaluating the story, the critic lists each event (in chronological order, not the order in which audiences learn of events) and notes who did what and where. Then, the critic notes the connections among the various events, ascertaining which events and characters cause other events. This process gives the critic an overarching perspective on the story.

For example, analyzing former president Bill Clinton's 2016 Democratic Convention speech about Hillary Clinton's adult life, a critic could isolate the story elements, starting with the mentors who shaped her childhood, then Bill and Hillary's meeting in college, her numerous activities and social justice efforts, their trip overseas (where Bill Clinton first proposed), her early career, his second proposal, her relocation to Arkansas, her work for a law firm, and her founding of a legal aid clinic. The story continues with Bill Clinton's third proposal (this one successful), their marriage, his political career, the birth of their daughter, Hillary Clinton's social justice work, and then her political career, ending with the 2016 presidential campaign. In addition, the critic would note that the speech characterizes Hillary Clinton as "insatiably curious," a "natural leader," a "good organizer," and a listener, as well as incredibly matter-of-fact and practical. The settings throughout this narrative vary from the Midwest (Chicago area), to the South (Arkansas), to the Northeast (DC and New York), to an international context.[28] Assessing these story elements, the critic would note recurring themes: almost every event features Hillary Clinton as likable and effective at making things better.

To assess the story, narrative critics distinguish between kernels and satellites. **Kernels** are *events and actions that are essential to the plot.*[29] These are big turning points in the story. One of the best ways to determine whether an event or action is a kernel is to imagine removing it from the story and then consider what would happen to the plot trajectory. If the plot would fundamentally change, then the action or event is a kernel. For example, Hillary Clinton's decision to marry Bill Clinton is a kernel in this story. Without their marriage, she would not have become First Lady, and her political advocacy during his presidency would not have given her the experience (and name recognition) necessary for her role as a New York senator and then as secretary of state.

In contrast, **satellites** are *unessential pieces of the story.* You could delete them without altering the overall plotline, but satellites typically provide greater understanding of a character or the setting. For instance, Bill Clinton's narrations of his two failed proposals are funny satellites. They add warmth and humility to his narrative—yet he could have skipped those events and the plotline (Hillary Clinton's political trajectory) would have still hung together. When a critic distinguishes between kernels and satellites, the decision is not which parts of the story are better or more influential to audiences, but how all the events, characters, and settings fit together.

Analyzing the Discourse

After achieving a thorough understanding of the story, the critic analyzes the **discourse,** which in narrative criticism refers to *how a story is told—the arrangement, tone, look, feel, and pace of the narrative.*[30] One of the best ways to start is to note the arrangement of the events: going back to the chronologically ordered list of events and noting the order in which audience members experience them. What comes first? Are some events flashbacks or flashforwards? Next, the critics notes how chronological shifts are communicated to audiences—if they are communicated at all. Does the narrative state, "seven years ago"? Does a flash of light and then a sepia-toned filter visually communicate temporal shifts? Or perhaps temporal shifts are not originally flagged in any way and the audience is invited to assume a simple chronological rendering of events until much later in the narrative. In that case, the critic must ask how the narrative reveals its temporal ordering to audience members.

Returning to Bill Clinton's 2016 Democratic Convention speech, a critic would note that although the events are generally laid out in chronological order, the speech opens with the first time Bill met Hillary. This opening is anachronistic, or out of chronological order: he later discusses her childhood and how family and mentors had shaped her political ideology. He does not begin at the beginning; instead, his discourse—more specifically, the sequencing of events in his narrative—invites audience members and voters to see Hillary Clinton as he had: through the eyes of an awestruck, love-smitten youth.[31]

Moreover, when analyzing narrative discourse, critics often grapple with **narration,** *the use of commentary (such as a voice over in a film or a character in a book who tells the story) to convey a narrative.* Narration can fundamentally shape how audience members experience the narrative and what conclusions they draw from it. For instance, the television series *Grey's Anatomy* is narrated by its central character, Meredith Grey. Many episodes begin and end with her voice-overs. These fundamentally shape how audience members interact with the series and with each episode: Grey's opening narration primes viewers to expect certain themes and the closing narration often offers a sense of meaning. When analyzing a narrative, a critic needs to consider whether there is narration, and if so, whether the narrator is omniscient and/or omnipresent, speaks in first, second, or third person (or a mixture thereof); whether the story is told in past, present or future tense, in active voice (where the characters do things) or in a distancing passive voice (where things happen in an impersonal, inevitable, fated sort of way). The critic also assesses whether the narrator's tone is optimistic, sarcastic, cynical, distant, ominous, and so on, and how that tone is communicated.

For example, analyzing tweets as narratives, communication critic Neil Sadler suggests that this fragmented and distributed narration style—full of interruptions and deeply personal—matches everyday storytelling practices.[32] That is, in conversation with friends and acquaintances, a person may narrate a story, but the narration will be full of interruptions and asides. So too with a tweet, which places a considerable burden of interpretation on the audience to sort through fragmented storytelling, without the contextual clues available in face-to-face conversations.

A critics also considers pacing in analyzing the discourse of a narrative. The pacing of a narrative can be slow, languid, fast, frantic, and so on. For example, the opening sequence of the breakout 1998 German thriller, *Run Lola Run,* combines a variety of filmic techniques in order to set a frantic pace.[33] Quick editing (fast-paced cutting from shot to shot) portrays the character, Manni, as feeling out of control by establishing a hectic quality. The characters speak quickly, darting questions at each other. The pacing of events is fast—reinforcing the title of the film and the central scenes of Lola running. In the conclusion, the pacing slows: a wide shot places Manni and Lola alone together in an intersection; the traffic and pedestrians fade from view, creating a sense of pause, or a slowing and relaxing of time, as the characters (at least temporarily) solve their problems. The pacing directly contributes to the narrative by first reinforcing the sense of danger that compels the plot and then by offering rest and relaxation as the characters are saved in its conclusion.

When analyzing a narrative's discourse, a critic needs to consider other elements, such as whether the characters and/or the narrator directly address the audience, whether the narrative uses dominant or recurrent metaphors or symbols, and, in audiovisual texts, how elements such as the cinematography and background music shape the narrative. For example, in Alfonso Cuarón's *Gravity* (2013), the camera pointedly lingers on a small Buddha statue as Sandra Bullock's character, Dr. Ryan Stone, begins her final descent to the earth. This imagery clearly conveys the spiritualism in the film as Stone passes through a life-altering experience—not just surviving space, but letting go of her daughter who had died in an accident.

Analyzing the Role of the Medium

When analyzing the discourse, critics focus on *how* the story is communicated. In other words, critics must pay attention to the **medium,** *the format and/or platform used to create and disseminate the narrative,* such as books, television, film, oral presentations, music, dance, and graphic novels. Each medium has things it does well and things it does not—for both story and discourse. For example, in terms of story, television lends itself to ongoing storylines, whereas films often have discrete plots that come to an end as the credits roll. In terms of discourse, an episode in a broadcast or basic cable television series takes advertisement breaks that disrupt the narrative (and therefore disrupt the audience's transportation into the narrative), whereas premium cable (such as HBO) and films have uninterrupted narratives.

Each medium is different—and the differences matter. A book can be hundreds of pages long, taking over twenty-four hours to read. A film usually maxes out at the three-hour mark, not only because audiences grow uncomfortable and restless after a few hours in a theater, but because the theater itself must resell those seats to new audiences if it is going to make a profit. The particular capabilities and limitations of a medium, as well as its economic context, affect the level of complexity that the story can have and the level of detail in the discourse.

A narrative critic assesses the story of a narrative, then analyzes how "the story is rendered as discourse" and then "manifested in a medium."[34] Although a critic breaks this analysis into steps (story, then discourse, then medium) to make the process manageable, it is ultimately necessary to make connections among the story, discourse, and medium, understanding how they influence and shape one another. For example, rhetorical critics David Levasseur and Lisa Gring-Pemble assess how story, discourse, and medium combined to fundamentally hamper Mitt Romney's political career.[35] During his 2012 presidential campaign, Mitt Romney and his campaign team routinely told a narrative of his role leading the finance firm Bain Capital to economic success. The reasoning of the narrative went something like this: Romney's experience making Bain Capital an extraordinarily successful company provided him with the insight and wisdom to lead the US economy. Levasseur and Gring-Pemble demonstrate how this narrative had strong plausibility and fidelity: it offered reasons that many Americans find culturally plausible. Throughout the early stages of Romney's presidential campaign and across various media platforms, the Bain Capital narrative argued that Romney would be good for the national economy. Romney featured this story in his speeches, emphasized it on his campaign website, and wrote about it in the *Wall Street Journal.*

Next, focusing on Romney's discourse, Levasseur and Gring-Pemble consider the specific word choices featured across these language-based media. Romney's discourse—specifically, his word choices—draw firm lines between politicians and businessmen, casting then-President Obama as a career politician and himself as a businessman. In so doing, Romney worked to identify with average citizens who work in businesses. His word choices suggest that all businesses are fundamentally the same: capitalist enterprises operating in a free market. Unfortunately for Romney's political aspirations, his rivals during the Republican primaries knew that under Romney's leadership, Bain Capital had transitioned from a venture capital company (which provides start-up loans to new businesses) to a private equity company (which borrows money to buy out companies, radically reduces those companies' expenses—often through layoffs—and then resells those companies at enormous profits).[36]

Levasseur and Gring-Pemble draw the story, discourse, and medium together to assess what went wrong for Romney in a narrative that had had such strong plausibility and fidelity with Republican audiences. Romney's story, discourse, and media outlets would have dovetailed quite nicely for this narrative—except that he also had to participate in live televised debates against well-informed, well-prepared, business-savvy opponents. Levasseur and Gring-Pemble suggest that if Romney could have saturated the nation in his narrative, he likely could have profited from this story. During the campaign season, however, the other Republican candidates revealed the difference between venture capitalist companies and private equity companies, breaking open Romney's discourse of a unified free market. Whereas Romney's discourse featured all companies as operating within a singular capitalist marketplace, the other candidates cast Romney's Bain Capital as participating in a "vulture" and "exploitive" economy, rather than "good capitalism."[37]

In conjunction with these debate attacks, the Republican candidates ran negative ad campaigns that were based on their version of the Bain narrative. These ads served as the basis for the Obama campaign's approach to that narrative after Romney received the Republican presidential nomination.[38] Although Romney's version had had strong narrative plausibility and fidelity with Republican audiences, and although its discourse featured important word choices that helped audiences identify with Romney and vilify Obama, the televised debates and larger campaign setting—complete with attack ads—largely undid Romney's carefully worded and reasoned narrative.

When analyzing the story, discourse, and medium of a narrative—and the ways these elements influence and shape one another—a critic works to understand the cultural popularity of a narrative and/or assess the reasoning embedded within it. A narrative critic must ultimately take a step back from the narrative and interpret it, revealing how the story and discourse demonstrate what reasoning the narrative assumes is true, how the discourse and medium communicate the narrative, and how the narrative guides human decision-making. Finally, the critic judges the narrative, typically arguing that the reasoning it offers to the audience is good or bad for society.

RESEARCH EXAMPLES

In the first example, Valerie Wee analyzes the Japanese horror narrative, *Ringu*, and its US adaptation, *The Ring*. Wee is particularly adept at demonstrating how each narrative reflects its audience's culture by showing how *The Ring* changed specific elements of *Ringu*'s plot and characterization to fit US norms for narrative probability and fidelity. In the second example, Leroy Dorsey and Rachel Harlow analyze how the mythic elements of Theodore Roosevelt's narrative history, *The Winning of the West,* guided—and continue to guide—US decisions on immigration policies. The third example explores the way then-President Ronald Reagan used a story form known as the jeremiad as he persuaded US citizens and Congress to enact a package of financial policies. This third example showcases the potential for overlap between narrative criticism and genre criticism (discussed in Chapter 5).

Valerie Wee
"Patriarchy and the Horror of the Monstrous Feminine" (2011)*

Entertainment industries often borrow, adapt, and retell narratives that originated in other cultures. For example, the long-running US reality TV show, *Survivor,* is an adaptation of the Swedish reality TV show, *Expedition Robinson.* However, given the ways in which narratives embody and convey culturally based assumptions, reasons, characters, plot structures, and endings, they usually must be adapted in order to fit a different culture's expectations for narrative probability and narrative fidelity. Analyzing Japan's 1998 horror film, *Ringu,* and its 2002 US adaptation, *The Ring,* Valerie Wee demonstrates what these films reveal about Japanese and US conceptualizations of women.

Both films share the same basic narrative. A girl who has supernatural abilities is murdered. Subsequently, she haunts our world through a videotape, killing people who watch the video seven days after they watch it. When a young boy accidentally watches the video, his mother—a reporter—goes to considerable lengths to understand the supernatural phenomenon and save her son's life. Analyzing the stories and discourses of these two films, Wee notices three key areas where the US adaptation is significantly different from the Japanese original.

First, the characters are fundamentally different. In *Ringu,* the girl's supernatural abilities are originally ambiguous—she is not necessarily an evil character—and she uses her psychic abilities to protect and defend her innocent mother. In contrast, in *The Ring,* the girl is inherently evil and uses her psychic abilities to torment and manipulate her adopted mother, who responds with violence. Thus, the Japanese version presents one good woman (the mother) and one ambiguous girl; the US version presents two bad females: a merciless mother and an evil girl.

Second, the originating kernels are different. Both plotlines functionally begin with the supernatural girls' murders, but offer different accounts of their deaths and thus attribute blame differently. In *Ringu,* the girl's father brutally murders her; in *The Ring,* the tormented but also vicious mother murders her adopted daughter.

Third, the discourses resonate differently with Japanese and US audiences. Audiences familiar with Japanese ghost stories recognize the ghost in *Ringu* as a traditional "vengeful ghost" who returns as a "terrifying" and "destructive" being, seeking vengeance for the wrongs committed against her by men who should have protected her.[39] Her appearance is visually similar to the traditional depiction of

---

*This essay may be found in *Feminist Media Studies* 11, no. 2 (2011): 151–165.

vengeful ghosts. The US version maintains the visually striking depiction of the ghost: long, dark, lank hair that obscures a disfigured face with swollen eyes, but US viewers do not associate this visual symbolism with any traditional or archetypal character; nor do they connect it with the concept of vengeance or the righting of social wrongs. The imagery is terrifying, but otherwise meaningless in US culture.

Focusing specifically on the differences between the two films, Wee concludes that both narratives demonstrate patriarchal reasonings: they both invite viewers to understand the female characters as out-of-control, violent forces. However, Wee suggests that *Ringu* taps into conservative Confucian values that hold men responsible for protecting others and hold women responsible for acting submissively. Thus, *Ringu* shares the blame between both genders: the girl's father is monstrous because he failed to uphold his role and killed his daughter; the girl herself becomes monstrous as she fails to accept her fate and turns vengeful instead. In contrast, *The Ring* "unambiguously associates femininity with evil." All the women in this film participate in the terrifying violence while the men are "innocent individuals haunted and/or killed by a malevolent female force."[40] Ultimately, Wee argues that the distinctions between these narratives and their "depictions of these female characters reveal the fundamental cultural and philosophical differences that structure Japanese/Eastern and Hollywood/Western views of femininity, women, and their roles in society."[41]

Leroy G. Dorsey and Rachel M. Harlow
"'We Want Americans Pure and Simple': Theodore Roosevelt and the Myth of Americanism" (2003)*

Between 1885 and 1894, Theodore Roosevelt published several best-selling volumes in his historical narrative, *The Winning of the West.* In this narrative, Roosevelt recounts the "American struggle for westward exploration and settlement."[42] He focuses on how the "north American frontier influenced" settlers' character and describes how immigrants cultivated frontier lessons and morals in order to ensure the success of their settlement—and the American experiment more broadly.[43] During this era, social-Darwinist science ran rampant in US society. Many believed that allowing widespread immigration and admitting immigrants from specific countries would be suicidal for the White American race.[44] Although far from recognizing racial equality, Roosevelt nonetheless had "'little use for the anti-immigrant ravings'" of white nationalists.[45] In *The Winning of the West,* he portrays the US frontier romantically, presenting a narrative that offers new immigrants a path toward what Roosevelt imagined as true Americanism and simultaneously affirms existing citizens' "understanding of American culture."[46]

Leroy Dorsey and Rachel Harlow argue that this narrative offers the United States a myth that imagines immigration and assimilation as equally necessary to the American experiment.[47] In an era when white nationalists were trying to

*This essay may be found in *Rhetoric & Public Affairs* 6, no. 1 (2003): 55–78.

close the door on immigration, Roosevelt crafted *The Winning of the West* as a persuasive narrative, replete with reasons why assimilationist immigration is the past, present, and future of the United States. He positioned the immigrant as the "archetypal hero" of the American story and narrated how immigrants learned the moral and social lessons through which they became "wholly American" on the frontier.[48]

For example, Roosevelt narrated how immigrants fought off the harsh elements of nature and evil humans (represented in *The Winning of the West* by Native American raiders and cattle rustlers).[49] He presented these frontier trials as rites of passage through which immigrants learned moral lessons and became American. Throughout, Roosevelt's immigrant protagonists succeeded when they learned to balance the need to toil individually for their own survival with the need to toil sacrificially to "sustain the community."[50]

Roosevelt's narrative conformed to broader cultural trends as he differentiated among immigrant communities, asserting that Irish, Scottish, German, and English immigrants had the "bloodlines" necessary to survive the frontier and become American. In contrast, the narrative portrayed people of Spanish, French, and Asian bloodlines as largely incapable of sustained noble toil (which Roosevelt called "the strenuous life") and therefore incapable of thriving on the American frontier.[51]

Throughout, Roosevelt's immigrant protagonists labored incredibly hard to ensure their own survival and help their communities thrive. They discarded their old ways of thinking and living, completely assimilating into US culture. The narrative offers a formula for becoming an American: by working hard to survive and settle the frontier, and then working hard to ensure the survival of the democratic community; while also completely abandoning prior languages, customs, traditions, and cultural identities. This is how an immigrant became American, "pure and simple," in *The Winning of the West*.[52]

Ultimately, Dorsey and Harlow demonstrate how Roosevelt offered people who were already US citizens reasons to accept immigrants as Americans. In Roosevelt's narrative, if immigrants had the right bloodlines and learned the right moral lessons on the frontier (to abandon their prior cultures, to solely accept ultimate responsibility for their own survival, and to generously toil in support of their neighbors), they could become purely and simply American.

Dorsey and Harlow conclude by suggesting that Roosevelt's narrative reasoning still holds sway in the American imagination. Many US citizens are still leery of immigrants and insist that immigrants earn their own way, support their American neighbors, and abandon prior cultural identities before qualifying as American. However, Dorsey and Harlow also suggest that Roosevelt's three-part formula for becoming an American is deeply connected to its narrative setting, the frontier. By settling the frontier, immigrants prove their ability to live "the strenuous life," thus qualifying as Americans. Without a frontier to settle, Dorsey and Harlow suggest, current immigrants are largely unable to prove their Americanism to today's white nationalists, even when they earn their own ways, contribute to their democratic communities, and abandon their prior cultures.

Meg Kunde
"Making the Free Market Moral: Ronald Reagan's Covenantal Economy" (2019)*

In Ronald Reagan's first major policy speech as president, he explained a four-part economic plan: (1) to cut government spending on welfare programs, (2) to lower taxes, (3) to reduce regulations on financial institutions, and (4) to protect the dollar against inflation.[53] These financial policies—collectively known as "Reaganomics"—overturned over forty years of federal financial policy. How did Reagan sell the US public on such radically new financial policies? Rhetorical critic Meg Kunde answers this question by demonstrating that Reagan told a very old story—a jeremiad—that made his new policies sound like the policies for which America's mythic Puritans would have voted.

The jeremiad is a type of narrative named after the Old Testament prophet Jeremiah. Jeremiah preached to a divided Israelite kingdom, prophesying that the city of Jerusalem in the Northern Kingdom of Israel would be destroyed and that the Southern Kingdom of Judah would face similar destruction if the people did not stop oppressing the poor and worshipping idols. Only by returning to their foundational covenant with Yahweh (their holy name for their monotheistic God) could the people experience peace, justice, and well-being.

A covenant is an oath between people and God, in which God promises an *if/then* commitment and God's power ensures the *then* outcome of the covenant. The covenant between the Israelites and God was that *if* the Israelites would worship only Yahweh and keep his commands, *then* Yahweh would bless and protect them. When the Israelites broke the covenant by worshipping other gods and disregarding Yahweh's commands by oppressing the poor, Yahweh removed his blessing and protection. Thus, Jeremiah prophesied, disaster (war, famine, conquest, and exile) was coming and could only be averted by returning to the covenant and thus receiving Yahweh's blessings and protection once again.

The jeremiad is a three-part narrative structure that starts by reminding everyone of how wonderful things were when the people kept the covenant. Second, it describes or forecasts doom, gloom, and disaster now that people have broken the covenant. Third, the narrative promises a thriving, beautiful future if people return to the covenant. The Puritans relied heavily on this narrative, claiming that the covenant between the Israelites and Yahweh transferred onto their New England community and the Christian God. They believed that if they maintained religious and behavioral purity (worshiping only God and keeping his commands) they would receive God's blessings and protection.[54] Narrativizing their decisions and governmental policies in the three-part jeremiad structure, the Puritans reminded themselves of the importance of the covenant and the special blessings they were to receive if they were good enough.[55] Over time, Americans secularized this narrative, replacing its specific religiosity with a more humanistic morality.[56]

Speaking in the 1980s, Ronald Reagan invoked this covenant, essentially claiming that *if* we were good people, *then* we would experience prosperity. His

---

*This essay may be found in *Rhetoric & Public Affairs* 22, no. 2 (2019): 217–252.

narrative utilized the three-part jeremiad structure. First, he recounted a time of prosperity (before the 1930s Great Depression) that he characterized as a free-market paradise in which entrepreneurs thrived and welfare was all but unnecessary because people had good work ethics and thus were motivated to work. Second, he cast the higher taxation rates and increased regulations of the post-WWII era as a breach of the covenant. In his telling, the United States lost its faith that by being good (fulfilling our part of the covenant) we would receive blessings (God's part of the covenant or a more secularized fate—which Reagan referred to as the "magic of the marketplace").[57] Having lost our faith in this "magic," Reagan's narrative continued, we turned to human solutions and asked the government to take care of the poor, which Reagan claimed was the cause for our high taxation rates. He described a gloomy reality of economic stagnation, unemployment, and a moral corruption that kept people dependent on welfare. Finally, Reagan claimed that by cutting taxes, slashing welfare programs, eliminating regulations, and preventing inflation, he would restore the covenant and thus return the nation to prosperity and blessings.

Analyzing this narrative, Kunde notes how its logic equates a good work ethic with morality. Within this narrative, cutting taxes restores prosperity for *all* Americans, because Reagan imagined wealth trickling down: if those with strong work ethics get to keep more of their money (and their company's money), then—because they are good—they will hire more employees, raise their employees' wages, and so on. Everyone benefits financially as the wealth trickles down. This logic directly equates a strong work ethic with morality, suggesting that those who directly receive the benefit (the tax cut) are going to share it (raising wages) instead of hoarding it for themselves. (For example, CEOs wouldn't give themselves bonuses instead of raising employee wages.) Within this narrative, slashing welfare is a moral action, a "tough love" type of goodness: Reagan claimed that cutting welfare would motivate poor people to get jobs. The logic of the covenant, as applied here, is that good people receive prosperity, so anyone without prosperity must be bad. Poverty is construed as proof of immorality (being lazy) and having broken the covenant. Within this logic, laziness is the cause of unemployment, not an economy in which there are no jobs, or no jobs that don't pay poverty wages. Cutting welfare, Reagan promised, would motivate poor people to work; thus, he said, they would learn a good work ethic, become good people, and be restored to the covenant and its blessings of prosperity.

Reagan's policies "increased the income gap" as those who were already prosperous became richer and the middle class began splitting—some becoming much richer and others becoming much poorer.[58] Reagan's free-market policies resulted in growing economic inequalities.[59] As it turns out, the rich are not necessarily good people and thus wealth "did not necessarily 'trickle down'";[60] many impoverished people could not find jobs with living wages, yet their safety net had been removed as Reagan slashed welfare programs.[61]

In 2019 (before the COVID-19 related rise in unemployment in 2020), unemployment levels in the United States were historically low. The GDP (gross domestic product, a measure of how strong our economy is) had seen more than ten years of consecutive growth.[62] Yet even in this "surging economy" in which the poor were definitely employed, their wages were actually going down in terms of real money. Adjusting for inflation and using 2016 dollars, the Pew Research Center reported that the median income for a three-person household of the lower class was $26,923 in 2000; by 2016, that number had dropped by over a thousand dollars, to $25,624.[63] Meanwhile, under the economic policies that had originated with Reagan, the middle class had shrunk. In 1971, before "Reaganomics," the middle class was considered to be 61 percent of the United States; by 2016, the middle class had shrunk to only 52 percent of the population. Meanwhile both the lower and upper classes grew, absorbing the shrinking middle class.[64]

Kunde argues that Reagan narrativized the "if we are good/then we will prosper" covenant that had been circulating in the US psyche since the Puritans.[65] Reagan's narrative tapped into our Puritan myths and thus our values, assumptions, and expectations, asking Americans to believe—not in God—but in a secularized "magic of the marketplace," and reasoning that prosperity was evidence of a good work ethic, which was equated with moral goodness, while poverty was evidence of a poor work ethic, which was equated with immorality.[66] In so doing, Reagan's narrative recast his policies as the epitome of American morality "rather than a form of social Darwinism."[67]

STRENGTHS AND WEAKNESSES OF NARRATIVE CRITICISM

Narrative criticism is a particularly strong method for (1) evaluating the popularity of a text, (2) assessing a culture's assumptions about the human experience through its culturally told narratives, and (3) demonstrating how a narrative persuades its audiences as it offers them not only entertainment, but reasons to use in making decisions.

Narrative criticism can reveal why a particular narrative is a "breakout" hit. For example, Andy Weir's first novel, *The Martian,* was extraordinarily popular—especially for a science fiction novel—and was quickly made into a 2015 blockbuster film, directed by Ridley Scott and starring Matt Damon and Kristen Wiig. A narrative critic would likely suggest that this novel resonated so deeply with US audiences because it utilizes an underdog storyline and centers on a persevering hero cut from the same cowboy cloth as Tom Hank's character in *Apollo 13. The Martian*'s narrative innovatively uses familiar and popular elements from our culturally told narratives. By understanding the narrative reasoning of a culture—that is, what a culture deems to be likely to occur and faithfully representative of the human experience—a narrative critic can assess how a breakout hit fits within the culture and resonates with its audiences.

By studying the narratives of a culture, critics assess how and why people think the way they think and make the decisions they make. Narrative critics study what a culture believes to be probable: which motives lead to which actions, what chains of cause and effect—plotlines—are realistic, how certain personalities—characters—are likely to act, and what types of conclusions are acceptable. Moreover, by studying narratives, critics evaluate what a culture believes to be fundamentally true about the human experience.

This is what Valerie Wee was doing in her comparison of *Ringu* and *The Ring.* Through the narrative of *Ringu,* Wee assessed that within Japanese narrative reasoning, women's violence can be framed as vengeance. Although this vengeance is portrayed as wrong and terrifying, there is still a sympathetic understanding of it. In contrast, *The Ring*'s purposeful revisions to *Ringu*'s storyline suggest that its directors believed that framing violent women as inherently and utterly evil would resonate more with US audiences' understandings of violent women—and *The Ring*'s box office success suggests they were right.

Finally, narrative criticism is a particularly strong method for evaluating how a narrative persuades its audience. By studying the narrative reasoning embedded within the text and analyzing the discourse of the story, a critic can assess the persuasive force of a narrative. Dorsey and Harlow's analysis of *The Winning of the West* beautifully exemplifies this strength of narrative criticism as it demonstrates how Theodore Roosevelt persuaded Americans to be more accepting of immigrants—so long as those immigrants worked hard to tame the frontier, supported their American neighbors, and abandoned their prior cultures.

Narrative criticism only works on narratives. The method is limited to texts that tell a story. Its insights are most meaningful when they reveal the narrative reasoning of a community. Consequently, narrative criticism is generally limited to studying narratives that matter—narratives that are demonstrably popular in a community or foundational to the identity of a community.

CHOOSING THIS METHOD

How do you know whether you should use narrative criticism to interpret a particular piece of public discourse? To answer this question, you need to consider your text, its context, and the research question animating your analysis.

First, consider your text. Is it a narrative? Does it have at least two linked events, a chronology, and a central subject, and is it told to an audience? If not, then narrative criticism is unlikely to be a good fit for analyzing your text.

Second, consider the context of your text. Does it matter to a community? Is the narrative widely popular within a community, or does it serve a foundational role in that community? For example, a particular narrative from the Bible would qualify as a narrative that matters to an evangelical community because it serves as its foundational text. Mel Gibson's film *The Passion of the Christ* would also qualify as a narrative that matters to an evangelical community because of its popularity within that community.

And third, consider your own research motives. What research question animates your analysis? Do you want to discover why a narrative is a box-office hit, enduringly popular, or suddenly popular again? Are you interested in how a culture thinks—what it considers probable and accurate about human experiences? Are you interested in how a narrative persuades audience members—how it invites them to reason and what it prompts them to do? Narrative criticism is particularly suited to answering research questions that stem from these types of motivating concerns.

Ultimately, narrative criticism is an insightful method. Metaphorically speaking, a narrative is like a prism. At first glance, a prism may appear to be like a small gemstone: it is lovely and there is something fun about its angular shape. But a light that shines through the prism refracts into a spectrum of colors. Similarly, narratives are fun and fascinating. Analyzing a narrative is often like refracting light through a prism—the narrative reveals a startling array of cultural reasons.

DISCUSSION QUESTIONS

1. Name a narrative that you love and explain why you love it. Specifically, what have you learned from the narrative and how have you used it?
2. Consider the four defining elements of a narrative: linked events, chronology, a central subject, and a communicative element of "teller" and "told to." Now list two specific discourses that qualify as narratives and two that do not.
3. In your own words, define narrative probability and narrative fidelity. Now describe a time when you were watching or reading a narrative and noticed that it broke your standards for narrative probability and/or fidelity. How did you react?
4. Describe a time when you were transported into a narrative. Is that narrative particularly persuasive to you?
5. Describe a time when you used the narrative of a film, TV show, or book to help guide a decision you made.
6. Make a list of three narrative plotlines and three character types that repeat across narratives in your culture.

NOTES

1. Robert L. Scott, "Narrative Theory and Communication Research," *Quarterly Journal of Speech* 70, no. 2 (1984), 197.
2. See Scott, "Narrative Theory," 197.
3. Hayden White, "The Value of Narrativity in the Representation of Reality," *Critical Inquiry* 7, no. 1 (1980): 11.
4. Scott, "Narrative Theory," 199.
5. Caren Deming, "*Hill Street Blues* as Narrative," *Critical Studies in Mass Communication* 2, no. 1 (1985): 2.
6. See Robin Clair, Stephanie Carlo, Chervin Lam, John Nussman, Canek Phillips, Virginia Sanchez, Elain Schnabel, and Liliya Yakova, "Narrative Theory and Criticism: An Overview toward Clusters and Empathy," *The Review of Communication* 14, no. 1 (2014): 3.
7. Clair et al., "Narrative Theory and Criticism," 3; Walter Fisher, "The Narrative Paradigm: In the Beginning," *Journal of Communication* 35, no. 4 (1985): 73–108.
8. J. David Cisneros, "Racial Presidentialities: Narratives of Latinxs in the 2016 Campaign," *Rhetoric & Public Affairs* 20, no. 3 (2017): 513–515.
9. Quoted in Cisneros, "Racial Presidentialities," 515.
10. Quoted in Cisneros, "Racial Presidentialities," 515–516.
11. Fisher, "Narrative Paradigm," 75.
12. Clair et al., "Narrative Theory and Criticism," 4.
13. Cisneros, "Racial Presidentialities," 517.
14. Cisneros, "Racial Presidentialities," 517.

15. Fisher, "The Narrative Paradigm," 75.
16. Clair et al., "Narrative Theory and Criticism," 4; Fisher, "The Narrative Paradigm," 75.
17. As cited in Robert Davies, James Farrell, and Steven Matthews, "The Dream World of Film: A Jungian Perspective on Cinematic Communication," *The Western Journal of Speech Communication* 46, no. 4 (1982): 328.
18. Carl G. Jung, "Approaching the Unconscious," in *Man and his Symbols,* eds. Carl G. Jung and M. L. von Franz (New York: Doubleday, 1964), 67.
19. Janice Hocker Rushing, "Evolution of 'The New Frontier' in *Alien* and *Aliens:* Patriarchal Co-Optation of the Feminine Archetype," *The Quarterly Journal of Speech* 75, no. 1 (1989): 2.
20. Leroy Dorsey and Rachel Harlow, "'We Want Americans Pure and Simple': Theodore Roosevelt and the Myth of Americanism," *Rhetoric & Public Affairs* 6, no. 1 (2003): 62.
21. Richard Slotkin, *Regeneration through Violence: The Mythology of the American Frontier, 1600–1860* (Middletown, CT: Wesleyan University Press, 1973), 8–9.
22. Rick Busselle and Helena Bilandzic, "Fictionality and Perceived Realism in Experiencing Stories: A Model of Narrative Comprehension and Engagement," *Communication Theory* 18, no. 2 (2008): 272.
23. Melanie Green, Timothy Brock, and Geoff Kaufman, "Understanding Media Enjoyment: The Role of Transportation Into Narrative Worlds," *Communication Theory* 14, no. 4 (2004): 312.
24. Neil deGrasse Tyson, *Astrophysics for People in a Hurry* (New York: Norton, 2017), 17.
25. deGrasse Tyson, *Astrophysics,* 17.
26. Walter Fisher, "Narration as a Human Communication Paradigm: The Case of Public Moral Argument," *Communication Monographs* 51, no. 1 (1984): 3.
27. Michael J. Porter, Deborah Larson, Allison Harthcock, and Kelly Berg Nellis, "Re(de)fining Narrative Events: Examining Television Narrative Structure," *Journal of Popular Film and Television* 30, no. 1 (2002): 24.
28. Bill Clinton, "Democratic National Convention Speech," CNN.com, July 27, 2016, https://www.cnn.com/2016/07/27/politics/bill-clinton-speech-transcript/index.html.
29. Porter et al., "Re(de)fining Narrative Events," 25.
30. Porter et al., "Re(de)fining Narrative Events," 25.
31. Clinton, "Democratic National Convention Speech."
32. Neil Sadler, "Narrative and Interpretation on Twitter: Reading Tweets by Telling Stories," *New Media & Society* 20, no. 9 (2018): 3266–3282.
33. Bridey Kenwick, "Run Lola Run and American Beauty," *Australian Screen Education* 34 (2004): 125.
34. Deming, "*Hill Street Blues* as Narrative," 2.
35. David Levasseur and Lisa Gring-Pemble, "Not All Capitalist Stories Are Created Equal: Mitt Romney's Bain Capital Narrative and the Deep Divide in American Economic Rhetoric," *Rhetoric & Public Affairs* 18, no. 1 (2015): 1–38.
36. Levasseur and Gring-Pemble, "Not All Capitalist Stories," 10.
37. Levasseur and Gring-Pemble, "Not All Capitalist Stories," 9.
38. Levasseur and Gring-Pemble, "Not All Capitalist Stories," 15.

39. Valerie Wee, “Patriarchy and the Horror of the Monstrous Feminine,” *Feminist Media Studies* 11, no. 2 (2011): 153–154.
40. Wee, “Patriarchy and the Monstrous Feminine,” 163.
41. Wee, “Patriarchy and the Monstrous Feminine,” 162.
42. Dorsey and Harlow, “‘Americans Pure and Simple,’” 57.
43. Dorsey and Harlow, “‘Americans Pure and Simple,’” 57.
44. Dorsey and Harlow, “‘Americans Pure and Simple,’” 57.
45. Dorsey and Harlow, “‘Americans Pure and Simple,’” 57.
46. Dorsey and Harlow, “‘Americans Pure and Simple,’” 57.
47. Dorsey and Harlow, “‘Americans Pure and Simple,’” 58.
48. Dorsey and Harlow, “‘Americans Pure and Simple,’” 58.
49. Dorsey and Harlow, “‘Americans Pure and Simple,’” 58, 67.
50. Dorsey and Harlow, “‘Americans Pure and Simple,’” 59.
51. Dorsey and Harlow, “‘Americans Pure and Simple,’” 57.
52. Dorsey and Harlow, “‘Americans Pure and Simple,’” 74.
53. Meg Kunde, “Making the Free Market Moral: Ronald Reagan’s Covenantal Economy,” *Rhetoric & Public Affairs* 22, no. 2 (2019): 218–219.
54. Kunde, “Making the Free Market Moral,” 223.
55. Kunde, “Making the Free Market Moral,” 223.
56. Kunde, “Making the Free Market Moral,” 223–224.
57. Kunde, “Making the Free Market Moral,” 229.
58. Kunde, “Making the Free Market Moral,” 238.
59. Kunde, “Making the Free Market Moral,” 238.
60. Kunde, “Making the Free Market Moral,” 238.
61. Kunde, “Making the Free Market Moral,” 238.
62. Bill Chappell, “U.S. Income Inequality Worsens, Widening to a New Gap” NPR.com, September 26, 2019, https://www.npr.org/2019/09/26/764654623/u-s-income-inequality-worsens-widening-to-a-new-gap.
63. Rakesh Kochhar, “The American Middle Class is Stable in Size, but Losing Ground Financially, to Upper-Income Families,” Pew Research Center, September 6, 2018, https://www.pewresearch.org/fact-tank/2018/09/06/the-american-middle-class-is-stable-in-size-but-losing-ground-financially-to-upper-income-families/.
64. Kochhar, “The American Middle Class.”
65. Kunde, “Making the Free Market Moral,” 223–224.
66. Kunde, “Making the Free Market Moral,” 229.
67. Kunde, “Making the Free Market Moral,” 225.

Chapter 4

Dramatistic Criticism

In 2018, John Allen Chau attempted to visit the uncontacted Sentinelese tribespeople on North Sentinel Island, off the coast of India. The Sentinelese have "shown again and again that they want to be left alone."[1] They attack any and all outside visitors—including firing arrows at low-flying helicopters. Because of the risk of infecting the tribespeople with outside diseases (and thus wiping out the tribe) the Indian government has made it illegal to visit them.

Chau visited the Sentinelese twice. The first time, he retreated when they fired arrows at him. The second time, he did not survive their attack. The fishermen who illegally transported Chau to the island witnessed the killing.[2]

In the days following Chau's death, US secular news media and Christian news outlets flooded my news feeds with very different accounts of these events. Indeed, the accounts were so different that they presented different victims. In secular news media, Chau was seen as the (potential) perpetrator and the Sentinelese as the victims: he invaded their land; he exposed them to dangerous germs and pathogens; and the Sentinelese defended themselves and their land. NPR's coverage featured the title, "American Reportedly Killed in Flurry of Arrows as Tribe Defends Its Island off India."[3] These secular news outlets emphasized the location as the central aspect of the story. The isolated nature of the island (and thus, its people) determines the other aspects: it makes Chau's illegal visit an endangerment to the Sentinelese people and makes their actions *defensive* actions.

In contrast, Christian news outlets told a story in which Chau was a brave missionary; his death was a tragic but heroic martyrdom; and the Sentinelese were aggressors who ought to be forgiven. *Christianity Today* quotes Mary Ho, the international executive leader of the missionary organization All Nations (through which Chau was a missionary), as stating that even as Christians grieve his death and pray for those mourning him, "we also know that he would want us to pray for those who may have been responsible for his death."[4] Similarly, Chau's alma mater, Oral Roberts University (a Christian affiliated university), released the following statement: "Oral Roberts University alumni have gone to the uttermost bounds of the earth for the last 50 years bringing hope and healing to millions. We are not surprised that John [Chau] would try to reach out to these isolated people in order to share God's love. We are deeply saddened to hear of his death."[5] These Christian news outlets emphasized the purpose of Chau's visit (to evangelize) as the central aspect of this story. His purpose transformed his visit into a God-sanctioned mission instead of the reckless endangerment of the tribe and transformed his death from a murder (for which the Sentinelese would be responsible) into a martyrdom (for which the Sentinelese should be forgiven).

The two types of news sources presented different aspects of the drama as the defining factor (location versus purpose), according to their worldviews or perspectives. Both attempted to explain an act—Chau's killing—but had different motivations in their explanations. The traditions and business model of secular news embody a worldview that focuses on material realities—existing persons, places, and events (things a reporter could touch and see)—to the extent that existing material situations are understood to determine or control future actions. Thus, secular news told a story that started with the land and featured other material aspects such as germs and pathogens.

In contrast, Christian news media embody a worldview in which all events are ordained or overseen by a merciful deity. They tell the drama of Chau's killing in a way that reinforces the idea of a good God who loves all people with a sacrificial love. With this worldview in place, Chau's death becomes a sacrifice (reminiscent of Jesus's sacrifice) that proves God's love for all people (in this case, the Sentinelese).

As I processed these news stories, my analysis was based on **dramatistic criticism,** *a method that is based on a theory, pioneered by communication theorist Kenneth Burke, that focuses on revealing rhetors' motives as they recount a drama.* Simply put, when rhetors use symbols to explain events, propose actions, and so on, they do so in ways that feature drama: something happened; someone did it; it happened in a specific location; and so on. Dramatistic criticism helps orient a critic to a text by focusing on a single aspect of its symbolic form—its dramatism—as the central approach to the text. By analyzing the way rhetors dramatize events, critics work to assess rhetors' motives—and the worldviews from which those motives are derived. The next section explores Kenneth Burke's theory of dramatism, in order to lay the foundation for learning how to use dramatistic criticism.

A THEORY OF DRAMATISM

Kenneth Burke introduced dramatism as a way of making sense of humans and acts.[6] He grounded his theory in his understanding of humanity and defined humans as symbol-using animals, "bodies that learn language."[7] (Whether other animals can or do use symbols does not matter for our purposes here.) According to Burke, the combination of symbol use and bodies is at the heart and core of what it means to be human; it is at the very center of human nature.

Symbols Screen Reality

The first chapter of this book defined a symbol as something (such as a word, sound, or image) that represents another thing, idea, or action. When humans think about symbols, we tend to imagine that our symbols are neutral, that they merely represent something that is real. Burke, however, offers a more complex understanding by demonstrating that symbols do not represent things as they really are.

Burke explains that when humans use a symbol to refer to something, we identify a "particular character" of the thing in order to "place the appropriate verbal label upon it."[8] In other words, in choosing a symbol, we choose what the "inherent character" of a thing *is.*[9] For example, consider smartphones. Although these devices can be used as phones to speak to people, our everyday usage of these devises only occasionally involves their "phone" technology. Instead, we use these devices primarily for text messaging, a host of social media apps, internet browsing, GPS, games, health and exercise apps, news apps, and entertainment apps that allow us to stream media either on the device's screen or by casting it to another screen. Yet by naming these devices "smart*phones,*" we identify a specific aspect of their capabilities and elevate that aspect as the character of these devices. In so doing, we fundamentally affect how "smart*phones*" operate within our society: they are primarily sold by telephone companies (such as T-Mobile, AT&T, and Verizon); they are typically sold in conjunction with other services offered by those telephone companies; and they are regulated—primarily as *phones*—by the Federal Communications Commission (FCC).

Burke also described humans as inventors of the negative,[10] meaning that referring to something through symbols also separates "it from that which it *is not.*"[11] For example, the symbol "tree" separates large, wood-based plants from smaller and softer plants such as "ferns." Consider, as another example, mothers who are not biologically related to their children. Shira Spector, a woman who is in a lesbian partnership with the birthmother of their child, stated that there is "no name for myself that doesn't begin with a lack. Consider *non*biological mother, *non*-birthmom."[12] These labels are *negatives*—they name what is *not* as they name what *is.*

Because symbols name what humans believe to be the essential aspect of a thing (not the real thing itself), and because our naming/labeling separates a thing from what it is not, Burke points out that our symbol systems are *context dependent.* That is, as Burkean scholar Bryan Crabble explains, depending on "the context's scope, the definition of the thing in question will vary greatly."[13] For instance, imagine moving to Chicago and quickly forming a group of friends—one of whom is closer than the others. In Chicago, you routinely refer to this close friend as your "bestie" or "best friend." And indeed, within the context of your Chicago-based friends, she is your "best friend." During the holidays, you return to your hometown and are surrounded by your long-standing, close-knit community of friends. When your hometown friends ask how Chicago is, you honestly explain that moving is tough, but you are making friends and even have one "close-ish" friend in Chicago.

This example demonstrates how the symbols we use (and the "essential nature" of the thing they refer to) are context dependent. Within the context of your Chicago friendships, one person is your "best friend." However, within the context of your larger social group, that person is only beginning to be a close friend. The idea here is that symbols are not mirrors that reflect reality, but rather, context-dependent labels that humans use to interpret and construct reality. Depending on how we understand a context, we use different labels and construct for ourselves (and our audiences) different realities.

Burke describes **terministic screens** as *terms (words and other symbols) that reflect reality by selecting one portion of reality to highlight while deflecting attention away from another portion of reality.* Thus, terms function like screens that filter our perceptions and understandings.[14] For example, the Sugar Association (a trade association that represents the US sugar industry) is hard at work ensuring that the public thinks of sugar as a "natural sweetener."[15] The use of the term "natural" *reflects* reality: sucrose (which becomes sugar when extracted from plants, fruits, and vegetables) occurs naturally in plants, fruits, and vegetables; moreover, when sucrose is extracted from these sources, it retains its naturally occurring molecular structure.[16] However, the term "natural" *selects* a portion of reality to emphasize: by describing sugar as natural, the Sugar Association highlights other meanings we associate with "natural," thus communicating that sugar is healthy, ecologically responsible, and generally good for you.[17]

In addition to selecting these aspects of reality, the term "natural" *deflects* attention from sugar's other realities. For instance, although sucrose is naturally occurring in sugar cane, there is nothing natural about the process of extracting sucrose from sugar cane, repackaging it as sugar, and then adding it to foods that already contain sucrose naturally. Additionally, because "natural" selects meanings that frame sugar as healthy, the term deflects attention from the reality of medical practitioners' advice concerning sugar intake. For example, the American Heart Association recommends that in order to avoid weight gain, which leads to heart disease and type 2 diabetes, women should eat no more than twenty-five grams (six teaspoons) and men should eat no more than thirty-six grams (nine teaspoons) of added sugar a day.[18] For context, the Coca-Cola Company reports in their nutritional facts that a twelve-ounce can of Coca-Cola contains thirty-nine grams of added sugar.[19] By describing sugar as "natural," the Sugar Association uses a term that screens reality for its audience: although the term does indeed reflect reality, it simultaneously selects and deflects realities for its audience to think of added sugar as healthy rather than linked to significant health problems.[20]

Larger discourses also function as terministic screens as they advance a particular way of interpreting reality, an interpretive worldview. A **worldview** is *a big-picture perspective or attitude regarding what the world is like: an overarching way of interpreting the world.* In Burke's terms, it is a "bundle of judgments as to how things were, how they are, and how they may be."[21] Each individual has a worldview that is voiced in the rhetoric that person creates. Through our discourses, we present our worldviews to others, inviting them to see the world as we do.

Consider, for example, the book on witchcraft that the Puritan clergyman Increase Mather published in 1684 during the lead-up to the Salem witch trials, in an attempt to convince his fellow Salem residents that the unusual events occurring in their village were acts of witchcraft. To counter other scholars and theologians who argued that individuals exhibiting strange behaviors were actually suffering from physical or mental diseases, Mather told seven detailed stories of demonic possession.[22] Then he presented an account of six symptoms "unique to episodes of possession" that his readers could use to "discern between natural Diseases and Satanical Possessions."[23] To modern ears, his six symptoms (which include items such as "When the Body is become inflexible") sound fairly unconvincing as a way to discern between demonic possession and natural diseases or disabilities.[24]

However, as rhetorical critic Lauren Lemley demonstrates, Mather's narratives and formal symptom-based assessments reinforced one another, creating a compelling argument for his audience.[25]

This example showcases two competing and context-dependent terministic screens: demonic possession and natural illness. Mather—and, ultimately, his audience—accepted a context in which a spiritual realm not only exists but regularly affects the natural realm. That context included a God, Satan, demons, and magic, and largely excluded medical knowledge and scientific principles. Other scholars were working in a different context, which largely excluded the spiritual realm and included the medical knowledge of the time.

When the Salem townspeople accepted Mather's argument, they—metaphorically speaking—placed Mather's screen between themselves and reality. They chose to interpret the world (the unusual events they witnessed) through the framework of demonic possession and witchcraft. Rather than seeing people becoming paralyzed or suffering convulsions through the screen of a natural ailment such as a seizure, they saw these symptoms through the screen of demonic possession.

Within this Burkean theory of language, there is no "outside" of terministic screens. Because humans are (according to Burke) "symbol-using, symbol-making, and symbol-misusing animals," our very nature is wrapped in symbols.[26] As such, humans can never be devoid of symbols, and thus we can never be devoid of terministic screens and worldviews. For Burke, there is always a screen (language, symbols, worldviews) between humans and reality.

Symbolic Action

The first chapter of this book began with a discussion of symbolic action that is fairly indebted to Kenneth Burke's ideas. To understand his ideas regarding symbolic action more fully, however, we must back up and consider the way Burke defined action in contrast to motion. For Burke, **motion** is *movement without purpose:* for example, a tree falls in the forest; the juices in your gut gurgle; gravity sends the Earth whirling around the sun. In contrast, **action** is *purposeful movement:* for example, a logging company cuts down a tree; a person knowingly takes a laxative; God speaks the solar system into whirling existence.

Burke considers symbols as action (hence the term "symbolic action"). When humans use symbols (whether one is speaking, interpreting a street sign, or coining a new word) we are engaged in symbolic action. Because symbols screen our reality, the use of symbols actively constructs our versions of reality. Rather than passively reflecting our world, symbols act upon us as they screen our realities; as we use them, we act to screen our realities.

Again, Burke considers humans to be symbol-using animals, which means that purposeful action is "a *way of being*" for humans.[27] Thus, purpose, or motive, is at the very center of symbol use and human existence. Burke theorizes human motives not as a "fixed thing, like a table, which one can go and look at."[28] Rather, he argued, human motives arise from and exist within our worldviews, thus bringing motive into an interlocking relationship with Burke's other key ideas of worldviews, terministic screens, action, and symbols.

Rhetorical theorist Charles Kneupper offers a version of the following example to explain motive and demonstrate how it fits with the rest of Burke's theory.

Imagine two people watch lumberjacks cut down trees in a forest. One person "describes this event [as] 'progress,'" happily noting that clearing this forest will make way for roads, commerce, and industry, and goes on to present a speech at the next city council meeting commending the deforestation as a significant achievement.[29] The other person observes exactly the same event but "describes it as 'the destruction of natural resources.'"[30] This person goes on to speak at a local ecological preservation club, condemning the deforestation.

These two people have different worldviews, which motivate them, first, to interpret the same event differently, and second, to present different speeches to their audiences. Here, we can see that worldview gives birth to motive. The worldview itself, however, is a terministic screen that acts upon us—shaping our understandings of reality. Burke understood motives as "distinctly linguistic products," meaning that *motives are derived from language (terministic screens that coalesce into worldviews) and conveyed through language.*

Burke's theory of dramatism understands humans as engaged in motivated action through symbol use. It also recognizes that symbols themselves act as they screen our interpretations of reality, coalescing into worldviews and thus giving birth to the motives that fuel our action—which involves further symbol use. On the basis of this theory, Burke developed a methodology that critics can use to (1) understand how symbols screen reality, and (2) discern the worldview that motivates a discourse.

DOING DRAMATISTIC CRITICISM

There are several ways to apply Burke's theory of dramatism critically. The following explanation features just one of Kenneth Burke's dramatistic methodologies, which he called the pentad. This method guides a critic to approach an analysis of a text through a focus on how it portrays its drama. It proceeds in three stages.

Identifying Pentadic Elements

Kenneth Burke's **pentad** is *a tool to help critics identify how a discourse screens reality. It consists of five elements: (1) act, (2) scene, (3) agent, (4) agency, and (5) purpose.* A critic can start ascertaining how any given discourse presents reality by understanding its presentation of these five terms.

- To discern the *act,* a critic asks questions such as "What took place?" "What happened?" and "What was done?"
- To discern the *scene,* a critic asks questions such as "When did the act happen?" "Where did it happen?" "What is the background while the act is happening?"
- To discern the *agent,* a critic asks questions such as "Who did the act?" "What kind of person performed it?"
- To discern the *agency,* a critic asks questions such as "How was the act accomplished?" "What instruments, materials, or means were used to perform it?"
- To discern the *purpose,* a critic asks questions such as "Why was the act accomplished?" "Why was this act was committed?"

Occasionally, a sixth element is conjoined with the original five pentadic elements. **Attitude** refers to *state of mind, which is largely understood as an aspect of the agent.* A critic who is considering the agent's attitude asks questions such as "What is the agent's state of mind in preparation for the act?"

Critics identify the pentadic elements within the text. For example, imagine a school principal gave a speech at an annual school board meeting, where she summarized the school's transition into a new building. A critic using the pentad to assess this speech would look at the drama presented within the principal's speech. When discerning the *act* by answering the question "what happened?" the critic would not respond with an account of the external context ("the school principal gave a speech at a school board meeting"), but would instead look within the speech to discern that the act, the thing that happened, was that the school moved to a new building.

Identifying the act is typically the first step because a critic will then identify the scene, agent, agency, and purpose in relation to that act. Sometimes, the act can be difficult to discern—especially if the critic is working with a narrative text, such as a film or a book, in which lots of things happen. Consequently, when discerning the act in a narrative text, it can be helpful for a critic to focus on the overarching, big-picture thing that is accomplished—typically the outcome that the whole narrative builds toward, and that is achieved or revealed in its conclusion.

For example, when using dramatistic criticism to analyze the 2011 film *The Help,* critics Mollie Murphy and Tina M. Harris determined that the act within this film—which is set in Jackson, Mississippi, during the early 1960s—is achieving the possibility for empowerment for Black maids and the characters' "journey toward better interracial relations."[31] Many things take place during this film. Some characters clean houses; some participate in interviews, one character writes and publishes a book, and so on, but the film builds toward a conclusion in which some of the Black maids are pursuing different jobs and the town has begun to reckon with racism.

Having identified the act, critics then identify the other four pentadic elements within the text, in relation to the act. Murphy and Harris identified the *scene* as Jackson, Mississippi, at the very beginning of the civil rights era. They identified the writer, Eugenia "Skeeter" Phelan (portrayed by Emma Stone), as the *agent:* it is Skeeter's work—observing, interviewing, and eventually writing the book that is published at the end of the film and titled *The Help*—that functions as the catalyst for the act. Without Skeeter's intervention, the act would not be accomplished in this narrative. Murphy and Harris identified multiple elements as the *agency*—the means through which the act is accomplished.

Broadly considered, Skeeters' writing of the book is agency, but that agency is made possible through three significant means. First, her knowledge of and access to a publishing company is a major portion of her agency. Second, her Whiteness is part of her agency: as a White person, she can safely traverse both the White and Black sections of the segregated town, while Black characters only have partial access (as maids) to the White sections. Thus, Skeeter's Whiteness plays a central role in how she is able to observe and interview the subjects of her book. Additionally, her agency is a mixture of personal "colorblindness" and awareness of racism. That is, she is the lone "colorblind" White person in this film: she "doesn't see color" and makes friends and loving relationships with people regardless of color. Yet she is also disturbed by something that "bothers *no one else.*"[32] She is the only White person who notices the racism in town. This combination of colorblindness in her personal relationships and ability to see color in the racism surrounding her is unique to Skeeter's character and is a significant part of her agency—how she is ultimately able to conceive of and complete her book project, which leads the townspeople into a reconsideration of racism.

Finally, Murphy and Harris identified two intertwined *purposes* in *The Help.* Skeeter's primary purpose is to fight the "enemy of blatant racism," but her work is also driven by her love for her former maid.[33] Similarly, the supporting characters, Aibileen and Minny (whom Skeeter interviews for the book), are also trying to fight racism. Yet they too are driven by their love—love for the White children and families for whom they work.

Assessing Pentadic Ratios

Once a critic has identified the pentadic elements within a text, the next step is to understand how those pentadic elements interact: for example, how the depiction of the scene shapes or affects the way the agent is understood, or how the way the agent is characterized shapes how the act is understood. For example, speaking in 1969, Senator Edward Kennedy attempted to explain the events surrounding his car crash—which resulted in the death of the passenger, Mary Jo Kopechne—by stating, "Little over one mile away the car that I was driving on an *unlit* road went off a *narrow bridge* which had *no guard rails* and was built on a *left angle* to the road. The car overturned in a *deep pond* and immediately filled with water" (emphasis added).[34] Analyzing this speech, rhetorical critic David Ling noted how the *scene* shaped how the other elements of the pentad were depicted.[35] The description of the scene makes the *act* (the car crash) seem inevitable—any car would have gone off such a dangerous road. The scene also constrained the *agent* (Senator Kennedy), who became a victim of the scene rather than the cause of the accident. The scene (the darkness of the road, the narrowness of the bridge, and so on) dominated this account, deflecting attention away from other pentadic elements, especially the agent.

By assessing how two pentadic elements interact, a critic considers what is known as a **pentadic ratio** by asking the following interpretive questions: (1) Does the *scene* shape, contain, influence, or determine how the act, agent, agency, or purpose is depicted? (2) Does the *act* shape, contain, influence, or determine how the scene, agent, agency, or purpose is depicted? (3) Does the *agent* shape, contain, influence, or determine how the scene, act, agency, or purpose is depicted? (4) Does the *agency* shape, contain, influence, or determine how the scene, act, agent, or purpose is depicted? (5) Does the *purpose* shape, contain, influence, or determine how the scene, act, agent, and/or agency is depicted? In asking these questions, critics consider all twenty possible ratios (thirty, if the critic includes *attitude*). Depending on the text, not all pairings have clear interactions: the way the purpose is portrayed might have very little bearing on the scene, and vice versa. If so, the critic just moves on to consider the next ratio pairing.

The point of considering how these elements interact is to determine which element dominates its ratios—that is, which element most frequently or emphatically shapes, constrains, influences, or determines how the others are depicted. Murphy and Harris's analysis of *The Help* demonstrates the utility of considering ratios. First, within the film's depiction or screening of reality, the *scene* of Jackson, Mississippi, helps determine the *agency* and—in turn—the *agent.* Jackson is a segregated town; to navigate it and thus observe and interview people (agency) requires that the agent be White, because only White people can safely navigate all portions of the town. The scene and the agency determine that the agent of the *act* (writing a book that reveals and counters racism) must be a White person within this screening of reality.

The 1960s were a time of intense civil rights activism in Mississippi—and Black activists led the movement.[36] However, within the fictional narrative of *The Help,* a White person emerges as the seemingly necessary instigator (the agent) of activism to improve race relations (the act). Indeed, Skeeter seems so fitting as the agent because of the way the scene and agency have been arranged within this narrative. Audience members—especially audience members who have little familiarity with the history of the civil rights movement—can watch a film that "paves over the legacy of Blacks' civil rights activism" without even noticing that the Black historical figures who led the activism in Mississippi have been replaced with a White person in this film.[37] Indeed, the terministic screen of this film (its selection and deflection of reality) can slip by unnoticed as its depiction of the scene and agency seemingly necessitate a White agent of racial reconciliation. Murphy and Harris conclude that the agent operates as the dominant element of the pentad because "what took place [the act] is inextricably linked to the kind of person [the agent] who committed the act."[38]

Determining Motive

A critic analyzes the pentadic ratios to interpret the terministic screen or worldview of the text, as well as the motivations embedded in that worldview. Essentially, the critic considers what would motivate a rhetor to describe a drama in such a way that it features the scene, act, agent, agency, or purpose as the dominant term that constrains or influences the other terms. At this point, the critic asks interpretive questions such as:

- What assumptions or beliefs would lead a rhetor to feature this element of the pentad?
- What priorities would lead a rhetor to describe the drama in this way?
- Who or what benefits from featuring this element of the pentad in this drama?
- What way of thinking would lead a rhetor to feature this element of the pentad as dominant?
- What is the outcome or result of featuring the drama this way?

Murphy and Harris's analysis of *The Help* demonstrates how critics can use dramatistic criticism to identify the rhetor's motive (or motives) and the worldview from which this motive arises. Murphy and Harris note that the film directs audiences' attention to a White character and "away from the non-White characters," even though the effect misrepresents both historic and current civil rights activism.[39] *The Help* presents a "White savior" narrative in which a "White lead character" (agent) lends "a helping hand" to "people of color" (act) out of the goodness of her heart (purpose).[40] By making *agent* the dominant term, the whole film revolves around Skeeter; the act is made possible exclusively through her agency. As a result, *The Help* presents a narrative that not only misrepresents history, but continues to depict a racist hierarchy. In a film about racism in the United States, a White character is portrayed as the morally superior character: it is Skeeter who shows the characters in *The Help* and the audience what goodness looks like in terms of race relations.

Murphy and Harris argue that the film's portrayal of *purpose* consistently minimizes the harm that racism perpetrates "against Blacks, thus freeing Whites of guilt and responsibility."[41] The film depicts Skeeter as truly loving her former maid, and the maids Aibileen and Minny as truly loving the White children and families for whom they work. Moreover, Skeeter, Aibileen, and Minny love one another. This love stirs the characters to action, providing a major component of the purpose—of why these characters are working toward the act of publishing the book and journeying toward better race relations. It also obscures the hierarchy in which Skeeter is the primary agent and Aibileen and Minny are subservient to her, grateful for her "willingness to liberate people of color."[42] It makes it seem as though Aibileen and Minny are not suffering from racism: their ability to love White people becomes proof that racism was not so bad. Indeed, Murphy and Harris note that *The Help* and similar Hollywood films frame race relations "as more egalitarian and harmonious than they have ever been."[43]

Through this analysis, Murphy and Harris demonstrate that *The Help* is motivated by a worldview that is able to recognize that racism is bad, but still fundamentally links Whiteness to goodness and importance while linking Blackness to subservience.[44] Even in a film that is meant to tackle America's historic and contemporary racism, audiences are presented with (and invited to accept) a terministic screen—a way of seeing the world—that focuses on how good and innocent White people are. Murphy and Harris conclude that *The Help* makes White people feel better about themselves, even as it maintains "a racist status quo."[45]

RESEARCH EXAMPLES

The first two research examples provide excellent demonstrations of how critics use the pentadic version of dramatistic criticism. In the first example, Janice Hocker Rushing uses dramatistic criticism to analyze the frontier myth (discussed in Chapter 3), specifically focusing on US portrayals of space as the next frontier. In the second example, Mari Boor Tonn, Valerie A. Endress, and John N. Diamond use dramatistic criticism to understand how controversy can grip a community when different worldviews actively construct radically different interpretations of reality. The third research example demonstrates a different version of dramatistic criticism, which is often known as the guilt, purification, and redemption cycle.

Janice Hocker Rushing "Mythic Evolution of 'The New Frontier' in Mass Mediated Rhetoric" (1986)*

When the United States entered the space race, frantically attempting to put satellites in orbit and a man on the moon, President John F. Kennedy used frontier language. Speaking in Houston, Texas, he stated that Houston, "once the furthest outpost on the old frontier of the West," would become an "outpost on the new frontier of science and space" as its spacecraft center and engineering community created rockets and designed manned missions.[46] His words tapped into the frontier myth to motivate Americans but, simultaneously, reimagined the frontier (which was actual land) as space—an emptiness with uninhabitable planets. Kennedy was hardly alone in this "space is the final frontier" sort of discourse. Politicians, scientists, and entertainment industries joined this "space = frontier" rhetoric by reworking the genre of Westerns, sending cowboys to space in narratives such as *Star Wars* and *Star Trek. Star Trek* opened every episode with the monologue, "Space, the final frontier! These are the voyages of the Starship Enterprise."

As rhetorical critic Hillary Jones explains, the traditional frontier myth focuses on a male hero who "lives at the edge of civilization,"[47] prefers "solitude to community" and is "more comfortable with savagery than most folks."[48] As such, the frontier hero (*agent*) develops the tools and strategies (*agency*) to survive the rugged frontier (*scene*), where he can live in undisturbed solitude. Despite his surly preference for solitude and freedom, he "consistently supports civilization," and people—typically weak townspeople, especially women and children—look to him for help.[49] Indeed, the plot structure of the frontier myth requires the frontier hero to do "society's dirty work" of subduing the frontier (*act*), whether that work is teaching people how to survive a blizzard or protecting them from marauding cattle rustlers.[50] He accomplishes this "dirty work" with "great skill" because he has developed the tools and strategies of survival (*agency*).[51] However, "his work might be very dirty" as the frontier myth often calls upon the hero to kill the "Other"—perhaps in a high-noon showdown with an outlaw, or by the massacre of an entire tribe of indigenous peoples.[52] By killing the "Other," the frontier hero reestablishes the expanding boundary between community and wilderness, civilization and savagery, us and them (*purpose*). In the end, the frontier hero journeys westward into the sunset, leaving civilization to find a new frontier on the ever-expanding vista of the plains.

Myths establish a community's collective sense of morality, purpose, and its place in the world. Thus, as media critic Susan Opt points out, when Americans tell ourselves this frontier myth, we tell ourselves "who we are, what our place is,

*This essay may be found in *Critical Studies in Mass Communication* 3, no. 3 (1986): 265–296.

and why we are here."[53] Communities routinely use their established myths to "make sense" of new complexities and "crisis situations." The myth helps us experience our collective identity and reaffirms our values in the midst of upheaval.[54]

The frontier myth moved from land to space during what President Kennedy celebrated as a surge in technological and scientific innovation. The subsequent decades have seen ever increasing—if occasionally worrisome—technological advances. Studying the frontier myth and its evolution into space, Janice Hocker Rushing noted that because pentadic elements are interconnected, changes in the *scene* (from land to space) affect the other elements of this myth. Because Americans use the frontier myth to ground "our public character," Rushing became increasingly concerned with understanding the evolution of the myth.[55] To that end, she analyzed three films from the early 1980s: *Outland, Bladerunner,* and *The Right Stuff.*

Outland stars Sean Connery and largely reproduces the classic frontier myth, but moves from the prairie to a mining outpost on Io—one of Jupiter's moons. Connery's character, Federal Marshall William T. O'Niel, discovers that the owners of the mining factory are drugging the workers to drive them into longer hours and higher productivity. The drugs are eventually fatal to the workers. O'Niel ultimately engages in a bloody showdown (strongly reminiscent of the Western *High Noon*) to singlehandedly save the community.

Although this film largely reproduces the frontier myth, the transition to space has wrought a significant change: the townspeople cannot farm or ranch outside because there is no atmosphere. Thus, they work in a mining factory, and technology itself (the industrialized factory and its efficiency-oriented owners) become the enemy. Rushing notes that this film foreshadows that "the problems of the space hero will be different from those of the old frontiersman" and that technology itself is featured as an *agency,* albeit an evil agency. (Technology is how the villains get things done.)[56] That is, rather than struggling against a blizzard, drought, or people (whether they are outlaws or stereotyped indigenous people) endemic to the land, and thus scene, this space-frontier hero struggles against technology, which is agency.

Bladerunner stars Harrison Ford as Rick Deckard, a "ruggedly individualistic bounty hunter" who is clearly recognizable as a chip off the old frontiersman block.[57] The narrative is primarily set in Earth's Los Angeles, but it is clear that space is settled, as blimps fill the skies and "gaudy commercials" advertise to take tourists into space.[58] This film, however, marks a clear shift in the evolution of the frontier myth: it incorporates the Frankenstein myth to portray technology as the problem that the hero faces. That is, just as the scientist, Frankenstein, created a monster without appropriately considering the ramifications of what he was doing or caring for the monster after its creation, so too *Bladerunner*'s scientists have created replicants—"mechanical carbon copies of human life" that are indistinguishable from humans.[59] Some of these replicants have rebelled against their human masters, and Deckard is recruited to exterminate them.

Deckard occasionally uses technological devices (*agency*) as he tracks the replicants; however, he has no real control over technology in this film. Indeed,

Rushing demonstrates that he can never have control over the technology because it is so bloated, so omnipresent, so overwhelming in every aspect of Los Angeles that this agency has metamorphized into the *scene.*

The plot represents a radical shift in the pentad's ratios. Typically, the agent makes use of the agency and both are contained within the scene. As the agency has morphed into the scene, however, it is beyond the agent's control. The technology itself becomes the villain—the replicants that (like Frankenstein's monster) humans made and failed to care for. The scene is manifested as an evil technological entity: Los Angeles is the *type of place* where replicants are ubiquitous. This "technology as agency-turned-scene" is depicted as grotesque. Notably, Deckard never gains control of his technological agency-fused-scene; indeed, he flees a scene "he cannot control" rather than choosing to leave a scene after conquering it.[60] *Bladerunner* concludes with the hero fleeing this technological landscape for the desolate mountains.[61]

Unlike *Outland* and *Bladerunner,* which are entirely fictional, *The Right Stuff* is a fictionalization of the early years of the US space program. Based on a novel by Tom Wolfe, the film covers real-life events such as Chuck Yeager's breaking of the sound barrier, the training of the first seven astronauts (known as the Mercury 7), and the first manned space flight. Rushing emphasizes that technological *agency* has become the dominant term in this film: no one can do anything without technology—whether it is a computer, an airplane, a rocket, or a spacecraft. Moreover, the film fuses the astronauts' *agency* with their *scene.* As a result, these astronauts are a far cry from the old frontier hero: they are not using technology; they are "en-capsule-lated" in space capsules while engineers fly the rockets; they are lab rats or test subjects, not pilots.[62] Indeed, the Mercury flights were only manned to "add drama to the politics of the space race," ensuring the average citizen cared about the technology.[63] The space race used the astronauts (agents) for publicity: "technology, once created to serve the agent as agency, had become the astronauts' prison"; it contained them.[64]

However, because space is space—limitless, a vacuum, deadly—these versions of the frontier myth are unfulfilling for US audiences. Rushing points out that in the Old West, "frontier was ultimately limited and conquerable": with the right tools and knowledge or character (*agency*) the old frontier hero (*agent*) traditionally conquered the *scene.*[65] But space is infinite and cannot be conquered. When humans turn to technology in an attempt to conquer the unconquerable in the evolution of this myth, we unknowingly unleash a monster: technology either manifests as Frankenstein's creation, or it traps and contains us.

Ultimately, Rushing's analysis demonstrates how the evolution of the frontier myth offered Americans a way to conceptualize the space race, as well as how it continues to offer Americans a way to process the fusion of technology into our daily lives. She observes that the frontier myth has not finished its evolution: Americans are still rearranging its pentadic elements in an attempt to tell a story that helps us navigate our lives. Rushing's dramatistic analysis points the way for scholars to make sense of more recent iterations of this myth in narratives such as *Firefly, Battlestar Galactica, I-Robot, Gravity, Interstellar,* and *The Martian.*

Mari Boor Tonn, Valerie A. Endress, and John N. Diamond "Hunting and Heritage on Trial: A Dramatistic Debate over Tragedy, Tradition, and Territory" (1993)*

For some communities, hunting season is not only highly anticipated, it feels like an annual rite of passage—a defining element of the community. As the demographics of a town change, however, new community members and hunters often clash over hunting and the role it plays in the community. Hermon, Maine, is one such hunting town. Its controversy came to a jarring crisis when Donald Rogerson, a "veteran hunter and native Mainer," shot and killed Karen Wood, a recent transplant from Iowa, while she stood in her backyard.[66] The controversy unfolded as the town's local news covered the tragedy and its ensuing legal drama. He was indicted by a grand jury and stood trial for manslaughter. Two years after killing Wood, he was acquitted of all charges.

Analyzing the news coverage, Mari Boor Tonn, Valerie Endress, and John Diamond use dramatistic criticism to reveal the motivations that animate this controversy. They demonstrate how different motivations led to radically different interpretations of reality. Some blamed Rogerson (who had been hunting illegally) for Wood's death, while others—including the local news media—blamed Wood herself, claiming she had been careless and was responsible for protecting herself during hunting season.[67]

The local news coverage defended Rogerson (and blamed Wood), heavily emphasizing the *scene*. Discourses that feature scene often present a deterministic or fated worldview: the *act* is portrayed as a necessitated response to the scene, rather than a rational, choice of the purposeful *agent*. In other words, "free will is supplanted largely by fate."[68] In discussing the scene, the news coverage emphasized that Wood was not on her lawn but in the thinly wooded area behind her house—which bordered a more densely wooded area. Although she was on her own property, the news coverage fixated on the location, routinely describing Wood as standing "in the woods" and going to great lengths to dispel the idea that Wood was in her own backyard.[69]

With the scene dominating this account of the shooting, Rogerson's actions are seen as a natural response. The news portrayed him not as "a moral, thinking agent," but rather as an "organism who merely responded to external stimuli."[70] He believed he saw a buck and he fired twice. Essentially, Rogerson—the "veteran hunter and native Mainer"—is contained by the scene.[71] The woods are his home and he acts on instinct within the woods.

In contrast, local news coverage portrayed Wood as an outsider—as someone who did not belong in the scene. She is portrayed as an *agent,* as a rational, purposeful person who made direct choices to endanger herself. These news media fixated on her apparel: they reported that she was wearing a jacket and that gloves were found near her body, and cited this as evidence that "her behavior was 'not spontaneous,'" but rather a premeditated choice to go outside during hunting season.[72] Moreover, after Rogerson stated that she had put her hands over her head, making the gloves look like deer tails, the news coverage focused on Wood as

*This essay may be found in *Quarterly Journal of Speech* 79, no. 2 (1993): 165–181.

having "*tempted*" Rogerson by disguising "herself as compelling prey."[73] Skipping over the inconsistencies that (1) Rogerson claimed to have seen a human put her hands over her head and also claimed to never have seen a human at all, and (2) Wood's gloves were found near her body and not on her hands, this coverage depicts Wood as the agent who caused the *act* (her own death) and Rogerson as part of the natural landscape of hunting season in Maine (*scene*). Indeed, although Rogerson was hunting illegally close to a residential area, Rogerson described himself as neither negligent nor neglectful; instead, he—and the local media—characterized himself as "a victim of circumstances."[74]

Tonn, Endress, and Diamond conclude by focusing on the motivation that animates this interpretation of the evidence and the news discourse. They emphasize that in a different town this drama would have unfolded quite differently in the news—and likely in the courts. They argue that when looking at the same evidence (a woman shot by an illegal hunter while she stood on her own property), different communities will—on the basis of their terministic screens—arrive at very different interpretations of reality. Long-standing residents of Hermon, Maine, were deeply motivated to absolve Rogerson of guilt in order to maintain the boundaries and values of their community. Focusing on the *scene* (and characterizing it as a hunting scene) absolves Rogerson and vilifies Wood. This focus maintains Hermon, Maine, as a characteristically rural, hunting town and demarcates the boundaries between the real "Hermon-ites" and the villainous interlopers (such as transplants from Iowa) invading their territory and destroying their community, values, and traditions.

Brian L. Ott and Eric Aoki
"The Politics of Negotiating Public Tragedy: Media Framing of the Matthew Shepard Murder" (2002)*

The pentadic approach explained in this chapter is only one approach to dramatistic criticism. Kenneth Burke wrote extensively about dramatism, and his ideas have been methodologically applied in many ways. The **guilt, purification, and redemption cycle** is *an application of dramatism in which critics identify a specific cycle of drama (guilt, purification, redemption) within a discourse.*

Guilt is *a stage in which someone has deviated from social expectations and thus feels guilty for their actions.* For Burke, these deviations may not be bad. Indeed, a person facing conflicting social expectations cannot avoid deviating from at least one of those expectations. For instance, if your boss expects you to put in long hours to finish a job with a tight deadline but your family expects you to be at your daughter's birthday party, you are going to disappoint either your boss or your family, and you are going to feel guilty about whichever expectation you did not meet.

Purification is *a stage in which those experiencing guilt attempt to set things right, typically through "mortification and/or victimage."*[75] As communication professor Rise Jane Samra explains, mortification means that the person who is guilty "makes a symbolic offering to appease society and thus restore balance

*This essay may be found in *Rhetoric & Public Affairs* 5, no. 3 (2002): 483–505.

and social order."[76] For instance, if you skipped your daughter's birthday party to finish something at work, you might apologize to your family, and then take your daughter on a special day trip for just the two of you. Victimage, on the other hand, is when the blame is placed on someone else, who then serves as a "scapegoat" who is sacrificed to atone for the "sin" and thus purge the guilt.[77] For instance, rather than apologizing and taking your daughter on a day trip, you might blame your boss, print out a picture of her/his face, and have your daughter set it on fire. Although it is not always violent, scapegoating is never pretty.

Redemption is *the stage when purification has succeeded and the social order is restored.* For redemption to be obtained, the act of purification "must be appropriate" or balance out the "sin of the guilty."[78] Because the guilt, purification, redemption cycle is theorized as a *cycle,* however, this redemption stage is never seen as final or absolute. Instead, this aspect of dramatism suggests that individuals and communities are continually reentering the guilt phase—and the cycle repeats.

Brian Ott and Eric Aoki used this aspect of dramatistic criticism to analyze the way news outlets framed the murder of Matthew Shepard. In 1998, Aaron McKinney and Russell Henderson brutally beat Shepard "for being gay,"[79] then left him bound to a fence in the fields of Wyoming. A mountain biker found Shepard the next day. He was still alive, but died five days later in the hospital without regaining consciousness.[80] Both McKinney and Henderson received life sentences for their crime.

Analyzing the news coverage of this murder and trial, Ott and Aoki demonstrate how the news media's fascination with this crime and the sensationalized reporting of the disturbing details profoundly disrupted the social order.[81] Many people were attacked and murdered in antigay hate crimes in 1998 but received scant news attention.[82] Thus, it was the news media's intense publicizing of this murder rather than the murder itself that created a social disruption at the national level—and social disruptions start the guilt, purification, and redemption cycle turning. Soon, the national press featured news stories that expressed a sense of national shame and guilt that such a crime could have happened *here.*

After guilt comes purification, and sure enough, Ott and Aoki point out, the news media swung their attention to the perpetrators, McKinney and Henderson, vilifying and dehumanizing them as the worst of the worst. This coverage scapegoated them by making them the sole icons and embodiments of antigay hate. Essentially, the news media funneled all of America's antigay sentiments into the portrayals of McKinney and Henderson, positioning them as the embodiment of ignorant and malicious homophobia. Having thus scapegoated them, society could then experience purification and redemption when the judicial system punished them.

Analyzing this news coverage through this particular drama cycle, these critics demonstrate how McKinney and Henderson came to represent more than just their crime in the national imagination. Indeed, Ott and Aoki demonstrate that the nation felt guilty, and purged that guilt by laying on McKinney and Henderson the (antigay) sins of the nation. By funneling the national guilt onto McKinney and Henderson and punishing them, the nation healed itself—restoring a social order in which Americans are assured of their own goodness without actually changing America's laws or culture to prevent anti-gay crimes.

STRENGTHS AND WEAKNESSES OF DRAMATISTIC CRITICISM

One clear strength of dramatistic criticism is the way it can be applied to a wide range of texts, from political speeches to news reportage and entertainment narratives. Kenneth Burke described dramatistic criticism as a method that critics can use whenever an act is posited in language (or other symbols). That is, he saw dramatistic criticism as an appropriate method to use whenever a happening is expressed symbolically.[83] Because Burke understood all human action as symbolic and all symbols as active, he understood dramatistic criticism as almost universally applicable.

A second clear strength of this method is that it focuses the critic's attention on the worldview that motivates a particular interpretation of reality and thus the way a text presents reality. This focus helps a critic articulate what the text is designed to accomplish in society and thus articulate the importance of the analysis of that text.

Sometimes, however, dramatistic criticism can feel formulaic. This is especially true when a critic simply identifies the elements of the pentad within a discourse and then stops. For a critical work to be substantive, a critic must progress to using the pentadic ratios to analyze the worldview and assess motive.

CHOOSING THIS METHOD

So how do you know whether you should use dramatistic criticism to interpret a particular text? To answer this question, consider your text, its role in society, and the research question animating your analysis.

First, does your text feature a clear *act?* Whether the act is a broad, overarching accomplishment achieved at the end of a narrative or a specific instance—such as a miscalculated shot in the woods that kills a woman—dramatistic criticism is oriented around an act that takes place within the text. This method will work best if you can identify a clear act in your text.

Second, is the *scene* a prominent element of the pentad within your text? Scene need not be the dominant element or even a prominent element for your analysis to be meaningful, but a significant portion of dramatistic criticism revolves around the role that scene plays.

Third, is your text prominent in society? This prominence can be accomplished through its widespread popularity or through its influence on a specific subculture, genre, or community. Dramatistic criticism ultimately focuses your attention on the text's symbolic action—on the terministic screen (worldview) that it uses to interpret and construct reality and that it offers to the audience. As a result, this method is most useful when a text is popular (offering its worldview to a large number of people) or when a text is particularly influential (meaning that people accepted its worldview and now see reality as the text portrayed reality).

Finally, consider your own research motives. What research question animates your analysis? Do you want to discover how symbols screen reality? Do you want to understand the worldview that motivated a particular discourse? Dramatistic criticism is particularly suited to answering research questions that stem from these types of animating concerns.

Ultimately, dramatistic criticism helps critics recognize how texts act in society and the role that symbols play in constructing our interpretations of reality. The pentad offers critics a tool through which they can assess any text, identifying what happened (act), who did it (agent), how (agency), where and when (scene), and why (purpose). Then, by identifying the relationships among these elements and the way they affect, shape, and constrain one another, a critic can identify the worldview that motivates the way a text interprets and presents reality. To some extent, this method is like doing a jigsaw puzzle: the critic considers whether and how each pentadic element (or puzzle piece) interlocks with the others, then pieces together the motivating worldview, the big picture of the text.

DISCUSSION QUESTIONS

1. Consider Kenneth Burke's insight that the symbols we use are context dependent. We identify people, places, things, ideas, and so on as having one character in one context (for example, describing someone as tall, or labeling a relationship as a dating relationship, or describing yourself as spiritual), but a different character in a different context (for example, describing someone as average height, or labeling a relationship as "just taking it slowly and seeing where it goes," or describing yourself as Christian). Describe a time when you have used different labels to describe something or someone, depending on the context.
2. Terministic screens are words and other symbols that filter our reality. They reflect reality by selecting certain aspects to focus on and deflecting attention away from other aspects of reality. Describe a time when you noticed how the terms used in a television advertisement were screening your interpretation of reality. Now describe a friend or family member's use of a terministic screen: what words do they use that shape how they understand reality?
3. In your own words, define motion and action. Then provide an example of motion and an example of action.
4. Consider an adult who has positively influenced your upbringing (such as a parent, legal guardian, grandparent, aunt or uncle, pastor, mentor, teacher, or coach). Describe that person's worldview: what is the big-picture terministic screen that filters how they see reality? For example, do they see the world as a dangerous place and, accordingly, are always suspicious and cautious? Do they see the world as a good place and, accordingly, trust and look for the best in others?
5. Identify a story from your childhood that you like to tell or that your family/friends like to tell about you. Using the pentad, label the act in the story and then identify the other elements: agent, scene, agency, and purpose. Now consider which of these elements is dominant in the pentad. In other words, which of these elements is characterized in such a way that it shapes or constrains the meaning or character of the other relevant elements?

NOTES

1. "American 'Killed in India by Endangered Andamans Tribe,'" BBCNews.com, November 21, 2018, https://www.bbc.com/news/world-asia-india-46286215.
2. "American 'Killed in India.'"
3. "American Reportedly Killed in Flurry of Arrows as Tribe Defends its Island off India," NPR.com, November 21, 2018, https://www.npr.org/2018/11/21/669909594/american-reportedly-killed-in-flurry-of-arrows-as-tribe-defends-its-island-off-i.
4. Kate Shellnutt, "U.S. Missionary Killed by 'World's Most Isolated' Tribe," ChristianityToday.com, November 21, 2018, https://www.christianitytoday.com/news/2018/november/missionary-killed-north-sentinel-isolated-island-tribe-chau.html.
5. "Statement on the Death of John Allen Chau," Oral Roberts University, accessed January 14, 2019, http://www.oru.edu/news/oru_news/20181121-john-chau-statement.php.
6. In Bernard Brock, Kenneth Burke, Parke Burgess, and Herbert Simons, "Dramatism as Ontology or Epistemology: A Symposium," *Communication Quarterly* 33, no. 1 (1985): 23.
7. In Brock et al., "Dramatism as Ontology," 28.
8. See Bryan Crable, "Defending Dramatism as Ontological and Literal," *Communication Quarterly* 48, no. 3 (2000): 328.
9. Crable, "Defending Dramatism," 328.
10. See Brock et al., "Dramatism as Ontology or Epistemology: A Symposium," 19.
11. Crable, "Defending Dramatism," 328; see also Kenneth Burke, *A Grammar of Motives* (Berkeley: University of California Press, 1969), 21–25, 77–79.
12. Shira Spector, "High-Femme Dad," *Confessions of the Other Mother: Nonbiological Moms Tell All!*, ed. Harlyn Aizley (Boston: Beacon, 2006), 28; see also Katrina Miller, "What Will They Call You? Rhetorically Listening to Lesbian Maternal Narratives," *The International Journal of Listening* 26 (2012): 134–145.
13. Crable, "Defending Dramatism," 328; see also Burke, *A Grammar of Motives*, 84.
14. Kenneth Burke, "Terministic Screens," in *Language as Symbolic Action*, ed. Kenneth Burke (Berkeley: University of California Press, 1966), 45; Paul Stob, "'Terministic Screens,' Social Constructionism, and the Language of Experience: Kenneth Burke's Utilization of William James," *Philosophy & Rhetoric* 41, no. 2 (2008): 139.
15. Sarah Heiss, "A 'Naturally Sweet' Definition: An Analysis of the Sugar Association's Definition of the Natural as a Terministic Screen," *Health Communication* 30, no. 6 (2015): 536–544.
16. "Sugar 101: What Is Sugar?" *The Sugar Association*, last modified 2018, https://www.sugar.org/sugar/what-is-sugar/.
17. Heiss, "A 'Naturally Sweet' Definition," 536–544.
18. "Sugar 101," *American Heart Association*, last modified 2018, http://www.heart.org/HEARTORG/HealthyLiving/HealthyEating/Nutrition/Sugar-101_UCM_306024_Article.jsp#.W0TuCaknZTY; "How Does Sugar in our Diet Affect our Health?" *National Health Services*, November 8, 2017, https://www.nhs.uk/live-well/eat-well/how-does-sugar-in-our-diet-affect-our-health/.
19. "Nutrition Facts," *Coca-Cola Company*, last modified 2018, https://www.coca-colaproductfacts.com/en/products/coca-cola/original/12-oz/.

20. Heiss, "A 'Naturally Sweet' Definition," 536–544.
21. Kenneth Burke, *Permanence and Change: An Anatomy of Purpose,* 3rd ed. (Berkeley: University of California Press, 1984), 13–14.
22. Lauren Lemley, "Crafting a Terministic Screen: The Rhetorical Influence of Increase Mather's *Illustrious Providences,*" (paper presented at the National Communication Association, Chicago, IL, November 2009), 12.
23. Lemley, "Crafting a Terministic Screen," 14; Increase Mather, *An Essay for the Recording of Illustrious Providences,* ed. James A. Levernier (Delmar, NY: Scholars' Facsimiles & Reprints, 1977), 169.
24. Lemley, "Crafting a Terministic Screen," 14; Mather, *Illustrious Providences,* 169.
25. Lemley, "Crafting a Terministic Screen."
26. Kenneth Burke, "The Nature of Human Action," in *On Symbols and Society,* ed. Joseph R. Gusfield (Chicago: University of Chicago Press, 1989), 60.
27. Burke, *A Grammar of Motives,* 310.
28. Burke, *Permanence and Change,* 25.
29. Charles Kneupper, "Dramatistic Invention: The Pentad as Heuristic Procedure," *Rhetoric Society Quarterly* 9, no. 3 (1979): 131.
30. Kneupper, "Dramatistic Invention."
31. Mollie Murphy and Tina M. Harris, "White Innocence and Black Subservience: The Rhetoric of White Heroism in *The Help,*" *Howard Journal of Communications* 29, no. 1 (2018): 59.
32. Murphy and Harris, "White Innocence and Black Subservience," 56.
33. Murphy and Harris, "White Innocence and Black Subservience," 57.
34. Edward Kennedy, "Chappaquiddick Speech," July 25, 1969, retrieved from https://www.americanrhetoric.com/speeches/tedkennedychappaquiddick.htm.
35. David Ling, "A Pentadic Analysis of Senator Edward Kennedy's Address to the People of Massachusetts, July 25, 1969," *Central States Speech Journal* 21, no. 2 (1970): 81–86.
36. Murphy and Harris, "White Innocence and Black Subservience," 54.
37. Murphy and Harris, "White Innocence and Black Subservience," 54.
38. Murphy and Harris, "White Innocence and Black Subservience," 60.
39. Murphy and Harris, "White Innocence and Black Subservience," 53.
40. Murphy and Harris, "White Innocence and Black Subservience," 52.
41. Murphy and Harris, "White Innocence and Black Subservience," 60.
42. Murphy and Harris, "White Innocence and Black Subservience," 60.
43. Murphy and Harris, "White Innocence and Black Subservience," 61.
44. Murphy and Harris, "White Innocence and Black Subservience," 61.
45. Murphy and Harris, "White Innocence and Black Subservience," 60.
46. John F. Kennedy, "Moon Speech—Rice Stadium," Nasa.gov, September 12, 1962, retrieved from https://er.jsc.nasa.gov/seh/ricetalk.htm.
47. Hillary A. Jones, "'Them as Feel the Need to be Free': Reworking the Frontier Myth," *Southern Communication Journal* 76, no. 3 (2011): 233.
48. Jones, "'Them as Feel the Need,'" 233.
49. Jones, "'Them as Feel the Need,'" 233.
50. Jones, "'Them as Feel the Need,'" 233.

51. Jones, "'Them as Feel the Need,'" 233.
52. Jones, "'Them as Feel the Need,'" 233.
53. Susan K. Opt, "American Frontier Myth and the Flight of Apollo 13: From News Event to Feature Film," *Film & History* 26, no. 1-4 (1996): 41.
54. Opt, "American Frontier Myth and the Flight of Apollo 13," 41.
55. Janice Hocker Rushing, "Mythic Evolution of 'The New Frontier' in Mass Mediated Rhetoric," *Critical Studies in Mass Communication* 3, no. 3 (1986): 267.
56. Rushing, "Mythic Evolution," 273.
57. Rushing, "Mythic Evolution," 274.
58. Rushing, "Mythic Evolution," 273.
59. Rushing, "Mythic Evolution," 274.
60. Rushing, "Mythic Evolution," 275.
61. Rushing, "Mythic Evolution," 274.
62. Rushing, "Mythic Evolution," 279.
63. Rushing, "Mythic Evolution," 278.
64. Rushing, "Mythic Evolution," 279.
65. Rushing, "Mythic Evolution," 281.
66. Mari Boor Tonn, Valerie Endress, and John Diamond, "Hunting and Heritage on Trial: A Dramatistic Debate over Tragedy, Tradition, and Territory," *Quarterly Journal of Speech* 79, no. 2 (1993): 165.
67. Tonn, Endress, and Diamond, "Hunting and Heritage," 165.
68. Tonn, Endress, and Diamond, "Hunting and Heritage," 166.
69. Tonn, Endress, and Diamond, "Hunting and Heritage," 172.
70. Tonn, Endress, and Diamond, "Hunting and Heritage," 173.
71. Tonn, Endress, and Diamond, "Hunting and Heritage," 165.
72. Tonn, Endress, and Diamond, "Hunting and Heritage," 173.
73. Tonn, Endress, and Diamond, "Hunting and Heritage," 173.
74. Tonn, Endress, and Diamond, "Hunting and Heritage," 171, 175.
75. Rise Jane Samra, "Guilt, Purification, and Redemption," *The American Communication Journal* 1, no. 3. (1998), http://ac-journal.org/journal/vol1/iss3/burke/samra.html.
76. Samra, "Guilt, Purification, and Redemption."
77. Samra, "Guilt, Purification, and Redemption."
78. Samra, "Guilt, Purification, and Redemption."
79. Brian L. Ott and Eric Aoki, "The Politics of Negotiating Public Tragedy: Media Framing of the Matthew Shepard Murder," *Rhetoric & Public Affairs* 5, no. 3 (2002): 484.
80. Ott and Aoki, "Negotiating Public Tragedy," 484.
81. Ott and Aoki, "Negotiating Public Tragedy," 488.
82. Ott and Aoki, "Negotiating Public Tragedy," 495.
83. Brock et al., "Dramatism," 24.

Chapter 5

Genre Criticism

In the early 2000s, *CSI: Crime Scene Investigation* became one of the most-watched series on television. Soon, other series (such as its three spin-offs *CSI: Miami, CSI: NY,* and *CSI: Cyber*) began replicating all or parts of the original series. These forensic crime series became a staple in my television viewing habits. Unlike more traditional police procedurals, where "cases are built on the street or in the interrogation room, through interviewing witnesses and confronting suspects," *CSI* (and its wannabes) builds each case in the laboratory.[1] The show emphasizes the role of scientific inquiry and evidence, and repeatedly makes statements such as, "Physical evidence cannot be wrong. It doesn't lie. It's not influenced by emotion or prejudice."[2] After *CSI*'s rise in popularity, many lawyers and others working in law enforcement reported experiences in which jurors were increasingly unmoved by their presentations of circumstantial evidence and witness testimonies. Legal scholars, prosecutors, and others began to talk about the "*CSI* effect," claiming that the television series leads jurors to "expect prosecutors to prove scientific certainty rather than to merely overcome reasonable doubt."[3]

Media and legal research, however, does not support this claim: watching *CSI* (and similar entertainment) makes no difference in how likely a juror is to convict someone for a crime or what type of evidence that juror will find convincing beyond a reasonable doubt.[4] Still, prosecutors and law enforcement officers have seen a marked shift in jurors' expectations for scientific evidence. Donald Shelton, a felony trial judge in Ann Arbor, Michigan, and criminology professors Young Kim and Gregg Barak explain this shift—and *CSI*'s popularity—by pointing to the technological revolution of recent decades. Their research suggests that culture itself has changed: that the new "scientific and information age comes marching through the courtroom door in the psyche of almost every juror who takes a seat in the box," regardless of whether that juror watches *CSI*.[5]

CSI participates in the genre of television crime dramas. Broadly speaking, **genres** are *fluid categories humans create that group discourses—such as action movies, romance novels, and policy speeches—together.* The shift in television crime dramas from "on the street" investigations (where police officers chase and interrogate suspects) to laboratory and high tech investigative methods reflects the broader shift in US culture toward technology and away from pounding the pavement. Rather than causing a change in jurors' expectations, *CSI* can be understood as an effect of the same cultural shift that changed jurors' expectations.

Genre Criticism is *a method for analyzing genres and how a culture creates and uses them.* This method helps orient critics by focusing on a single aspect of symbolic form—genre—as a critic's central approach to a text (or texts). To understand how to use this method, we need a more precise understanding of what genres are, as well as how humans create and use them.

A THEORY OF GENRES

On the surface, genres seem pretty basic—labels for groups of similar texts (RomCom, Sitcom, Action Flick, and so on). When critics study how genres function in society, however, we ask broad questions such as: Why do we currently have so many dystopian young adult novels? Why do genres such as "cover letters" or "caution labels" exist? Why would someone watch more than one romantic comedy when these films are so incredibly similar? Answering these questions and others like them reveals the importance, complexity, and function of genres in society.

Generally speaking, genres exist because they are culturally convenient.[6] Humans (within cultures) make and use genres for our own convenience. For example, genres help us decide what type of entertainment to watch. If you know you like a genre—such as horror films—you can easily find more entertainment that you will likely enjoy by selecting a film from within this genre. Similarly, if you know you do not like horror films, you can easily avoid these frightening films by choosing a movie that is not included in the horror genre.

Genres also provide other important conveniences. Aristotle famously divided speeches into three genres: **forensic speeches,** *speeches that typically take place in courts and present arguments about what happened* (for example, accusing someone of murder and presenting evidence of how that person committed the crime); **epideictic speeches,** *speeches that affirm "communal values and virtues" during good and bad times to help a community orient itself toward the future* (such as eulogies at funerals and toasts at weddings); and **deliberative speeches,** *speeches that typically take place in legislative assemblies and other public spaces, and argue that specific policies should be adopted or rejected* (for example, when someone proposes a new policy at a school board meeting).[7] Genres such as these are convenient because they help rhetors think about what to say in a given situation.

For example, political candidates who realize they have not been elected typically give concession speeches. The possibilities for what a losing candidate might say are virtually endless, yet a politician typically adheres to the same six elements in a concession speech: first, acknowledging defeat and congratulating the victor; second, calling for unity in support of the victor; third, reaffirming the importance of her or his own central platform; fourth, briefly articulating future goals; fifth, calling supporters to continue fighting for that central platform; and finally, expressing gratitude to supporters.[8] By reviewing prior concession speeches and responding to the felt needs of their particular circumstances, politicians participate in the genre of concession speeches and deliver remarks that audiences find quite fitting.

Explaining how humans create and use genres for cultural convenience, theorist Carolyn Miller returned to Lloyd Bitzer's key insight that rhetoric is a response to a rhetorical situation.[9] As discussed in Chapter 2, a rhetorical situation is comprised of three elements: an exigence (an urgent problem that can be resolved through communication), an audience (people who are capable of being influenced and effecting change), and constraints (elements that shape the discourse—such as cultural values). Metaphorically speaking, we can imagine a rhetorical situation as a question and a text as an answer: the text is drawn forth and elicited by its situation.[10] Accordingly, to fully understand any rhetorical text, a critic must attend to the situation as well as the text. Miller argues that in order to understand how genres function in society—how and why people create and use genres—we need to understand the situations that call them forth.

Generic Responses

Miller argues that people make connections by imagining similarities between or among different rhetorical situations.[11] For example, imagine you are late for work because your car got a flat tire. After changing the tire, you rush into work and apologize to your boss, explaining that you had car trouble. Your boss is a little frustrated from being short-staffed, but she understands and even lets you rearrange your schedule to get your tire patched tomorrow. Later that day, you tell your coworkers your story. The next week, your coworker sleeps through her alarm and comes into work late. Having heard your story, she figures that if the excuse worked for you it will work for her too. She apologizes to your boss, explaining that she had car trouble. Your coworker, however, has a history of being late for work. Your boss does not believe her excuse and issues her an official reprimand for lateness. In this example, the two situations are not the same: different people were late and their lateness was caused by different events (car trouble versus oversleeping), and ultimately the boss's response was different. Yet despite significant differences, people tend to imagine similarities between situations, and reason that if a rhetorical response worked in the prior situation it will work again in a situation they deem similar.

Within a culture, different situations are considered similar. For example, although different people with different skills and backgrounds apply for different types of jobs in different locations, US culture groups all these situations together as "job searches." Similarly, although different people in different places graduate with different degrees from different institutions, US culture groups all these situations together as "graduation ceremonies." Genres—such as cover letters and commencement speeches—are generic responses to the situations a culture imagines being similar.

Thinking of a genre as a generic response emphasizes that genres are expected to accomplish something in society: genres act, they do something. Just as carpeters have hammers and screwdrivers on hand for the problems they expect to encounter, so too, cultures have ready-made responses (such as concession speeches) for the situations that we expect will routinely arise and that can be improved through discourse. Genres, then, are responses to the recurring exigencies, or problems of our lives; responses to the rhetorical situations we deem most repetitive and familiar. As such, genres express a culture's "rationality": they reveal the situations a culture deems important and routine.[12] Ultimately, then, genres are useful and practical templates for solving—through symbolic action—the problems we expect to arise.

Fusions of Form and Substance

As discussed in the first two chapters of this book, rhetoric acts symbolically. Something actually happens through rhetoric (voters are reassured, values are celebrated, attitudes are changed, and so on). Like close textual analysis (discussed in Chapter 2), genre criticism recommends that a critic attend to the fusion of form and content in a text in order to discern what this action is and how it is achieved—although genre criticism uses the terminology of "form" and "substance" rather than "form" and "content." **Formal elements** are *the elements of a text's form; its organizational pattern, tone, style, metaphors, color schemes, and so on.* **Substantive elements** are *the ideas presented in a text.* Genres, then, feature fusions of formal and substantive elements so that particular ideas are expressed through particular forms in order to achieve specific symbolic actions.[13]

For example, as critic Chandler Harriss documents, crime dramas are typically organized in the following way: a crime is discovered and an investigation begins; investigators discover partial answers from evidence and interrogation; the investigators review their evidence, noticing any inconsistencies; the investigators identify and apprehend a perpetrator or false perpetrator, who then provides partial answers (if the investigators have apprehended a false perpetrator, some previous steps are repeated); the investigators solve the crime, revealing the villain, method, and motive; and finally, the villain faces punishment and the investigators reflect on the case.[14] Crime dramas share this organizational form. Even long-form crime dramas, such as *Broadchurch* (which solves a single murder over the course of an entire season), use this same form; they simply slow down the pace so that each episode completes one of these stages rather than completing all the stages in a single episode, as a more traditional crime drama would. Crime dramas share other formal elements as well, such as featuring police or other law enforcement officers as recurring, if not central, characters.

Fused to these formal elements are the substantive elements of crime dramas. Crime dramas revolve around interpersonal conflict (between the villain and victim, as well as lesser conflicts among the investigators), amplifications of human motivations (such as the villain's greed, anger, impatience, obsession, or pride), moral boundaries, the genius of the investigator(s), and the ultimate restoration of law and order.[15]

The fusion of form (its predictable organization) and substance (ultimately, the righting of wrongs) in crime dramas acts in society by inviting audiences to feel that all is right in the world. Crime dramas feature dark and dangerous material as they delve into human psyches and human violence, yet they predictably end with justice and the restoration of order. Moreover, they move toward that order in an orderly fashion. The form and substance are fused: both prioritize order, reassuring viewers as they find chaos "restitched into harmony" in both the plot sequence and conclusion.[16]

Genres respond to particular situations by featuring fusions of form and substance to achieve a symbolic action. For example, imagine you climbed Mount Everest and lost an arm to frostbite during the experience. After you recover, a Fortune 500 company invites you to be the keynote speaker at its company retreat. You tell your story as an inspirational speech and earn a lot of money by speaking at this event. Soon, you travel the country presenting this inspirational speech at a wide variety of corporate events. Then you partner with a Hollywood director to create an action film that tells your story. The film is a blockbuster hit. Much later in life, you write a philosophical memoir that retells your Everest story, but this time you focus on how pain and loss shape the meaning of life. All these texts feature the same content: the same things happen—you climb Mount Everest and lose an arm to frostbite. However, these three versions of your story do not belong in one genre (mountain climbing stories), but rather, in three different genres: inspirational speeches, action films, and memoirs. They respond to different situations (company events, summer film entertainment, and philosophic contemplation). Their substance (your Everest story) is fused to different forms that inhabit different media (speech, film, and book). And they ultimately accomplish different symbolic actions (inspiring, entertaining, and illuminating).

Genres are created by humans. It is humans—in cultural communities—who decide which situations are similar enough that a response that worked in one situation will work again in another situation. It is humans who recognize patterns across texts: for example, we see violence (such as fist fights and explosions) and fast-paced editing as a pattern across blockbuster action films, ignoring all the other elements that have no pattern in this genre (the particular actors; the locations; the presence or absence of superheroes, romantic plotlines, and motivating emotions such as greed, pride, or heroism; comedic sidekicks; and so on). And it is humans—again in cultural communities—who decide which symbolic actions genres should accomplish to resolve cultural situations. Rhetorical theorists Joshua Gunn and Thomas Frentz describe genres as existing "in the minds of a given public or audience."[17]

Change over Time

Because cultures change, genres change too. Over time, and in response to economic, political, technological, and social changes, the situations that a culture considers important and recurrent change, and thus the genres we create to address those situations change too. For example, prior to cheap long-distance phone calls and the internet, letters were routinely used in situations where people wanted to communicate across distances; thus, we had genres for letter writing.[18] Now, letter genres have all but disappeared as we use phone calls, emails, text messaging, instant messaging, and social media posts to communicate across distances. As they disappear, however, their elements are reincorporated into our current means of communication. For instance, most phone calls and business emails still begin with salutations, such as "Hi Paul, how's it going?" (phone) or "Dear Paul, I hope you are well" (email), thus incorporating the first part of a letter's generic form.[19] Genres are fluid. We change and adapt them, combining and recombining elements—creating mixed genres—as we respond to new and newly conceived cultural situations.

Ultimately, genre theory suggests that critics should use genre criticism when (1) attempting to understand the emergence of several similar, popular texts (such as hit music singles or television series) that seem cut from the same cloth, because this emerging or reconceived genre indicates a new or newly conceived symbolic action; (2) tracking social, economic, technological, and/or political changes in a culture, because these changes will be reflected in generic changes; and (3) assessing the values and assumptions of a culture, because genres indicate the situations a culture sees as important and recurrent, as well as the symbolic actions through which a culture expects to resolve those situations.

DOING GENRE CRITICISM

This method has several phases: a critic becomes familiar with a genre and chooses a text (or texts); analyzes the text(s); analyzes the rhetorical situation; and finally, assesses the role or function of the genre in society. These phases are not exactly a linear progression—one does not complete the first phase and then move on to the next without ever looking back. Rather, the critic revisits prior phases throughout the research process, as each phase helps inform the others.

Becoming Familiar with a Genre and Choosing Texts

When conducting genre criticism, a critic begins by becoming familiar with the genre: reading, watching, and/or listening to a wide variety of discourses within the chosen genre while paying attention to its form, substance, situation, and symbolic action (or intended effects). By reviewing the literature (see Chapter 2) a critic can learn what other scholars have already discovered about a genre, and thereby build upon established knowledge rather than reinventing the proverbial wheel. During this process, the critic begins deciding whether to analyze one or several generically representative texts.

A **generically representative text** is *a text that represents the central elements (form and substance) and functions of its genre.* Such texts are typically popular, earn critical acclaim, and/or are particularly memorable and influential. For example, if you want to study vampire novels, Bram Stoker's *Dracula,* Anne Rice's *Interview with a Vampire,* Octavia Butler's *Fledgling,* and Stephanie Meyer's *Twilight* would all be texts that are representative of the genre. By widely surveying the genre (reading, watching, and listening to texts in that genre) and considering contextual elements (such as the popularity, enduring notoriety, and critical acclaim for a text) a critic gets a sense of which texts are generically representative.

A critic who wants to track change over time (comparing and contrasting texts from different eras) will probably work with multiple texts. Similarly, a critic may work with multiple texts when demonstrating the emergence of a new or newly conceived genre (such as teen zombie romance stories), and thus a new or newly conceived cultural situation. However, working with multiple texts can be difficult, because it requires critics to divide their analytical attention among texts and, ultimately, to describe and interpret multiple texts in a limited amount of space. (See Appendix B.) Therefore, although critics ought to broadly familiarize themselves with their genres, they need to be quite selective when deciding how many texts to analyze in their critical essays.

Analyzing a single text may seem paradoxical, as genres are fundamentally about a collection of texts. Analyzing a single text allows a critic to narrow focus and thus to go into greater detail in the analysis. A critic can analyze a single text when making an argument about how it fits within, updates, or extends a genre. Once you have a clear understanding of the whole genre and have chosen your text(s), it is time to begin your analysis.

Analyzing Generic Texts

Focusing on the text or texts, a critic assesses the *substance* or content of a genre—as represented by the text(s). For example, a critic studying a narrative genre such as true-crime novels ought to consider what plotlines, characters, settings, morals, and so on emerge across the genre, as well as how those elements appear in the text. When studying a nonnarrative genre such as policy speeches, the critic considers substance by asking what themes, ideas, recommendations, policies, persuasive appeals, and so on emerge across the genre, as well as how those elements appear in the text.

For example, imagine analyzing the genre of protest songs, and specifically U2's "Sunday Bloody Sunday" as a generically representative text. The critic would assess the song's lyrics for their substance, noting the way they allude to the "Troubles" in Northern Ireland and specifically the incident known as "Bloody Sunday," when British troops shot dead thirteen people and injured many others who were peacefully protesting internment. The critic would also note the lyrics' use of Christian scriptures and the contrast between seemingly endless cycles of violence and Easter Sunday—which is also referred to as a bloody Sunday.

Additionally, a critic considers the *form,* or the organization and style of the genre as represented by the text(s). Here, the critic needs to identify elements such as the organizational patterns, tones, metaphors, styles, narration, visuals, and sounds that emerge across the genre, as well as how those elements appear in the text(s). In the "Sunday Bloody Sunday" example, a critic would consider its form by noting the military quality of the opening snare-drum rhythm, the minor chord progressions during the verses, and the increasingly furious guitar during the verses. In contrast, during the chorus, major chords are featured; the guitar is muted; and the snare drum is silent.

Having observed the substance and form, a genre critic interprets how those elements are *fused:* how form shapes substance and vice versa. In "Sunday Bloody Sunday," the critic might note that the militaristic snare drum is "evocative of a call to struggle," creating and conveying the sense of violence and state-mandated conflict.[20] Meanwhile the clarity and power of Bono's vocal style creates and conveys a sense of the magnitude of the problem of violence, yet also conveys optimism in the choruses when he sings in major harmonies. The lyrics' repeated attention to "time and place" (its focus on bloody Sundays), creates and conveys a sense of realism—insisting that violence takes place in real times and places.[21] Throughout the music and lyrics, form and substance fuse to create and convey meaning.

A genre critic also considers how the genre—represented by the text(s)—invites audiences to respond. Here, the critic interprets the fused form and substance of the genre to assess the symbolic action—what it encourages audiences to think, feel, value, do, and/or be. A genre critic might determine that "Sunday Bloody Sunday" invites audiences to respond by rejecting oppression, standing against injustice, and thinking in a realistic but optimistic framework. After all, the song is very clear and realistic about the nature of violence and its historic effects, yet the chorus calls audiences to optimism by envisioning unity. Ultimately, "Sunday Bloody Sunday"—like the protest genre more broadly—calls audiences to understand that they likely will experience violent oppression as they protest injustice.

Analyzing the Rhetorical Situation

Genres are fundamentally responses to culturally conceived rhetorical situations. Therefore, a critic must analyze the situation in order to understand the genre. Accordingly, the critic examines the exigence or multiple exigences, audience, and constraints of the genre.

To begin, a critic might consider whether there is a clear *exigence* or a set of exigences for the genre, as represented by the text(s). For example, the critic asks whether there is a problem, qualm, crisis, concern, or motive, or some combination thereof to which the text responds. To answer this question, the critic is likely to start by looking for clues in the text that indicate how the text imagines or defines the situation. A speaker may refer to exigences within the speech itself. For instance, Martin Luther King, Jr., opened his "I have a Dream" speech by stating, "I am happy to join with you today in what will go down in history as the greatest demonstration for freedom in the history of our nation."[22] He continued by referring to the location, stating that he and the audience stood in the "symbolic shadow" of President Lincoln, who signed the Emancipation Proclamation.[23] These opening lines provide clues to the exigences to which King responded: racist oppression and segregation, wide-scale civil rights protests, his physical location on the Lincoln Memorial steps, and the Emancipation Proclamation, which proclaimed freedom for enslaved Black people in the states that had seceded from the Union.

In addition to considering how the text itself frames its exigencies, a critic assesses cultural reviews, news reports, the hype surrounding the text, any interviews with the text's speakers, writers, actors, musicians, directors, and so on. By assessing these surrounding texts, the critic can consider how audience members, cultural critics, journalists, and the creators of the text understood its connections to real-world exigences. Finally, the critic considers whether there are medium-specific exigences for the text, such as profit-seeking motivations for entertainment genres.

Next, the critic considers the *audience* for the genre, as represented by the text(s). Here, the critic broadly considers who watched, read, or heard the text. Studying reviews, news reports, box-office data, exit polls, and social media trends can provide important information about the audience. Cultural reviews often contain clear information about who the audience was and how it responded to the text. Published interviews with the rhetor of the text will probably demonstrate how the rhetor imagined the audience.

The text itself also provides clues regarding the type of audience it targeted. For example, it might mention its audience, directly address it, or use a fused form and substance to target a particular audience age, demographic, or ideology. Returning to Dr. King's "I have a Dream" speech, we see that the opening provides clear information regarding how King understood his audience: "I am happy to join with you today in what will go down in history as the greatest demonstration for freedom in the history of our nation."[24] This direct address reveals whom the speech intended as its primary audience—civil rights protesters. Moreover, King's repeated use of Judeo-Christian references, quotes, and allusions throughout the speech suggest that he expected his primary audience would be fluent in the Judeo-Christian tradition.

Finally, the critic considers the *constraints* that influence the genre, as represented by the text. The critic will probably start by looking for clues in the text itself that indicate how outside elements shaped it. For example, it might mention or allude to prior generic examples, name cultural values, call attention to its medium, or allude to the rhetor's reputation. Then, the critic considers more broadly how the genre draws on particular cultural values, interacts with religious beliefs, and/or recounts particular histories. Physical and material realities matter here as well: the critic considers how the text is shaped by technological capabilities, contained by time limits, influenced by the spatial layout, and so on.

Next, the critic assesses how the medium functions as a constraint for the genre. For example, the critic might consider whether there are norms or traditions that limit the text, such as industry expectations for how long a music album typically is or how many advertisement breaks a television series needs to accommodate. Finally, the critic considers how the rhetor's reputation, as well as prior examples or forerunners of the genre, influenced the text. For example, Dr. King's reputation, his experiences in Birmingham, the physical realities of the Lincoln Memorial area, the sabotaged sound technology, the audience size (over 250,000 people), and the pending civil rights legislation (introduced by President Kennedy) all functioned as constraints that shaped the speech.[25]

Analyzing "I have a Dream" and its rhetorical situation, communication critics David Bobbitt and Harold Mixon persuasively argue that this speech participates in the genre of apocalyptic rhetoric. Apocalypse means "revelation" (not "disaster"), and apocalyptic rhetoric responds to a crisis by revealing a visionary narrative—a story of the future.[26] Bobbitt and Mixon specifically point to the intertwining exigencies of racist oppression and civil rights protests as the crisis to which this apocalyptic speech responds. Moreover, they demonstrate how Dr. King drew on Judeo-Christian motifs and central documents of the United States (the Declaration of Independence, the Constitution, and the Emancipation Proclamation) as he cast a new vision for America's future—a future of equality that made good on what he presented as both America's and Christianity's founding principles. By analyzing the rhetorical situation of "I have a Dream," Bobbit and Mixon not only identify how this speech participates in the apocalyptic genre, they demonstrate that this speech was so successful because the apocalyptic genre "resonated with the largely church-based and Biblically-literate audience who composed the rank and file of the civil rights movement."[27]

Analyzing the Symbolic Action

In addition to analyzing the text and its situation, a critic needs to account for how a genre functions within its culture—how the society values the genre and what roles that genre plays within its culture. Genre theorist Jason Mittell recommends that genre critics ask interpretive questions such as the following:[28]

First, what does this genre mean to the community that uses it? To answer this question, a critic considers the text, its situation, its audience, and its intended effects on the basis of the critic's prior research and analysis. Because virtually nothing is universally applicable or has the same meanings in every community, a genre critic makes precise and well-supported arguments about the role of the genre in a specific community instead of making large, all-encompassing claims that cannot be robustly supported about the supposedly universal meanings of that genre. For instance, Bobbitt and Mixon's conclusion identified the role apocalyptic rhetoric plays within communities who are "church-based" and "Biblically-literate." In such a community, the apocalyptic genre is popular and sets the identity of the community as it interweaves the past into a narrative vision of the future.

Second, is this genre socially defined in a way that offers it prestige or that diminishes it? Here, a critic considers how a culture values the genre. For example, plenty of sports fans causally wear athletes' jerseys and other merchandise. In so doing, they essentially dress like their favorite athletes while going about their normal lives. But when people dress like their favorite anime or historical drama characters while going about their normal lives, they are usually mocked, teased, and socially ostracized. This difference indicates that some genres (such as sports) are socially defined in ways that have more prestige than other genres (such as anime or historical drama). A critic considering the role of a genre in society needs to assess whether the culture considers it prestigious—and if so, how and why. A critic can do this by assessing the popularity of the genre and how cultural reviews treat it.

Third, how do people use this genre? When, where, and why do people watch, read, use, or listen to a genre? To answer this question, a critic assesses her or his prior research and analysis, considering the situation, the audience, the responses the text invites from audiences, and the effects it attempts to elicit.

Finally, does this genre represent, engage in, criticize, and/or disrupt the hierarchies and established power relations in its culture? If so, how? For example, if local television coverage of minor league baseball games routinely avoided showing or mentioning players who knelt during the anthem as part of Black Lives Matter protests, a critic could argue that this genre of sports broadcasting accepted and reinforced established hierarchies and power relationships, inasmuch as its cinematography and commentary hid these protests from audiences watching the games at home. To assess how a genre functions in society and the roles it plays in society, a critic needs to consider how the genre interacts with the established hierarchies.

RESEARCH EXAMPLES

The following three research examples provide excellent demonstrations of how critics study the representative texts, situations, and societal roles of a genre. In the first example, James A. Herrick analyzes several technofuturist texts, demonstrating how the genre offers solutions to both physical problems and spiritual malaise—and, in so doing, provides a road map for legislative and practical decisions concerning technology. In the second example, Erin J. Rand uses Ruth Bader Ginsburg and Sonia Sotomayor's judicial dissent from the Supreme Court case *Burwell v. Hobby Lobby* to demonstrate the roles that the genre of judicial dissent plays in US culture. The third example features Jason Mittell's analysis of Michael Jackson's *Beat It,* in which Mittell demonstrates how the traditions and racist politics of the music video industry constrained the genre of music videos, temporarily excluding *Beat It.*

James A. Herrick
Visions of Technological Transcendence: Human Enhancement and the Rhetoric of the Future (2017)*

What role should technology play in our lives? Although many of us adore our smart phones and think free Wi-Fi is a basic human right, other technology may make us pause. For example, what role should drones play in policing peaceful protests?[29] Who is culpable in accident fatalities involving self-driving cars?[30] Should companies, industries, or the government retrain/reeducate coalminers for different jobs before replacing up to 80 percent of them with automated machines?[31] Legislators answer these questions as they pass laws regulating technology. Tech leaders (such as Elon Musk) answer them as they finance—and therefore steer—technological advances. But what cultural logic guides the decisions? James Herrick analyzes the genre of technofuturist rhetoric to assess the reasoning that US culture uses to shape the role of technology in society.

Technofuturist rhetoric presents a vision of "inevitable technological progress" that builds on human evolution and ultimately conceptualizes "the person as information."[32] This genre philosophically imagines humanity's future as fundamentally fused with and dependent upon technology. It includes science fiction narratives (such as Christopher Nolan's 2014 film, *Interstellar*) as well as prose that philosophically envisions the future of humanity (such as Francis Bacon's novel, *New Atlantis,* published in 1626).

Herrick identifies the form of this genre as fundamentally philosophical and visionary, its substance as technological renderings of the future. When fused together, the form and substance create texts that meditate on what it means to be human. They present technology as the answer to this philosophical question. Thus, technology becomes humanity's salvation and transcendence.

Herrick begins his book-length analysis by evaluating initial versions of the genre, demonstrating how writings from as early as the 1600s began the work of "imagining a comprehensive technological culture" and established the frameworks

---

*This book is published by Parlor Press (Anderson, SC: 2017).

that continue to echo throughout the genre.[33] In the subsequent chapters, Herrick analyzes a wide variety of technofuturist texts, repeatedly demonstrating how the "myth of progress" and "the story of evolution" recur throughout the genre.[34] He combines genre criticism and narrative criticism (discussed in Chapter 3) as he demonstrates how these myth and narrative structures animate the genre.

Analyzing the technofuturist genre, Herrick focuses on the situations that call it forth. He identifies cultural moments of "technological breakthroughs that promise to deliver dramatic social, cultural, and commercial change" as a key exigence.[35] As turbulent scientific advancement intersects with the ongoing exigences of disease, poverty, mortality, environmental disasters, and spiritual/philosophical ennui (as humans question the meaning of life in light of our own frailty and mortality), these combined exigences form the locus of a powerful rhetorical situation. Technofuturist rhetoric then forms a generic response to this situation, addressing humanity's philosophical/spiritual questions and imagining the role of technology in the future of humanity. This genre is ultimately optimistic; it ameliorates our concerns and the despair humans can feel when facing loss and death.

Herrick argues that the technofuturist genre plays a crucial role in modern societies. First, it offers humans a vision for controlling their own lives and their environments—a vision that we might never be subject to disease or disaster again. Second, it offers humans a vision of what it means to be human—a vision that elevates our spirit, will, and memories as more meaningful than our physical embodiment. Third, the genre offers humans a vision of human perfection that celebrates our potential for greatness, while sacrificing as unworthy the humans who cannot or do not genetically contribute to cultivating this greatness (for example, those whose genes are considered inferior or those who refuse to reproduce). Fourth, it offers humans a new vision of ethics based on progress: that which is right is that which advances technological innovation. Finally, the genre offers humans a vision of spiritualism and religion; that is, it offers humans something to believe in—technology—that will supposedly save us by providing transcendent meaning and improving the physical and relational elements of our lives.

Herrick is deeply concerned by the role this genre is playing in our world. He finds that its animating myth is ethically and spiritually suspect, but that it dominates our lives as technological advancement increasingly shapes our work environments, our children's educational environments, the medical treatments we undergo, the homes we live in, the relationships we value, and the "systems of defense and justice" we champion.[36] Considering how this technofuturist genre supported and fueled the US and Nazi eugenics projects, Herrick is alarmed to find the technofuturist genre steering US visions of technology again.[37]

Herrick recognizes that humans use genres to respond to the situations we imagine as important and recurrent; that we will use some myth, narrative, or other fusion of form and substance to address the questions that arise during periods of technological advancement. However, we need not wed ourselves to this technofuturist genre and its mythology. Herrick argues that the technofuturist genre cannot satisfy humanity's persistent questions concerning the meaning of life and, moreover, that the genre contains a dangerous recasting of social Darwinism (racism and ableism) even as it downplays our embodied experiences. He concludes that this genre harms us as it guides legislation, research grants, company investments, and consumer choices.

Erin J. Rand
"Fear the Frill: Ruth Bader Ginsburg and the Uncertain Futurity of Feminist Judicial Dissent" (2015)*

Imagine that your family is deciding where to go for spring break: Florida or Minnesota. Incredulously, you find the majority is leaning toward Minnesota and is unmoved by your arguments that a warm beach is preferable to snow. Your family takes a vote and the majority wins. Suddenly—against your will—you find yourself headed to Minnesota for spring break. Now, imagine you spend days, maybe weeks, crafting a sharply worded argument condemning their decision. You read your dissent to your family from the back seat of the car as you all drive across the country.

Sound ridiculous? Well, the US judicial system regularly engages in this genre—the genre of dissent—even though dissents do not affect the ruling or application of the law in any way. Judicial dissents explain why a justice disagreed with the majority, but that explanation has no immediate legal function.

Studying this genre, Erin Rand analyzed the role these seemingly useless dissents play in society. Specifically, she analyzed the dissent Justice Ruth Bader Ginsburg read aloud from the bench at the conclusion of the Supreme Court case of *Burwell v. Hobby Lobby*. Hobby Lobby won the case, successfully arguing that if a business's owners have religion-based objections (even if the business employs thousands of employees and has franchises across the nation), the business should be excused from the Affordable Care Act (ACA) mandate that employer-based health insurance include particular forms of contraceptives.

Ginsburg's judicial dissent argued that the Supreme Court majority had misapplied the 1993 Religious Freedom Restoration Act (RFRA) by considering a "for-profit corporation" to be a "person" and deeming the "ACA's required contraceptive coverage" to be a "substantial burden" on its religious beliefs.[38] Rand notes that the form of this dissent utilizes a "fiery" and personal tone and that its substance criticizes the decision of the ruling majority by arguing for alternative interpretations of the 1993 RFRA as more appropriate.[39]

Judicial rulings are typically expressed in neutral and objective terms—as if they were impartial forces of nature rather than decisions crafted by individuals. Judicial dissents, by contrast, reveal the personal and contingent nature of judicial rulings as they incorporate subjective perspectives and reveal alternative logics—different ways of thinking and interpreting laws—that expose the majority ruling as a similarly subjective, human decision rather than an objective force of nature.

Rather than dwell on the Hobby Lobby dissent, however, Rand focuses primarily on the situations to which judicial dissents respond and the role they play in democratic practices in the United States. Rand stipulates that judicial

*This essay may be found in *Quarterly Journal of Speech* 101, no. 1 (2015): 72–84.

dissents respond to situations in which a ruling was "hotly contested among the justices" and a minority of justices believes the majority decision egregiously misadministers the law.[40] She demonstrates how dissents respond to and ameliorate this tense situation by playing several social roles. First, dissents signal to the citizenry that a ruling was disputed, thereby inviting cases that revisit the ruling in future years. Second, they perform and signal the arguments that future cases could use to contest the current ruling.[41] And third, judicial dissents reveal the personal and rhetorical nature of the law itself.

While these three roles subvert and challenge the majority ruling, the genre of judicial dissent has two more social functions that, surprisingly, sustain and legitimate the judicial system in the United States. First, judicial dissents restrain populist revolts. By arguing back, publicly and officially resisting the majority decision, they speak on behalf of those who disagree with it, thus providing an official record of their dissent and ensuring that this portion of the population feels heard and represented by government authorities. Like a steam valve that lets out the pressure, dissents can prevent populist uprisings if the people maintain faith in the system—if they feel represented by government officials—even though the dissents do not affect the outcomes of the cases or provide precedent for future cases. Second, judicial dissents function to "uphold the legitimacy of the judicial system" even as they "challenge its particular conclusions."[42] Essentially, the genre of judicial dissent offers a way for justices to voice their grievances without trying to change the ruling or questioning the right of the majority to make that ruling. It is an official form of protest that works "within the system" and ultimately trusts the system to eventually set things right.[43] By analyzing the Hobby Lobby dissent, Rand focuses on how judicial dissents function, showing how the genre responds to its complex originating situation.

Jason Mittell
"A Cultural Approach to Television Genre Theory" (2001)*

If you want to watch a music video, you probably type the title of the song into the search bar on YouTube.com, Vimeo.com, or some other website. But during the 1980s, if you knew what a music video was and wanted to watch one, you turned on cable television and found the MTV channel. MTV—which stands for Music Television—launched in 1981. Its original programming featured "video jockeys" who introduced music videos before playing them.[44] Analyzing how MTV initially rejected Michael Jackson's audiovisual *Beat It* (arguing that it was not a music video) Jason Mittell demonstrates how industries shape our cultural understandings of genres.

By modern standards, Michael Jackson's audiovisual *Beat It* is quintessentially a music video: it seems to be the very definition of its genre. Jackson and other performers sing and dance; the video features a gang fight narrative that is only hinted at in the lyrics alone; and it ends with a large choreographed dance. However, when *Beat It* was released in 1983, MTV's industrial practices—how they defined music videos and which videos they featured—played a big role in how people understood this emerging genre.

---

*This essay may be found in *Cinema Journal* 40, no. 3 (2001): 3–24.

MTV was the dominant outlet for music videos, which it defined as videos exclusively set to rock music. This may now seem like an odd but innocuous choice, but in practice during the 1980s, it narrowed the genre to videos performed by White artists such as Duran Duran and ignored the "racially hybridized origins of rock as a musical style."[45] MTV's industrial practices dominated the "conception of the genre": other mainstream outlets for music videos, such as NBC's *Friday Night Videos,* followed MTV's lead by also featuring "white-centric lead" singers.[46]

MTV refused to play Michael Jackson's *Beat It* (along with *Thriller* and *Billie Jean*), claiming that it did not fit their genre of music videos because it was not rock and because it began with approximately twenty seconds during which there was no musical accompaniment. (The opening scene, in which two men leave a diner to join their gang, has no music.) MTV used formal, textual elements in their attempt to define the genre: a video had to be rock and it had to have music during the entire video to qualify as a "music video." However—as we have seen—genres are not only defined according to their textual elements (form and substance), but also the situations to which they respond and the effects they produce.

Rightly understanding *Beat It* in terms of its situation and effects, Jackson's label, CBS Records, saw the "commercial potential of Jackson's album" (which included *Beat It, Thriller,* and *Billie Jean*) and allegedly threated to "withdraw all CBS artists from MTV if Jackson continued to be excluded."[47] MTV bowed under this pressure, first airing *Billie Jean* and then—due to its "tremendous audience response"—*Beat It.*[48] The two videos performed so well that they were in "heavy rotation" by March of 1983. Subsequently, MTV featured *Thriller* with "significant promotion and fanfare" that December.[49] Jackson's success on MTV changed its "racially segregated programming policies," opening the door to Prince, Tina Turner, and other Black artists—and ultimately widening the genre of music videos to incorporate musical styles such as soul, R&B, rap, and hip-hop.[50]

Mittell's analysis highlights the role that industries play in creating and understanding genres. Studying the genre of music videos in a moment of generic definition, Mittell demonstrates how MTV's original definition of music videos had textual elements (rock styles and continuous music), but also situational elements. The race of the artist was a constraint on the genre (only White artists qualified, according to MTV). MTV's profit-driven nature served as an exigence as it targeted only White suburban youths as the primary audience, simplistically imagining that this audience was the most likely to spend money on music. Jackson's audiovisual creations, *Beat It, Billie Jean,* and *Thriller* ultimately broke through MTV's generic boundaries largely because of situational elements: Jackson's "growing star persona," pressure from CBS Records, and growing "public protests" over MTV's segregationist programming served as clear exigences that pushed MTV to widen its definition of the music video genre.[51]

STRENGTHS AND WEAKNESSES OF GENRE CRITICISM

Genres are fluid categories that a society creates in order to group texts for its own convenience. Consequently, genres reveal how a culture thinks: they reveal not only how a culture categorizes texts, but what situations routinely occur, what the situations are that it deems important and recurrent enough to create a generic way of addressing through rhetoric. For example, if a dictator ruled the United

States, it would have no elections. If it had no elections (the situation), it would need no campaign speeches (the genre). The existence of campaign speeches as a genre points to the needs of our culture as a democracy. Genre criticism is particularly good at showing how a culture understands reality and the situations it deems recurrent and important.

Moreover, genres reveal how a society expects speakers, authors, directors, and so on to respond to given situations. Here again, the logic of the culture is on display. At a campaign debate, we expect gubernatorial candidates to humbly explain their qualifications, explain how their policies will improve conditions in the state, and argue that their character and policies are demonstrably better than their opponent's—thus following the standard fusion of form and substance for a campaign debate. We do not expect gubernatorial candidates to spend their time during a debate singing and dancing to entertain the audience. Genre criticism is particularly good at demonstrating a culture's expectations for how a discourse should go—and thus, how a society wants a rhetorical situation to be resolved.

Genre criticism, however, is often quite poor at working with a given text in a close, detailed way. Because it often studies multiple texts and carefully attunes itself to the situation that calls forth the genre and the function it serves in its culture, a critic typically needs a panoramic lens to practice this method: genre criticism lacks the nitty-gritty details provided by other methods that use a more zoomed-in lens. Consider, for example, that Erin Rand only quoted from the *Burwell v. Hobby Lobby* dissent six times in her entire analysis and provides no sense of the organization of the dissent. Similarly, Jason Mittell is focused on the cultural elements (the industry norms and racist politics) surrounding *Beat It*'s contested classification as a music video, and all but ignores the lyrics, dance moves, and gang-related narrative of the text itself. These critics are doing excellent genre criticism—but because this method is concerned with more than the specific features of the text, it does not produce critical essays that focus on those features.

CHOOSING THIS METHOD

So how do you know whether you should use genre criticism to analyze a particular piece or several pieces of public discourse? To answer this question, you need to consider your text, its context, and the research question animating your analysis.

First, consider your text. Does your text meaningfully participate in a genre? Do people—audience members, industry personnel, or cultural critics—generally consider this text to be part of a larger genre and/or liken it to other similar texts? You might consider whether reviews of your text name other texts that are similar to yours or suggest that your text draws inspiration from a famous older text. If your text does not noticeably participate in a genre, genre criticism is unlikely to be the best method for your analysis.

Second, consider the context of your text: the situation that called forth your text and its influence in society. Research your text to see how much information is available about its situation and its influence. For example, if I were considering conducting a generic analysis of *Black Panther* (2018), I would look up its box office figures, its critical reviews, its social media references, and its role within the Marvel Universe. If you cannot find much information about the situation and influence, it will be difficult to make a coherent argument about how the genre functions in society.

Third, consider your research motives. Are you intrigued by a suddenly emergent genre or a change in an existing genre? Are you interested in tracking cultural change over time? Are you interested in the values and assumptions of a culture? Genre criticism is particularly suited to answering research questions that stem from these types of motivating concerns.

Genre criticism can be a deeply rewarding rhetorical method. To some extent, this method is like a panoramic lens. It helps critics assess the role of a text (or of several texts) within a wide cultural context, and thus make sense of whole swaths of public discourse.

DISCUSSION QUESTIONS

1. Name a genre you love or hate. How would you describe that genre? What are its key elements? Why do you love or hate it?
2. Consider the genres of romantic comedies, sermons, and presidential inaugural addresses. Explain what rhetorical situation(s) call these genres into existence. Specifically, list at least one exigence, audience, and constraint for each genre.
3. List two situations you consider important and recurrent in your life and for which you have developed generic responses. Explain the situations and your generic response. To answer this question, you might first think about what generic responses you currently have; for example, do you have a standard apology, break-up approach, compliment, or pick-up line? Then think backwards to consider the "situations" in which you use your generic statements.
4. Reconsider the genre you discussed for the first question. Specifically, look at how you described the genre and identified its key elements. Now separate those elements into formal and substantive elements. Are any of those formal and substantive elements fused together in this genre?
5. Describe a genre that you think has changed over time. How has it changed? What cultural shifts (economic, political, technological, social, and so on) do you think led to those changes?
6. Name a genre and then name a generically representative text for that genre. How did you decide that text was a good representative of its whole genre?

NOTES

1. Simon Cole and Rachel Dioso-Villa, "*CSI* and Its Effects: Media, Juries, and the Burden of Proof," *New England Law Review* 31, no. 3 (2007): 442.
2. *CSI: Crime Scene Investigation,* season 6, episodes 7–8, "A Bullet Runs through It: Part 1" and "A Bullet Runs through It: Part 2," directed by Danny Cannon and Kenneth Fink, aired November 10, 2005, and November 17, 2005, on CBS.
3. Chandler Harriss, "The Evidence Doesn't Lie: Genre Literacy and the *CSI* Effect," *Journal of Popular Film and Television* 39, no. 1 (2011): 4.

4. Donald Shelton, "The '*CSI* Effect': Does it Really Exist?" *National Institute of Justice Journal,* vol. 259 (2008), https://www.nij.gov/journals/259/pages/csi-effect.aspx; Donald Shelton, Young S. Kim, and Gregg Barak, "A Study of Juror Expectations and Demands Concerning Scientific Evidence: Does the '*CSI* Effect' Exist?" *Vanderbilt Journal of Entertainment & Technology Law* 9, no. 2 (2006): 331–368.
5. Shelton, "The '*CSI* Effect.'"
6. Jason Mittell, "A Cultural Approach to Television Genre Theory," *Cinema Journal* 40, no. 3 (2001): 5.
7. Craig Rood, "The Gap between Rhetorical Education and Civic Discourse," *Review of Communication* 16, no. 2–3 (2016): 135.
8. Ryan Neville-Shepard, "Triumph in Defeat: The Genre of Third Party Presidential Concessions," *Communication Quarterly* 62, no. 2 (2014): 217.
9. Carolyn Miller, "Genre as Social Action," *Quarterly Journal of Speech* 70, no. 2 (1984): 151–152.
10. Lloyd Bitzer, "The Rhetorical Situation," *Philosophy & Rhetoric* 1, no. 1 (1968): 2, 5–6.
11. Miller, "Genre as Social Action," 156–157.
12. Miller, "Genre as Social Action," 165.
13. Miller, "Genre as Social Action," 153.
14. Chandler Harriss, "Policing Propp: Toward a Textualist Definition of the Procedural Drama," *Journal of Film and Video* 60, no. 1 (2008): 46.
15. Karen Riggs, "The Case of the Mysterious Ritual: Murder Dramas and Older Women Viewers," *Critical Studies in Mass Communication* 13 (1996): 310–311.
16. Riggs, "Case of the Mysterious Ritual," 311.
17. Joshua Gunn and Thomas Frentz, "*The Da Vinci Code* as Alchemical Rhetoric," *Western Journal of Communication* 72, no. 3 (2008): 216.
18. Andy Kirkpatrick, "The Arrangement of Letters: Hierarchy or Culture? From Cicero to China," *Journal of Asian Pacific Communication* 17, no. 2 (2007): 245–258.
19. Marian M. Extejt, "Teaching Students to Correspond Effectively Electronically," *Business Communication Quarterly* 61, no. 2 (1998): 57–67.
20. Michael Drewett, "The Eyes of the World Are Watching Now: The Political Effectiveness of 'Biko' by Peter Gabriel," *Popular Music and Society* 30, no. 1 (2007): 41.
21. Drewett, "The Eyes of the World Are Watching Now," 42.
22. Martin Luther King, Jr., "I Have a Dream," *American Rhetoric,* August 28, 1963, https://www.americanrhetoric.com/speeches/mlkihaveadream.htm.
23. King, "I Have a Dream."
24. King, "I Have a Dream."
25. "10 Fascinating Facts about the 'I Have A Dream' Speech," *National Constitution Center,* August 28, 2017, https://constitutioncenter.org/blog/10-fascinating-facts-about-the-i-have-a-dream-speech.
26. David Bobbitt and Harold Mixon, "Prophesy and Apocalypse in the Rhetoric of Martin Luther King, Jr.," *Journal of Communication and Religion* 17, no. 1 (1994): 30.
27. Bobbit and Mixon, "Prophesy and Apocalypse," 36.
28. Mittell, "A Cultural Approach," 9, 14–19.

29. Sun-Times Editorial Board, "Editorial: Chicago Police Drones at Rallies Smack of Red Squad Snooping," *Chicago Sun-Times,* May 4, 2018, https://chicago.suntimes.com/opinion/police-drones-surveillance-red-squad-illinois-law/.
30. Daisuke Wakabayashi, "Self-Driving Uber Car Kills Pedestrian in Arizona, Where Robots Roam," NYTimes.com, March 19, 2018, https://www.nytimes.com/2018/03/19/technology/uber-driverless-fatality.html.
31. Patrick Thibodeau, "Robotics, Driverless Tech are Taking over Mining Jobs," ComputerWorld.com, October 28, 2016, https://www.computerworld.com/article/3136675/it-careers/robotics-driverless-tech-are-taking-over-mining-jobs.html.
32. James Herrick, *Visions of Technological Transcendence: Human Enhancement and the Rhetoric of the Future* (Anderson, SC: Parlor Press, 2017), 10.
33. Herrick, *Visions of Technological Transcendence,* 25
34. Herrick, *Visions of Technological Transcendence,* 36.
35. Herrick, *Visions of Technological Transcendence,* 153.
36. Herrick, *Visions of Technological Transcendence,* 167–168.
37. Andrea DenHoed, "The Forgotten Lessons of the American Eugenics Movement," *The New Yorker,* April 27, 2016, https://www.newyorker.com/books/page-turner/the-forgotten-lessons-of-the-american-eugenics-movement; Edwin Black, "Eugenics and the Nazis—The California Connection," SFGate.com, November 9, 2003, https://www.sfgate.com/opinion/article/Eugenics-and-the-Nazis-the-California-2549771.php.
38. Erin Rand, "Fear the Frill: Ruth Bader Ginsburg and the Uncertain Futurity of Feminist Judicial Dissent," *Quarterly Journal of Speech* 101, no. 1 (2015): 74.
39. Rand, "Fear the Frill," 74.
40. Rand, "Fear the Frill," 75.
41. Rand, "Fear the Frill," 77.
42. Rand, "Fear the Frill," 78.
43. Rand, "Fear the Frill," 79.
44. "MTV Turns 30: MTV VJs: Where are they Now?" *NYDailyNews.com,* http://www.nydailynews.com/entertainment/music-arts/mtv-turns-30-mtv-vjs-gallery-1.33602.
45. Mittell, "A Cultural Approach," 13.
46. Mittell, "A Cultural Approach," 13.
47. Mittell, "A Cultural Approach," 14.
48. Mittell, "A Cultural Approach," 14.
49. Mittell, "A Cultural Approach," 14.
50. Mittell, "A Cultural Approach," 14.
51. Mittell, "A Cultural Approach," 16.

Chapter 6

Metaphor Criticism

As a child, I started reading the poetry of Emily Dickinson. Her poetry is full of nature: she writes about birds, flowers, and sometimes even squirrels. One of Emily Dickinson's poems starts with the line, "The Lightning is a yellow Fork."[1] The poem goes on, musing that this "fork" is dropped by the clumsy fingers of someone eating at a table in the sky. As a child, one of the key reasons I liked (and at least partly understood) Dickinson's poetry is that it uses striking metaphors—turning lightning into forks.

A **metaphor** *imagines one thing as another thing, so that something unfamiliar, abstract, or complex is reimagined as something familiar, concrete, or simple.* In the line, "The Lightning is a yellow Fork," lightning is unfamiliar: although we may see lightning fairly often, it is typically far away. Few of us have any firsthand experience with lightning or scientific understanding of it. In contrast, forks are familiar: we encounter, use, wash, and drop forks on a regular basis. By reimagining lightning as a yellow fork, Emily Dickinson's metaphor renders the unfamiliar familiar. As a child, I knew Dickinson was often not being literal in her poetry. Obviously, lightning is not actually forks dropped from heavenly tables. But the metaphor reimagines lightning in a way that makes it less scary.

Poets, like Dickinson, use metaphors because they are part of our everyday thought, speech, and action. Consider these metaphors, for example: America is a melting pot; life is a roller coaster; time is money; the world is a stage; that solution is just a Band-Aid; my roommate is a night owl; you are my sunshine; my room is a disaster zone; she is a walking dictionary; love is a battlefield; and don't kill the goose that lays the golden egg. Like Dickinson's metaphor, "The Lightning is a yellow Fork," each of these metaphors takes something unfamiliar, abstract, complex or unknown and reimagines it as something familiar, concrete, simple, or known. For instance, you might use the metaphor "my roommate is a night owl" to explain your roommate's behavior to someone. In so doing, you take something unknown (your roommate and her behavior) and make it known by reimagining her as an owl, thus conveying that she typically stays up late into the night.

Metaphors can communicate ideas in striking and memorable ways. In the process, they often fundamentally change how we understand something. We can see that Dickinson's lightning metaphor renders lightning familiar, domestic, and benign—like a fork. Telling a child that lightning is a yellow fork dropped from a table in the sky allows that child to imagine lightning in a new way: it is no longer scary and dangerous, but rather common, homey, and harmless.

Metaphors' ability to affect meaning may seem like a trick that would only work on children, but metaphors also affect how adults understand meaning. For example, in 2010, Australia faced a policy question—a proposed tax—regarding how to regulate mining industries that produce significant pollution. These highly profitable industries lobbied against this regulatory tax, often claiming, "the tax is the equivalent of killing the goose that lays the golden egg."[2] This metaphor characterized the mining industry itself as the "goose," thereby characterizing it as not only good and innocent, but also extraordinarily good for Australia. Once this metaphor captured the Australian public's imagination, the taxation policy was no longer viable. No one wants to kill the goose that lays the golden egg.

The metaphors we have been discussing have all been verbal metaphors, but visual metaphors exist as well. Consider the way *The Bachelor/Bachelorette* franchise features dates in which a couple jumps into the ocean while holding hands or rappels down a cliff together to express that they are *falling* in love. Visual metaphors—like verbal metaphors—can be striking and memorable, and often have a clear impact on meaning. (Chapter 10 will provide more guidance on how to consider the visuality of a metaphor.)

Metaphor criticism is *a method for understanding how metaphors (1) shape meaning, (2) appeal to audiences, and (3) influence the decisions of a community.* This method helps orient a critic toward a text by focusing on a single aspect of its symbolic form—its metaphor(s)—as the critic's central approach. Critics use this method to focus on how metaphors not only convey meaning but also shape our perceptions of reality. To understand how to use this method, we need a more precise understanding of what metaphors are and how humans use them.

A THEORY OF METAPHORS

In 1936, communication theorist I. A. Richards developed terminology to help critics study how metaphors shape meaning.[3] Metaphors work by imagining one idea in terms of another idea, so they always involve two "different things."[4] Richards names the "underlying idea or principle subject" the **tenor,** *the abstract, complex, or unfamiliar idea (or thing) that the metaphor has reimagined or made known to the audience.*[5] In Emily Dickinson's metaphor "The Lightning is a yellow Fork," lightning is the tenor. The poem is about lightning; lightning is what Dickinson reimagines and makes known to the reader through her metaphor. Richards named the other idea in a metaphor the **vehicle,** *the familiar, concrete, or simple idea (or thing) through which the tenor is reimagined.* In Dickinson's metaphor, the fork is the vehicle: the fork is known and lends its meaning (domestic, harmless, and commonplace) to the tenor (lightning).

Richards further notes that metaphors ask audiences to put the two different concepts (the vehicle and tenor) into interaction with one another. That is, the tenor has one meaning and the vehicle has another, but combined in the metaphor the two meanings interact to generate a new meaning—a new way to understand the tenor. For example, George W. Bush, during a presidential debate with his opponent, Al Gore, asked citizens whether they wanted a "*big exploding* federal government."[6] Here, the federal government is the tenor: Bush's metaphor was designed to help his audience make sense of the complex idea of the federal government. The vehicle is the idea of a big explosion. Separately, the federal government means one thing (the arrangement designed in the Constitution: the electorate and a federal Congress, presidency, and judiciary, along with their agencies, committees, and cabinets), but a big explosion means a different thing (a huge fire bomb combined with a large outward propulsion of debris). In Bush's metaphor, these two different meanings interact, creating one new meaning for the tenor: a rapidly expanding, messy, destructive federal government that obliterates life as we know it.

A metaphor is far more than a nice turn of phrase. Metaphors can profoundly shape how we understand reality. Building on Kenneth Burke's theory of terministic screens (Chapter 4), metaphor theorist Leah Ceccarelli explains how metaphors shape our thinking. Burke wrote that a metaphor is "a device for seeing something *in terms of* something else."[7] As such, Ceccarelli says, metaphors "select some aspects of a subject to emphasize, while deflecting our attention from other aspects of that subject."[8] They work like screens, filtering and transforming our perceptions of reality.[9]

Burke's theory of terministic screens suggests that everyday terms (words and other symbols) reflect, select, and deflect how reality is understood. For example, if I introduce my colleague as "a friend I happen to work with," the term "friend" faithfully reflects reality. It also selects our personal relationship as salient and deflects attention away from my colleague's expertise as a professor. Burke argued that every term functions in this "screening" way—hence his phrase, "terministic screens." Metaphors, then, are like terministic screens on steroids: they take one term (such as lightning) and wrap it in a second term (such as forks).

Types of Metaphors

Linguistic theorist Cornelia Müller notes that people use metaphors in different ways. Some metaphors are used so routinely they barely even register as metaphors; others use familiar concepts; and still others are fresh and striking.[10] Categorizing these different types of metaphors helps us understand how metaphors function in our discourse.

Dead metaphors are *metaphors that have become the conventional, routine way to describe a particular concept or thing within a culture; they are used so conventionally that people often fail to notice them.* For example, when my spouse described an argument he had with a plumber who had unexpectedly demolished our flooring, he said, "the plumber started off really *defensive* and *attacked* me as if the flooring was my fault." In this statement, my spouse used dead metaphors when he described the plumber's angry response as defensive and an attack. He did not intend for me to conjure up the image of combat in order to understand his experience with the plumber—and indeed, I did not imagine his confrontation through the concept of combat.

War metaphors are used so conventionally to describe arguments ("I *defended* my claims"; "s/he *shot down* my argument") that we generally forget that they are metaphors.[11] Other dead metaphors include falling metaphors to imagine love (*falling* in love); bird metaphors to imagine flying machines (*wings* of an airplane); economic metaphors to imagine time (I *wasted* my time); directional metaphors to imagine moods (that *lifted* my spirits; I'm just *down* today); and body metaphors to imagine inanimate objects (*face* of a clock; *legs* of a chair).

Dead metaphors reveal how a culture conceptualizes a concept or thing. For example, Americans' conventionalized use of war metaphors for arguments demonstrates an assumption that arguments are destructive and have victors and vanquished foes. Moreover, by imagining arguments as war, US culture ignores other aspects of argumentation. For instance, many arguments are not destructive but cooperative: two people take turns in a conversation, explaining their own reasons, asking questions to better understand the other person's reasons, and working to find a mutually satisfying path forward. However, people in healthy interpersonal relationships and civic communities often dread arguments because we think of them in destructive terms, even when we go about arguing in cooperative and mutually beneficial ways.

Because we think of arguments as war, we are far more likely to approach an argument in a hostile state than in a calm and cooperative state of mind. As a result, a dead metaphor shapes our lived realities as we *fight* with our family members, friends, neighbors, and civic communities. The argument-as-war metaphor then becomes a self-fulfilling prophesy: because we think of arguments as war, we are more likely to argue in destructive and hostile ways. Thus, even though such metaphors are known as "dead," they powerfully shape a community's perceptions, values, assumptions, and experiences. Given how powerful they are, some theorists prefer to refer to them as "conventionalized," "literalized," "deeply entrenched," or "historical" metaphors.[12]

Unlike dead metaphors that typically slide by as "routine language choices," **entrenched metaphors** are *metaphors that reimagine ideas (or things) in familiar ways.*[13] They are entrenched within their communities: although people recognize them as metaphors, they are familiar and carry familiar values and meanings. For example, in the Old Testament, the prophet Isaiah gives the people of Israel a comforting message from their God, saying, "this is what the Lord says . . . when you *pass through the waters,* I will be with you" (Isaiah 43:1–2, NIV). In this historical context, the sea was a deeply frightening concept: given their lack of nautical capabilities, the Israelites quite rightly feared having to cross large bodies of water. The passage is metaphorical (the Israelites are not anticipating a sea voyage) and the metaphor is entrenched: the sea-as-danger was a familiar metaphor in this time and place, so this message made sense to the Israelites and comforted them.

In contrast to dead metaphors, which are so familiar we have forgotten they are metaphors, and entrenched metaphors, which feature familiar vehicles, **novel metaphors** are *unusual and fresh ways to imagine a concept or thing.* For example, President Barack Obama addressed the nation in 2013, explaining that Syria's ruler, Bashar al-Assad, had used chemical weapons to brutally massacre over a thousand people, and announcing that the United States would respond through a targeted military strike. He then stated, "Let me make something clear: The United States military doesn't do *pinpricks.* Even a limited strike will send a message to Assad that no other nation can deliver."[14] Obama used a sewing metaphor, *pinpricks,* to assure the US public that a targeted strike would sufficiently deter Assad from using chemical weapons in the future. This was a novel metaphor: we do not commonly think of the military as a seamstress who accidentally pricks herself or her client with an errant pin. Indeed, we are not in the habit of thinking about war, soldiers, combat, and weapons in terms of fabric, thread, patterns, and pins. Obama's novel metaphor works by contrasting the US military to this metaphorical pinprick.

Novel metaphors are often striking and memorable, and therefore tend to grip an audience's attention. Audience members must grapple with the tension a novel metaphor creates by placing two ideas (or things) that do not typically interact into interaction with each other. For example, in 2012 Gary Kovacs (then the CEO of the Mozilla Corporation) explained how digital entities collect Internet users' personal data (which websites you visit, what you click on, the content of your social media posts, and information such as your birthday and purchasing preferences) in an industry he called behavioral tracking.[15] He provided a demonstration that visually charts all of the entities that track his data as he navigates to fairly common websites (email, the news, and so on). As his demonstration unfolds, Kovacs states, "*I am being stalked* across the Web."[16] He elaborates on this stalking metaphor, discussing his daughter's internet usage and likening the internet tracking to a real person following his daughter around, taking pictures of her, and taking notes on all of the things she does and says.[17] Kovacs closes by calling his audience to action as he reminds them, "*We are being watched.*"[18] Kovacs's novel metaphor is striking and memorable. It makes what could have been a rather dry topic (website cookies, data sharing, and legal loopholes) into a gripping speech while portraying behavioral tracking as a nefarious industry that ought to be stopped.

When a novel metaphor is routinely used across a culture, it can become entrenched. For example, in 1908, when Israel Zangwill opened his play, *The Melting Pot,* in Washington, DC, this "melting pot" metaphor for America was novel. As the final curtain came down on opening night, Theodore Roosevelt "leaned over his box and shouted to Zangwill: 'That's a great play, Mr. Zangwill, that's a great play.'"[19] President Roosevelt's endorsement helped make the play a success. It enjoyed significant popularity—and launched the term "melting pot" into US discourse.[20] With use, this novel metaphor lost its novelty, settling into an entrenched metaphor for the American experience.

By studying the metaphors in a text, a critic studies what the text asks its audience to imagine as reality—a reality that is filtered or screened through metaphors. Studying dead metaphors offers the critic an opportunity to study how a community conventionally interprets reality. Studying entrenched metaphors allows a critic to study the go-to concepts, histories, and experiences that a culture recurrently uses to screen its reality. After all, entrenched metaphors typically draw on culturally held values, cultural histories, symbols, landmarks, and experiences that are familiar to the audience. Studying novel metaphors offers the critics an opportunity to analyze new meaning-making possibilities and their effectiveness within a given context.

A Continuum: Sleeping to Awake

Depending on how a metaphor is used, it falls on a continuum from sleeping to awake. **Awake metaphors** are *metaphors that are "activated in a given text" by (1) repetition, (2) contextual clues, such as visual aids that depict the vehicle of the metaphor or gestures that point toward or enact the vehicle, (3) elaboration, and (4) the clustering of terms related to the vehicle.*[21] Returning to Gary Kovacs's stalking metaphor, we can see that it is an awake metaphor: although his speech does not *repeat* the word "stalk" or "stalking," his visual aid *contextually* activates this metaphor as it shows an animated map that visualizes being followed; he *elaborates* (draws out, or further explains) this metaphor when imagining a person following his daughter around and writing down her actions; and he presents a *cluster* of stalking-related terminology as he repeatedly refers to this digital phenomenon as behavioral "tracking," describing it as "following us," "compiling a profile on us," and "watching" us.[22] Kovacs goes to considerable lengths to use this metaphor, weaving it throughout his speech. The metaphor is activated—brought to the audience's attention—throughout the speech. It is awake.

In contrast, **sleeping metaphors** are *metaphors that—like a sleeping person—are present but not particularly active.* The text does not draw attention to these metaphors; they are more of a passing reference than a focal point. For example, consider how an inspirational speaker discussing insomnia might describe a low point in her life through entrenched metaphors, saying, "at this point, *my career was on thin ice* and *my relationship was on life support,*" before going on to explain how she learned healthier ways to manage insomnia. Both of these metaphors are sleeping. *On thin ice* and *on life support* are not active metaphors: there is no repetition, contextual activation, elaboration, or surrounding cluster of metaphoric terms. The metaphors add color and variety to the speech, but they are not particularly active or meaningful.

Sleeping metaphors are at one end of the continuum of metaphoricity and awake metaphors are at the other end, but, as Müller states, there are no "clear-cut boundaries between sleeping and waking metaphors."[23] Kovacs's stalking metaphor was clearly on the "awake" end of the continuum, but it did not fulfill all of the possible criteria for "wakefulness": he did not directly repeat the "stalking" metaphor but instead gestured to it through his contextual activation, elaboration, and clustering of metaphoric terms. In comparison, Obama's "pinprick" metaphor falls somewhere in the middle of this continuum: he repeated the metaphor twice, but did not contextually activate it, elaborate on it, or surround it with a cluster of metaphoric terms. Both Kovacs's and Obama's metaphors were novel, so it makes sense that they are on the middle-to-awake side of the continuum. Novel metaphors tend to draw attention to themselves by being fresh and unusual ways to imagine a concept.

Typically, when speakers or writers use dead metaphors, they use them in sleepy ways. Dead metaphors are often sleeping metaphors—a passing reference that calls no attention to itself. However, just like entrenched and novel metaphors, dead metaphors can be used in ways that are more or less sleeping or awake. Any metaphor can be more or less activated depending on how much its "metaphoric nature" is emphasized and highlighted in the text.[24] For example, philosopher Daniel Cohen awakens the argument-as-war metaphor by clustering terms as he describes many Americans' approach to argumentation, saying that we want "arguments that *have a lot of punch,* arguments that are *right on target.* We want to *have our defenses up* and *our strategies all in order.* We want *killer* arguments."[25]

We regularly use metaphors. They are often deeply influential as they shape, filter, and transform meaning. Although all metaphors select and deflect meaning, they do so in different ways depending on whether they are dead, entrenched, or novel. Moreover, they are used—and experienced by audiences—in different ways depending on how sleepy or awake they are.

A critic should use metaphor criticism when (1) a text features metaphors heavily or when a metaphor dominates how a culture routinely talks about a thing, concept, strategy, or issue; (2) the critic is working to understand how meaning is shaped—how reality is reflected, selected, and deflected—within a text; and (3) when the critic is analyzing the meaning systems that structure a community's decisions.

DOING METAPHOR CRITICISM

When doing metaphor criticism, a critic usually focuses on a single text that features multiple metaphors or that relies heavily on a metaphor to convey its meaning. Alternatively, a critic may use metaphor criticism to analyze how a culture thinks about a topic, by assessing the metaphor(s) that the culture uses to discuss it. Here, the critic analyzes how a particular metaphor (or set of metaphors) operates in multiple texts. When conducting metaphor criticism (whether dealing with a singular text or multiple texts), a critic will typically assess the metaphors and then interpret the metaphors.

Assessing Metaphors

When assessing a metaphor, the critic must first determine the tenor and vehicle of the metaphor. Many texts clearly state the tenor and vehicle; the critic need only label them as such. For example, Emily Dickinson's line "The Lightning is a yellow Fork," clearly states both the tenor and vehicle. The critic need only mark "Lightning" as the tenor and "yellow Fork" as the vehicle. Other metaphors, however, present more complicated relations between the tenor and the vehicle. For example, consider the first stanza from another poem by Emily Dickinson:

> I dwell in Possibility—
> A fairer House than Prose—
> More numerous of Windows—
> Superior—for Doors—[26]

At first, it seems that "Possibility" is the tenor and "House" is the vehicle. After all, possibility is an abstract concept: it is the unfamiliar, which is made known through the familiar concept of a house. Dickinson seems to contrast possibility with prose, suggesting that they are both houses and that possibility is the better place to live. However, possibility and prose do not make sense as a contrasting pair.

Poetry and prose, however, work perfectly as a contrasting pair. If we consider "possibility" itself to be a metaphor, a vehicle for the unstated tenor (poetry), then the stanza begins to make sense. It invites readers to understand poetry as inherently involved in possibility (a playful, future-oriented mindset) and makes both abstract concepts—poetry and possibility—familiar through the house metaphor. In other words, this poem offers readers a layered metaphor that represents poetry (often thought of as obscure, abstract, and generally useless) as a house (the very epitome of practical, concrete, and useful) that is open and full of life (that is, possibility). Poetry itself becomes the habitable space: Emily Dickinson lives in poetry.

In other instances, the vehicle or tenor could go partially unstated. Consider again George W. Bush's metaphor "big exploding federal government."[27] Here the vehicle—a bomb—goes mostly unstated, only gestured at through the verb "exploding." When labeling the tenor and vehicle, a critic considers the metaphoric language and the surrounding content, while bearing in mind that the metaphoric elements may be complex or only partially stated. By deciphering and labeling the tenor and vehicle, the critic is able to understand how a metaphor works—how its different ideas or concepts interact—and thus, identify surrounding clusters of metaphoric language, and perhaps how cultural experiences shape the meanings of the metaphor.

Next, the critic determines whether the metaphors are dead, entrenched, or novel. Here, the critic considers how the metaphor is used in the text and in wider contexts. Analyzing speeches given at Japanese wedding receptions, linguistic anthropologist Cynthia Dickel Dunn identifies how the metaphor of a journey operates as an entrenched metaphor for marriage. For example, during toasts at a wedding reception, speakers regularly wish the couple well as they *set out* on a *new path*, or *set sail* together, or *walk together* through life, and so on.[28]

By identifying whether a metaphor is dead, entrenched, or novel, the critic takes a first step toward assessing how the metaphor functions. Dead metaphors shape meaning while flying under the radar. They affect how we think about a wide variety of concepts, but because those meanings are so deeply accepted, we often fail to notice that a selection of reality has even been made. Entrenched metaphors are familiar to audiences, often draw on cultural experiences, and frequently activate cultural assumptions and values. Moreover, because audiences understand how entrenched metaphors work (up is good, down is bad; daylight is safe, nighttime is scary) these metaphors can convey established meanings efficiently. Novel metaphors tend to function in more arresting ways, creating a tension for audiences who are confronted by an unusual association of tenors and vehicles. Thus, novel metaphors often function in striking and memorable ways as they create new possible meanings.

Finally, a critic assesses metaphors by identifying how sleepy or awake they are. Here, the critic primarily looks to the surrounding content of the text. Metaphors that are more awake are typically repeated throughout the text and elaborated upon. They also feature a clustering of related terminology. Additionally, contextual clues can awaken metaphors. Thus, a critic considers aspects such as a speaker's body language or visual aids, the images embedded in a blog, the cover image on the dust jacket of a novel, or a speaker's location during a speech. Here, the critic analyzes how the surrounding context might emphasize or activate a metaphor. For instance, a speech might use a mountain-climbing metaphor in passing, but if that speech is given on a mountainside the context can awaken the metaphor even if the metaphor is not repeated or elaborated on in the speech itself.

When assessing metaphors, these concepts and categories (tenor and vehicle; dead, entrenched, and novel metaphors; and the sleeping-to-awake continuum) help a critic ascertain how the metaphors function in the text(s). The point is to use these concepts to consider how a metaphor works: whether it slips by unnoticed while shaping meaning (dead), or piggybacks on an audience's patriotic spirit (entrenched), or guides audiences into an epiphany of new meaning (novel and awake). A critical essay need not label metaphors as dead, entrenched, or novel, or note how sleepy or awake a metaphor is, but these concepts are important analytical tools that can help a critic understand how a metaphor functions.

Interpreting Metaphors

After assessing how metaphors function in the text, a critic works to interpret those metaphors, specifically identifying how each metaphor represents reality. Rhetorical critic Leah Ceccarelli models this stage of metaphor criticism by describing three interpretive questions that shape her analysis, and that she used to interpret how frontier metaphors shape scientific research. Among these metaphors were genetic science as the *final frontier, maverick* scientists, science *pioneers,* and the *wild wild west* of stem cell research.

Ceccarelli first asks, "what is selected and what is deflected by this metaphor?"[29] With this question, a critic interprets how a metaphor represents reality. For instance, frontier metaphors select "ruggedly individualistic men" as the people qualified to undertake cutting-edge scientific research, while deflecting female scientists and less cowboyesque male scientists from that pool.[30] Similarly, Ceccarelli found that these frontier metaphors selected competitive, fast, and exploitive methods as the proper way to conduct research (for example, science as a land grab), while deflecting careful, cooperative, nonprofit-driven methods as inappropriate for scientific and technological advancements.

Second, Ceccarelli asks, "what effects might these selections and deflections" have on the given topic?[31] Ceccarelli demonstrates that, beyond shaping which scientists ("ruggedly individualistic men") are considered nationally recognized as experts in their field, the science-as-frontier metaphor negatively affects scientific communities.[32] For instance, scientific research is—in most cases—a cooperative effort. Scientists work together in research teams. The frontier metaphor negatively affects scientific research by reframing scientists as competitors, pitting researchers—who would make good cooperative partners—against one another.

The third interpretive question is applicable primarily when a critic studies how a metaphor saturates a community. This question asks, what "moves" do rhetors make "when they try to escape" this metaphor?[33] Answering this question reveals how a metaphor works by considering what rhetors are up against, if and when they try to counter a metaphor or escape its meanings. Asking this question can show a critic how much falls within a metaphor's domain by pushing the critic to consider how rhetors try to get around the power of the metaphor. For example, Ceccarelli analyzed President George W. Bush's first "Stem Cell Research" speech, in which Bush attempted to reject and postpone stem cell research by refusing to allocate federal money for it. To do so, he had to deny the frontier metaphor: instead of commending *pioneering* scientists for pushing into the unknown, he condemned scientists for crossing into Aldous Huxley's "brave new world," in which babies are grown for spare parts.[34] Bush reworked the frontier metaphor, reimagining it as an ethical line in the sand—a line that should not be crossed—rather than an ever-expanding zone of opportunity.

As Bush tried to escape the entrenched positive associations of exploring new frontiers, Ceccarelli sees him make two intertwined moves. First, he changed the "frontier" into a fixed line rather than a (westward) moving boundary. Second, he attempted to change the frontier from a large area that can be profitably settled by pioneers into a line that divides two distinct areas—civilization and wilderness. Through this analysis, the power of the frontier metaphor becomes clearer. To counter it, rhetors must contend with the frontier on at least two levels: its expansion and its profitable allure.

Given the ways in which metaphors orient communities toward particular policies and actions—such as how to spend tax money on different types of scientific research—it is not unusual for metaphors to compete. Speakers, authors, activists, lobbyists, experts, pastors, and politicians have different perspectives of reality and different goals, and thus they use different metaphors as they work to orient their communities toward their goals and perspectives—or, to use Kenneth Burke's phrase, to adopt their "terministic screens." Communication critic Monica Brown notes that "competing metaphors often signal a conflict of values" within a community.[35] That is, critics can see competing value systems and goals as they analyze how rhetors utilize opposing metaphors, attempt to renegotiate an existing metaphor (as Bush did in his stem cell speech), or to resist a dominant metaphor, its version of reality, and its ensuing policies.

Metaphor criticism reveals how reality is portrayed to the audience and how meaning is created through the interaction of two different concepts (or things), in order to reflect reality by selecting particular aspects to emphasize while deflecting attention away from others. Metaphor criticism can reveal the realities a culture accepts as de facto truths by analyzing dead metaphors. It can also reveal the persuasive touchstones that communities find particularly useful by studying entrenched metaphors. A critic can also reveal new meaning-making possibilities by studying novel metaphors.

RESEARCH EXAMPLES

The following three research examples provide excellent demonstrations of how critics use this method. In the first example, Emily Martin analyzes the metaphors in biology textbooks and scientific research publications. Focusing on the biological explanations of conception, Martin finds that this scientific discourse heavily relies on sleepy entrenched metaphors to explain biological processes—and that those metaphors profoundly shape our understanding of human anatomy and conception. In the second example, Theon Hill examines Barack Obama's campaign speech in Selma, Alabama, in which Obama used the biblical figure of Joshua as a novel metaphor for his leadership. The third example analyzes economic metaphors that imagine the federal government as a person and the federal budget as a household budget.

Emily Martin "The Egg and the Sperm: How Science Has Constructed a Romance Based on Stereotypical Male-Female Roles" (1991)*

Medical textbooks seem an unlikely place to find metaphors. After all, scientific communities are not known for being poetic, and textbooks in general seem like improbable repositories for figurative language. However, given the ways in which metaphors—especially dead and entrenched metaphors—sleepily suffuse our everyday language, Emily Martin became concerned that culture shapes scientists' discoveries of "the natural world."[36] She suspected that rather than letting observations of nature create new understandings of reality, scientists allow cultural assumptions to influence how they make sense of the natural phenomenon they observe. She analyzed undergraduate scientific textbooks, medical school textbooks, and scientific research publications, focusing on the ways scientists explained their discoveries surrounding (1) female/male reproductive organs, (2) eggs and sperm, and (3) the interaction between eggs and sperm.

Analyzing how scientists describe female and male reproductive organs, she found two primary metaphors: ovaries are described through a clustering of loss or waste metaphors, while testes are described through metaphors of creation and production. For example, at birth, a woman's ovaries contain several hundred germ cells that are then developed into eggs and released: typically one egg per lunar month during a woman's reproductive years.[37] Rather than describing this process through production metaphors (where the ovaries produce mature eggs), scientific textbooks and research publications refer to this process as "*overstocked inventory*" where eggs "*sit on the shelf,* slowly degenerating."[38] This process is described as *wasteful,* as each egg that does not result in a fetus is seen as a wasted egg or lost opportunity.[39] At birth, a man's testes do not have their whole set of germ cells; rather, they develop germ cells and then mature them into sperm throughout his reproductive years. Describing this process, scientific discourse uses production metaphors, emphasizing the act of creation. For example, testes are described as *manufacturing plants* that *produce* "hundreds of million sperm per day."[40] Remarkably, this production is not considered wasteful even though male bodies generate approximately a hundred million sperm per day and thus "well over two trillion sperm" during a man's reproductive years, in contrast to a woman's approximately five hundred eggs.[41] Essentially, Martin is pointing out that men "waste" exponentially more developed germ cells than women do. Yet these metaphors situate each sperm as a valuable production in and of itself, while women's developed eggs only have value if they result in an embryo.

*This essay may be found in *Signs* 16, no. 3 (1991): 485–501.

Analyzing how this scientific discourse imagines eggs and sperm, Martin finds a different set of metaphors: highly feminized metaphors cluster around eggs so that they are cast as sacred princesses in distress, while sperm are imagined as adventurous heroes. For example, eggs have a protective barrier that scientific discourse calls *vestments*—a term "usually reserved for sacred, religious dress."[42] Although holy, the egg is also passively feminine, referred to as "'a dormant *bride* awaiting her *mate's magic kiss.*'"[43] In contrast, sperm are described as being on a *mission* or *quest* in which they undertake a *perilous journey* in order to surround the *prize* and *assault* the egg. These metaphors situate the egg as a feminized, passive, fragile, holy (or perhaps virginal) entity waiting to be rescued by a competitive, active, adventurous hero. Indeed, the scientific discourse explicitly stipulates that an "'egg will die within hours unless *rescued* by a sperm.'"[44] The concept of being rescued by a sperm is highly suspect, as sperm typically "also only live for a few hours."[45] Martin points out that an egg and sperm continue in a merged existence only if they fuse, but neither ensures the other's survival; rather, each acts upon the other. More important to Martin, however, is the way these feminized and masculinized metaphors personify the egg and sperm, changing them from genetic material into women and men. These metaphors shape how readers imagine reality, and readers can come to root for an egg and sperm to *survive* in a similar way we might root for *Sleeping Beauty*'s Princess Aurora and Prince Phillip to survive the evil fairy, Maleficent. In other words, imagining eggs and sperm as people fundamentally changes our goals for these entities. Ultimately, these personifying metaphors convey this personhood onto the embryo that an egg and sperm create if they fuse.

Finally, Martin analyzes the metaphors used to imagine how eggs and sperm interact while fusing. She finds that the feminizing and masculinizing metaphors (which turns eggs into sacred princesses in distress and sperm into adventurous heroes) affect the types of actions of which scientists imagine eggs and sperm being capable. For example, the scientific community has conclusively discovered that sperm have very little forward thrust and thus cannot simply push through the membrane of an egg—the zona pellucida. Moreover, the zona pellucida is not simply a protective layer around the egg; rather, it contains binding molecules that interact with the binding molecules on sperm, thereby binding the egg and sperm together and ultimately dissolving part of the zona pellucida so that the egg and sperm can fuse. Despite these discoveries, scientific textbooks and research publications continue describing the sperm as *harpooning* the egg, *penetrating* the egg, *attacking* the egg, *entering* the egg, and *burrowing into* the egg—as if the sperm were the only active (and rather violent) entity and the egg simply sat there.

Analyzing the research publications of Paul Wassarman, who discovered and thus named the binding molecules on eggs that interact with the binding molecules on sperm, Martin notes how strongly the prior metaphors shape scientific thought. Publishing his discovery, Wassarman named the binding molecules on the egg "sperm *receptors,*" as if they were the receiving part of the pair of binding molecules; he even likened them to *locks* and the sperm's binding molecules to *keys.*[46] The lock/key metaphor positions the egg in the passive role (lock) even as the name (sperm receptor) given to the binding molecule of the egg similarly denotes passivity.

However, biological research typically refers to the type of binding molecules on sperm as "receptors" and the type of binding molecules on eggs as "ligands."[47] Bucking these traditional names, Wassarman gave the name "sperm receptors" to the binding molecules of eggs, and then had to invent a new name ("egg-binding proteins") for the binding molecules of sperm.[48] Moreover, the diagrams of these molecules show that the sperm's binding molecules have pockets (almost like locks) and the egg's binding molecules have knobs that stick out (almost like keys).[49] Martin points out that the established metaphors for eggs and sperm (which frame eggs through feminine passivity and sperm through masculine activity) fundamentally shape how scientists recount their observations—even leading them to invert and distort their findings. She observes that eggs and sperm interact in fairly mutual terms, making scientific discourse's "refusal to portray them that way all the more disturbing."[50]

Ultimately, Martin urges her readers to "wake up sleeping metaphors in science."[51] She observes that such metaphors are often sleeping in scientific discourse: they are not particularly prominent and rarely call attention to themselves. Rather, they tend to slip by without much fanfare. Martin asks readers to become aware of these metaphors and of the ways in which we project "cultural imagery" onto scientific investigations of nature.[52] She concludes that only when audience members can wake up these metaphors can we "rob them of their power to naturalize our social conventions about gender."[53]

Theon E. Hill
"Sanitizing the Struggle: Barack Obama, Selma, and Civil Rights Memory" (2017)*

On Sunday, March 7, 1965, a large group of nonviolent protesters gathered in Selma, Alabama, and began marching toward Montgomery to protest the racist practices that prevented Black citizens from voting. Led by Hosea Williams and John Lewis, and in coordination with Martin Luther King, Jr., these peaceful protesters made their way through Selma and across the Edmund Pettus Bridge, where they encountered Alabama state troopers. "Cheered on by white onlookers" and under orders from their commanders, the "troopers attacked the crowd," breaking Lewis's skull, beating many protesters, and killing one.[54] Mounted police then chased and beat the retreating marchers. The television coverage of this state-sanctioned violence "triggered national outrage." The events became known as "Bloody Sunday."[55] Martin Luther King, Jr., subsequently joined the Selma protesters in several peaceful demonstrations and led a march later that month from Selma to Montgomery. Recounting these events, Dr. King credited the protests in Selma with pressuring President Lyndon B. Johnson and the federal government to produce the Voting Rights Act of 1965.[56]

Roughly forty years later, Senator Barack Obama made a campaign stop in Selma to "woo Black voters."[57] Delivering his speech at Brown Chapel—which served as a "gathering place," "staging area," and ultimately "refuge for wounded protesters on Bloody Sunday," Obama stood at a symbolic center of the civil rights movement.[58]

---

*This essay may be found *Communication Quarterly* 65, no. 3 (2017): 354–376.

His speech was a political success. He secured "Black support without alienating White voters" and thus built a political coalition that would ultimately lead to his election as president.[59] Analyzing this speech, however, Theon Hill argues that its central metaphor severely limited the scope of justice toward which Obama could lead America. Moreover, he argues that Obama's metaphor threatens "the future of the Black freedom struggle" by curtailing how other activists understand their own roles and what types of justice and paths toward justice are possible within the metaphor's selection and deflection of reality.[60]

Obama's central metaphor was built on the biblical account of Joshua. The book of Exodus, in the Old Testament, tells the story of God raising up Moses to lead the Israelites in Egypt out of slavery and into the Promised Land of Canaan. This story has shaped "Black consciousness since the dawn of American slavery," providing not only hope, identity, and purpose, but also offering a "prophetic critique of pervasive forms of injustice."[61] The Christian scriptures describe prophesy as a person hearing a message from God and delivering that message to the audience, as directed by God. Within this context, prophets speak the truth (a word from God) and typically speak that truth to those in power—the rulers, the rich, the religious leaders. For example, in a prophetic role Moses spoke truth to power as he confronted Pharaoh, telling Pharaoh, "This is what the Lord says: Let my people go" (Exodus 8:20, NIV).

Communication scholars use the term "prophetic voice" to refer broadly to the act of speaking truth to power, especially when that truth reveals systemic injustice. During the 1950s and 1960s, civil rights leaders routinely spoke in the prophetic voice. Activists drew upon Exodus and Moses as entrenched metaphors. Martin Luther King, Jr., explicitly operated "as the Moses of the civil rights movement."[62] In the Biblical narrative, Joshua is Moses's successor: he leads the Israelites during their conquest of Canaan. Although Joshua is a familiar biblical figure, Obama's metaphoric use of Joshua is fairly novel—especially in contrast to the entrenched Exodus/Moses metaphors. Essentially, Obama is trying to do something different (successfully campaign for president) from what Dr. King was attempting (end racism); thus, he uses a novel metaphor to seize new meaning-making possibilities.

Analyzing Obama's Joshua metaphor, Hill argues that it accomplishes an important task for Obama: it sets him up as a legitimate leader of Black Americans. The metaphor embeds Obama within the legacy of the civil rights movement and metaphorically positions him as Dr. King's direct successor. Moreover, Obama used the metaphor to juxtapose the "Moses generation" and the "Joshua generation," thereby contrasting the civil rights leaders and his own leadership.[63] Obama is gracious and celebratory of the "Moses generation," crediting their leadership with his own opportunity to campaign for president. However, this metaphoric juxtaposition enabled him to graciously usher the civil rights leaders (such as John Lewis, who represented Alabama in the House of Representatives in Congress) out of sight, making way for his own leadership.

Hill demonstrates that the Joshua metaphor shaped and reinforced Obama's emphasis on personal responsibility during his campaigns and first term as president. That is, the biblical Joshua did not free enslaved people or speak truth to an oppressive Pharaoh, but rather led people as they settled into Canaan, exhorting the Israelites to keep the Law of Moses and to remain faithful to their God (Joshua 23:1–13). In a similar vein, Obama casts his role not as freeing enslaved people or speaking truth to power, but rather, as exhorting African Americans to take greater personal responsibility for living good lives. Specifically, he urged his audience to personify the "Joshua generation" by renouncing their supposed "poverty of ambition" and "materialism."[64]

Obama specifically blamed the high levels of children who live in poverty in the United States on "daddies not acting like daddies."[65] This remark played off negative stereotypes and reinforced the idea that fatherlessness causes wide scale poverty—a claim that is not supported by data.[66] In the United States, the rate of single-mother households is fairly low: in 2013 only 8.8 percent of working-age households are headed by single mothers; the remaining 91.2 percent are headed by cohabitating adults, single fathers, or childless adults.[67] Moreover, although 16.1 percent of working-age US households are in poverty, only 1.3 percent are in poverty *and* headed by a single mother.[68] In other words, blaming wide scale poverty on fatherlessness is statistically inaccurate. Only 1.3 percent of working-age households are impoverished and fatherless; 14.8 percent are impoverished and have fathers.[69]

Hill notes that Obama has fundamentally deviated from King's legacy. King routinely discussed "responsibility and personal conduct in the Black community," but he did so while also speaking truth to power and calling out systemic racism.[70] Obama, however, identified personal responsibility as the future of the civil rights movement while ignoring systemic injustice, such as "labor market inequality, mass incarceration, and educational achievement gaps."[71]

For Hill, however, the most important change that the Joshua metaphor ushers into civil rights activism is the stripping away of the prophetic voice. The Joshua metaphor lays claim to the heritage of the civil rights movement and takes up residence as the future of civil rights activism. But unlike Moses, the biblical Joshua did not speak truth to power; and neither—Hill contends—did Obama during his campaigns or first presidential term. Hill fully recognizes the political brilliance of the Joshua metaphor and the conundrum facing Obama: he could not prophetically oppose the powerful while campaigning to become the powerful. However, Hill is deeply concerned that Obama's persuasive, novel metaphor alienates activists from the prophetic tradition, making it harder for activists to confront systematic injustice and call oppressive leaders to account for their abuses of power.

William Rodney Herring "The Rhetoric of Credit, The Rhetoric of Debt: Economic Arguments in Early America and Beyond" (2016)*

US politicians, from Republican Paul Ryan to Democrat Barack Obama, use a metaphor for the national budget: the family budget. Former House Speaker and Republican John Boehner said, "Every family in America has to balance their

*This essay may be found in *Rhetoric & Public Affairs* 19, no. 1 (2016): 45–82.

budget. Washington should, too."[72] Likewise, former President Obama cautioned Americans that we need to get "our fiscal house in order."[73] The metaphor is simple: the country is like an individual, and just as an individual must balance a family budget, so too must the nation balance its budget. Politicians use this metaphor when they argue that the country should decrease what is known as the "national debt" or "national deficit."

The metaphor can be traced back to at least the early republic, when Alexander Hamilton and James Madison argued about Hamilton's 1790 proposal for "administering the public debt."[74] Analyzing their arguments, rhetorical critic William Rodney Herring demonstrates that Hamilton and Madison used the metaphor in different ways—and that far from wanting to reduce the national deficit, Hamilton would likely see the national deficit as an opportunity.[75]

The War of Independence was expensive, leaving the early republic in massive debt. In 1784 Congress owed $39.3 million to foreign and domestic creditors, many of whom were former soldiers whose salaries had been "deferred" during the war.[76] By 1790 that debt had grown to almost $53 million; in addition, the states collectively owed an additional $18 million.[77] Congress and many of the states were largely unable to pay their debts, and therefore had bad international credit. As a consequence, it was hard to borrow more money since the republic had to borrow at steep interest rates. Since the republic was newly founded and could not pay its debts, citizens (such as the former soldiers) had little faith in their new federal government. Within this context, Hamilton and Madison employed the *individual = government* metaphor and its corresponding *family budget = national budget* metaphor.

James Madison was the leader of the House of Representatives. He argued that just as a court would find a man delinquent if he could not pay his family debts, so too an imaginary court would find the republic delinquent if it did not pay its debts. Herring demonstrates that for Madison, debt was evil (if sometimes necessary) because it strained the relationship between two people or entities. Debt was personal for Madison—it was about relationships and honor—so he wanted to repay the republic's debts as fast as possible.

Herring demonstrates that Madison's relationship-focused, honor-focused perspective is represented by and derived from the *individual = government* and *family budget = national budget* metaphors. Madison was holding the nation accountable for a debt in the same way that people might feel honor bound to do well by their neighbors who had lent them aid during a time of need. Paying back the republic's debt, Madison imagined, would reclaim the honor of the republic and put it back into good relationships with its citizens and international "neighbors."

Alexander Hamilton—who was then the secretary of the newly created Treasury—employed the same metaphor to different ends. Rather than thinking about debt in terms of what one individual owes another and how that affects their relationship, Hamilton was concerned with what type of person is worthy of credit. That is, rather than thinking about debt as a burden owed, Hamilton thought about the worthiness or credibility of the person to whom one is willing to loan goods and money. Accordingly, increasing debt at low interest rates is a marker of credibility (good credit), because people (or entities) are willing to lend to you.

Understanding a loan as a form of trust, Hamilton created financial policies that asked people to trust the republic. He reimagined national debt as an investment and a never-ending flow of cash. If its creditors would agree to be paid only the interest on their loans, then the republic could be in good standing (deemed trustworthy), because it could make those payments. Why would creditors agree to this? Because if the republic never paid the principles on its loans, it would pay interest in perpetuity (which would turn out better for the creditors in the long run). Hamilton reimagined these loans as long-term investments: indeed, creditors could sell and resell these debts to others (much as stocks and bonds are investments that are sold and resold). Meanwhile, the republic would have strong credibility—like a trustworthy person—and thus would always have a fresh influx of cash. Because people and other countries would be willing to invest in the republic on the basis of its credibility—its trustworthiness—our interest rates would remain low.

Linking trustworthiness and loans, Hamilton's policies essentially turned the republic into what we might currently consider a bank: other countries gave the republic money (like opening a savings account with a bank) and the republic paid those countries interest on that money. Meanwhile the republic invests that money—often by loaning it out at higher interest rates to other countries—and thus makes a profit. Hamilton (and his visions of endless debts that are never due and good credibility that generates endless influxes of cash) won the argument. Congress passed his proposal even though Madison voted against it, and the republic successfully renegotiated its debt contracts with its creditors.

Hamilton's metaphor was wildly effective. The federal government has been loaned trillions and has loaned trillions to other countries. As of November 2019, the US government has accepted more loans than it has given out, which means that the amount it "owes" is approximately $17 trillion. Only $4.1 trillion of this "debt" is owned by foreign countries; the rest is owned "by the American people."[78] Additionally, the government "owes" itself almost $6 trillion in intragovernmental holdings—money "loaned" from funds such as Social Security).[79] These numbers are incomprehensibly large. However, in 2019 the federal government spent only 8.7 percent of its fiscal budget to pay the interest on its loans.[80]

Herring demonstrates that Hamilton used the *government = an individual* metaphor and the corresponding *national budget = family budget* in order to explain the importance of trust and trustworthiness for his newly designed financial system. The entire system works because people (and entities) trust the US government, believing the United States is a safe investment. Yet when current politicians use the *government = an individual* and *national budget = family budget* metaphors, they do so in a way that is fundamentally different from the way Hamilton used them. They ignore the resources Hamilton made available to them: unlike a family, a nation state can act like an international bank. Indeed, as current politicians bemoan the national deficit and liken it to a family's frivolous spending, they erode some of the trustworthiness Hamilton carefully cultivated and which the

United States needs in order to maintain the system. After all, who wants to trust a frivolous spender?

Trustworthiness—credibility—is rhetorically created: Hamilton talked people into imagining the republic as a trustworthy person. To this day, trust and its rhetorical construction remain at the center of US finances. For example, while campaigning for president, Donald Trump suggested that if the United States faced a recession during his presidency, he would attempt to "make a deal" with our creditors, convincing them to accept less than the amount owed.[81] These statements sent economists reeling, as they argued that such a breach of trust would cause our interest rates to skyrocket. Without good credibility we would be a risky investment and thus have to pay much higher interest rates—leading, economists believe, to an economic collapse.[82]

STRENGTHS AND WEAKNESSES OF METAPHOR CRITICISM

Metaphor criticism is a particularly strong method for assessing how language and symbols shape meaning, and thus affect our choices, policies, and actions. Metaphors control perception: they filter how we "see and encounter the world in which we live."[83] As such, metaphor criticism offers critics a particularly insightful way to analyze how speakers, authors, and cultures perceive the world, and therefore, how we act in the world.

One of the clear strengths of metaphor criticism is its relevance. Metaphors matter: by shaping our perceptions, they wield considerable guidance over our public policies and our understandings of ourselves and others.[84] Moreover, metaphors can limit the scope of our imaginations, placing constraints on what we—through the metaphor—can imagine as possible. For instance, Emily Martin is deeply alarmed by the way in which gendered metaphors for eggs and sperm shape our understanding of nature, our policies concerning birth control, and the enduring character of gender inequality in the United States. Similarly, Theon Hill is deeply concerned that the Joshua metaphor hijacks civil rights activism, stripping it of its central feature: the ability to speak truth to power. Through metaphor criticism, these critics demonstrate how metaphors influence our communities, our worldviews, our actions, and our policies.

However, when dealing with sleeping, dead metaphors, critics can find themselves grasping at straws. Some metaphors are "dormant-unto-literality" and no longer function as metaphors.[85] For example, "airplane *wings*" is such a very sleepy, dead metaphor that perhaps it no longer functions as a metaphor and is now simply the name of that airplane part. Generally speaking, metaphor criticism is unlikely to serve a critic well as the primary approach to a single text that only contains sleeping, dead metaphors.

CHOOSING THIS METHOD

So how do you know whether you should use metaphor criticism to interpret a particular piece of public discourse? To answer this question, consider the metaphoricity of your text(s) and the research question animating your analysis.

That is, does your text feature metaphors? When analyzing a single text (such as a speech or blog post), a critic should ask whether the text features several different metaphors or repeatedly features a particular metaphor. Moreover, the critic should consider whether the metaphors are at least somewhat awake. If not, then metaphor criticism might not be the most insightful method of analysis.

When analyzing multiple texts, a critic should consider whether a particular family of metaphors infuses the discourse (as Emily Martin discovered in scientific textbooks) or whether competing metaphors are shaping different policy positions within a community. Working with multiple texts is likely to allow more leeway to analyze sleeping metaphors, because the critic is probably working to reveal an "overall orientation" or cultural worldview rather than to make definitive links between a metaphor and policy choices.[86]

Additionally, critics should consider their own research motives. What research question animates your analysis? Are you concerned with how metaphors shape audience members' interpretations of reality? Are you intrigued by the way a culture routinely uses metaphors to talk about a thing, concept, strategy, or issue? Are you broadly interested in studying the meaning systems that structure the values and decisions of a community? Metaphor criticism is particularly suited to answering research questions that stem from these types of motivating concerns.

Ultimately, metaphor criticism helps critics recognize how language and symbols shape our understanding of reality and thus guide our actions and beliefs. This method offers critics double vision, enabling us to analyze the thing under consideration (the tenor, such as lightning, eggs, sperm, political leadership, the federal budget) and the thing it is being called (the vehicle, such as forks, princesses in distress, adventurous heroes, the Joshua generation, a family budget). This double vision is essential: a critic must understand both halves of the equation in order to unpack how the tenor and vehicle collide in public and popular discourse, fundamentally shaping meaning and filtering reality.

DISCUSSION QUESTIONS

1. List three metaphors. Now use each of them in a sentence.
2. Consider the metaphors you listed in answering the prior question. For each metaphor, label the tenor and the vehicle. Keep in mind that the tenor might not be explicitly stated in your sentence.
3. Rhetorical theorist Kenneth Burke elaborated on his phrase "terministic screens" by explaining that symbols screen our experiences. Briefly explain a scenario in which you or someone else used a term (a word or other symbol) to screen reality. Specifically identify how the term *reflected* reality by *selecting* some aspects of reality to highlight and *deflecting* attention away from other aspects of reality.
4. In your own words, explain the differences between dead, entrenched, and novel metaphors.
5. Identify two songs, one that uses a sleeping metaphor and another that uses an awake metaphor. Explain why you consider the metaphors either sleeping or awake. Identify where on the continuum of metaphoricity you would place these two songs' metaphors.

NOTES

1. Emily Dickinson, "The Lightning is a yellow Fork" (1140), in *The Poems of Emily Dickinson,* ed. R. W. Franklin (Cambridge, MA: Belknap Press of Harvard University Press, 1998), 457.
2. D. McKnight and M. Hobbs, "Public Contest through the Popular Media: The Mining Industry's Advertising War against the Australian Labor Government," *Australian Journal of Political Science* 48, no. 3 (2013): 311.
3. David Douglass, "Issues in the Use of I. A. Richards' Tenor-Vehicle Model of Metaphor," *Western Journal of Communication* 64, no. 4 (2000): 407.
4. I. A. Richards, *The Philosophy of Rhetoric* (London: Oxford University Press, 1936), 93.
5. Richards, *The Philosophy of Rhetoric,* 96–97.
6. "October 3, 2000 Transcript," *Commission on the Presidential Debates,* October 3, 2000, http://debates.org/index.php?page=october-3-2000-transcript; Alan Cienki, "Bush's and Gore's Language and Gestures in the 2000 US Presidential Debates," *Journal of Language and Politics* 3, no. 3 (2004): 409–440.
7. Kenneth Burke, *A Grammar of Motives* (Berkeley: University of California Press, 1969), 503–504.
8. Leah Ceccarelli, *On the Frontier of Science: An American Rhetoric of Exploration and Exploitation* (East Lansing: Michigan State University Press, 2013): 19.
9. Ceccarelli, *On the Frontier of Science,* 20.
10. Cornelia Müller, *Metaphors Dead and Alive, Sleeping and Waking: A Dynamic View* (Chicago: University of Chicago Press, 2008).
11. Ceccarelli, *On the Frontier of Science,* 20.
12. For example, Leah Ceccarelli occasionally uses the terms "conventionalized" and "literalized" when discussing these types of metaphors while Cornelia Müller occasionally uses "deeply entrenched" or "historical." See Ceccarelli, *On the Frontier of Science,* 20–21; Müller, *Metaphors Dead and Alive,* 193.
13. Ceccarelli, *On the Frontier of Science,* 21.
14. Barack Obama, "Remarks by the President in Address to the Nation on Syria," *The White House,* last modified September 10, 2013, https://obamawhitehouse.archives.gov/the-press-office/2013/09/10/remarks-president-address-nation-syria.
15. Gary Kovacs, "Tracking our Online Trackers," TED2012, last modified 2012, https://www.ted.com/talks/gary_kovacs_tracking_the_trackers.
16. Kovacs, "Tracking our Online Trackers."
17. Kovacs, "Tracking our Online Trackers."
18. Kovacs, "Tracking our Online Trackers."
19. Guy Szuberla, "Zangwill's *The Melting Pot* Plays Chicago," *Melus* 20, no. 3 (1995): 3.
20. Szuberla, "Zangwill's *The Melting Pot,*" 3.
21. Ceccarelli, *On the Frontier of Science,* 22.
22. Kovacs, "Tracking our Online Trackers."
23. Müller, *Metaphors Dead and Alive,* 197.
24. Ceccarelli, *On the Frontier of Science,* 22.
25. Daniel Cohen, "For Argument's Sake," *TedxColbyCollege,* last modified 2013, https://www.ted.com/talks/daniel_h_cohen_for_argument_s_sake/up-next?language=en.

26. Emily Dickinson, "I dwell in Possibility—" (466), in Franklin, *The Poems of Emily Dickinson,* 215.
27. "October 3, 2000 Transcript," *Commission on the Presidential Debates.*
28. Cynthia Dickel Dunn, "Cultural Models and Metaphors for Marriage: An Analysis of Discourse at Japanese Wedding Receptions," *Ethos* 32, no. 3 (2004): 359–360.
29. Ceccarelli, *On the Frontier of Science,* 3.
30. Ceccarelli, *On the Frontier of Science,* 3.
31. Ceccarelli, *On the Frontier of Science,* 3.
32. Ceccarelli, *On the Frontier of Science,* 3–4.
33. Ceccarelli, *On the Frontier of Science,* 3.
34. George W. Bush, "President Discusses Stem Cell Research," *The White House,* last modified August 9, 2001, https://georgewbush-whitehouse.archives.gov/news/releases/2001/08/20010809-2.html.
35. Monica Brown, "Woman as Mysterious Machine: Metaphor, Rhetoric and Female Sexual Dysfunction," *At the Interface/Probing the Boundaries* 55 (2009): 132.
36. Emily Martin, "The Egg and the Sperm: How Science has Constructed a Romance Based on Stereotypical Male-Female Roles," *Signs* 16, no. 3 (1991): 485.
37. Martin, "The Egg and the Sperm," 487–488.
38. Martin, "The Egg and the Sperm," 487.
39. Martin, "The Egg and the Sperm," 488.
40. Martin, "The Egg and the Sperm," 486.
41. Martin, "The Egg and the Sperm," 488–489.
42. Martin, "The Egg and the Sperm," 490.
43. Martin, "The Egg and the Sperm," 490.
44. Martin, "The Egg and the Sperm," 490.
45. Martin, "The Egg and the Sperm," 490.
46. Paul Wassarman, "Fertilization in Mammals," *Scientific American* 259, no. 6 (1988): 78–84.
47. Martin, "The Egg and the Sperm," 496.
48. Martin, "The Egg and the Sperm," 496.
49. Martin, "The Egg and the Sperm," 496.
50. Martin, "The Egg and the Sperm," 499.
51. Martin, "The Egg and the Sperm," 501.
52. Martin, "The Egg and the Sperm," 501.
53. Martin, "The Egg and the Sperm," 501.
54. "Selma to Montgomery March," *The Martin Luther King, Jr., Research and Education Institute,* Stanford University, accessed December 31, 2018, https://kinginstitute.stanford.edu/encyclopedia/selma-montgomery-march; John Murphy, "Barack Obama, the Exodus Tradition, and the Joshua Generation," *Quarterly Journal of Speech* 97, no. 4 (2011): 387–410.
55. "Selma to Montgomery March."
56. "Selma to Montgomery March."
57. Theon Hill, "Sanitizing the Struggle: Barack Obama, Selma, and Civil Rights Memory," *Communication Quarterly* 65, no. 3 (2017): 355.

58. Hill, “Sanitizing the Struggle,” 356.
59. Hill, “Sanitizing the Struggle,” 355.
60. Hill, “Sanitizing the Struggle,” 367.
61. Hill, “Sanitizing the Struggle,” 358.
62. Hill, “Sanitizing the Struggle,” 359.
63. Hill, “Sanitizing the Struggle,” 359–360.
64. “Candidate Barack Obama Remarks at Selma,” *Campaign 2008* (Selma, AL: C-SPAN, March 4, 2007), http://www.c-span.org/video/?c4530352/candidate-barack-obama-remarks-selma.
65. “Candidate Barack Obama Remarks at Selma.”
66. Hill, “Sanitizing the Struggle,” 363, 364; David Brady, Ryan Finnigan and Sabine Hübgen, “Single Mothers Are Not the Problem,” *New York Times,* February 10, 2018, https://nyti.ms/2BPxhtb; Rebekah Levine Coley and Bethany L. Medeiros, “Reciprocal Longitudinal Relations between Nonresident Father Involvement and Adolescent Delinquency,” *Child Development* 78, no. 1 (2007): 132–147; Daphne C. Hernandez and Rebekah Levine Coley, “Measuring Father Involvement within Low-Income Families: Who is a Reliable and Valid Reporter?” *Parenting* 7, no. 1 (2007): 69–97; Jo Jones and William D. Mosher, “Fathers' Involvement with Their Children: United States, 2006–2010,” *National Health Statistics Reports* (Hyattsville, MD: Center for Disease Control and Prevention, December 20, 2013).
67. Brady, Finnigan, and Hübgen, “Single Mothers”; David Brady, Ryan Finnigan, and Sabine Hübgen, “Rethinking the Risks of Poverty: A Framework for Analyzing Prevalences and Penalties,” *American Journal of Sociology* 123, no. 3 (2017): 740–786.
68. Brady, Finnigan, and Hübgen, “Single Mothers”; Brady, Finnigan, and Hübgen, “Rethinking the Risks,” 740–786.
69. Brady, Finnigan, and Hübgen, “Single Mothers”; Brady, Finnigan, and Hübgen, “Rethinking the Risks,” 740–786.
70. Hill, “Sanitizing the Struggle,” 364.
71. Hill, “Sanitizing the Struggle,” 364.
72. Quoted in Tamara Keith, “How the Federal Budget Is Just Like Your Family Budget (Or Not),” NPR.com, March 19, 2013, https://www.npr.org/sections/itsallpolitics/2013/03/19/174762184/how-the-federal-budget-is-just-like-your-family-budget-or-not.
73. Obama, Barack. “Remarks by the President on Fiscal Policy,” *The White House: President Barack Obama,* April 13, 2011, https://obamawhitehouse.archives.gov/the-press-office/2011/04/13/remarks-president-fiscal-policy.
74. William Rodney Herring, “The Rhetoric of Credit, The Rhetoric of Debt: Economic Arguments in Early America and Beyond,” *Rhetoric & Public Affairs* 19, no. 1 (2016): 49.
75. Herring, “Rhetoric of Credit,” 45–82.
76. Herring, “Rhetoric of Credit,” 50.
77. Herring, “Rhetoric of Credit,” 50.
78. “Debt Position and Activity Report,” *TreasuryDirect,* November 2020, https://www.treasurydirect.gov/govt/reports/pd/pd_debtposactrpt_1119.pdf; Kimberly Amadeo, “US Debt to China, How Much It Is, Reasons Why, and What if China Sells,” The Balance, November 24, 2019, https://www.thebalance.com/u-s-debt-to-china-how-much-does-it-own-3306355.

79. "Debt Position," *TreasuryDirect.*
80. Drew Desilver, "5 Facts About the National Debt," *Pew Research Center,* July 24, 2019, https://www.pewresearch.org/fact-tank/2019/07/24/facts-about-the-national-debt/.
81. Quoted in Binyamin Appelbaum, "Donald Trump's Idea to Cut National Debt: Get Creditors to Accept Less" NYTimes.com, May 6, 2016, https://www.nytimes.com/2016/05/07/us/politics/donald-trumps-idea-to-cut-national-debt-get-creditors-to-accept-less.html.
82. Appelbaum, "Donald Trump's Idea."
83. Michael Osborn, "The Trajectory of My Work with Metaphor," *Southern Communication Journal* 74, no. 1 (2009): 83.
84. Ceccarelli, *On the Frontier of Science,* 20.
85. Randy Harris, "Review of *Tropical Truth(s),* ed. Armin Burkhardt and Brigitte Nerlich," *Quarterly Journal of Speech* 97, no. 4 (2011): 474.
86. Ceccarelli, *On the Frontier of Science,* 21.

PART III
Ideological Critique

Chapter 7

Ideological Criticism

During February 2019—Black History month—Bernice A. King tweeted about her father's assassination, remarking that Martin Luther King, Jr., was murdered while he was dressed "respectably."[1] Her tweet included a picture of her father, taken shortly before he was murdered, walking between two other Black men. All of them were wearing suits. King argues that wearing suits or other professional clothes—instead of hoodies or sagging pants—does nothing to cure racism and nothing to end, avoid, or protect against racist violence.

In a similar vein, Bree Newsom (the activist and filmmaker known for climbing the South Carolina Statehouse flagpole to remove its Confederate flag in June 2015) recounts that some people recommended she and her colleagues wear professional clothes when they went to protest the death of Trayvon Martin and his killer's acquittal at the Florida Statehouse.[2] For Newsom, this recommendation was juxtaposed with the way "many pundits" assumed in their talking points that Trayvon Martin was killed "not because of racism" but because he was "wearing a hoodie."[3] Remembering the assassination of Martin Luther King, Jr.—murdered while he was wearing a suit—Newsom and her colleagues decided to wear hoodies to the protest as an "act of rejecting" the ideology of respectability politics.[4]

Communication scholars Tom Daniels, Barry Spiker, and Michael Papa explain that an **ideology** is *"a set of assumptions and beliefs that comprise a system of thought."*[5] Our ideologies are like default settings: we are rarely conscious of them. Yet our ideologies guide our thoughts and interpretations of reality.

Respectability politics is *a longstanding US ideology that emphasizes "reform of individual behavior and attitudes both as a goal in itself and as a strategy for reform of the entire structural system of American race relations."*[6] The term "respectability politics" was coined by Evelyn Brooks Higginbotham in her 1993 book, *Righteous Discontent: The Women's Movement in the Black Baptist Church, 1880–1920*. The ideology itself is much older.[7]

As an ideology, respectability politics links different ideas and things together. This ideology sees one's value in society—and therefore one's treatment in society—as directly related to how one presents oneself and behaves. Here, several ideas are linked: individual behavior and fashion (how you speak and dress, how politely you interact with others, and so on) are linked to the idea of your value in society, which is then linked to ideas about how others will treat you. People operating in the ideology of respectability politics might see some aspect of reality, such as a hoodie or sagging pants, and—using this ideology to guide their interpretations of reality—assume that the lack of respectability in wearing a hoodie or sagging pants is the cause for others' suspicion, maltreatment, and even violence.

This ideology shifts "responsibility away from perpetrators" and onto the victims.[8] Instead of trying to change institutions (such as housing and school segregation), respectability politics asks "the people harmed" by racism to change their lifestyles "in order to stop being harmed."[9] As Damon Young, a writer on race issues, says, this is like "getting shot and then getting blamed for standing in front of the bullet."[10] Activists, advocates, and intellectuals such as Bernice A. King and Bree Newsom reject respectability politics, pointing out that its interpretations of reality are false and that being "respectable" does not cure racism or protect racial minorities from racist violence.

Everyone has ideologies and relies on them to make sense of the world. We act in the world—even at the level of our clothing choices—on the basis of our ideologies. Moreover, the rhetoric we create reflects and expresses our ideologies. That is, rhetoric attempts to make sense of reality through the rhetor's ideology and offers that interpretation to audience members, inviting them into this sense-making system of thought.

Part III, Ideological Critique, introduces **ideological criticism,** *a mode of criticism that focuses on understanding the system of beliefs and assumptions that guide a rhetorical discourse in its interpretation of reality.* Using this approach to criticism is no easy task. Ideologies are complex because they link concepts together in complicated and often surprising ways. Moreover, they function as default settings; as such, people are often unaware of them as they construct their discourse, and they only rarely explain their ideologies to audiences. As a result, ideological criticism is difficult but important: it directly focuses on understanding how others interpret reality and what assumptions guide their thinking.

Ideological critiques are fundamentally concerned with the **political,** *the way power is achieved and used in society.*[11] The word politics is usually linked with the idea of government, because governments have achieved power and use it to manage society. However, the political encompasses far more than just the government: power is achieved and used by many people in a wide variety of ways. Indeed, generally speaking, both rhetoric and rhetorical criticism are political: they are fundamentally concerned with power and its usage. Rhetoric often acts politically through symbolic action—affecting how people think and feel, what they believe, and how they behave. As rhetorical theorist Jeremy Engels put it, rhetoric acts politically as it tries to influence people, by changing minds, motives, and worlds.[12] Similarly, rhetorical criticism acts politically by revealing and assessing the power of rhetoric. Ideological critiques, however, are particularly overt in their politics. They have political goals that inform how the critics conduct their research.[13]

This chapter introduces the principles of ideological criticism and the ways in which it often borrows from the methods discussed in earlier chapters (narrative, dramatism, genre, and metaphor). Because ideological critiques analyze various types of power relations, there are various types of ideological critiques.

For example, Marxist criticism analyzes texts in ways that support a particular vision of economic justice. Queer criticism analyzes texts in ways that challenge gender binaries. Antiracist criticism analyzes texts in ways that reveal the ubiquitous nature of racism and ethnocentrism; it works to support and empower racial and ethnic minorities. Feminist criticism analyzes texts in ways that seek to end sexism, empower women, and build a society based on mutuality instead of domination. The next chapter, on feminist criticism, offers one example of ideological critique.

To understand ideological criticism, we must first explore its foundational theory of hegemony.

A THEORY OF HEGEMONY

Antonio Gramsci was an Italian intellectual who died during World War II. As fascism swept across Italy, he resisted and publicly urged others to resist. In 1926, the fascist government—led by Mussolini—had Gramsci arrested and imprisoned. During his life and especially his imprisonment, he was perplexed by how easily normal, everyday people accepted the new fascist order that only benefited the elite.

The changes happening in the Italian government and culture did not benefit the majority of Italians, and yet they went along with it—even though they were not coerced or threatened. Gramsci thought this was illogical. He expected working-class people to revolt, to throw off the oppressive government and demand a fair shake. But they did not. Moreover, people all around the world were going along with ideas and government policies that only benefited a small, dominant group of elites. No one was coercing, threatening, or forcing everyday, working-class people to accept this domination, but they accepted it all the same. Writing in prison, where he resisted Italy's fascist state until his death in 1937, Gramsci developed the theory of hegemony.

The theory of **hegemony** explains how *processes within capitalist societies convince average people to support the status quo, even though it primarily benefits only elite members of society, not the average person.*[14] Gramsci stated that average people seemed to consent spontaneously to "the general direction imposed on social life by the dominant."[15] By using the term *spontaneous,* Gramsci emphasizes that the consent of the masses is not coerced or forced in any way. Instead, people simply allow the dominant elite to steer social life, or everyday habits, practices, beliefs, and values. Gramsci argued that people consent to polices (such as fascism) that ultimately hurt them because the elites have already dominated the way they think. Extending Gramsci's ideas, television scholar Todd Gitlin remarked that elites—such as television executives, media moguls, and so on—have dominated the "thought, the common sense, the life-ways and everyday assumptions of the working class."[16] In other words, the masses accept and share the ideologies of the elite.

Dominant Ideologies

Communication scholar Brenda Allen explains how people come to hold **dominant ideologies,** *ideologies that "reflect perspectives and experiences of ruling groups, whose members construct and circulate beliefs that will most benefit them."*[17]

For instance, when I was growing up, my parents were the "ruling group" or the elites in the household: they made the rules, controlled the money, and were capable of disciplining my sister and me. I could have rebelled against their power, but my rebellions were few and far between because they had taught me to think the way they thought. Throughout my childhood, I "spontaneously consented" to the "general direction imposed on social life" by this ruling group; that is, I willingly and happily cleaned and tidied the house, believing that cleanliness was next to godliness. This largely benefited my parents, not me. After all, I could have been playing instead of cleaning.

While certain ideologies can be dominant within family units, rhetoricians are generally interested in those that dominate whole cultures, societies, and nation states. For example, in the United States, the idea that "if you try hard enough, you will succeed" is a dominant ideology. It is linked to a whole system of thought: that hard work is a moral good; that success is the result of hard work; that those who are successful have earned their prestige through hard work; that those who are not successful are lazy and/or immoral; and that luck and unequal advantages do not really affect people's success.

This system of thought guides how Americans interpret reality. It shapes how we think of poverty and therefore the policies we advance (such as drug testing as a prerequisite for assistance programs) and the programs (such as food stamps) we fund—or don't fund. It directly benefits those who are already economically successful in at least two ways. First, we treat them with respect and prestige because we assume they are hard workers (which we consider morally good) who have earned their status. Second, the way we design our tax systems benefits those who are already rich because this ideology leads us to reward "morally good" hard workers, who we trust will continue to work hard, thus creating more jobs for more hard workers.

Because dominant ideologies are widely circulated, they show up throughout public discourse. For example, then-Congressman Paul Ryan celebrated the Tax Cuts and Jobs Act of 2017, which provides "steep tax cuts for businesses and the wealthy," by saying it would ultimately benefit "hard-working families."[18] His reasoning was that businesses and the wealthy would "reinvest in their workers, reinvest in their factories, pay people more money, [and pay workers] higher wages."[19] Ryan's logic directly embodies the ideology that "if you try hard, you will succeed": it posits that "hard workers" are the people who should be benefiting and assumes that the wealthy have acquired their wealth through hard work and thus will continue to work hard—creating a trickle-down effect that cascades into more opportunities for more hard workers. We assume these hard workers will be fairly paid because they are being paid by rich people—who we assume are hard workers and thus morally good. Because this ideology tightly links success to hard work and morality, it fundamentally ignores the possibility that the wealthy might not embody the moral good of hard work (by reinvesting the tax cut), but might instead participate in what US culture considers a moral failure (greediness) by keeping the tax cut in order to become even wealthier.

Hegemony is not coercive or threatening. No one is compelled to believe that "if you try hard enough, you will succeed" or any other dominant ideology. Rather, capitalist societies have developed processes that continually and persuasively invite the population to accept these dominant ideologies as common sense. These processes are largely known as "cultural productions."[20]

Take the Miss America pageant, for example. It is the "world's largest provider of scholarships for women," which it awards on the basis of experts' judgments of women's attractiveness.[21] Although in recent years, the pageant has attempted to broaden the idea of "attractiveness" to include women's intellect and character, it is primarily a beauty pageant.[22] It is a cultural production (it is produced by and through cultural institutions—it is not a government issued program). It features a dominant ideology: that women's value primarily lies in their attractiveness. Indeed, only after one accepts this ideology does it become reasonable to reward women financially on the basis of their physical beauty. This dominant ideology benefits the elites (heterosexual men and beautiful women). No one is compelled to watch the pageant or participate in it. However, its presence and prestige in US culture continually and persuasively invite Americans to believe it is reasonable—common sense—to value women based on their attractiveness and to reward women who best embody this attractiveness.

Resisting Hegemony

People can and do resist hegemony and its dominant ideologies. Individuals and communities—through education, critical thinking, and human ingenuity—realize that the dominant ideologies they believe are not entirely accurate and not in their own best interests. These people and communities (1) try to stop thinking in and through the dominant ideologies and (2) develop their own ideologies that more accurately suit their lives.

For example, in 1963 Betty Friedan wrote *The Feminine Mystique*, in which she identified a dominant ideology: that White middle- and upper-class women were not suited to work outside the home. She explained how and why she had stopped thinking in and through this dominant ideology and offered her readers a different ideology—one based on gender equality. Throughout the 1960s and 1970s, women protested, rallied, and met in small groups for what they called "consciousness raising" in order to help other women and men reject the dominant ideology of sexism. These groups, called "women's liberation groups," resisted hegemony.

To some extent, this movement represented what Antonio Gramsci originally expected to happen: the masses rising up to throw off their oppressors. And indeed, the women's liberation groups made progress toward their goal of equality. For instance, as a result of their activism, which was in concert with that of other civil rights activist groups, Congress passed the 1964 Title VII Civil Rights Act, which prohibits discrimination against employees based on sex, race, color and national origins. Because of this law, businesses (like restaurants) can no longer only hire men to some positions (managers) and only hire women to other positions (waitstaff).

However, just as Gramsci noticed resistance groups failing to throw off fascism in Italy during the 1920s, women's liberation groups never got large enough or successful enough to throw off their oppressors. Although they resisted dominant ideologies, their progress was slow and ultimately incomplete. To understand why social activist groups rarely garner widespread support for their resistant ideologies, we have to reconsider hegemony.

Resilience of Hegemony

The processes of hegemony largely ensure that those who are currently rich and powerful will stay rich and powerful—and those who are poor and marginalized will stay poor and marginalized. In order to maintain these relations of power, however, dominant ideologies have to evolve in response to resistance. Todd Gitlin points out, for example, how television (a cultural production) often airs programming that seems to give voice to resistant ideologies. For instance, in 1965 the sitcom *I Dream of Jeannie* aired an episode in which Jeannie reads a magazine published by a women's liberation group, subsequently stops doing the housework, and gets a job. Here, *I Dream of Jeannie* seems to join forces with Betty Friedan by disrupting the established relations of power and resisting the dominant ideology of sexism.

Gitlin demonstrates, however, that in such instances resistance is absorbed and domesticated by hegemonic processes.[23] Resistance is **absorbed** *when cultural productions change their messages by incorporating the terminology or symbols of a resistant ideology.* Yet even as cultural productions absorb this resistance, they **domesticate** it by *featuring reduced, tamed, and less radical versions of the resistant ideology.*

The *I Dream of Jeannie* episode in which Jeannie joins the women's liberation movement provides a good example of this absorption and domestication. This episode absorbed feminism into the mainstream: you could turn on a popular sitcom and watch feminism! But the story line also domesticated the women's liberation movement by portraying it as a much less radical movement. In this episode, Jeannie (a magical genie) never really wanted to stop doing the housework or get a job; she only wanted her "Master," Tony, to thank her for doing the housework and spend time with her. Women's liberation was about radical equality, but this cultural production absorbed and then domesticated it to look like women just wanted a little more appreciation and attention from the men in their lives. By simultaneously absorbing and domesticating resistance, dominant ideologies remain hegemonic and thus maintain the status quo relations of power. In this case, men continue to be powerful, valued breadwinners and White middle-class women retain their positions as homemakers. The only difference is that the men occasionally say "thank you."

Communicating Ideology

To understand how ideologies are communicated, rhetorical theorist Edwin Black recommends that we pay attention to the implied audiences of a discourse.[24] A speaker invites an audience to imagine her or him in a particular way. This is the **first persona,** *what a discourse implies about its rhetor.* For example, speaking at Southern New Hampshire University, former First Lady Michelle Obama embodied her first persona throughout the speech in which she famously stated, "when they go low, we go high." She wanted her audience to think of her as the First Lady and as a "Black feminist intellectual"; the way she talked—and talked about herself—emphasized these roles.[25] The **second persona** is *what a discourse implies about its audience.* For example, if a speech uses formal and reserved language, it implies that the audience members are professional, well-respected, and authoritative people. This is how one might speak at a business meeting while the CEO visits. In contrast, if a speech uses casual and casually profane language, the audience members are likely young and the speaker's peers. This is how one might speak to kick off a party at a fraternity or sorority.

The second persona of a discourse is largely characterized by ideology. For instance, a campaign speech in Michigan might praise audience members for their work ethic and ingenuity in developing auto factories and then promise to revive the auto-manufacturing industry. The second persona in this speech embodies the ideology that hard work leads to success and the ensuing assumption that communities only need more opportunities for hard work in order to thrive. The second persona is not an exact representation of the real audience. Instead, it is a "model of what the rhetor would have his [or her] real auditor become"—as if the discourse projected an ideological cutout onto a screen and asked audience members to mold themselves into that image.[26] By studying the second persona, critics can understand the ideology a discourse wants its audience to believe.

For example, imagine taking your dog to run in a dog park. The dog park is being renovated, so there is currently a small gap in the fence. As your dog, Buddy, dashes around the park, he gets close to the gap and begins to run toward it. You call out, "Hey Buddy! Who's a good boy? Who's a good boy? You are! Buddy!" Hearing your praise, your dog exuberantly loops back toward you. Though simplistic, this example demonstrates how a second persona is designed to work. Your dog fulfilled your optimistic imagination of him: you spoke like he was a good dog and in response he acted like a good dog.

In human communication, the second persona is often far more complicated. Rather than directly telling audiences what to think, believe, and assume as true, rhetoric often uses **stylistic tokens,** *repeated, emphasized symbols (words, phrases, visuals) that conjure up particular associations.* In language-based texts (such as speeches and essays), stylistic tokens are often devices such as analogies, metaphors, metonymy, synecdoche, euphemisms (and their opposite, dysphemisms), allusions, paraleipsis, personification, and humor. In audiovisual discourses, stylistic tokens additionally include elements such as color schemes, editing, cinematography, staging, background music, and laugh tracks.

Speakers, journalists, political cartoonists, directors, pundits, authors, artists, and other rhetors very rarely state their ideologies in their discourse—indeed, they may not be fully aware of the whole systems of thought guiding their interpretation of reality. Stylistic tokens, however, indicate a second persona. For example, Edwin Black explained how the use of dysphemism—using a harsh word instead of a neutral word—in a speech about school segregation in the 1950s would indicate the second persona's ideology:

> Let the rhetor, for example, who is talking about school integration use a pejorative term to refer to black people, and the auditor is confronted with more than a decision about school integration. He is confronted with a plexus

> of attitudes that may not at all be discussed in the discourse or even implied in any other way than the use of the single term. The discourse will exert on him the pull of an ideology. It will move, unless he rejects it, to structure his experience on many subjects besides school integration.[27]

In other words, Black argues that a single pejorative term in an otherwise seemingly neutral policy speech can indicate the second persona's ideology, and that the ideology calls out to the audience members, urging them to adopt a whole *system of thought,* which would affect their *interpretations of reality* on a myriad of topics—not just school desegregation.

In this case, a stylistic token clearly communicates ideology to an audience while keeping the explicit logic of that ideology out of sight. This school official could avoid making overtly racist arguments in support of his segregationist policy, yet could still convey a racist ideology to the audience members—and invite them to share it—by using a pejorative term for Black people. Here, ideology hides in plain sight.

Ideographs

In addition to stylistic tokens, some commonplace, widely used words, phrases, and visual images function in particularly powerful ways to telegraph an ideology to the audience. Rhetorical theorist Michael McGee coined the word **ideograph** to represent *a symbol that is (1) fairly common in a culture, (2) has historical roots or connotations in that culture, and (3) "invoke[s] identification with key social commitments" in that culture.*[28] An ideograph works like a magnet, drawing people who identify with its sponsoring ideology into greater commitment with the related cultural values. In so doing, ideographs often function as "imperatives," hindering the audience's ability to think through the persuasive appeal and make informed decisions.[29] Ideographs telegraph an ideology to the audience: they invoke a whole set of meanings, commitments, beliefs, attitudes, and assumptions about how the world works, what is right, and what (and who) has value.

For example, students at the Pennsylvania State University annually lead the "largest student-run philanthropy in the world" as they participate in THON, an annual forty-six-hour dance marathon that, since its founding in 1973, has raised over one hundred and fifty million dollars to sponsor pediatric cancer research and support families "impacted by childhood cancer."[30] THON's mission statement and tag line is "For The Kids," a phrase that is commonplace across the campus.

While I was teaching at Penn State, a student approached me one day after class and asked me to sign a form. He handed me a lengthy, detailed document with lots of fine print and—seeing me pause to try to read the document before signing—stated, "it's for the kids." I replied something along the lines of, "yes, but what is it?" and he repeated by way of explanation, "it's *for the kids.*" Without further hesitation, I signed it. I later learned that I'd agreed to be a faculty advisor for a small portion of THON's activities.

Within Penn State's culture, the phrase "for the kids" functions as an ideograph. It is a magnet; it draws on Penn Staters' social commitments, pulling people into agreement with the persuasive message and guiding their behavior.[31] It functioned as an imperative for me, short-circuiting my thinking as I signed the document without reading it. Rhetorical scholars often use angle brackets to indicate that words or phrases (such as <freedom>, <liberty>, <law and order>, <equality>, and <choice>) are ideographs.[32] In Penn State's culture, <for the kids> functions as an ideograph.

PARTICIPATING IN IDEOLOGICAL CRITIQUE

The theories of hegemony, ideology, the second persona, and ideographs are crucial to ideological criticism. Critics who participate in ideological critique are almost always motivated by "ethical or political concerns" regarding ways in which a small, powerful subset of a population benefits from cultural patterns of thought (dominant ideologies) at the expense of the masses.[33] Ideological criticism, then, is not a method like those introduced in the previous chapters. Rather, critics engage in ideological critique by adopting certain strategies or principles—and quite often combining this approach with others. As the following pages discuss, the strategies or principles of ideological critique share much in common with the methods discussed earlier—such as carefully attending to the text and its stylistic features. However, ideological criticism emphasizes an analysis of relations of power—the power hierarchies within a text, as well as between the text and its broader social context.

Attending to Stylistic Tokens

When participating in ideological critique, a critic identifies every stylistic token (references, jokes, sarcastic statements, metaphors, and so on) in the text. The critics will probably need to use internet and library resources to track down unusual stylistic tokens or unknown references in the text. For example, when analyzing a commencement speech by the science fiction author Ursula Le Guin, I noticed that she described our world as a "war-games world."[34] This phrase seemed odd in the context of this speech, so I flagged it as one that my ongoing research would need to make sense of. I later learned that the movie *WarGames* (starring Matthew Broderick) premiered less than two weeks after Le Guin's speech. It would have been heavily promoted through trailers and posters when Le Guin delivered her speech. This contextual research provided a likely explanation for this unusual stylistic token.

Because different media enable different types of stylistic tokens, critics need to work in medium-specific ways. For example, some texts (such as newspaper editorials and novels) only have verbal stylistic tokens. Other texts (such as spoken poetry and podcasts) have both verbal and delivery-based stylistic tokens. Still others (such as recorded speeches, films, music videos, and television episodes) have audio, visual, and verbal stylistic tokens. A critic needs to be generally familiar with the technological, industry-based, and cultural contexts of the medium in order to recognize the stylistic tokens that are directly related to that medium.

While identifying stylistic tokens, a critic may find it useful to become familiar with other examples of the rhetor's work. For example, a critic studying *The Shape of Water* (2017) should also view director Guillermo del Toro's other critically acclaimed feature films, such as *Pan's Labyrinth* and *Crimson Peak.*

Such background research allows a critic to compare and contrast a text with other similar texts, gaining a sense of how this text engages with the rhetor's stylistic trends.

Moreover, critics often familiarize themselves with texts that are contextually similar to their texts in order to see how those texts differ in their stylistic choices. For example, communication critic James Schiffman compared and contrasted the stylistic tokens in NBC's coverage of the 2008 opening ceremony for the Summer Olympic Games in Beijing with China Central Television's coverage. In so doing, he was able to clearly see the various stylistic choices the commentators, camerapersons, editors, directors, and so on made.

At this point, critics often find it useful to reflect on their observations and to identify trends or themes within the stylistic tokens. For instance, communication critic Randall Livingstone analyzed Apple's "Get a Mac" advertising campaign.[35] This campaign was a series of more than sixty advertisements featuring actor Justin Long as a human embodiment of a Mac and writer/actor John Hodgman as a human embodiment of a PC. The two men would stand side by side and discuss their relative merits as computers. Analyzing these advertisements, Livingstone made lists of all of the metaphors, references, allusions, and so on, and compared the style of these advertisements to those of prior Apple advertisements. Then, he noted trends and themes in his observations. For instance, the PC (Hodgman) and Mac (Long) always dressed differently from each other, but had their own consistent styles: the PC wore unflattering business attire while the Mac wore more casual but trendier and slimmer styles. Another clear trend was that the PC was often sick (Hodgman regularly coughed and complained of colds) but the Mac was always healthy.

The principle of attending to stylistic tokens is hardly unique to ideological critique. Indeed, rhetorical criticism is consistently concerned with stylistic elements, as demonstrated in the earlier chapters. Critics who participate in ideological critique often draw on elements of narrative criticism, dramatistic criticism, genre criticism, or metaphor criticism, depending on the type of stylistic tokens featured in their texts.

Attending to Power Relations

In observing a text, a critic needs to assess how power is distributed. For example, is anyone referred to by a specific honorific or by a derogatory term? Does the speaker sound sarcastic or mean when mentioning a person or place? For example, referring to a Supreme Court judge as, "His Honor, Justice Kennedy," uses several honorifics. The speaker could have simply said "Justice Kennedy," or possibly just referred to him as "Kennedy." By adding the honorifics, this speech attributes a place of power and prestige to Kennedy.

An ideological critic pays particular attention to **hierarchies,** *rankings of people, places, or things according to their authority, prestige, or value in a culture.* For example, in addition to noting how characters in a film are organizationally ranked (who the bosses and employees are), a critic would consider who gets their way most of the time, who is portrayed as the smartest or richest, which characters typically acquiesce (in word or deed) to which other characters, and which characters demean, belittle, or control which other characters.

Additionally, critics assess power relations by noting **stereotypes,** *brief sets of characteristics used to identify groups of people or regions.*[36] A critic might consider how elements such as adjectives, nicknames, visual depictions, or audio elements classify a person, character, or region. For example, consider how the word "feisty" often appears as a descriptor of female athletes—especially in ranking lists, such as lists for the "Hottest Female Athletes" or "Female Athletes Who Were Born to Wear Leggings"—but also in children's books and broader sports commentary.[37] According to the Women's Media Center, "feisty" is almost exclusively used to describe individuals (or animals, such as Pekingese dogs) who are not considered powerful.[38] Referring to female athletes as "feisty players" instead of "powerful players" or "excellent athletes" activates a stereotype of women as inherently not powerful. Thus, by describing strong, powerful, and authoritative women as "feisty," discourses activate a stereotype that classifies those women as less than strong, powerful, or authoritative—even as they demonstrate their power.

Attending to Ideographs

To identify ideographs operating in a text, a critic looks first for repeated words or phrases. These words or phrases may be repeated within the text itself and more broadly in similar discourses. For example, rhetorical critics Benjamin Bennett-Carpenter, Michael McCallion, and David Maines note that the ideographic phrase <personal relationship with Jesus> is not only prominent in protestant US discourses, but features repeatedly in US Catholic texts.[39] Variations of this phrase occur four times in quick succession in the 1999 statement of the council now known as the United States Catholic Conference of Bishops.

Ideographic words or phrases are resonant yet commonplace. A critic looks for words or phrases that will be familiar to the audience and resonate with the audience's deeply held values. These words or phrases seem to sum up the rhetor's entire argument or are offered as the "because" or "so that" in a text. For example, a speaker might say something like, "because we value <freedom> we must vote for Jane Doe. Only by casting our votes for Jane Doe do we ensure America remains a land of <freedom>." This example demonstrates how an ideograph (such as <freedom>) can operate as both the rationale and the result of the action a speech asks of its audience. In the <personal relationship with Jesus> example, Bennett-Carpenter, McCallion, and Maines noted how Pope Benedict XVI situated a <personal relationship with Jesus> as the "because" that would lead toward an inevitable good. Benedict stated that only by living in an "ever deeper <personal relationship with Jesus>" can we "begin to understand what he is asking of us."[40]

When analyzing a text for ideographs, a critic considers whether a word or phrase "galvanizes people" toward a political agenda.[41] Because many ideographs—especially those related to US democratic processes and political parties—have already been identified by rhetorical critics, reviewing the literature on ideographs in general, as well as considering any prominent, galvanizing, and/or repeated phrases in a text, can help a critic identify ideographs.

The ideographs discussed in this chapter have primarily been language based. Chapter 10 provides more guidance on how to consider visual ideographs.

Strategies for Interpreting Ideology

After identifying the stylistic tokens, relations of power, and ideographs in a text, a critic considers what meanings these elements are meant to evoke. The idea is to brainstorm the "suggested ideas, references, themes, allusions, and or concepts" that these elements present.[42] For example, Randall Livingstone suggests that by consistently portraying PCs as "sick," through their human embodiment's chronic colds and illnesses, the Apple ads "bring the metaphors of computer problems—viruses, freezing, crashing—to life."[43]

A critic also considers the primary objective of the text in grappling with its ideology. For instance, is the text a campaign speech that is intended to get someone elected? An advertisement intended to sell a product? A sermon intended to change congregants' behaviors? To identify the primary purpose of a text, the critic analyzes the text itself and its contextual clues.

Politicians' speeches and professors' lectures often state their goals: to persuade the audience toward some policy or educate it on some topic. Some texts are cagey, however, announcing one goal while furthering others. In their analysis of Abraham Lincoln's speech at Cooper Union, rhetorical scholars Michael Leff and Gerald Mohrmann note that Lincoln is ostensibly not campaigning; yet, the speech clearly and persuasively argues that Lincoln is the best leader for what was then known as the Republican party. Lincoln was not persuading citizens to support his party, but to support him.[44] Leff and Mohrmann base this conclusion on their analysis of the text itself and its context—what Lincoln said in the speech and when, where, and to whom he presented this speech. Similarly, an ideological critic ought to consider the purpose of a text not only by considering its stated purpose (if it has one), but also its content and its context.

To interpret the ideologies of their texts, critics put all their prior work together: (1) their observations—the stylistic themes and trends, the power relations, and any ideographs, (2) their connotative understandings of those themes, trends, power relations, and ideographs, and (3) the purposes of the texts. Communication scholar Celeste Wells recommends that a critic ask the following two interpretive questions while working to identify the ideology of a text: First, in order for this text to be compelling to its audience, what systems of "meaning/belief" must this audience adopt or already rely on?[45] And second, how does this text demonstrate that its product, purpose, or end goal is in the audience's "best interest," and how might this be not "entirely accurate?"[46]

Returning to the "Get a Mac" advertising campaign, we can see how Livingstone answered these questions to determine the ideology of the advertising campaign. He had already identified three clear trends in the stylistic tokens and the following meanings: PCs are sick, Macs are healthy; PCs are for work, Macs excel at both work and play; and PCs are difficult to use, Macs are easy to use. The overarching purpose of these advertisements is to produce positive brand associations with Macs and, ultimately, to sell Mac computers.

Interpreting his findings and noting the overarching stylistic device (that the computers appear as humans—they are embodied by actors), Livingstone answers the first question. He identifies the ideology this text invites its audience to adopt: buying the right commodities leads to personal fulfillment. Actor Justin Long's embodiment of a Mac computer enables the Mac itself to represent the "lifestyle for individual and social fulfillment."[47] Essentially, Mac has it all (interesting work, creative leisure time, fun, excitement, health, speed, friends, a cool factor, and so on), and offers all this to audiences if they choose to buy Macs rather than PCs. For these advertisements to be compelling, the audience must already believe or assume that buying the right commodities will lead to personal fulfillment. Only with this assumption in place do these advertisements—which feature virtually no demonstrations of how Mac computers actually work—become persuasive.

Livingstone offers two clear answers to the second question. First, looking at the evidence—his observations of the text and its connotative meanings—he persuasively argues that these advertisements present PCs as sick, largely by featuring their operational upgrades as "patches." The advertisements further mock the Windows Vista upgrade as "glitchy"—further proof of PC's illness. However, during this advertising campaign, Mac computers underwent two operating upgrades (Mac OS 10.5 Leopard and Mac OS 10.6 Snow Leopard), about which these advertisements are all but silent.[48] Thus, Livingstone suggests that the ad campaign is disingenuous and not motivated by the audience's ultimate good. More substantively, however, buying a Mac will not lead to a fulfilling life. It might make your computer time more fun, but it will not make you, your work, your family, or your friends more fun. It will not grant you leisure time or make you cool. Indeed, while buying a Mac directly benefits Apple, the benefits to consumers are more ambiguous—and certainly do not include life fulfillment.

Consequences

An ideological critique is fundamentally concerned with how the ideology of a text affects audiences and communities.[49] Edwin Black's theory of the second persona captures this focus on consequences: the second persona beckons to audience members, urging them to reshape themselves in its image, adopt its values, think through its systems of thought, and use its assumptions to guide their interpretations of reality. In practical terms, ideological critics are not done analyzing their texts until they understand and can articulate how the ideologies of their texts affect their audiences.

Essentially, a critic asks the interpretive question, what happens if audience members accept this text's ideology and are persuaded to its end goals? The "Get a Mac" campaign provides a useful example. Livingstone considered what would happen if an audience member accepted the ideology that buying the right commodities leads to personal fulfillment, and then accomplished the goal of the text by buying a Mac computer. The immediate effect is that the person would be a few thousand dollars poorer but would have a new computer, while Apple made a tidy profit. However, if audiences truly adopt this ideology, they are shaped into consumers—people who routinely make purchases in order to experience personal fulfillment.

Livingstone identifies how this ideology benefits those who are already elite at the (literal) expense of the masses: we spend money on commodities (such as Mac computers). We then spend our leisure time watching screens and submerged in digital spaces that are saturated in advertisements that shape and mold our desires—aiming us toward the next commodity and the next fulfillment—and thus spend more money buying new items. The cycle continues. Essentially, Livingstone suggests that by accepting the ideology of these ads, audience members enter a cycle where the money they earn from work is endlessly handed back to "the top—i.e. producers, owners, the upper class."[50] The rich get richer while the lower classes never keep their wages and remain poor.

Ultimately, an ideological critic focuses on the ideology a text wants its audience (the second persona) to believe, and discerns this ideology by observing and then interpreting the stylistic tokens, power relations, and ideographs present in that text. When I imagine an ideological critique, I envision the text as a large lake. Rather than looking across the surface of the water, an ideological critique asks us to look down into the depths—to see what lies on the floor of the lake. Stylistic tokens, power hierarchies, stereotypes, and ideographs are like buoys floating on the surface of the lake, marking particularly clear patches of water where we can see all the way to the ideology at the bottom.

RESEARCH EXAMPLES

Ideological critiques often make readers uncomfortable because they point out how dominant ideologies—the things we think and believe—benefit a subset of the population at the expense of others. In the first example, Rachel E. Dubrofsky persuasively demonstrates that far from promoting diversity and equality, the television series *Glee* (2009–2015) absorbs and domesticates antiracist ideology, repackaging it in a way that makes audiences comfortable with the (racist) status quo. In the second example, Myra Washington analyzes the ideology disseminated in TV portrayals of interracial couples, specifically focusing on the portrayal of Drs. Yang and Burke in the first three seasons of *Grey's Anatomy.* In the third example, Fernando Delgado demonstrates how critics can make sense of ideographs by analyzing Fidel Castro's use of the ideographs <*la Revolución*> and <*revolucionarios*> as Castro crafted a new national identity for Cubans.

Rachel E. Dubrofsky
"Jewishness, Whiteness, and Blackness on *Glee:* Singing to the Tune of Postracism" (2013)*

When the TV series *Glee* premiered on Fox, it self-consciously focused on issues of diversity and explicitly promoted an "everyone is welcome" ethic, as a wide range of high school students—from jocks and cheerleaders to social misfits—learned to sing together in their school's glee club. However, by studying the stylistic tokens (both verbal and audiovisual), Rachel E. Dubrofsky demonstrates that this series

*This essay may be found in *Communication, Culture & Critique* 6, no. 1 (2013): 82–102.

is ultimately hegemonic. Essentially, it absorbs and domesticates antiracist social activism, repackaging this resistant ideology in a way that enables viewers to feel good (nonracist) about themselves without changing the current (racist) social hierarchies.

For instance, focusing on humor as a stylistic token, Dubrofsky examines a joke from the second season's episode, "Audition." In this fairly typical scene, Rachel Barry (a main character known for being obnoxious, overbearing, and often rude) approaches Sunshine Corazon (a Filipino foreign exchange student) and invites her to join the glee club. When Sunshine appears not to understand, Rachel shouts in broken English, "Oh, you don't speak English. You like me sing. You like me sing very much." Sunshine then removes her ear buds and responds in perfect US English, "I totally speak English."

In this scene, Rachel acts in an overtly racist way—seeing Sunshine's skin color, she assumes a negative stereotype about Sunshine's intellectual and social abilities. The scene is funny as it invites us to laugh at Rachel's overt racism, yet it is humorously designed in the same way as scenes in which Rachel is being bossy or otherwise socially awkward. This scene signals that overt racism is a problem, but simultaneously likens racism to bossiness and social awkwardness—a cringe-worthy but humorous personality quirk with no great consequences, something to laugh at. Like other similar scenes, this one absorbs antiracist ideology by incorporating a rebuke of racist behavior; yet it and others like it also domesticate antiracist ideology by downplaying the consequences of racist actions.

Dubrofsky also analyzes the musical numbers, camerawork, and lighting, studying these stylistic tokens to understand the ideology of *Glee*'s second persona. The glee club has many talented vocalists, but Rachel Barry and Mercedes Jones are their strongest female soloists in the early seasons. Rachel, though ethnically Jewish, is White; Mercedes is Black. Throughout *Glee*, Rachel has considerably more musical numbers than Mercedes—she sings her way through many more featured solos as part of the glee club's practices and performances and through many more "time out" songs, during which (in true musical fashion) she sings while others either freeze, fade out, or seem oblivious to the music. These musical numbers "function the way background stories do in films": they offer "insight about a character's home and personal life, giving the character depth so audiences can connect and empathize."[51]

Rachel's many solos also span a wide range of musical genres. In contrast, Mercedes' rare solos are limited to stereotyped music, such as gospel, jazz, and hip-hop. Analyzing their performances, Dubrofsky demonstrates that the music invites viewers to resonate emotionally with Rachel (who is White), while Black characters—including the vocally talented Mercedes—are "made one-dimensional" through the lack of emotionally insightful "time out" songs, and through the stereotyped genres in which *Glee* features their solos.[52]

Moreover, the camera and lighting treat Rachel differently during the solo performances. Studying the stylization of camerawork and lighting, Dubrofsky notes that when Rachel performs solos, the camera provides tight close-ups on her emotion-laden face; the lighting illuminates her so that she glows softly while the rest of the cast fades into the background. Then, the camera often circles around her, enveloping and celebrating her. These stylistic choices—the camerawork and lighting—invite audiences into Rachel's perspective, giving viewers a sense of Rachel's "feelings and motivations, enabling empathy."[53]

Dubrofsky explains that these stylistic devices function by encouraging audiences to identify with Rachel: she is presented to audiences as a complex character with understandable and relatable dreams, motives, and goals. In contrast, during the first several seasons of *Glee,* Mercedes is a one-dimensional, stereotypical character: *Glee*'s stylistic devices do not invite audiences to empathize or identify with her. *Glee* recreates the hegemonic status quo by granting White characters more emotionally resonant musical numbers and stylizing their portrayal in ways that draw audiences to identify with White characters, while denying Black characters similar camera and lighting treatments. Dubrofsky argues that *Glee*'s ideology is that White people are normal and relatable and that racial minorities are stereotyped aberrations from the norm, even as this series champions a pro-diversity ethos.

Like most ideological critiques, Dubrofsky's analysis of *Glee* is motivated by an ethical concern. She is primarily interested in how a radical, resistant ideology (antiracism) has become mainstream, and yet has not resulted in significant social change. Hegemony theory includes the idea that resistant ideologies can be absorbed and domesticated, and Dubrofsky demonstrates exactly how *Glee* absorbs and domesticates antiracist ideologies. Watching *Glee,* viewers are invited into a second persona that feels good (nonracist) about itself, without changing behavior or even empathizing with characters who are not White.

Myra Washington "Interracial Intimacy: Hegemonic Construction of Asian American and Black Relationships on TV Medical Dramas" (2012)*

In the 1960s, approximately 5 percent of White Americans approved of interracial marriage between White and Black people.[54] Interracial marriage between Whites and racial minorities in the United States was legalized in 1967 through the landmark Supreme Court case *Loving v. Virginia.* Mildred Loving (a Black woman) and Richard Loving (a White man) had been sentenced to a year's imprisonment in 1958 for having married each other. The Supreme Court ultimately overruled their conviction, thus decriminalizing marriages between Whites and racial minorities.

Since then, significant changes have taken place. As of 2015, approximately 85 percent of White Americans report in polls that they approve of marriage between White and Black people.[55] Analyzing television entertainment, however, Myra Washington notes that very few series feature interracial romances, and even fewer of those romances mature into happy, healthy, marriages that also result in children. Essentially, Washington suggests that although White Americans claim to support interracial marriage in polls and surveys, the entertainment industries

*This essay may be found in *The Howard Journal of Communications,* vol. 23, no. 3 (2012): 253–271.

do not believe that mainstream White audiences will consume media that features interracial romance, marriage, and babies.

Washington's research delves into the historical context of antimiscegenation laws in the United States—such as Virginia's Racial Integrity Act of 1924, under which Mildred and Richard Loving's marriage was a crime. These laws applied only to marriages between White people and racial minorities; a marriage between members of different minority races was not a crime in the United States.[56] In other words, these laws focused on Whiteness and distinguishing Whites from other races.[57] As Brendon Wolfe explains, these laws were designed to prevent White people from producing "mixed-race" children, and thus to "protect 'Whiteness'" from what was perceived as "the negative effects of race-mixing."[58] Through this contextual research, Washington demonstrates how the history of interracial marriage in the United States focuses on Whiteness and maintaining Whites—as a race—at the top of a racial hierarchy by preventing interracial progeny.[59]

Washington then rhetorically analyzes the medical dramas *Grey's Anatomy* and *ER* because—unlike the vast majority of mainstream TV series—these shows broadcast multiepisode story arcs featuring interracial romance. The diverse ensemble casts and interracial storylines were "applauded" throughout media outlets as a "newfound celebration of racial diversity."[60] One of the key goals of Washington's analysis is to evaluate whether these series make good on the premise that modern America doesn't "blink at interracial relationships," but rather embraces a multiethnic, multiracial population.[61]

Washington engages in ideological criticism, analyzing the ideology embedded within these series and their "mediated impact" upon audiences.[62] She focuses on the representation of sex and romance between "Black and Asian/American characters" in an effort to study interracial romance without the focus on Whiteness that is embedded in the history of US antimiscegenation laws.[63] In the following pages I highlight Washington's analysis of Cristina Yang and Preston Burke's relationship in the first three seasons of *Grey's Anatomy.*

Focusing on the context surrounding *Grey's Anatomy,* Washington notes the "very celebratory response" that greeted Yang and Burke's interracial relationship, which was praised for moving "past race" and for "crossing racial boundaries."[64] Washington reminds her readers that "Black-Asian pairings" have never been prohibited in the United States and are in fact quite common, especially in the context of "U.S. military interventions in Asian countries."[65] She reminds us that there is no "boundary" for Yang and Burke to "cross." Although their relationship is depicted as progressive, within the context of US history it is not—it is an instance of something that has always been legal.[66]

Washington's ideological analysis also demonstrates that Yang and Burke are portrayed in ways that recreate racist stereotypes. Analyzing the portrayal of Cristina Yang, Washington recognizes the stereotype of "the dragon lady," which (along with the geisha stereotype) has historically dominated the portrayal of Asian/American women.[67] This stereotype presents Asian/American women as cold, calculating, often mean, and sexually aggressive.[68] As Washington demonstrates, this stereotype fits Yang exactly. *Grey's Anatomy*'s website describes Yang as "aggressive, cutthroat and arrogant."[69] She is depicted throughout the series as "brilliant" but "über-competitive"; her "abrasive and cold personality" makes it difficult for her to relate to patients.[70] Moreover, she sexually pursues Burke while resisting the more romantic and emotional aspects of their relationship.

Meanwhile, Washington argues, Burke is portrayed through the stereotype of a "tom." Black men are often portrayed in US entertainment as either "toms" or "brutal Black bucks."[71] These racist stereotypes are inversions of each other. The "buck" stereotype is physically powerful, animalistic, hot-tempered, and sexually aggressive. In contrast, the "tom" stereotype (named after "Uncle Tom" in Harriet Beecher Stowe's *Uncle Tom's Cabin*) is "submissive, stoic, generous, selfless, and oh-so-very kind."[72] Burke epitomizes the "tom" stereotype: he is endlessly composed, loyally submissive to the hospital (even when passed over for promotions), and contains himself in ways that are not required of the White male doctors on the series.

Analyzing these characters' story arc, Washington notes that the way their relationship is dramatized withholds the privileges of healthy relationships, marriage, and progeny from interracial couples. Both *Grey's Anatomy* and *ER* deny their interracial couples the ability to have sexy and loving romances that culminate in the gold standard of successful relationships, according to US culture: marriage and babies. Indeed, on *Grey's Anatomy,* Yang's pregnancy ends in a miscarriage—eliminating the on-screen depiction of a multiracial child—and Burke ultimately abandons her at the altar in a surprise twist of the plot.

Ultimately, Washington argues that the first three seasons of *Grey's Anatomy* uphold dominant ideologies that privilege Whiteness as normal and that situate Whites at the top of a racial hierarchy. The racist stereotypes function hegemonically in the depictions of Yang and Burke and the dooming of their progeny and marriage. Indeed, these television shows recirculate dominant ideology by portraying people of color through one-dimensional racist stereotypes, even while claiming to celebrate a diverse ensemble cast. Similarly, these shows function hegemonically, as they claim to celebrate interracial relationships while denying interracial couples a "happily ever after" and eliminating interracial offspring.[73] Meanwhile, same-race couples on *Grey's Anatomy* and *ER* are situated in plotlines that let them combine sexiness, marriage, and babies. Through ideological criticism and the specific examination of stereotypes and power hierarchies, Washington argues that far from being progressive, these shows offer "stagnant, if not regressive" portrayals of race, gender, and interracial relationships.[74]

Fernando Delgado
"The Rhetoric of Fidel Castro: Ideographs in the Service of Revolutionaries" (1999)*

What does it mean to be American? A student asked this question as he led discussion in my classroom one morning. His peers immediately answered with "freedom," and then settled into murmured conversations as he pressed them

*This essay may be found in *The Howard Journal of Communications,* vol. 10, no. 1 (1999): 1–14.

for more concrete answers. Eventually, the class agreed that "being American" involved being "unpretentious" or having "basic" pleasures. They named "burgers and beer" as the quintessential American experience.

The student leader followed up by asking how they knew that freedom, simplicity, burgers, and beer are the cornerstones of the US national identity. The class pointed to the political news articles they had been reading and the television commercials they had been watching. For instance, Budweiser's advertisements were a touchstone in the conversation, grounding the assumption that Americans enjoy simple pleasures—like basic beer.

As realistic (or unrealistic) as this implied ideology for a national identity might be, Americans have spent decades cultivating this identity. In fact, the discussion in my classroom was about Theodore Roosevelt's presidency and similarities in what it meant to be American then and now.

National ideologies, however, can undergo significant change—especially in times of political, economic, and social upheaval. Fernando Delgado uses an ideographic analysis to study just such an upheaval in Cuba, demonstrating how Fidel Castro used the ideographs <*la Revolución*> and <*revolucionarios*> to craft a new national identity for Cubans. *La Revolución* translates into English as "the Revolution." *Revolucionarios* translates as "revolutionaries."

Castro was Cuba's *Máximo Lider* (maximum leader) for roughly fifty years. He rose to power in 1959, when he overthrew the brutal dictator Fulgencio Batista.[75] As journalist Anthony dePalma wrote, Castro "held on to power longer" than any of his contemporary national leaders "except Queen Elizabeth II."[76] He had significant time in which to establish and cultivate a national identity; however, at the beginning of his reign, Castro faced a significant cultural problem. Cuba's writers, artists, and others working in the news and entertainment industries were not necessarily supportive of his communist vision for Cuba. Indeed, many of these cultural workers had lived through significant socioeconomic and political upheaval and had their own visions of Cuba's national identity.

The islands now known as Cuba had been colonized by Spain from the fifteenth century until the Spanish-American War of 1898, when Cuba became a protectorate of the United States as part of the treaty between the United States and Spain. In 1902, Cuba became an independent republic; however, its constitution reflected US interests and granted the United States continued influence in its governance. The next fifty years were politically turbulent. Vast economic inequality swept the islands, largely connected to US corporations' control of the sugar industry in Cuba, trade agreements between the United States and Cuba that undercut Cuba's ability to build and maintain its own industries rather than importing US goods, and corruption within Cuba's political governance.[77] In 1952, Fulgencio Batista overthrew Cuba's democratic government and established himself as a dictator.

Responding to Batista's regime, the prior decades of corruption, the economic inequality, the failures of Cuba's supposedly democratic government, and US political and economic interventions, Fidel Castro led Cuba into a communist revolution that not only overthrew Batista's tyrannical governance (executing many of its agents), but also threw off US corporations' control of the sugar industry.

Two years later, in 1961, the United States responded by arming and training approximately fourteen hundred Cuban refugees who had fled from Castro, and facilitating their invasion of Cuba. This attempt to overthrow Castro, known as the Bay of Pigs invasion, failed.[78]

A few months later, Castro gathered Cuba's journalists, documentary film makers, artists, and writers together for a speech known as "*Palabras a los Intelectuales*" (words to the intellectuals). Keenly aware of Cuba's history, Delgado analyzes this speech, identifying how Castro developed and used the ideographs of <la Revolución> and <revolucionarios> to craft a new national identity for Cubans. The intellectuals Castro addressed in his speech worked in "the culture industries," creating the art and entertainment and writing the news that Cubans interacted with on a daily basis.[79] Some of these artists and writers had become critical of Castro's governance and what they perceived as censorship of their work. In this famous speech, Castro works to convince these culture workers to support his vision for Cuba and to engage in hegemonic processes by disseminating his ideology as the dominant ideology throughout Cuba.

According to the "meaning system" that Castro constructs in this speech, the revolution was an ultimate good: it had thrown off Batista's repressive regime and (according to Castro) ushered in freedom for Cubans—freedom from tyranny, foreign political interference, economic inequality, and so on.[80] Castro, however, reimagines <la Revolución> as an ongoing, personified entity, not as a moment in time. Within his framework, <la Revolución> has the same rights ("the right to exist, the right to develop, the right to win") as it bestows on Cubans.[81] Imagined in this way, Castro's "revolutionary government is not the revolution but renders service to it by protecting all Cubans' rights, including those of the revolution."[82] Within this circular framework, by protecting and serving <la Revolución>, Cubans protect and serve themselves.

By situating <la Revolución> as both the means to and the goal of freedom, Castro invites the artists and writers into an identity of <revolucionarios>, or those who serve <la Revolución>. He calls them into "a powerful new existence and identity" as <revolucionarios>.[83] This identity involves self-censorship, as opposed to imposed censorship by the state. That is, if one serves the revolution, one would not publish or broadcast content that criticizes a government that also serves the revolution. Similarly, if one serves the revolution, one would publish and broadcast content that encourages others to serve the revolution. Delgado argues that through this speech, Castro worked to establish a hegemony, as he called the culture makers into an identity as <revolucionarios> who would then create a culture that called each Cuban into this new national identity.[84]

While responding to writers' and artists' very real fears of censorship and repression, Castro offers them seats of honor within his vision of Cuba's future. As long as these writers and artists accepted Castro's vision and took up their roles as <revolucionarios>, Castro assures them prestige and a meaningful role in directing Cuba's future. Indeed, within Castro's framework, artists' and writers' creative works and cultural labor would play a central role in Cuba's future by cultivating this revolutionary identity in other Cubans. Moreover, Delgado notes,

Castro incentivized artists' and writers' consent to his ideology with considerable "material benefits."[85] If they accepted his vision, they could be assured the government would support their cultural labor.[86]

Throughout this analysis, Delgado studies not just the repetition of the phrases <la Revolución> and <revolucionarios>, but the way they function as the master terms or driving force of an entire meaning system in Castro's "*Palabras a los Intelectuales*"—and in his rhetoric more broadly. Delgado argues that it was not enough for Castro to overthrow Batista's regime. To retain his role as the Máximo Lider, Castro had to unite the Cuban people by offering them a new identity that squarely and unquestionably supported his authority. He crafted just such a national identity in his <revolucionarios> ideograph. Offering this identity to Cuba's culture makers (and significant material benefits for the culture workers who accepted this identity), he set into motion a hegemonic process that would ensure Cubans' support of his government for many years.

Ultimately, Delgado concludes that from the outside of Castro's hegemonic system, his regime appears "repressive, authoritarian, [and] dictatorial."[87] However, within this hegemonic system—which Castro set into motion through Cuba's culture workers—Castro offered Cubans a coherent meaning system and national identity grounded in the ideas of self-actualization and freedom.

STRENGTHS AND WEAKNESSES OF IDEOLOGICAL CRITIQUE

An ideological critique can effectively identify the systems of belief and assumptions at work in a text, and thus the way that the text invites its audience to understand reality and therefore think and act within the world. By focusing on stylistic tokens, power relations, stereotypes, and ideographs, ideological criticism makes sense of public discourse, revealing the systems of thought that guide our interpretations of reality while remaining just beneath our conscious logic.

One of the core strengths of this mode of criticism is that its relevance is fairly obvious. Ideological criticism is fundamentally concerned with ethics. The critic is ethically troubled by the dominant ideologies and hegemonic processes shaping society, and believes that a small, elite subset of the population has shaped a culture's logic, beliefs, assumptions, and values to benefit themselves. An ideological critic who can demonstrate this through an analysis of discourse can prove that the culture is fundamentally unfair—unethical.

Well-argued ideological critiques clearly matter. However, these arguments are generally unpopular. Nobody likes being told that their own thoughts and beliefs are unfair—whether they are unfair to themselves or others. Nobody likes thinking of themselves as mindless sheep, easily duped by the elite, or as part of the elite, making life unfair for others.

To argue an ideological critique successfully, therefore, a critic needs significant evidence. This evidence is usually hard to compile because it is stylistic. The critic points to particular word choices, metaphors, camera angles, and so on as evidence of complex systems of thought that call out to audiences, persuasively inviting the audience to accept the whole system. Thus, to successfully argue an ideological critique, critics typically need a lot of evidence.

A critic must compile so much evidence that although readers might dismiss any particular piece of evidence as indicative of an ideology, they cannot dismiss the preponderance of evidence. To return to my lake metaphor for ideological criticism, it is as if you (the ideological critic) are standing on a lakeshore with a friend. You turn to your friend and say, "Guess what! The bottom of this lake is entirely smooth. There are absolutely no rocks on the bottom of this lake." Your friend is naturally incredulous. After all, who ever heard of a rock-less lake? So you climb into a rowboat with your friend and take a tour of the lake. You visit every buoy that marks clear water areas so your friend can peer down to the bottom. After the first couple of buoys, your friend admits that she has yet to see a rock, but quite logically explains that this doesn't prove anything. There could be—and probably are—a million rocks at the bottom of the lake, they just aren't in the few square feet of lake floor she has been able to see. In order to convince your friend, you will have to show her a preponderance of evidence—a whole lot of lake floor with no rocks—before she will be ready to agree with you.

CHOOSING THIS APPROACH

How do you know whether you should use ideological criticism to interpret a particular piece of public discourse? I recommend a process through which you evaluate the text's qualities, the context surrounding the text, and the research question animating your analysis.

First, does your text feature a lot of stylistic tokens? If the text is primarily verbal, does it feature stylistic devices (such as analogies, metaphors, metonymy, synecdoche, euphemisms, dysphemisms, allusions, paraleipsis, personification, and/or humor)? If the text is audiovisual, what is the stylistic function of the color scheme, editing, cinematography, staging, and/or sound? Texts that feature multiple or recurring stylistic tokens are good candidates for ideological criticism.

Second, does your text feature an ideograph or multiple ideographs? If it uses commonplace words, phrases, or images to justify its call to action or to represent a community's sense of identity and their commitments, then it might be relying on ideographs. Texts that feature ideographs can be good candidates for ideological criticism.

Third, does the context provide some clues to the place of your text within the hegemonic system? The theory of hegemony suggests that dominant ideologies are widely circulated. Thus, critics can expect mainstream texts to reproduce dominant ideologies. Given the ways resistant ideologies are absorbed and domesticated by hegemonic processes, critics can also expect mainstream texts to absorb and domesticate resistant ideologies. In contrast, texts that are produced by social activist groups are more likely to advance resistant ideologies. Critics need to be aware of these contextual trends, but should not let context overdetermine their interpretations of their texts. Some activist texts espouse one resistant ideology but simultaneously feature other dominant ideologies. Some relatively mainstream texts can be surprisingly radical.

Finally, examine your own research motives. Are you interested in understanding why large groups of people are thinking and acting against their own best interests? Are you trying to understand the thought structures shaping a culture? Do you want to study how an activist group resists the elite? Or do you want to understand how a radical idea (like equality) has become mainstream without resulting in significant social changes? Ideological criticism is particularly suited to answering research questions that stem from these types of concerns and goals.

Moreover, ideological criticism is almost always motivated by an ethical concern. You need to ask yourself whether you are morally motivated to analyze your chosen text. Communication theorist and environmental activist Peter Andersen notes that ideological critics are engaging in activism. He states that "writing [an ideological critique] itself constitutes a form of action" that often "leads to other kinds of actions," such as signing petitions, protesting, marching, showing up to school board meetings and neighborhood association meetings, voting, campaigning, donating, volunteering, speaking out, running for office, boycotting, unionizing, striking, and sharing your opinions by calling or writing your local, state, and federal representatives.[88] Clearly such activities are not prerequisites for or compulsory follow-ups to ideological criticism. Still, Andersen is right to call our attention to the fact that ideological criticism changes us—the critics—and that this change often deepens our commitment to moral action and activism.

Ultimately, ideological criticism is political. Flowing from the theory of hegemony, this mode of criticism is concerned with who has power (the elite) and how that power is used to shape and disseminate dominant ideologies. In a world riddled with texts whose second personae beckon audiences into ideologies that are not only inaccurate but also only benefit an elite group of people, ideological criticism is a challenging but necessary mode of criticism.

DISCUSSION QUESTIONS

1. What is an ideology that you learned in your childhood? Who taught you this ideology? Do you still think that way? If not, what changed your mind?
2. Make a list of three ideologies you think are dominant in US culture. For each of these ideologies, explain whom you think the ideology benefits (who are the elite for this dominant ideology?) and give a specific example of where you've seen this ideology represented in US culture.
3. In your own words, define and explain the "second persona."
4. Why are stylistic tokens useful for helping a critic discern the second persona's ideology?
5. Identify a word or phrase that you believe operates as an ideograph in one of your cultures. What ideology does it represent? What communally felt commitment does it invoke the audience to act on?
6. Pick one of the dominant ideologies you identified in question 2. Now imagine a text that resists that ideology. What ideology would this resistant text want its audience to embody? What types of stylistic tokens could it use to communicate this resistant ideology?
7. What are some of the risks and rewards of the ethical concern at the heart of an ideological critique?

NOTES

1. Bernice A. King, “Please Don’t Use My Father to Suggest or Assert that Respectability Cures Racism,” Twitter.com, February 12, 2019, 7:42 PM, https://twitter.com/berniceking/status/1095483194785316865?lang=en.
2. Bree Newsom, “The Civil-Rights Movement’s Generation Gap,” *The Atlantic*, March 27, 2018, https://www.theatlantic.com/magazine/archive/2018/02/bree-newsome-generation-gap/552554/.
3. Newsom, “Civil-Rights Generation Gap.”
4. Newsom, “Civil-Rights Generation Gap.”
5. Tom Daniels, Barry Spiker, and Michael Papa, *Perspectives on Organizational Communication,* 4th ed. (Madison, WI: Brown & Benchmark, 1997), 255.
6. Evelyn Brooks Higginbotham, *Righteous Discontent: The Women’s Movement in the Black Baptist Church, 1880–1920* (Cambridge, MA: Harvard University Press, 1993), 187.
7. Damon Young, “The Definition, Danger and Disease of Respectability Politics, Explained,” The Root.com, March 21, 2016, https://www.theroot.com/the-definition-danger-and-disease-of-respectability-po-1790854699.
8. Young, “Definition, Danger and Disease.”
9. Young, “Definition, Danger and Disease.”
10. Young, “Definition, Danger and Disease.”
11. Natalie Fixmer and Julia T. Wood, “The Personal is *Still* Political: Embodied Politics in Third Wave Feminism,” *Women’s Studies in Communication* 28, no. 2 (2005): 235–236.
12. Jeremy Engels, *The Politics of Resentment: A Genealogy* (University Park, PA: Pennsylvania State University, 2015), 14.
13. Sandra Harding, “Introduction: Is There a Feminist Method?” in *Feminism and Methodology,* ed. Sandra Harding (Bloomington: Indiana University Press, 1987), 3.
14. Kevin Carragee, “A Critical Evaluation of Debates Examining the Media Hegemony Thesis,” *Western Journal of Communication* 57, no. 3 (1993): 330.
15. Antonio Gramsci, *Selections from the Prison Notebooks,* ed. and trans. Quintin Hoare and Geoffrey Nowellsmith (New York: International, 1989), 12.
16. Todd Gitlin, “Prime Time Ideology: The Hegemonic Process in Television Entertainment,” *Social Problems* 26, no. 3 (1979): 251.
17. Brenda Allen, Difference Matters: Communicating Social Identity, 2nd ed. (Long Grove, IL: Waveland Press, 2011), 32.
18. “Paul Ryan Talks Tax Bill, Trump and Sexual Harassment on *Today,*” *Hollywood Reporter,* December 20, 2017, https://www.hollywoodreporter.com/news/paul-ryan-talks-tax-bill-today-show-1069605.
19. “Paul Ryan Talks Tax Bill.”
20. Carragee, “A Critical Evaluation,” 331.
21. Ed Mazza, “John Oliver Explains Everything That’s Wrong with the Miss America Pageant,” Huffpost.com, September 22, 2014, https://www.huffpost.com/entry/john-oliver-miss-america_n_5859726.
22. Bonnie Dow, “Feminism, Miss America, and Media Mythology,” *Rhetoric & Public Affairs* 6, no. 1 (2003): 127–149.

23. Gitlin, "Prime Time Ideology," 264.
24. Edwin Black, "The Second Persona," *The Quarterly Journal of Speech* 56, no. 2 (1970).
25. R. A. Griffin, "Black Feminist Reflections on Michelle Obama's Tribute to Maya Angelou," in *Michelle Obama: First Lady, American Rhetor,* eds. E. J. Natalle and J. M. Simon (Lanham, MD: Lexington, 2015), 121–139.
26. Black, "Second Persona," 112–113.
27. Black, "Second Persona," 113.
28. See Dana Cloud, "To Veil the Threat of Terror: Afghan Women and the <Clash of Civilizations> in the Imagery of the U.S. War on Terrorism," *Quarterly Journal of Speech* 90, no. 3 (2004): 288.
29. Janis Edwards and Carol Winkler, "Representative Form and the Visual Ideograph: The Iwo Jima Image in Editorial Cartoons," *Quarterly Journal of Speech* 83, no. 3 (1997): 297.
30. *THON,* accessed September 4, 2018, https://thon.org/.
31. Cloud, "To Veil the Threat," 288.
32. Cloud, "To Veil the Threat"; Edwards and Winkler, "Representative Form"; and Celeste Condit, *Decoding Abortion Rhetoric* (Urbana: University of Illinois, 1990).
33. Sharon Crowley, "Reflections on an Argument That Won't Go Away: Or, A Turn of the Ideological Screw," *Quarterly Journal of Speech* 78 (1992): 452.
34. Ursula Le Guin, "A Left-handed Commencement Address," in *Words of a Century: The Top 100 American Speeches, 1900–1999,* eds. Stephen E. Lucas and Martin J. Medhurst (New York: Oxford University Press, 2009), 562–564.
35. Randall Livingstone, "Better at Life Stuff: Consumption, Identity, and Class in Apple's 'Get a Mac' Campaign," *Journal of Communication Inquiry* 35, no. 3 (2011): 210–234.
36. James Schiffman, "Chinese Soft Power and Its Reception: A Critical Comparison of the CCTV and NBC Presentations of the Opening Ceremony of the 2008 Beijing Summer Olympic Games," *China Media Research* 13, no. 2 (2017): 14.
37. "Top 8 Hottest Female Athletes," Profascinate.com, accessed December 31, 2018, https://www.profascinate.com/hottest-female-athletes.html; Bhav Patel, "15 Female Athletes Who Were Born to Wear Leggings," TheSportster.com, September 20, 2017, https://www.thesportster.com/entertainment/15-female-athletes-who-were-born-to-wear-leggings/; *The Berenstain Bears Say Their Prayers,* created by Stan Berenstain and Jan Berenstain, written by Mike Berenstain (Grand Rapids, MI: Zonderkidz, 2011).
38. Rachel Joy Larris and Rosalie Maggio, "Media Guide to Gender Neutral Coverage of Women Candidates and Politicians," *Women's Media Center,* last modified 2012, https://wmc.3cdn.net/b2d5a7532d50091943_n1m6b1avk.pdf.
39. Benjamin Bennett-Carpenter, Michael McCallion, and David Maines, "<Personal Relationship with Jesus>: A Popular Ideograph among Evangelical Catholics," *Journal of Communication and Religion* 36, no. 1 (2013): 1–24.
40. Bennett-Carpenter, McCallion, and Maines, "<Personal Relationship with Jesus>," 7; Pope Benedict XVI, "Encounter of His Holiness Benedict XVI with the Youth," *World Youth Day,* April 6, 2006.
41. Bennett-Carpenter, McCallion, and Maines, "<Personal Relationship with Jesus>," 2.
42. Livingstone, "Better at Life Stuff," 215.

43. Livingstone, "Better at Life Stuff," 216.
44. Michael Leff and Gerald Mohrmann, "Lincoln at Cooper Union: A Rhetorical Analysis of the Text," *Quarterly Journal of Speech* 60, no. 3 (1974): 147.
45. Celeste Wells, "Diapers Full of . . . Pampered, Hugged and 'Luved' Babies: Teaching Ideological Criticism through Diapers," *Communication Teacher* 30, no. 2 (2016): 74
46. Wells, "Diapers Full," 74.
47. Livingstone, "Better at Life Stuff," 224.
48. Livingstone, "Better at Life Stuff," 221–222.
49. Livingstone, "Better at Life Stuff," 215.
50. Livingstone, "Better at Life Stuff," 228.
51. Rachel Dubrofsky, "Jewishness, Whiteness, and Blackness on *Glee:* Singing to the Tune of Postracism," *Communication, Culture & Critique* 6, no. 1 (2013): 90.
52. Dubrofsky, "*Glee,*" 90.
53. Dubrofsky, "*Glee,*" 90.
54. Maria Krysan and S. Moberg, *Trends in Racial Attitudes,* University of Illinois Institute of Government and Public Affairs, August 25, 2016, http://igpa.uillinois.edu/programs/racial-attitudes.
55. Krysan and Moberg, *Trends in Racial Attitudes.*
56. Myra Washington, "Interracial Intimacy: Hegemonic Construction of Asian American and Black Relationships on TV Medical Dramas," *The Howard Journal of Communications* 23, no. 3 (2012): 266–267.
57. Virginia Health Department, "Instructions on Preserving Racial Integrity," *Encyclopedia Virginia,* 1924/2015, https://www.encyclopediavirginia.org/media_player?mets_filename=evm00001754mets.xml.
58. Brendan Wolfe, "Racial Integrity Laws 1924–1930," *Encyclopedia Virginia,* November 4, 2015, https://www.encyclopediavirginia.org/racial_integrity_laws_of_the_1920s#start_entry.
59. Washington, "Interracial Intimacy," 253–271.
60. Washington, "Interracial Intimacy," 257–258.
61. S. Jayson, "New Generation Doesn't Blink at Interracial Relationships," *USA Today,* February 8, 2006, 1A.
62. Washington, "Interracial Intimacy," 255.
63. Washington, "Interracial Intimacy," 255.
64. Washington, "Interracial Intimacy," 266.
65. Washington, "Interracial Intimacy," 254.
66. Washington, "Interracial Intimacy," 266
67. Washington, "Interracial Intimacy," 259.
68. Washington, "Interracial Intimacy," 259.
69. Washington, "Interracial Intimacy," 259.
70. Washington, "Interracial Intimacy," 259.
71. Washington, "Interracial Intimacy," 260.
72. Washington, "Interracial Intimacy," 260.
73. Washington, "Interracial Intimacy," 265.
74. Washington, "Interracial Intimacy," 256.

75. Fernando Delgado, "The Rhetoric of Fidel Castro: Ideographs in the Service of Revolutionaries," *The Howard Journal of Communications* 10, no. 1 (1999): 3; Anthony DePalma, "Fidel Castro, Cuban Revolutionary Who Defied U.S., Dies at 90," NYTimes.com, November 26, 2016, https://nyti.ms/2g1IaMO.
76. DePalma, "Fidel Castro, Cuban Revolutionary."
77. Nora Hamilton, "The Cuban Economy: Dilemmas of Socialist Construction," in *Cuba: A Different America,* eds. Wilbur Chaffee and Gary Prevost (Lanham, MD: Rowman & Littlefield, 1989), 37.
78. Richard Crooker, *Cuba* (Broomall, PA: Chelsea House, 2005), 43–44.
79. Delgado, "Rhetoric of Fidel Castro," 6.
80. Delgado, "Rhetoric of Fidel Castro," 7–8.
81. Delgado, "Rhetoric of Fidel Castro," 8
82. Delgado, "Rhetoric of Fidel Castro," 8.
83. Delgado, "Rhetoric of Fidel Castro," 7.
84. Delgado, "Rhetoric of Fidel Castro," 9.
85. Delgado, "Rhetoric of Fidel Castro," 10.
86. Delgado, "Rhetoric of Fidel Castro," 10.
87. Delgado, "Rhetoric of Fidel Castro," 12.
88. Peter Andersen, "Beyond Criticism: The Activist Turn in the Ideological Debate," *Western Journal of Communication* 57, no. 2 (1993): 249.

Chapter 8

Feminist Criticism

Phoebe Robinson is a comedian, actor, and, with Jessica Williams, cocreator of the podcast *Two Dope Queens.* In her book *You Can't Touch My Hair: And Other Things I Still Have to Explain,* Robinson describes how she understood her hair as an African American tween, how others treat her hair, and how she has come to reimagine her hair as an adult. Recounting the different ways she wears her hair (braids, dreadlocks or twists, straightened, bald, natural, in an Afro, and so on), she notes that how her hair is styled affects how others treat her.[1] For instance, she remarks that "the word *angry* doesn't get hurled at me nearly as much when my hair is straight as when it's in an Afro."[2] After describing experiences interviewing for jobs, shopping at stores, and other daily activities, Robinson concludes that "black women know that the quality of their life and how others will treat them is riding on the presentation of their hair."[3] She also makes a connection between her hair, how she thought about her hair, and how she understood beauty. She writes that as a teenager, "I assumed that if I had better hair, I would finally get my first boyfriend."[4]

Robinson observes that hairstyles are part of heterosexual beauty standards in the United States and that heterosexual beauty standards are sexist. They advantage women who are able and willing (and disadvantage women who are not) to style themselves in ways that cater to heterosexual men's preferences within their culture. For instance, the Miss America Scholarship Pageant financially rewards women who embody heterosexual beauty standards.[5] Robinson further recognizes that this sexism is racialized: that light, straight, nonfrizzy hair is equated with "good hair" in US society.[6] Her reflections are rooted—at least in part—in feminist ideology. Feminist theorist bell hooks (a feminist theorist who spells her name in all lower-case letters) defines **feminism** as "*a movement to end sexism, sexist exploitation, and oppression.*"[7]

Feminist criticism is *a type of ideological critique that is animated by the political goal of ending sexism.* In general, sexism is a system that values one sex over the other. Seeking to end sexism, feminist criticism excels at (1) analyzing discourse in ways that reveal the realities of women's lives, (2) assessing how discourse represents femininity and masculinity and how this representation affects people, and (3) celebrating discourses that model healthy communication strategies and build healthy communities. As an ideological critique, feminist criticism is emphatically concerned with the political (the way power is achieved and used in society, as discussed in Chapter 7).[8] Moreover, as an ideological critique, feminist criticism is emphatically concerned with the processes of hegemony, and the dominant ideologies that permeate society. More specifically, it is concerned with the hegemonic processes that support sexism and the way sexism operates as a dominant ideology.

Feminist criticism aims to empower and emancipate "women and other marginalized groups," promoting social change and justice for women.[9] This chapter will explain the principles that guide critics as they participate in this type of ideological critique. To understand how to participate in feminist criticism—and how to interweave it with other methods—we first need to explore the feminist theory that motivates feminist ideological critique.

A THEORY OF FEMINISM

Feminism is fundamentally focused on ending **sexism,** *a hegemonic system that ranks people, valuing masculinity over femininity, and affects who has power and how that power is used in society.* By identifying sexism as hegemonic, feminist critics recognize that sexism benefits the few at the expanse of the many. By identifying it as a dominant ideology, feminist critics recognize that the masses—women, men, and nonbinary people—regularly believe sexist ideology, even though this ideology is not in our best interests and does not accurately reflect the reality of human equality. Feminists often use the term **patriarchy** to refer to *sexist hegemonic processes and sexist ideology,* which feminist activist Allan Johnson describes as a "system," or "an it, not a he, a them, or an us."[10] To recognize patriarchy as a system is to understand that sexism is not simply people occasionally choosing to be rude (or worse) to one another, but that humans are situated within cultures and institutions (such as the family, religion, and the economy), and that our lives are shaped by and in relation to our cultures and institutions.[11] Just as a car's engine is a system with distinct but interlocking parts, so too is our society a system with distinct but interlocking parts—and *the system itself is sexist.*

Scholars Rita Hardiman, Bailey Jackson, and Pat Griffin help explain this system by identifying some of the parts within it. First, the system is made up of individuals (such as you and me), institutions (such as schools, companies, government agencies, and so on), and culture itself. Second, the system includes both attitudes and behaviors. Third, those attitudes and behaviors can be either conscious or unconscious.[12] All these elements can overlap. For instance, a school could have a dress code forbidding female students from wearing leggings. This policy happens at the institutional level, is conscious, and reflects an attitude that assumes girls' bodies must be covered up and obscured.

When Johnson says the system itself is sexist, he does not mean it is a simple hierarchy that puts all men as equals at the top and all women as equals at the bottom. Rather, it is a complex matrix of power relationships that ranks everyone based on a shifting pattern of values. Feminist theorist bell hooks describes sexism as an "imperialist white-supremacist capitalist patriarchy."[13] She identifies three key values that structure the power relations: capital (how rich one is and the role one plays in the economy), White supremacy (how much one affirms Whiteness and White cultures as normal and right), and imperialism (how much one values one's own nation state's success at the expense of other people, countries, and the Earth). These values shape and inform which types of masculinity and femininity are valued and how they are ranked in patriarchal societies. In the United States, sexism is a political system that stacks the deck in men's favor, especially when those men are rich (and/or serve important economic roles in a community), affirm Whiteness and White cultures as normal and right, endorse their nation/community at the expense of others, have strong bodies, act tough, and successfully engage in heterosexual conquests.[14]

As a system, sexism results in many real-world consequences. At the individual level, some men believe in their own superiority and authority to control women and women's bodies. This belief leads to the manipulation, coercion, control, and abuse of women. For instance, the CDC (Centers for Disease Control and Prevention) reports that 30.3 percent of women in the United States have been "slapped, pushed or shoved by an intimate partner" and 24.3 percent have experienced "severe physical violence by an intimate partner."[15] The CDC includes a range of behaviors (including being choked, burned, wounded by a knife or a gun, and being hit with a hard object) as "severe physical violence."[16] Such abuse is so pervasive that, on average, a woman is beaten in the United States every nine seconds.[17] Although intimate partner abuse is perpetrated by individuals, it is perpetrated by so many individuals and the victims are so overwhelmingly female that a clear trend emerges. These are not merely the actions of individuals, but rather these behaviors are incubated through unconscious attitudes in our broader culture and supported by institutional attitudes and behaviors. For instance, entertainment media—television, films, video games, advertisements, news, magazines, and so on—often use humor "to make light" of intimate partner violence, while law enforcement practices and legal systems can make it very difficult for victims of intimate partner violence to protect themselves.[18]

At the institutional level, conscious and unconscious sexist attitudes result in economic consequences commonly known as the "wage gap." Essentially, people who have the same qualifications and do the same work receive different wages—and women are systematically paid less. However, sexism is not a simple ranking of masculinity over femininity: it is not as if all men are paid the same and all women are paid the same, but less than men. The value of Whiteness plays a significant role in the sexist system. For example, among college-educated employees over twenty-five, in 2015 the median hourly earning for White men was $32; for Black men, $25; and for Hispanic men, $26.[19] Meanwhile, the median hourly earning for White women was $25; for Black women, $23; and for Hispanic women, $22.[20] In 2015, the average college-educated Black man and White woman earned $7 less per hour than the average college-educated White man. The difference amounts to $56 per eight-hour day, $280 per five-day week, and $14,000 per year if one works fifty weeks a year.

At the unconscious level, individuals, institutions, and the broader culture often assume that men are the norm, the standard or representative human. The practice of referring to all of humanity as "mankind" reflects the assumption that men are representative of all humans. This attitude has incredibly negative consequences for women's health. When men are considered normal, scientists, medical researchers, and health professionals study men's bodies and men's health, and then create treatments designed for men—which can negatively affect women. For example, men and women often experience different symptoms during heart attacks. Men's typical symptoms (chest pain and a numb or painful left arm) are widely known, but women's typical symptoms (such as "shortness of breath, nausea/vomiting and back or jaw pain") are not—even among medical practitioners.[21] Because medical practitioners often cannot identify women's heart attack symptoms and dismiss women's pain as "psychosomatic," women are "seven times more likely than men to be misdiagnosed and discharged mid-heart-attack."[22] As a result, women under fifty are "twice as likely to die from heart attacks as men of the same age."[23]

Sexism at the institutional level affects how people create our daily environments in ways that position men as the norm and thus disadvantage women. For example, seat belts and airbags are tested using dummies that are modeled after male bodies. As a result, seat belts and airbags are "designed primarily for male bodies."[24] Thus, women "are 47 percent more likely to sustain injuries in a crash" than men when wearing seat belts.[25]

Conscious and unconscious attitudes at the cultural level seep into individuals' attitudes and behaviors, affecting our relationships. For example, parents are "2.5 times more likely to query Google about whether their 2-year old is a genius if that 2-year-old is a boy."[26] Similarly, when heterosexual couples are given tests, men's self-esteem plummets when they are told their female partners outscored them, but rises when told that their female partners did poorly; women, however, are unaffected by hearing that their male partners outscored them.[27]

Moreover, patriarchy—the sexist system—has imperial aspects, which creates international consequences. For instance, the US Justice Department (an institution) revised its policies in 2018 to exclude domestic violence as a rationale for asylum.[28] Many women live in countries where their systems result in policing practices, divorce laws, property laws, child custody laws, and so on that make it impossible for women to leave abusive partners safely while staying in that country. Previously, these women could apply for asylum in the United States. By revoking its policy, the Justice Department acted as an imperialist patriarchy. The new policy helped it look tough on immigration, but at the expense of women's safety.

Recognizing the reality of patriarchy ups the ante for feminist action. Simply being kind and impartial to everyone may make you a nice and decent person, but it does nothing to end sexism. Sexism is a system; individuals' behaviors are only one part of it. To change the system at the level of institutions and the broader culture requires feminist activists to directly address the processes of hegemony that maintain the whole system.

Feminist rhetorical theorist Karma Chávez invites rhetoricians to reconsider how the discipline of rhetoric (an institution) participates in patriarchy.[29] She points out that the field of rhetorical criticism has a center. Rhetoricians primarily orient themselves around certain types of theories and certain types of texts (such as news reportage, political speeches, blockbuster films, and so on) that (1) are primarily made by people and institutions that benefit from systematic sexism, (2) espouse a narrow understanding of power, politics, democracy, morality, and rhetoric, and (3) feature a narrow range of communicative techniques. Chávez explicitly invites critics to acknowledge that this "center" exists and to recenter the discipline so that we are no longer constituted by what bell hooks calls the "imperialist white supremacist capitalist patriarchy."[30]

Intersectionality

Feminist theory champions what feminist legal scholar Kimberlé Crenshaw termed an "intersectional" approach to the analysis of sexism. **Intersectionality** is *the concept that one's gender is shaped by one's race, ethnicity, class, nationality, physical ability, mental ability, sexuality, ideology, religion, and so on, and vice versa.*[31] Essentially, everyone comes in "different classes, races, and cultures."[32] There is no universal representative of any demographic group (for example, no universal woman, universal man, or universal nonbinary person) and thus no universal experience for members of a demographic group (for example, no universal woman's, universal man's, or universal nonbinary person's experience).[33]

Feminist theorists recognize that different identities shape and inform each other. They pay attention to how "masculine and feminine are always categories within every class, race, and culture" and that "class, race, and culture" are always categories within gender.[34] Being a rich, female, Latinx lesbian is a different experience from being a poor, female, Latinx lesbian, because identities interact: whether you are rich or poor shapes how you experience your sex, gender, ethnicity, sexuality, and so on. The reverse is also true: how you experience poverty or wealth is shaped by your sex, gender, ethnicity, sexuality, and so on. Because identities are communicated (by the appearance of our bodies and how we dress, speak, and act), communication scholars are particularly attuned to the ways in which identities are symbolized and interpreted.

Because identities interact, feminist theorists pay attention to the ways that "different types of discrimination" also interact.[35] For example, in a recent TedTalk titled "The Urgency of Intersectionality," Kimberlé Crenshaw describes developing the concept of intersectionality while she was working on the legal case of Emma DeGraffenreid, a Black woman who applied for a job at an automobile factory. According to Crenshaw, DeGraffenreid "believed that she was not hired because she was a black woman."[36] She sued for "race and gender discrimination."[37] The judge dismissed the suit in 1976, citing that the manufacturing plant hired both Black people and women; however, the plant hired Black men only for industrial and maintenance jobs, and only hired women who were White, and only for secretarial and front office jobs.[38] The court refused to see how DeGraffenreid's identities intersected and how that intersection shaped her experiences. DeGraffenreid "needed to combine race and gender" to "tell the story of discrimination" she was experiencing.[39]

Unearned Advantages

Sexism creates **unearned advantages** (sometimes known as privilege) in society.[40] Unearned advantages are when someone has *benefits, assistance, bonuses, head* *starts, or such that they did not make or achieve through their own labor.* For example, my parents were recently in a car crash: they were T-boned by a truck that ran a red light and crashed into my father's side of the car. Their car was demolished. Both my parents were wearing their seat belts; my father (despite being on the impact side) more or less walked away from the crash. My mother, however, who was not on the impact side (but who was 47 percent more likely to be injured than my father because seat belts and airbags are designed primarily for male bodies), was severely injured, underwent a significant surgery, spent nearly a year recuperating, and will never have full mobility again. In this scenario, my father had an advantage: the seat belt and airbags were designed for someone with his mass and proportions. This advantage was unearned; my father has never done anything to earn or merit better car safety than my mother. This unearned advantage should be available to everyone: everyone should be equally protected by seat belts and airbags.

Feminists such as Peggy McIntosh argue that many unearned advantages are positive advantages—good things that should be available to everyone. Everyone should be safe; in democratic nation-states, everyone should be represented; and no one should experience injustice when trying to buy a house, rent an apartment, get a loan, or get an education. In contrast, however, some unearned advantages are negative advantages. Instead of being a universal good (for example, everyone should be as safe in cars as adult men are), a negative advantage allows some to dominate others. For example, #MeToo activists argue that men—especially rich men in positions of workplace authority—often escape justice. These men abuse others without facing any consequences.[41] This is a negative advantage: feminists argue that no one should be allowed to abuse others and escape justice. Feminists work carefully to distinguish between positive and negative unearned advantages. They use activism to try to increase everyone's access to positive advantages and to end negative advantages that lead to domination.

Sexism's unearned advantages often go unnoticed by those who experience them. For example, consider some of the unearned advantages I have as a heterosexual person in a heterosexist society. On an anniversary dinner with my spouse, I can expect the waitstaff to enthusiastically congratulate us; no doctor has ever asked me if I've recently taken an AIDS test; my marriage is not only recognized in every US state, but in every country on this planet; my parents do not love me "in spite of" my sexual orientation; I will never have to explain to my children why they have parents of different sexes; I've never considered how to "come out" to anyone; I could join the US military while still "living my truth"; I never worry that holding hands with my spouse will incite someone to commit a hate crime against us; and I have never wondered whether my spouse and our children will be covered by my employment-based health insurance.[42] The vast majority of the time, people never notice their unearned advantages; they simply take them for granted as the status quo. Within sexist systems, men, heterosexuals, and heterosexually attractive women often enjoy significant unearned advantages that remain invisible to them.

Positive, unearned, unnoticed advantages are built into the system: people who have these advantages typically cannot give them up or decide not to use them.

Regardless of what my father does, he is safer in a car than my mother. There is no way for him to "opt out" of this advantage because it is not an individual thing, it is part of a system of institutions (car manufacturers, test-dummy manufacturers, and so on) that are embedded in cultural attitudes that treat men as if they represent all of humanity. Feminists recommend that, rather than feeling guilty or trying to divest one's self of these unearned advantages, people use any positive unearned advantages they have to try to expand these advantages so all people enjoy them.

Sexism and Power

As a hegemonic system, sexism is fundamentally about how power is attained and used—and there are two clearly distinct ways that power operates. The first is through **institutional operations of state,** *laws and policies through which governments and organizations officially regulate society.* The US Justice Department's definition of the criteria for asylum and its revocation of domestic violence as a rational for asylum is a clear example of how power is wielded through institutional operations of state. This type of power is generally thought of as top-down power.[43] Historically, feminist activism countered institutional operations of state through organized rallies, prolonged court cases, and other large-scale protests. This is how feminists successfully argued for the vote, for legalizing birth control, and for same-sex marriage.

The second form of power is associated with philosopher Michel Foucault's theories. This power is known as **disciplinary power,** *a bottom-up, ubiquitous form of power through which people punish one another (as opposed to the state punishing a citizen) in order to bring greater conformity to cultural norms.*[44] For example, imagine that a fairly average, straight, White, male student wore a pink T-shirt to class, and a couple of his classmates gently teased him for wearing pink. The teasing is an act of disciplinary power: it lets the student know that he has done something wrong, something out of step with cultural norms.

Disciplinary power is everywhere. For example, no laws prohibit men from becoming dental hygienists or public school teachers, but 99 percent of dental hygienists and 73 percent of public school teachers are female.[45] Likewise, there are no laws against women being dentists or public school principals, but only 16.6 percent of dentists and 34.5 percent of principals are female.[46] Disciplinary power explains these staggeringly sex-segregated statistics. Men are teased, prodded, advised, encouraged, mentored, and (financially) supported into dentistry and principalships; women are teased, prodded, advised, encouraged, mentored, and (not financially) supported into careers as dental hygienists and teachers. Disciplinary power is communicated through our daily interactions.

One prominent form of disciplinary power is **gender roles,** which are *(1) cultural assumptions of what men and women are* (for example, men are rational, women are emotional, and so on); *(2) cultural expectations for how men and women should behave* (for example, men should have full-time jobs outside the home, women should be very present at home, especially when they have young children, and so on); *and (3) cultural norms for men and women's roles within society* (for example, men are principals and dentists, women are teachers and dental hygienists, and so on). Gender roles echo across culture, constantly showing up in mass media, entertainment, hiring and promotion strategies, mentoring relationships, advertising stereotypes, religious teachings, self-help books, family structures, and fashion standards. Feminist communication critics often study how public discourse establishes cultural assumptions about gender.

Feminist theorist Judith Butler explains that gender is a performance.[47] Her perspective calls attention to the way people's actions (how we dress, move, talk, interact, and so on) constitute gender. Gender is not like a tree or computer: there is no "thing" we can point to and say "that's gender!" Instead, there are only behaviors, actions—performances—that people live out in society. We can see gender when people wear pink or blue, cross their legs while sitting, or throw a football, but apart from people's actions, there is no gender.

One of Butler's key insights is that gender is not natural. There is nothing about a female body that would naturally entail putting on mascara or preferring a job as a dental hygienist instead of as a dentist. Similarly, there is nothing about a male body that would naturally cause one to wear a baseball cap or prefer a job as a dentist instead of as a dental hygienist. Butler further demonstrates how unnatural gender is by noting that it is performed differently in different cultures. If gender (how we act) were caused by our bodies there would be no cultural differences: around the globe, every female would act the same and every male would act the same. Cultural differences are evidence that gender is constructed by each culture and performed by individual people—not caused by chromosomes or genitalia.

Butler's explanation of gender as a performance emphasizes that gender is something we do—it is communicated through our clothing, actions, body language, and speech. Accordingly, feminist communication critics often focus on how gender is performed and how those performances are interpreted in public discourse. When individuals fail to perform their gender as their culture expects, they typically experience some form of discipline. In best-case scenarios, someone might tease, chide, or mock them. In more punitive scenarios, they might be passed over for a hiring or promotion, socially ostracized, or publicly shamed. In worst-case scenarios, they might be beaten, raped, or murdered.

Within feminist theories, power itself is often considered a fairly ubiquitous fact of life: power exists. It exists in knowledge, in eloquence, in relationships, in organizations, in social structures, in government systems, and so on. Having power is not bad. Having more power than someone else is not bad either. After all, both the president and provost of my college hold considerably more power in my institution than I do, and this is right and fitting—the president's and provost's experience, expertise, and vision qualify them for these powerful positions. Power only becomes a problem when it is wielded to dominate and control others.

Feminist theorist bell hooks urges us to **use power for mutuality** instead of domination, which means *interacting with others in a way that emphasizes mutual growth and flourishing.*[48] Within relationships, institutions, and society, hooks urges us to champion each other's growth and development instead of exclusively focusing on what benefits ourselves and trying to control others in order to benefit ourselves. Mutuality is giving support instead of demanding respect, an orientation of love and well-being instead of a self-concerned attitude of suspicion and derision. Feminist rhetorical scholars Sonja Foss and Karen Foss argue that as a movement to end sexism, feminism is not just moving "away from something" bad, but "moving toward" something good: mutuality.[49] Feminist scholars often study women's lives to offer glimpses of what mutuality can look like and theorize broader ways to organize society around mutuality.[50]

Feminism works to end the oppression of women and queer people, as well as the real-life consequences sexism has on women, men, and nonbinary people. Feminist theory provides an understanding of the complexity of intersecting discrimination, unearned advantages, the functioning of power in both top-down and bottom-up systems, and ways in which mutuality can lead to flourishing relations of power. Feminist criticism challenges the assumptions, biases, practices, and sexist ideology that oppress women. It is particularly useful when critics work to (1) document women's real-life experiences, (2) analyze how sexism—including intersecting discrimination, unearned advantages, and power structures—works in a given instance and how it affects people, and (3) reveal communication strategies that model mutuality.[51]

PARTICIPATING IN FEMINIST IDEOLOGICAL CRITIQUE

As an ideological critique, feminist criticism coheres around political goals that inform how critics approach texts. Specifically, the feminist goals to live out mutuality, to recognize the complexity of intersectional identities in order to counter the interlocking nature of oppression, and to embrace ethical uses of power lead to three key principles that shape feminist criticism. These principles are fundamentally feminist—they are derived from feminist politics and utilized by feminist critics. Feminist critics, however, see these principles as hallmarks not only of good feminist criticism but of all good criticism, principles that partner well with other methods and modes of rhetorical criticism—such as narrative criticism, genre criticism, and metaphor criticism. Feminist critics invite all rhetorical critics to practice these principles, which we believe improve the quality and utility of all rhetorical criticism. To understand how to participate in feminist ideological critique, we will first work through these three key principles and then review the types of research questions feminist critics often ask.

The Principle of Mutuality

The **principle of mutuality** means that *as critics think about, interact with, analyze, and write about a text, they emphasize the humanity surrounding the text:* real people said these words, directed this film, watched this television episode, and so on. This principle promotes a "golden-rule" approach to the text: do unto the text as you would have done unto you. The idea is to be respectful—even generous—when working with texts.

Literary critic Alan Jacobs describes this principle as "intelligent charity."[52] Essentially, feminist critics, like all critics, should be "faithful" to a text, first, by representing it well (rather than exaggerating it or taking pieces out of context—see Appendix B), and second, by having faith in the "answerability" of a text.[53] To consider a text "answerable" brings us back to the idea of recognizing the humanity of the text: by conducting feminist criticism, we answer the text's surrounding humanity, joining it in conversation. Here, we think of the text's surrounding humanity as conversation partners, as people who want an answer—a response—and who deserve human dignity.

A feminist approach, like other approaches to rhetorical criticism, should neither attempt to obliterate a text nor dispassionately dissect and display it like a bug collection. These approaches embody a spirit of domination. To obliterate a text (treating it as stupid and its audience as idiots or dupes) or to dismantle it dispassionately is to dominate the text and its surrounding humanity, positioning yourself as superior to the text, its creators, and its audience. Instead, feminist criticism urges us to be good to texts—even when they are not good texts. Even when texts operate through domination, feminist criticism operates through mutuality. This does not mean pretending texts that are sexist are not, or that the sexism of a text does not matter, or that a lousy text is eloquent. Such pretenses would be unfaithful to the text by misrepresenting it. Moreover, feminist critics do not tiptoe around issues or ignore problems. Instead, the principle of mutuality means that feminist critics engage with a text by working for the good of the people who surround that text.

This principle suffuses feminist critics' entire approach to their analyses. It specifically affects how feminist critics choose which texts to analyze and the tone in which they write. By foregrounding the idea of being in conversation with the surrounding humanity of a text, the principle guides critics as they select which texts they want to analyze. Feminist critics tend to think more in terms of whom they want to talk with and which cultural conversations they want to join, rather than simply which texts catch their eyes, are the most popular, or are the most eloquent. By foregrounding the humanity surrounding the text and enacting mutuality in relationships, feminist critics are particularly attuned to the tone they use when writing. When experts write, their tone often reflects their expertise and authority; this is true of feminist criticism, yet feminist critics also strive to reflect a sense of human dignity and respect throughout their writing.

The Principle of Reflexivity

Feminist critics recognize that everyone has **positionality:** *specific beliefs, knowledge, values, and political goals that develop over the course of one's life based on one's experiences in society.*[54] The word "positionality" employs a helpful spatial metaphor to suggest that people are located in different positions and therefore see the world in different ways. For example, imagine people standing on different floors of a skyscraper: those positioned on lower floors might see into a neighboring building and therefore know about the lives of office workers in that building; others positioned on a higher floor might look down on busy roads and therefore know the city's complicated traffic patterns; finally, those positioned on the roof might have a thorough knowledge of cloud formations and wind patterns. The people know about different aspects of the city because they are positioned in different places. This hypothetical example focuses on only one aspect of positionality (what floor of the building a person is standing on), but people's real lives have nuanced and complex positionalities because we all have intersectional identities and a wide range of life experiences.

Feminist critics openly proclaim that a critic's positionality is an important factor in the analysis and interpretation of a text. The **principle of reflexivity** means that *critics consider how their own intersectional identities, positionality, political goals, and experiences shape their research.*[55] This principle shapes feminist criticism in two ways.

First, critics consider how their positionality affects their interpretations. This means that you think about how your intersectional identity and life experiences might predispose you to certain interpretive assumptions or create blind spots where you overlook possible interpretations of a text. For example, R. City's song "Locked Away" opens by featuring Adam Levine plaintively crooning as he asks a woman whether she will still love him if he loses everything and becomes incarcerated. A White, female, middle-class, straight, protestant, feminist critic might hear those opening lines and condemn this love song as sexist, as trying to shame women into blindly loving grievous criminals, on the basis of her assumptions that the court and prison systems are bulwarks of justice and that only violent crimes result in incarceration. This assumption, in turn, rests on the White, female, middle-class, straight, protestant, feminist critic's experiences (and lack thereof) with the court and prison systems.

By practicing reflexivity, however, this critic would interrogate her interpretation of the song, considering why she assumed that only violent criminals were incarcerated and then tracing that assumption back to her experiences within White, middle-class, straight, protestant communities. She might realize that she had a blind spot: that she is not well acquainted with how R. City's singers/songwriters Theron Thomas (known as Uptown AP) and Timothy Thomas (known as A.I.) might understand incarceration. Recognizing her blind spot, she would begin to research incarceration in the United States, and learn that the incarceration rate has recently quadrupled—leaping from approximately 500,000 in 1980 to over 2.2 million in 2015.[56] This rate is at odds with the rate of violent crime in the United States, which has been declining since the 1990s. Analyzing the FBI's annual reports of serious crimes, the Pew Research Center's editor John Gramlich reports that the national violent crime rate "fell 49% between 1993 and 2017," meaning we currently have approximately half the violent crime that we had in 1993 but four times as many incarcerations.[57] Pressing further, the critic would find that racism affects law enforcement and sentencing. For example, "African Americans and whites use drugs at similar rates," but the "imprisonment rate of African Americans for drug charges is almost 6 times that of whites."[58] Following this research, the critic would then reevaluate her initial interpretation, considering that the love song's opening question likely does not ask women to love violent criminals blindly, but rather reflects a reality in which racial disparities have led to one in fifteen adult Black men being incarcerated in the United States.[59] Through reflexivity, the critic would then reinterpret the song as much less sexist, and far more engaged with criminal justice reform than she had previously considered.

Second, feminist critics reflexively approach their research by being clear about their "goals and political commitments" in their analyses.[60] Feminist critics, first, recognize that their arguments have power; second, are up front about their political commitments and how those political commitments shape and motivate their analyses; and third, clearly highlight the real-world, political relevance of their analyses.

As a form of ideological critique, feminist criticism is fundamentally concerned with "the distribution of power."[61] Feminist critics reflexively approach their research by recognizing that they "participate in those power moves" and therefore ought to be aware of their "political and ethical choices" as they develop their arguments, target specific audiences, and produce their critical essays.[62] Ultimately, the principle of reflexivity encourages critics to offset their own limitations (interrogating their assumptions and working to counteract their blind spots) and to recognize the power—and therefore the moral and political importance—of their own argumentation.

The Principle of Agency

Agency refers to *a person's capacity to act—to make decisions with real-world effects* (discussed in Chapter 4). The **principle of agency** means that *critics recognize their own role (agency) in shaping a text.* Feminist critic Bonnie Dow explains this principle using Christopher Columbus as an example. When Columbus landed in the Bahamas in 1492, he declared that he had discovered a New World. This "New World" was quite obviously already occupied: he encountered many people. Regardless, he renamed the land and "thus began the construction of a myth of origins for the Americas."[63] This self-proclaimed discovery earned him an enduring legacy. Many states in the United States continue to celebrate Columbus Day. His version of the story is routinely told in elementary schools and throughout mass media entertainment. But although Columbus encountered something absolutely real (land), he seized a "discursive opportunity" when he claimed to have "discovered" something, claimed it was a "new" land, and named it the "New World."[64]

Similarly, a critic may encounter something absolutely real (a text) and then, in analyzing that text, claim to have discovered something, to offer a new interpretation or insight. The critic might even rename the text or some function of how it operates in society. Much like Columbus, critics often claim that we are discovering, exploring, investigating, and examining texts when in fact we are discursively constructing them. Essentially, even though texts exist in their own right (they are real), how we talk about them (and write about them) matters. How Columbus talked about the land he encountered absolutely mattered, it shaped how European society understood and interacted with that land, leading to the next several decades of conquest, colonization, and genocide. Similarly, although critics encounter something real (the text), how we talk about it matters. We have agency. Through our discourse—our analyses—we can fundamentally shape how others understand and interact with texts.

The principle of agency guides feminist critics to acknowledge their own authority and artistry. Criticism is authoritative because it establishes meaning.

It is artistic because it is a creative process of interpretation and argumentation. When critics recognize their agency—their authority and artistry—it "opens up significant ethical and philosophical issues" that are not obvious when they ignore their agency, thinking that they only "discover" meaning in the text.[65]

For example, imagine analyzing the 1848 Declaration of Sentiments, a document modeled after the Declaration of Independence in which a wide coalition of individuals advocated for women's rights, including suffrage. If you simply explore the text and report your discoveries, your ethical and philosophical burden is quite light: you owe your conversation partners (your readers) very little beyond an honest description of the Declaration of Sentiments. However, if you recognize your agency, then you must consider the ethics and philosophical considerations of your analysis and argumentation. Specifically, because you have authority and because the argument you develop is essentially a work of art, you bear a responsibility to "move," to "interest," and to help your readers think and act in ethical ways.[66] Accordingly, it is ethically and philosophically incumbent upon you to create an analysis of the Declaration of Sentiments that—in addition to representing the document honestly—makes it relevant to people's current lives, helps them imagine ways to think, speak, and act in effective and morally good ways, and eloquently motivates people into those moral choices.

Ultimately, the principle of agency foregrounds the civic and social relevance of criticism. This principle stems directly from feminism's goal to end sexism and its commitment to use power in morally ethical ways. The political motivations of feminism clearly shape this critical approach, urging critics to emphasize the civic and social relevance of their analyses and to demonstrate how people can make morally good decisions. This principle is foundational to feminist ideological critique, but it is also broadly applicable—virtually all critics benefit from holding themselves accountable to (1) make the text and their argumentation relevant to people's current lives, (2) help people imagine how to think, speak, and act in effective and moral ways, and (3) persuasively motivate people toward moral choices.

Asking Feminist Questions of the Text

In addition to enacting the principles of mutuality, reflexivity, and agency, feminist ideological critiques tend to ask certain types of research questions. Research questions derived from prompts such as those outlined below can help critics focus on projects that resist and disrupt sexism.

Feminist critics often ask what women's lives are really like. They work with texts that document women's lives, often analyzing women's speeches, novels, and art. For example, feminist critic Karlyn Kohrs Campbell analyzed the rhetoric of the women's liberation movement (what we now think of as feminism during the 1960s and 1970s), essentially asking, "How do women speak when advocating for their own liberation?"[67] By studying what women's lives are really like, feminist critics can demonstrate how sexism affects women and how women think, speak, and act in creative, effective ways to survive and resist sexism.

Feminist critics often ask how sexism operates hegemonically to affect people. They often work with texts that are widely popular cultural productions, such as films, television series, music, novels, and widely circulated speeches. They also often work with texts that shape the laws and policies of a society, such as judicial rulings, legislation, and political speeches. For example, feminist critic Tasha Dubriwny analyzed how women's health is represented in media such as popular "blogs, memoirs, advertisements, and news."[68] In this award-winning analysis, Dubriwny persuasively argues that media sources discuss US women in ways that individualize women: each woman fights her own battle and each woman is asked to manage her own problems by altering her lifestyle.[69] Rather than positioning women as a collective and connecting women's health to larger social issues (such as access to health insurance), this discourse individualizes women and distances them from collectively lobbying for better (and more affordable) health care. By studying how sexism hegemonically infuses a culture and operates throughout a community, feminist critics demonstrate what sexism is, what it is doing, and how it acts upon our world. Their analyses work to end sexism by helping us see it so that we can resist it.

Feminist critics often ask what rhetorics of mutuality can look like in society. These critics often work with texts that directly espouse or model feminist ideology. For example, Niyi Akingbe and Christopher Babatunde Ogunyemi analyzed popular novels by Nigerian female writers—such as Chimamanda Ngozi Adichie's *Purple Hibiscus*—arguing that these narratives help Nigerians (and people more broadly) reimagine family roles and socioeconomic roles in ways that help men live without dominating others and help women step into assertive lifestyles that maintain robust connections to social and spiritual traditions.[70]

Critics also consider what rhetorics of mutuality can look like by analyzing and theorizing from texts that reflect women's and minorities' rhetorical styles, knowledge, or communities. For example, Sonja K. Foss and Cindy L. Griffin theorize how society can use language for mutual flourishing. They draw on women's speech and conversational patterns to demonstrate how women invite others into this mutual flourishing.[71] They describe this type of rhetoric as "invitational rhetoric."[72]

RESEARCH EXAMPLES

The following research examples demonstrate the utility and versatility of feminist ideological critiques. In the first example, Kathryn M. Olson analyzes the animated Disney film *Beauty and the Beast,* focusing on how Beast's violent acts toward Belle are explained and justified to the child character, Chip. In the second example, Erica B. Edwards and Jennifer Esposito analyze an Instagram photo that went viral. These examples demonstrate how critics practice feminist ideological critique even as they draw on other methods: Olson draws upon the Aristotelian genre of epideictic rhetoric to analyze *Beauty and the Beast.* Edwards and Esposito's article offers a gateway example to our next chapter, on audience rhetoric. The third example showcases how critics can demonstrate what rhetorics of mutuality can look like: Andre Favors analyzes transgender activist Laverne Cox's rhetoric, identifying specific rhetorical strategies that Cox uses successfully.

Kathryn M. Olson
"An Epideictic Dimension of Symbolic Violence in Disney's *Beauty and the Beast:* Inter-Generational Lessons in Romanticizing and Tolerating Intimate Partner Violence" (2013)*

The story of Belle and Beast is an enduringly popular fairytale with many tellings and retellings. Disney's animated version is undoubtedly the most popular version in the United States, yet it is a radical departure from the early versions of this story. For example, in Madame Le Prince de Beaumont's 1757 version, written as a story to improve girls' morality and reinforce their intellect and education, both the Beast and Belle have important life lessons to learn as they develop morally.[73] In contrast, Disney's animated version significantly shortens Belle's role, eliminates her moral development, and changes the story from a dialogue-driven plot in which Beast and Belle "eat dinner together every night" into a romance driven by violence and made humorous by the invention of an "enchanted household staff."[74]

To analyze this film, Olson draws on the Aristotelian concept of epideictic rhetoric, a genre of rhetoric that praises what a culture considers praiseworthy, and blames or denounces what a culture considers blameworthy or objectionable (as discussed in Chapter 5). Epideictic discourse reinforces or celebrates cultural values.

Analyzing Disney's *Beauty and the Beast,* Olson is particularly concerned with the enchanted household staff's epideictic speech and actions as they help the child teacup, Chip, make sense of Beast's violence toward Belle. And Beast *is* violent toward Belle: he forces her to promise to never leave him, imprisons her in his home, separates her from her family, and controls her access to food. (When Belle refuses to join him for dinner, Beast yells at her "Fine! Then go ahead and starve!" and then tells the staff, "If she doesn't eat with me, she doesn't eat at all.") Beast spies on Belle (using the magic mirror), yells at her, and threatens her. He breaks objects in an uncontrolled rage and blames his outbursts on Belle's stubbornness.[75] Despite this violence toward Belle, and despite how scared the household staff is of Beast (they regularly recoil from him in fear), the household staff coaxes Belle to interact with Beast, asking her to "give him a chance" and claiming that he is "not so bad once you get to know him."[76]

Throughout the film, Chip is learning about love as he watches Beast and Belle interact. He explicitly asks, "Are they gonna live happily ever after, Mama?" as the film concludes, demonstrating his active interest in their romance. Mrs. Potts responds "Of course, my dear," cementing the magic and romance of this story by confirming its fairytale ending. Olson's analysis suggests that as the household staff prod Belle into this romance and encourage her to see beyond Beast's violence, the film encourages viewers to "overlook, excuse, or romanticize not only isolated acts but *patterns* of intimate partner violence" that "bode ill in real-life relationships."[77] Rather than blaming or denouncing Beast's violence, the staff's epideictic discourse excuses it; moreover, as the staff praises the romance between Beast and Belle, this epideictic discourse frames their troubled relationship as praiseworthy. The adult

---

*This essay can be found in *Quarterly Journal of Speech* 99, no. 4 (2013): 448–480.

characters witness the "danger signs" in Chip's presence, yet their behavior and comments repeatedly "convey lessons to Chip, and so to viewers" that "one should accept, enable, and romanticize a relationship that exhibits repeated signs of intimate partner violence rather than intervene or discourage it."[78]

Throughout this analysis, Olson demonstrates how sexism has seeped into US entertainment—even children's entertainment. She enacts the principle of mutuality, engaging with the humanity surrounding *Beauty and the Beast* (its audience members) and helping us recognize and resist sexist relational violence in the real world. Specifically, she explains two different forms of relational violence: expressive aggression, in which someone acts in dangerously angry ways, and coercive control, in which someone controls another person by isolating them from friends and family and keeping track of their whereabouts and movement. Olson explains Lenore Walker's psychological theory of relational violence as a three-part cycle that moves from tension (the aggressor becomes increasingly hostile and the victim attempts to placate the aggressor), to violence (which could be psychological or physical and might manifest as either expressive aggression or coercive control), and then to "loving-contrition" (the aggressor often apologizes and shows kindness to the victim).[79] This cycle of relational violence repeats as the couple moves back into the first phase of mounting tension.

Erica B. Edwards and Jennifer Esposito "Reading the Black Woman's Body via Instagram Fame" (2018)*

Patrice Brown, a Black woman, took a photo of herself while at work—teaching in a fourth-grade classroom—and posted it to Instagram. She posed for the photo by smiling and making the two-fingered peace sign with each hand. She wore a tight, pink, crew-neck dress and nude heels, and styled her hair in long waves.[80] In the photo, Brown looks happy, comfortable, and excited to teach.

In response, the internet—and the news media—exploded in a public debate, using the hashtag #teacherbae. One side shamed Brown for her attire, claiming it was unprofessional because it could cause students to be distracted by her body. The other side celebrated her choice of dress as a mark of her empowerment and saw the photo as proof of Brown's refusal to be ashamed of her curves. Some people even suggested that being "sexy" made her a better teacher by drawing her students' attention.[81] In response to the controversy, the school district for which Brown works publicly reprimanded her, required her to submit to some form of supervision, and then announced that she was cooperating by improving her social media presence.[82] Brown deleted the photo—along with many others—from her Instagram account and temporarily made her account private.

Analyzing Instagram as a site of cultural production and the discourse surrounding this photo, Erica Edwards and Jennifer Esposito foreground intersectionality and Black feminist theory in their critique. Edwards and Esposito do not reprint the photo—which would continue the dehumanization that Brown experienced in the public debate—because their analysis is not about passing

---

*This essay may be found in *Communication, Culture & Critique* 11, no. 3 (2018): 341–358.

judgment on Brown's attire. Rather than focusing readers' attention on Brown's body and clothing, Edwards and Esposito focus their analytical gaze—and thus their readers' attention—on the discourse surrounding the photo. They examine the hegemonic processes of Instagram as a site of cultural production and analyze the ideology at work in the ways people judged this photo in their public comments.

Edwards and Esposito note that although Instagram appears as a free leisure activity, it provides jobs not only for Instagram's employees, but also for Instagram users with over five thousand followers. These users, known as "influencers," typically attract sponsors who pay them to showcase products in their photos—thus influencing their followers, who function as the influencers' "customers."[83] To maintain their profitability, then, influencers must "sell" what customers—their followers—want. Edwards and Esposito explain that within a White supremacist capitalist patriarchy, women who wish to profit by selling their images must present glamorous images that are hyperfeminine and hypersexualized. The authors also note that ideas of femininity and sexiness are racialized. When they wrote their analysis, Brown had 315,000 followers—a substantial following that is many times the popularity typically needed to attract sponsors.[84] Brown's Instagram account clearly showcases her body and participates in the racialized hyperfemininity routinely seen in female Instagram influencers' accounts.[85]

Edwards and Esposito offer a thorough analysis of Brown's Instagram account, explaining that they conducted their analysis in order to see how Brown presents herself, and thus to humanize Brown rather than continue to objectify her by treating her as if she were only the controversial photo.[86] Although Brown presents herself as an influencer, she foregrounds her qualifications as a teacher (she has both a bachelor's degree and a master's degree), her passion for teaching, and her politics.[87] She uses her account to support her students and their school: she promotes her students, artistically documenting their learning, requesting donors (successfully) to support their learning, and thanking community members for their donations of classroom equipment and their participation in her career days.[88] Additionally, as she engages in politics regarding education policies, she promotes herself in ways that demonstrate confidence in her leadership as well as in her race and sex. For example, in one photo, Brown wore a T-shirt featuring a quotation by Senator Maxine Waters that says, "I am a STRONG BLACK WOMAN. I cannot be intimidated, and I'm not going anywhere!"[89] Edwards and Esposito work to humanize Brown—to see her as she presents herself, rather than seeing only her body and debating the "appropriateness" or "empowerment" of her attire.

When analyzing the comments made on this viral photo and in the broader media debate that criticized Brown as "too sexy," Edwards and Esposito foreground their own positionality to clarify the ways in which Brown is being held to standards of White femininity. Specifically, Edwards notes that "as a Black woman," she understands how "difficult it is to make [her] body 'acceptable' according to standards of White femininity."[90] She details the difficulties of finding "professional" clothes that fit her body and that are comfortable and not produced through the exploitive labor of other women of color. She specifically notes that she finds the cut and material of body-con dresses (which is what Brown wears in the photo) comfortable.[91] Similarly, Esposito identifies herself as "a Latina with curves" and describes a workplace encounter in which her pencil skirt was described by a colleague as something men "must love looking at" while she instructs college courses.[92] Essentially, while wearing the gold standard of feminine professional attire—a pencil skirt—Esposito nonetheless found her body sexually objectified. The admonishing response to Brown's attire, the authors note, disciplines Brown for the visibility of her body, while ignoring the fact that professional clothing in the United States is primarily designed for slim White women's bodies and that "women of color's bodies are often hypersexualized" regardless of what they are wearing.[93] Essentially, those who shame Brown for her clothing are using standards of "professionalism" that are rooted in both White supremacy and sexism.[94]

Analyzing the discourse that celebrates Brown's clothing as empowered, Edwards and Esposito question this perspective by suggesting that empowerment and self-objectification are not the same. Although women often find pleasure in wearing clothing that heterosexual men find attractive, the decision to wear "sexy" clothing is usually not exclusively based on a woman's own experiences of pleasure. Edwards and Esposito link back to the economic profitability of Instagram accounts and the more general ways in which women showcase their heterosexual attractiveness in order to obtain goodwill, goods, and services that patriarchal men would otherwise refuse them. Moreover, as a Black woman, Brown's sexuality is culturally fraught in the United States because of racist myths and stereotypes of exoticism and hypersexuality.

Both sides of the debate assess Brown and her attire from White supremacist and patriarchal perspectives, and thus both sides demand something impossible from Brown. The side that admonishes her for her "sexy" attire implies that there is professional clothing that could somehow hide Brown's curves—and that those curves must be hidden in order for Brown to be "professional." But this is impossible: Brown is a real person with a real body that she must clothe every day. Her body does not fit clothing designed for slim White women—which is the only clothing deemed "professional" for women in the United States. Moreover, due to hegemonic racism, Black women's bodies are often hypersexualized in public discourse regardless of their attire—which means Brown could have worn a pencil skirt and still been accused of dressing unprofessionally.

Similarly, those who celebrated the "sexiness" of Brown's dress assumed her choice was entirely free and reflected only Brown's pleasure.[95] Edwards and Esposito point out, however, that as long as we live in a "white supremacist capitalist patriarchy," Brown's choices (and other women's choices) will never be pure reflections of women's pleasure. Instead, women negotiate their pleasure in relation to the risks and rewards inherent in that patriarchy. Whether shaming Brown or championing her, both sides of this public debate defined Brown by her body rather than seeing her as a person.[96]

Throughout their analysis, Edwards and Esposito purposefully focus on an everyday facet of life—a viral photo and a social media debate. By choosing this text, Edwards and Esposito focus on the day-to-day realities of "Black sexual politics" and demonstrate how structures (Instagram economies, heterosexism, patriarchy, White supremacy) operate within our day-to-day realties—such as Instagram posts.[97] Their analysis directly reveals how hegemony works. Brown's

Instagram account is a crucial source of income, yet to be popular on Instagram requires that Brown discipline her body into racialized performances of hyper-femininity that influence other women to spend money and time discipling their bodies into racialized heterosexual beauty standards.

This is the essence of hegemony: women's empowerment is achieved through their sexualized self-objectification—which ultimately further reinforces sexism. It's one step forward and two steps back. Moreover, there is no coercion, force, or top-down power; women watch themselves (and watch influencers' Instagram accounts), thus enacting what Foucault described as "disciplinary power."[98] Women "choose" this lifestyle and become their own disciplinarians. In the short term, the benefits may outweigh the costs; Edwards and Esposito acknowledge that while living in a "white supremacist capitalist patriarchy," dressing according to its standards may be some women's best option. However, they caution that this choice ultimately reinforces rather than resists the dominant ideology.

Andre Favors
"Coming Out as a Transgender Advocate: Laverne Cox, Intersectional Rhetoric, and Intersectionality" (2016)*

Media depictions of people who are transgendered often focus on the "transition and surgery of the trans body," creating a spectacle of transgender people.[99] For example, in 2018 the cable channel *TLC* began to air a reality TV program, *Lost in Transition,* that chronicles four people's transitions.[100] Although such media attention may seek to demystify transgenderism, feminist and queer critics argue that by focusing exclusively on transitions, it reduces transgender people to "the genital question."[101]

Analyzing the way Laverne Cox rejects these reductionist and sensationalist frameworks of transgender people, Andre Favors identifies key elements of Cox's activism that successfully "shift the terrain on transgender issues" and build a "coalitional" social movement.[102] First, Favors notes how Cox uses a multimodal approach to her activism. Cox is best known as an actor from *Orange is the New Black,* but she has purposefully stepped beyond her acting career to address the public as a transgender activist. She speaks across the country, participates in media interviews, writes for national publications such as *The New York Times,* and actively participates in multiple social media platforms (Twitter, Instagram, and so on). A documentary she cocreated, *Free CeCe,* streams on Amazon Prime.[103] Through her multimodal activism, she not only reaches a wide audience, she places "speech, embodiment, and image" on what Darrell Enck-Wanzer considers "relatively equal footing.[104] Favors argues that Cox's activism seizes the different opportunities these different types of communication can afford, and also that her activism is open and equitable—it refuses to privilege one type of communication but instead embraces all forms freely.

Second, Favors notes that Cox's "approach" to activism is "non-leader-centered."[105] Cox does not set herself up as the leader of transgender activism.

*This essay may be found in *Journal of Contemporary Rhetoric* 6, no. 1/2 (2016): 15–22.

Instead, she chooses to speak "alongside other trans women of color," and to appear with other transgender activists at media events instead of going alone.[106] She consistently tells audiences about other activists' work, featuring their efforts and giving them credit.[107] Moreover, she situates current transgender activism within histories of feminist, queer, abolitionist, antiracist, and civil rights activism: she tells audiences about the work of activists who have gone before her, from Sojourner Truth to bell hooks.[108] Favors demonstrates that by refusing to "lead" the transgender movement, Cox builds a coalition of activists, thus broadening and strengthening the movement.

And third, Favors analyzes the way in which Cox and the people with whom she advocates shift the conversation toward "the violence and injustice that occurs to marginalized bodies."[109] Cox repeatedly drives the conversation back to the crimes committed against transgender people. As reported by Jamie Wareham, a journalist writing in Forbes Magazine, in 2008 the Transrespect Versus Transphobia Worldwide organization began releasing a report on all homicides of "gender diverse" individuals.[110] As of 2019, the organization had "recorded 3,314 deaths."[111] In 2019 alone, at least twenty-two "transgender killings" occurred in the United States—and the vast majority of those killed were black women.[112] When Cox speaks, she draws attention to these hate crimes and recenters the conversation on how "we create a culture where we love trans women."[113] Rather than letting interviewers or news anchors focus on transitioning, she reframes the conversation to focus on "the harm and abuse committed upon the bodies of transgender women."[114]

Ultimately, Favors identifies these rhetorical strategies as key aspects of Cox's "successful approach" to shifting the public discourse surrounding "trans and queer" persons.[115] Favors models how feminist criticism can showcase what rhetorics of mutuality can look like. Cox's multimodal, non-leader-centered approach, and her ability to shift the conversation toward ending hate and hate crimes provide a clear blueprint for how social movements can prioritize mutuality through their rhetoric.

STRENGTHS AND WEAKNESSES OF FEMINIST IDEOLOGICAL CRITIQUE

Feminist ideological critique is designed to change lives by making arguments that matter in society. It aims to help readers recognize the pernicious effects of sexism, reject sexist ideology in their own thinking and in society more broadly, and cultivate mutuality instead. For critics who are concerned with what women's lives are like, how sexism affects people, and what communication strategies can foster mutuality instead of domination, feminist ideological critique is an excellent mode of rhetorical criticism. Moreover, because feminist criticism pairs with other methods and critical approaches, it offers a particularly nuanced mode of analysis.

Feminist ideological critique is predominantly concerned with women's lives. To some, this focus might feel like a weakness or limitation because it only concerns the lives of one-half of the world's population. To some extent, however, feminist criticism is a necessary corrective to the ways in which other methods and critical approaches tend to focus only on men's lives. Consider that the vast majority of politicians are male; the vast majority of popular authors are male; the vast majority of news anchors, news editors, and nationally ranking journalists are male; the vast majority of television and film writers, directors, producers, and camerapersons are male; the vast majority of lines in films and television are spoken by male actors; the vast majority of pastors are male; the vast majority of record label executives are male; and so on. As a result, the vast majority of critical analyses focus on texts made by men and is concerned with only one-half of the world's population: men. Within this frame of reference, feminist criticism's insistence that women's lives matter and are worthy of rhetorical analysis is less exclusionary and more of a necessary corrective.

CHOOSING THIS APPROACH

So how do you know whether you should use feminist criticism to interpret a particular piece of public discourse? To answer this question, you need to consider your text, its context, and the research question motivating your analysis.

First, consider your text. Does your text document the lives of women, queer, trans, and/or other nonbinary people? Or demonstrate the pervasiveness of sexism and its effects? Or reveal a way people can live in mutuality with one another? If not, then this text is unlikely to warrant a feminist analysis.

Second, consider the humanity, the human context, surrounding your text. Is there a clear community, audience, or public connected to your text? Here, you need to consider with whom you would engage in conversation (either hypothetical or real) as you analyze the text. Because feminist criticism is designed to be socially useful, critics often work with texts that already have either considerable audiences or deeply committed audiences, or, alternatively, that they can make relevant to specific communities.

And third, consider your own research motives. Do you want to understand women's and/or nonbinary lives better? Are you interested in understanding how sexism works in culture? Are you intrigued by communication strategies that aim at mutuality instead of domination? Are you working to expand how rhetoricians understand what rhetoric is and what counts as rhetoric? Feminist criticism is particularly suited to answering research questions that stem from such concerns. Also, consider whether you are you willing to (1) submit your research process to the demands (and humility) of reflexivity, (2) submit your writing style to the demands of mutuality (generosity, faithfulness, respectfulness, and so on), and (3) submit the entirety of your research efforts to the responsibility of social engagement.

Ultimately, feminist criticism works to end sexism while modeling mutuality. This mode of analysis pairs well with other rhetorical approaches, creating nuanced, socially engaged analyses. As a feminist critic, I think of this mode of analysis as an oxygen mask in an airplane with a slow leak. Because the plane is depressurizing slowly, most of the occupants don't notice and can't be bothered to put a mask on—after all, the masks are uncomfortable and seem irrelevant. But those who use the masks find they can breathe—and therefore think—more clearly. Looking around the cabin and seeing their drowsy, oxygen-deprived neighbors, these individuals find a moral necessity to persuade others to use their masks too.

Though a little dramatic, this analogy describes feminist criticism: feminism may seem uncomfortable and outmoded, but using feminist criticism helps you make sense of this world—recognizing its dangerously low oxygen levels—and reveals the moral necessity of working to end sexism by socially and civically engaging with others.

DISCUSSION QUESTIONS

1. List six of your identities (sex, race, ethnicity, class, national origin, physical ability, mental ability, sexuality, popularity, ideology, religion, and so on). Now explore how those identities intersect by describing how one of them shapes your experiences of the others.
2. Think about a friend, family member, or coworker. List and explain an unearned advantage that person has. Is that advantage positive (a good thing everyone should have access to) or negative (a bad thing no one should have the power to do)? Now consider your own life, and list and explain an unearned advantage you have. Is that advantage positive or negative?
3. Explain a situation (from real life or from a film, television show, or novel), where you have seen disciplinary power used to make someone conform to culturally established gender roles.
4. In your own words, explain what it means to approach a text through mutuality, reflexivity, and agency. For each of these principles, list at least one concrete way that it shapes how you would do this type of criticism.

NOTES

1. Phoebe Robinson, *You Can't Touch My Hair: And Other Things I Still Have to Explain* (New York: Plume, 2016), 4.
2. Robinson, *You Can't Touch My Hair,* 4.
3. Robinson, *You Can't Touch My Hair,* 6.
4. Robinson, *You Can't Touch My Hair,* 18.
5. Ed Mazza, "John Oliver Explains Everything That's Wrong with the Miss America Pageant," Huffpost.com, September 22, 2014, https://www.huffpost.com/entry/john-oliver-miss-america_n_5859726.
6. Robinson, *You Can't Touch My Hair,* 19.
7. bell hooks, *Feminism is for Everybody: Passionate Politics* (New York: Routledge, 2015), 1.
8. Natalie Fixmer and Julia T. Wood, "The Personal is *Still* Political: Embodied Politics in Third Wave Feminism," *Women's Studies in Communication* 28, no. 2 (2005): 235–236.
9. Abigail Brooks and Sharlene Nagy Hesse-Biber, "An Invitation to Feminist Research," in *Feminist Research Practice: A Primer,* eds. Sharlene Nagy Hesse-Biber and Patricia Lina Leavy (Thousand Oaks, CA: Sage, 2007), 4.
10. Allan Johnson, "Patriarchy, the System: An It, Not a He, a Them, or an Us," in *Readings for Diversity and Social Justice,* 3rd ed., eds. Maurianne Adams, Warren Blumenfeld, Carmelita Castañeda, Heather Hackman, Madeline Peters, and Ximena Zúñiga (New York: Routledge, 2013), 334.

11. Johnson, "Patriarchy, the System," 335.
12. Rita Hardiman, Bailey Jackson, and Pat Griffin, "Conceptual Foundations," in *Readings for Diversity and Social Justice,* 3rd ed, eds. Adams et al., 27.
13. bell hooks, "Understanding Patriarchy," ImagineNoBorders.org, http://imaginenoborders.org/pdf/zines/UnderstandingPatriarchy.pdf.
14. Victoria Kerry, "The Construction of Hegemonic Masculinity in the Semiotic Landscape of a Cross Fit 'Cave,'" *Visual Communication* 16, no. 2 (2016): 212–213.
15. "National Intimate Partner and Sexual Violence Survey, 2010 Summary Report," Centers for Disease Control and Prevention, November 2011, https://www.cdc.gov/violenceprevention/pdf/nisvs_report2010-a.pdf, 43, 10.
16. "National Intimate Partner and Sexual Violence Survey," 43, 10.
17. *Partnership against Domestic Violence,* 2018, http://padv.org/.
18. Stephanie Kohlman, Amber Baig, Guy Balice, Christine DiRubbo, Linda Placencia, Kenneth Skale, Jessica Thomas, Jessica Flitter, Fereshte Mirzad, Hillary Moeckler, and Shane Aquino, "Contribution of Media to the Normalization and Perpetuation of Domestic Violence," *Austin Journal of Psychiatry and Behavioral Science* 1, no. 4 (2014): 1018.
19. Eileen Patten, "Racial, Gender Wage Gaps Persist in U.S. Despite Some Progress," Pew Center Research, July 1, 2016, https://www.pewresearch.org/fact-tank/2016/07/01/racial-gender-wage-gaps-persist-in-u-s-despite-some-progress/.
20. Patten, "Racial, Gender Wage Gap."
21. "Symptoms of a Heart Attack," *American Heart Association,* last modified 2008, https://www.goredforwomen.org/about-heart-disease/symptoms_of_heart_disease_in_women/symptoms-of-a-heart-attack/.
22. Kayla Webley Adler, "Women Are Dying because Doctors Treat Us Like Men," MarieClaire.com, April 25, 2017, https://www.marieclaire.com/health-fitness/a26741/doctors-treat-women-like-men/.
23. Adler, "Women Are Dying."
24. M. B. Roberts, "What Do Men Need to Know about Working with Women? Joanne Lipman Breaks It Down in *That's What She Said,*" Parade.com, February 9, 2018, https://parade.com/644646/m-b-roberts/what-do-men-need-to-know-about-working-with-women-joanne-lipman-breaks-it-down-in-thats-what-she-said/.
25. M. B. Roberts, "What Do Men Need to Know?"
26. Robbie Myers, "Review: That's What She Said: What Men Need to Know (and Women Need to Tell Them) about Working Together," NYTimes.com, January 30, 2018, https://www.nytimes.com/2018/01/30/books/review/joanne-lipman-thats-what-she-said-women-at-work.html.
27. Myers, "Review."
28. Katie Benner and Caitlin Dickerson, "Sessions Says Domestic and Gang Violence Are Not Grounds for Asylum," NYTimes.com, June 11, 2018, https://www.nytimes.com/2018/06/11/us/politics/sessions-domestic-violence-asylum.html.
29. Karma Chávez, "Beyond Inclusion: Rethinking Rhetoric's Historical Narrative," *Quarterly Journal of Speech* 101, no. 1 (2015): 162–172.
30. Chávez, "Beyond Inclusion," 163.
31. Patricia Hill Collins and Sirma Bilge, *Intersectionality* (Cambridge, UK: Polity, 2016).
32. Harding, "Introduction." 7.

33. Harding, "Introduction," 7.
34. Harding, "Introduction," 7.
35. Bim Adewunmi, "Kimberlé Crenshaw on Intersectionality: 'I Wanted to Come Up with an Everyday Metaphor that Anyone Could Use,'" NewStatesman.com, April 2, 2014, https://www.newstatesman.com/lifestyle/2014/04/kimberl-crenshaw-intersectionality-i-wanted-come-everyday-metaphor-anyone-could.
36. Quote from Kimberlé Crenshaw, "The Urgency of Intersectionality," TEDWomen, last modified 2016, https://www.ted.com/talks/kimberle_crenshaw_the_urgency_of_intersectionality/up-next#t-462925; see also Kimberlé Crenshaw, "Why Intersectionality Can't Wait," *The Washington Post,* September 24, 2015, https://www.washingtonpost.com/news/in-theory/wp/2015/09/24/why-intersectionality-cant-wait/?noredirect=on&utm_term=.53715d5a9896.
37. Crenshaw, "Urgency of Intersectionality."
38. Crenshaw, "Urgency of Intersectionality."
39. Crenshaw, "Urgency of Intersectionality."
40. Peggy McIntosh, "White Privilege: Unpacking the Invisible Knapsack," in *Introduction to Women's, Gender and Sexuality Studies: Interdisciplinary and Intersectional Approaches,* eds. L. Ayu Saraswati, Barbara L. Shaw, and Heather Rellihan (New York: Oxford University Press, 2018), 72–75.
41. *Time's Up,* last modified 2017, https://www.timesupnow.com/.
42. Devon Carbado, "Privilege," in *Readings for Diversity and Social Justice,* 3rd ed., 395–396.
43. Fixmer and Wood, "Personal is *Still* Political," 235.
44. Fixmer and Wood, "Personal is *Still* Political," 235–236.
45. "Affirmative Action and What It Means for Women," *National Women's Law Center,* last modified July 1, 2000, https://nwlc.org/resources/affirmative-action-and-what-it-means-women/.
46. "Affirmative Action and What it Means."
47. Judith Butler, *Gender Trouble: Feminism and the Subversion of Identity* (New York: Routledge, 1999).
48. hooks, *Feminism Is for Everyone.*
49. Sonja Foss and Karen Foss, "Our Journey to Repowered Feminism: Expanding the Feminist Toolbox," *Women's Studies in Communication* 32, no. 1 (2009): 50.
50. Karen Foss, Sonja Foss, and Cindy Griffin, eds., *Feminist Rhetorical Theories* (Thousand Oaks, CA: Sage, 1999).
51. Brooks and Hesse-Biber, "An Invitation to Feminist Research," 4.
52. Alan Jacobs, *A Theology of Reading: The Hermeneutics of Love* (Boulder, CO: Westview, 2001), 1.
53. Jacobs, *A Theology of Reading,* 63.
54. Harding, "Introduction." 9.
55. Brooks and Hesse-Biber, "An Invitation to Feminist Research," 15.
56. "Criminal Justice Fact Sheet," *NAACP,* last modified 2018, http://www.naacp.org/criminal-justice-fact-sheet/.
57. John Gramlich, "5 Facts about Crime in the U.S.," *Pew Research Center,* January 3, 2019, https://www.pewresearch.org/fact-tank/2019/01/03/5-facts-about-crime-in-the-u-s/.

58. "Criminal Justice Fact Sheet."
59. Adam Liptak, "More than 1 in 100 U.S. Adults are in Prison," NYTimes.com, February 29, 2008, https://www.nytimes.com/2008/02/29/world/americas/29iht-29prison.10561202.html.
60. Bonnie Dow, "Authority, Invention, and Context in Feminist Rhetorical Criticism," *Review of Communication* 16, no. 1 (2016): 70.
61. Dow, "Authority, Invention, and Context," 69; Sara Hayden and D. Lynn O'Brien Hallstein, "Placing Sex/Gender at the Forefront: Feminisms, Intersectionality, and Communication Studies," in *Standing in the Intersections: Feminist Voices, Feminist Practices in Communication Studies,* eds. Karma R. Chávez and Cindy Griffin (Albany, NY: SUNY Press, 2012), 97–124.
62. Dow, "Authority, Invention, and Context," 69; Hayden and O'Brien Hallstein, "Placing Sex/Gender," 97–124.
63. Bonnie Dow, "Response," *Western Journal of Communication* 65, no. 3 (2001): 336.
64. Dow, "Response," 336.
65. Dow, "Response," 339.
66. Dow, "Response," 346–347.
67. Karlyn Kohrs Campbell, "The Rhetoric of Women's Liberation: An Oxymoron," *Quarterly Journal of Speech* 59, no. 1 (1973): 74–86.
68. Tasha N. Dubriwny, *The Vulnerable Empowered Woman: Feminism, Postfeminism, and Women's Health* (New Brunswick, NJ: Rutgers University Press, 2013), 2.
69. Dubriwny, *The Vulnerable Empowered Woman,* 13.
70. Niyi Akingbe and Christopher Babatunde Ogunyemi, "Countering Masculinity: Chinua Achebe's *Things Fall Apart* and the Rise of Feminist Assertiveness in the Novels of Nigerian Female Writers," *Studia Universitatis Petru Maior: Philologia* 22 (2017): 81–93.
71. Sonja K. Foss and Cindy L. Griffin, "Beyond Persuasion: A Proposal for an Invitational Rhetoric," *Communication Monographs* 62, no. 1 (1995): 5.
72. Foss and Griffin, "Beyond Persuasion," 6.
73. Kathryn Olson, "An Epideictic Dimension of Symbolic Violence in Disney's *Beauty and the Beast:* Inter-Generational Lessons in Romanticizing and Tolerating Intimate Partner Violence," *Quarterly Journal of Speech* 99, no. 4 (2013): 451.
74. Olson, "An Epideictic Dimension of Symbolic Violence in Disney's *Beauty and the Beast,*" 451; Rick Martin, "Sexy Enough for Adults, Magical for Kids," *TV Guide,* November 16–22, 1991, 15.
75. Olson, "An Epideictic Dimension," 465–467.
76. Olson, "An Epideictic Dimension," 472.
77. Olson, "An Epideictic Dimension," 467.
78. Olson, "An Epideictic Dimension," 471.
79. Lenore Walker, *The Battered Woman Syndrome,* 2nd ed. (New York: Springer, 2000), 127.
80. Erica Edwards and Jennifer Esposito, "Reading the Black Woman's Body via Instagram Fame," *Communication, Culture & Critique* 11, no. 3 (2018): 346, 342.
81. Edwards and Esposito, "Reading the Black Woman's Body," 349.
82. Edwards and Esposito, "Reading the Black Woman's Body," 349.
83. Edwards and Esposito, "Reading the Black Woman's Body," 346.

84. Edwards and Esposito, “Reading the Black Woman’s Body,” 347.
85. Edwards and Esposito, “Reading the Black Woman’s Body,” 348.
86. Edwards and Esposito, “Reading the Black Woman’s Body,” 347.
87. Edwards and Esposito, “Reading the Black Woman’s Body,” 347.
88. Edwards and Esposito, “Reading the Black Woman’s Body,” 348.
89. Edwards and Esposito, “Reading the Black Woman’s Body,” 348.
90. Edwards and Esposito, “Reading the Black Woman’s Body,” 350.
91. Edwards and Esposito, “Reading the Black Woman’s Body,” 350.
92. Edwards and Esposito, “Reading the Black Woman’s Body,” 351.
93. Edwards and Esposito, “Reading the Black Woman’s Body,” 351.
94. Edwards and Esposito, “Reading the Black Woman’s Body,” 352.
95. Edwards and Esposito, “Reading the Black Woman’s Body,” 352.
96. Edwards and Esposito, “Reading the Black Woman’s Body,” 355.
97. Edwards and Esposito, “Reading the Black Woman’s Body,” 344.
98. Fixmer and Wood, “Personal is *Still* Political,” 235–236.
99. Andre Favors, “Coming Out as a Transgender Advocate: Laverne Cox, Intersectional Rhetoric, and Intersectionality,” *Journal of Contemporary Rhetoric* 6, no. 1/2 (2016): 15.
100. “Lost in Transition,” *TLC,* 2019, https://www.tlc.com/tv-shows/lost-in-transition/.
101. Favors, “Coming Out,” 20.
102. Favors, “Coming Out,” 15.
103. Favors, “Coming Out,” 17.
104. Darrell Enck-Wanzer, “Trashing the System: Social Movement, Intersectional Rhetoric, and Collective Agency in the Young Lords Organization’s Garbage Offensive,” *Quarterly Journal of Speech* 92, no. 2 (2008): 177.
105. Favors, “Coming Out,” 18.
106. Favors, “Coming Out,” 18.
107. Favors, “Coming Out,” 18.
108. Favors, “Coming Out,” 18.
109. Favors, “Coming Out,” 15.
110. Jamie Wareham, “Murdered, Hanged and Lynched: 331 Trans People Killed this Year,” Forbes.com, November 18, 2019, https://www.forbes.com/sites/jamiewareham/2019/11/18/murdered-hanged-and-lynched-331-trans-people-killed-this-year/#44ad87382d48.
111. Wareham, “Murdered, Hanged and Lynched.”
112. Tim Fitzsimons, “Transgender Day of Remembrance: At least 22 Trans People Killed in 2019,” NBCNews.com, November 20, 2019, https://www.nbcnews.com/feature/nbc-out/transgender-day-remembrance-least-22-trans-people-killed-2019-n1086521.
113. Favors, “Coming Out,” 20.
114. Favors, “Coming Out,” 20.
115. Favors, “Coming Out,” 22.

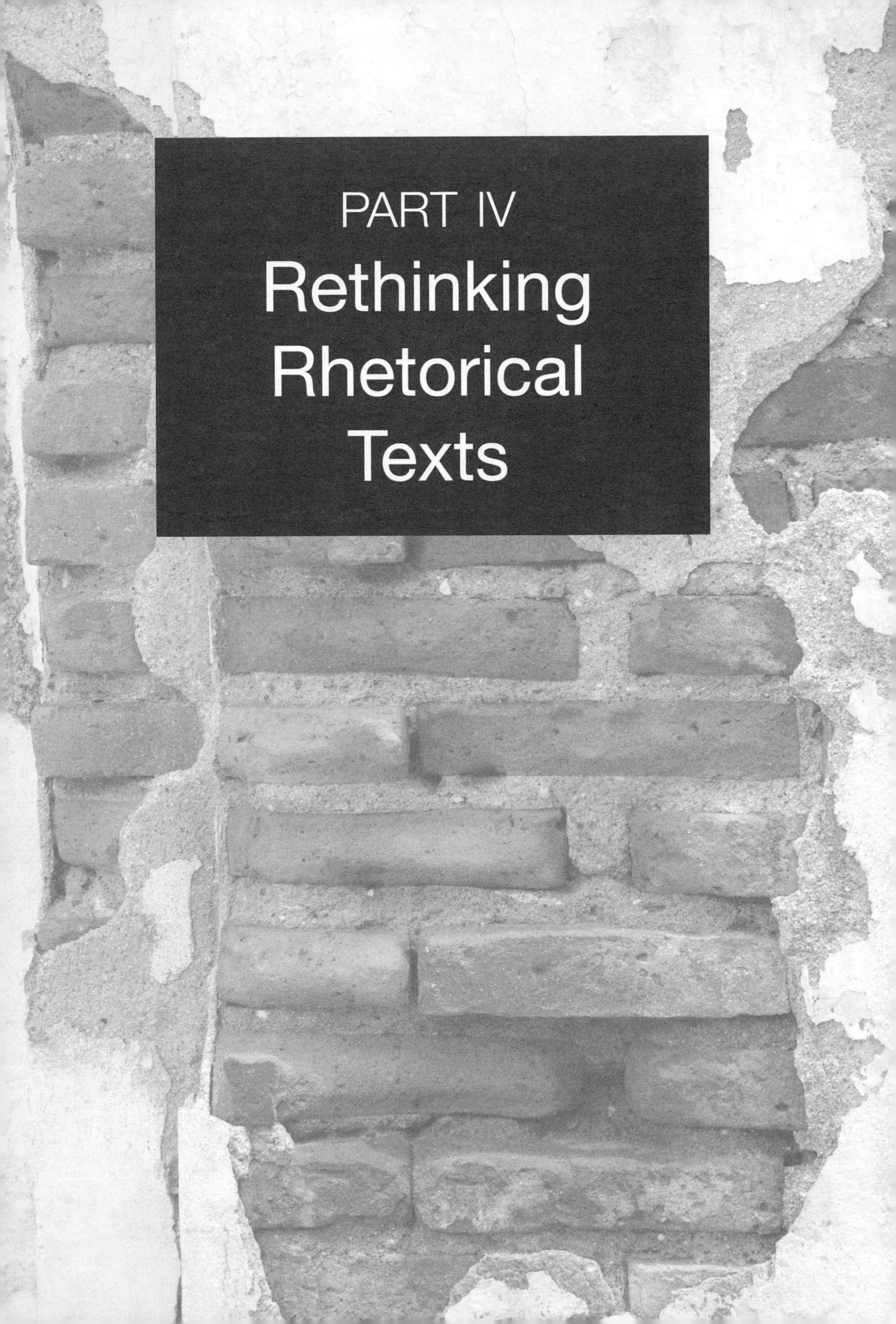

PART IV
Rethinking Rhetorical Texts

Chapter 9

Audience Rhetoric

During the summer of 2013, law student Shana Knizhnik (now an attorney) launched the Notorious R.B.G. Tumblr account. The name of the account riffs on the hip-hop artist Notorious B.I.G. The site, which operates as "a virtual shrine of irreverent reverence" for Supreme Court Justice Ruth Bader Ginsburg, features a "variety of Ginsburg quotes, photoshopped images, bits of news, and links to products emblazoned with her name, face, or words, including a Notorious R.B.G. T-shirt."[1]

Ginsburg's notoriety soared after the Supreme Court heard the case of *Burwell v. Hobby Lobby.* The company Hobby Lobby had sued the government—citing religious reasons—for the right not to cover some types of birth control for its female employees in its health insurance policies. In a 5-4 split, the Court ruled in Hobby Lobby's favor. Justice Ruth Bader Ginsburg read her dissent from the bench, lampooning the Court for ruling that corporations qualify as people capable of holding religious beliefs. Many people recirculated portions of this famous dissent, along with memes and images of Ginsburg. The independent journalism website *Mother Jones* featured an article titled, "The 8 Best Lines from Ginsburg's Dissent on the Hobby Lobby Contraception Decision."[2]

Ginsburg functions as a popular feminist icon. Her image is routinely circulated on the internet, commodified into apparel, used motivationally on protest picket signs, and featured in memes on social media. Shana Knizhnik, the "followers" of the Notorious R.B.G. Tumblr account, the Ginsburg memesters, and I can be considered as Ginsburg's audience members or perhaps as audience members of the *Burwell v. Hobby Lobby* dissent. Yet we could also consider Knizhnik and the Ginsburg memesters as rhetors: in response to Ginsburg and her *Burwell v. Hobby Lobby* dissent, they created discourse and disseminated it to the public. Indeed, these are audience members turned rhetors—but much of their rhetor-ship revolves around their ongoing role as Ginsburg's audience members. That is, even as they produce their own rhetoric, they continue being Ginsburg's audience; their rhetor-ship stems, in part, from the overflow of their audience-ship.

Audience texts are *texts that are created by audience members.* By analyzing audience members' rhetoric, rhetorical critics study (1) how audiences interpret, interact with, respond to, and use rhetoric; and (2) how audience members develop relationships with rhetorical discourses. When critics study audience texts, they often analyze many small or fragmented audience texts instead of a seemingly discrete entity (such as a film).

For example, a critic who used narrative criticism to study the television series *Game of Thrones* would likely choose a story arc and then analyze several hours of this series and its relevant contexts. The story arc might be divided across several episodes, but it still largely feels like a cohesive text—a discrete entity around which one could metaphorically draw a circle. A critic studying audience texts related to *Game of Thrones,* however, might analyze what audiences said in response to the episode "The Bells" (Season 8, Episode 5), in which Daenerys Targaryen (known throughout the prior seasons as "Mother of Dragons, Breaker of Chains") surprisingly engaged in the "mass murder" of the "exact same kinds of people she lifted up to forge her savior reputation."[3] During and immediately after the airing of this episode, audiences took to message boards, social media, blogs, fan forums, and news discourse to express their frustration with this plot decision—especially lamenting the ways it countered what they understood as Daenerys's character and the feminist ethos of the prior Season 8 episodes. A critic might gather these audience responses—from memes, to hashtags, to scathing reviews in the *New York Times*—and analyze it as a text. Here, the *Game of Thrones* episode or story arc becomes the context and the audience response becomes the critic's text.

Especially when studying audience texts, a rhetorical critic might engage in a **field study,** *a study in which a critic might directly observe a rhetorical environment, or use programming software to identify relevant social media discourses, or interview audience members and then analyze their responses.* The research example later in this chapter that features Christine Gardner's analysis of LGBTQ+ students at Christian colleges is an example of a rhetorical field study.

By learning to analyze audience texts, critics are able to study a variety of texts that other methods are not as well equipped to analyze. They can learn how audiences are thinking about, relating to, and using a wide variety of public discourse, such as news updates, political speeches, policy decisions, films, television series, social media platforms, and so on. They might learn that audiences use public discourse in creative and unexpected ways. Studying audience texts, then, can serve as a corrective to cultural assumptions. For instance, the research example featured later in this chapter that focuses on audience interactions with *The X-Files* offers its analysis as a correction to assumptions that cultural critics made about this series in TV reviews published in popular news outlets.

A critic can use this approach to supplement an analysis of a traditional text (such as a film) in order to assess the audience's reaction to and use for that text and the text/audience relationship. For instance, rhetorical critic Erin Rand's analysis of the Hobby Lobby dissent (discussed in Chapter 5) primarily used genre criticism to study the dissent itself. The full critical essay, however, concludes with a section that analyzes audience texts to address ways in which audience members used the dissent in their own efforts toward "cultural transformation."[4] Similarly, Erica Edwards and Jennifer Esposito analyzed audience texts in their feminist ideological critique of the debate surrounding the viral photo known as #teacherbae (discussed in Chapter 8); they focused on what people said about the photo rather than on the photo itself. Edwards and Esposito inverted the traditional relationship between text and context as they used what is typically considered "context" (how audiences received the text) as the "text" itself.

This chapter is in tricky terminological terrain. Other chapters in this book refer to films, speeches, and so on as "texts," but in this chapter, the audience's response is the "text." Therefore, this chapter refers to audience rhetoric as "texts" and refers to the films, campaign speeches, and so on that audiences react to as "existing discourses," as simply "discourse," or sometimes as "symbolic forms." To understand how to analyze audience texts, we need to understand what audiences are, how they use existing discourses (such as films and campaign speeches), and how they form relationships with existing discourses.

A THEORY OF AUDIENCES

Many media critics explain that audience members interact with existing discourses by being **active.**[5] By describing audiences as active, media critics emphasize that audiences are *engaged in mental activity while making sense of discourse and its meaning, and responding to it.* Although watching TV might be relaxing, being an audience member is not a passive experience where you mindlessly accept whatever a discourse tells you. Instead, while lounging on a couch or absently skimming through a news feed, you are fundamentally active as you make sense of, evaluate, and respond to the discourse.

Cultural theorist Stuart Hall described this process in his landmark theory **encoding/decoding,** *a theory that explains that meaning never pings from one mind straight into another, but rather is encoded by one person (or group of people, such as a film's writers and directors) into a discourse during its creation and then decoded by another person (or group of persons, in other words, an audience).*[6] For example, imagine that a film's writers and directors conceptualize a character as an evil person. To convey that meaning to audiences, they must first encode it, which they might do by playing sinister music when the character is on screen and situating the character in dark environments. For audience members to understand the meaning—that this character is evil—they must decode the symbols, recognizing the music and dark environments as coded symbols that indicate a sinister character.

Following the encoding/decoding model, for people to accurately convey meaning to one another, they must know the same codes. This is usually not a problem: a society socializes its members so that the vast majority of them understand the **culturally established codes,** *systems of verbal, visual, physical, aural, and technological symbols that a culture widely and repeatedly uses to convey meaning.* For example, languages themselves, body language, and tone of voice are all culturally established codes. Moreover, there are visual codes, such as road signs; audio codes, such as car alarms, building alarms, fire alarms, and fire sirens; and physical codes. Consider, for example how the floor plan and furniture of a home communicate a family's wealth and values, as well as what behaviors are appropriate in what spaces.

Additionally, technologies and industry traditions can function as culturally established codes. For example, imagine a film introduces two sinister characters—an evil mastermind and his evil assistant—at the same time. This film would likely cast those roles so the assistant is shorter than the mastermind, then use angled reverse-shots for their scenes: the camera looks upward at the mastermind so he looms over it while speaking to the assistant, then downward at the assistant so he appears small and insignificant while he makes his groveling reply. This medium-specific, technologically facilitated portrayal is able to communicate the evil mastermind's authority (and the assistant's lack thereof) because this type of camerawork has been used so often to communicate characters' relative authority.

Culturally established codes are connected to power systems. Part of what codes convey is power, authority, and/or class. For example, made-for-TV movies that play on the Hallmark Channel are much cheaper to produce than theatrical films because they use less expensive equipment and typically hire B-list actors, writers, directors, and crew members. As a result, although the storylines are often delightful, these movies have a look and feel—a code—that mark them as "made-for-TV movies." US audiences decode that look and feel, determining that any given made-for-TV movie is less important, popular, valuable, and interesting than a film made for theatrical release. The platform of distribution itself can become coded: television productions are coded as less valuable than theatrical releases.[7] The fact that a movie is distributed by television marks it as less important (and therefore less likely to be watched in its entirety) than a theatrical release.

Indeed, the medium, platform, and setting for a discourse often function together as a code that signals the importance and even tone of that discourse. Consider how political pundits decode the location of a presidential address. A speech given from the Oval Office is typically decoded as an issue "of national importance," whereas speeches in other White House rooms, "such as the Vermeil, Roosevelt, and Green Rooms," are often decoded as personal interest stories.[8]

Our life experiences inform the codes we use to encode and decode meaning. Consider how inside jokes work: a group of people who share a life experience develop code words or phrases that are meaningful only to that group. Only insiders—those who lived the experience together—can correctly encode an inside joke or decode the word or phrase as a joke. Similarly, your family background, interests, hobbies, education, subcultures, friend groups, class, political identities, and other social identities can profoundly shape the codes in which you are fluent, as well as how likely you are to accept the power and authority of any given code.

Relating to Existing Discourses

Hall's encoding/decoding theory laid the foundation for current understandings of active audiences. Audience members actively decode a discourse, sifting through a wide variety of culturally established codes and working to understand the verbal, visual, physical, aural, and/or technological symbols in that discourse. Although this process often happens at a commonsense level that seems rather unremarkable, Hall draws our attention to how active and remarkable it actually is. Not only are we actively decoding complex codes, but as we do so, we establish our relationship with a discourse (such as a TV series or a political critic's weekly editorial column).

Broadly speaking, Hall suggests that audiences develop one of three types of relationships with a discourse as they decode it. First, audience members can use a **dominant-hegemonic code** to make sense of the meaning: *audience members wholly accept the meanings encoded in the discourse and develop a relationship with it that accepts and endorses the discourse.* (See Chapter 7 for a discussion of hegemony.) Second, audience members can use a **negotiated code:** *audience members accept part of the meaning and reject, nuance, expand, or qualify other parts.* These audience members neither accept nor reject the discourse, but rather walk a swerving line in and out of agreement with it. And third, audience members can use an **oppositional code:** *audience members wholly reject the meaning of the discourse.* These audience members oppose the discourse, developing an antagonist relationship with it.

For example, imagine a choir member, a Catholic visitor, and an agnostic teenager listening to a sermon in a protestant church. The choir member loves this church, attends every Sunday, and is friends with the pastor. She wholly accepts the sermon: she operates "inside the dominant code" at this church and entirely accepts the meanings encoded in the sermon.[9] The Catholic visitor generally agrees with the sermon: much of it matches up with her worldview, doctrine, and life experiences, but she disagrees when the pastor talks about Communion. This visitor is using a negotiated code to make sense of the sermon, accepting some parts while considering, reviewing, and partially rejecting others. Finally, the agnostic teenager wholly rejects the sermon's meaning: she fundamentally disagrees with the pastor, doubting that one can ever "know God." She uses an oppositional code; she understands the pastor's words and arguments but decodes them in an oppositional manner. Every time the pastor exhorts the congregation to "have faith" she interprets him as asking the congregation to blindly believe in what she thinks ought to be rigorously questioned. In this example, the three audience members' life experiences lead them to decode the sermon differently and, therefore, to have different relationships with it.

Media scholars often celebrate the audience's activity, seeing audience members as reclaiming their own power and agency instead of being "duped" by the discourse—especially as they use oppositional codes to reject a discourse's meanings.[10] For example, for feminist media scholars, there is something celebratory and exciting in the way a YouTube.com user who goes by Sloane spliced together visual clips from J. J. Abrams's film *Star Trek* and set them to music from the comedy band Flight of the Conchords. The lyrics sing about heterosexual men's experiences going out clubbing, hoping to pick up women, only to be frustrated by finding very few women at the dance clubs. Pairing this music with shots from *Star Trek* starkly reveals how many male characters and how very few female characters populate the film.[11] Here, Sloane used an oppositional code to interpret *Star Trek* as sexist rather than a fun action blockbuster, then went a step further by creating a humorous rebuttal to the film and posting it on YouTube.

Media scholar David Buckingham, however, reminds us that although audiences are active, they "act under conditions that are not of their own choosing."[12] He reminds us that the codes audience members use to decode discourses are, by and large, culturally established. The cultures and subcultures in which we participate largely determine the codes we use to decode discourses and, therefore, our relationships with various discourses. Further, we should not equate an audience member's activity in decoding a discourse as having the same power or authority as the activity of the discourse in society.

To return to the hypothetical sermon example, the Catholic visitor does not have the same authority as the pastor who gives the sermon in the protestant church. If she were to stand up during the sermon and argue with it, explaining how she understands Communion to the congregation, her arguments would be unlikely to convince many people in this context. Existing discourses and audience members are not equal. Existing discourses operate within contexts that imbue them with power and authority to which audience members typically do not have access. Indeed, J. J. Abrams' *Star Trek* was a global phenomenon but Sloane's YouTube.com video only has about ninety thousand views. And finally, the audience members' activity is a response, a reaction to an existing discourse; audiences act "under conditions" that are not entirely "of their own choosing."[13]

Multiple Meanings

Audience members approach discourses from different life experiences and use different culturally established codes; accordingly, they often derive different meanings from discourses. Communication scholars describe this phenomenon as **polysemy**—which means *many meanings.*[14] For example, in an interview with *The Advocate,* Elizabeth Banks discussed directing the 2019 film reboot of *Charlie's Angels* and how important it was that the character that Kristen Stewart played "telegraphed as queer."[15] Stewart identifies as bisexual and her character in the film, Sabina, is one of the three "angels" the Charlie's Angels franchise traditionally features.[16] Banks included other queer "nods and cameos" throughout the film, such as featuring Laverne Cox in the closing credits.[17] Banks commented that throughout the film, showing Sabina flirting with other women is "a little callout that just tells the entire audience that this movie is inclusive and loves and accepts everyone."[18] For audience members, however, this queer "telegraphing" and the film's other "nods," "cameos," and "callouts" seem to exhibit polysemy. For instance, journalist Lucy Wood reported that the film was "affectionally dubbed by LGBTQ+ fans as *Charlie's Gayngels,*" indicating that some audience members recognized these queer meanings in the film's messages.[19] Other audience members, however, seemed to interpret these "callouts" in other ways, not recognizing them as queer. For instance, Darren Franich's negative review of the film for *Entertainment Weekly* never mentions these aspects of the film and never addresses Sabina's sexuality—even though he remarks at length about casting Stewart as a "generational figure for *Twilight* kids" who has spent a decade in "Indieland," and says the film missed its opportunity of being Stewart's "thrilling reintroduction to the mainstream."[20]

Discourses such as films, speeches, and even policies exhibit polysemy when audience members derive different meanings from the same content. However, it is important to consider ways in which some discourses encourage audience members to decode different meanings. Some discourses are **polyvocal,** which means *many voices.* Polyvocal discourses use strategic ambiguity and/or layer multiple culturally established codes (essentially speaking multiple languages) to reach a broad audience, knowing that audience members will take away different meanings from the discourse. For example, in the children's movie *Cars*, Lightning McQueen is a famous race car. At a press conference, twin cars approach him saying, "We're like your biggest fans! Ka-chow!" and flash their lights at him. McQueen responds, "I love being me." This scene speaks differently to children and adult audiences: children are meant to interpret that McQueen is popular and enjoys his popularity, but many adults can see the double entendre—groupies are flashing McQueen. Because entertainment and political discourses profit from large, diverse audiences, it is fairly common for these discourses to appeal polyvocally to multiple audiences.

How audience members encounter and interact with a discourse shapes their understandings of it. Media scholar Jonathan Gray focuses on these meaning-making possibilities in his analysis of **paratexts,** *artifacts that are connected to an existing discourse and that guide or extend audience members' interactions with that discourse.*[21] The entire "Notorious R.B.G." Tumblr account and the surrounding paraphernalia (T-shirts, twitter feeds, and memes) are all paratexts surrounding Supreme Court Justice Ruth Bader Ginsburg. Paratexts can be created by industry executives (producers, directors, and so on) and by audience members. For example, the production teams working on *Star Trek* with J. J. Abrams created its posters, toy figurines, and so on, but it was an audience member—Sloane—who created the oppositional YouTube.com video.

Paratexts such as trailers, promos, and posters can shape audience's interactions with a text by guiding their initial interactions with the text. Such paratexts welcome audiences into an existing or upcoming discourse, pique our interest, and offer us curated first glimpses of the discourse. They shape what a discourse means to audience members before they encounter the discourse. For instance, when I saw the original television promos for the opening episodes of *The Office*, I was repulsed by the characters of Michael Scott and Dwight Schrute and refused to watch the series. The meaning I gleaned from the paratexts shaped the way I would think about *The Office* for the next several years.

Alternatively, some paratexts are continuations or extensions of an existing discourse, and can shape an audience's ongoing understandings of a text. For instance, season recaps and snarky online summaries often help audiences keep track of plot lines; online discussion forums and fan merchandise on Etsy.com help audiences maintain and proclaim their emotional investment in a discourse; and spin-offs, sequels, prequels, and reboots keep audiences connected to the discourse and its characters.[22] Gray argues that paratexts fuel our interactions with discourses and the meanings we derive from them, thereby shaping audience members' understandings of what a discourse is and determining how audiences use it.[23]

Audience Fandom

Audience members generally develop relationships with discourses as they decode them. Some audience members bond with a discourse, however, and are considered

fans: *audience members who emotionally connect with an existing discourse, intellectually ruminate on that discourse, and alter their behavior to engage the discourse more deeply.*[24] For example, a fan of *The Bachelor* may form an emotional attachment to one of the contestants, identify with her, and feel happy when things are going well for her. This fan also engages intellectually with the series by trying to figure out which scenes and characterizations are manipulated by the producers and directors and which are more "real." Finally, the fan engages in behaviors that draw her into greater connection with *The Bachelor:* she reads magazine articles about the series and contestants, plays a *Bachelor* game on her smart phone, reads RealitySteve.com's snarky spoiler-filled blog, and follows @BachelorNation's twitter feed. We often think of fans developing these intense bonds with television, film, and book series, but fandom is as varied as people are. People are fans of sports, politicians, political parties, genres, actors, directors, musicians, board games, brands, pastors, venues, podcasts, and a wide variety of other cultural discourses.

Fans often form online communities where they engage in discussion and solidarity with one another. For example, a Harry Potter fan might participate in MuggleNet.com. A fan of Ruth Bader Ginsburg might follow Tumblr's Notorious R.B.G. account and use @notoriousRBG and #notoriousRBG in their own social media posts to interact with other fans and account moderators. Joining fan communities can strengthen fans' emotional, intellectual, and behavioral bonds with an existing discourse as these fans invest more time and socially engage their fandom.

Fans' activity can create a **feedback loop** as *industry executives (directors, producers, and so on) listen in on fans' online conversations and use the feedback to shape their productions.*[25] For example, J. J. Abrams described listening to fan sites as "integral" to producing a television series.[26] He likened online fan communities to the audience in a theatrical play, explaining that by listening "to the applause, the missing laughs, the boos" the actors can adapt to their audience.[27] Similarly, television series, politicians, business organizations, and so on, can adapt to their audiences by listening to their fan communities.

Ultimately, audience members meaningfully—and often noticeably—interact with discourses. They are active as they decode discourses and relate to them. Moreover, some audience members develop intense bonds with discourses, even, or perhaps especially, as those discourses diffuse across various paratexts. Understanding audiences in this way suggests that critics ought to analyze audience texts when (1) demonstrating how audiences decode and interact with existing discourses and (2) attempting to understand how audiences and discourses relate to one another.

ANALYZING AUDIENCE TEXTS

When analyzing audience texts, a critic studies how audiences respond to and in relation to an existing discourse. A critic can combine this approach with other methods—for example, by using narrative criticism to analyze a film and then also studying the audience texts surrounding that film. Regardless of whether a critic only analyzes audience texts or combines this approach with a more traditional method, this analytical process is hardly linear: the critic must toggle among—or hover over—the audience texts in relation to their contexts, including the existing discourse.

The advice that follows focuses on analyzing existing audience texts that are publicly available and accessible to a critic—such as the comment sections on a political blog. The research examples, however, also provide a glimpse into field methods. Rebecca Williams used programming software to sort through audience texts regarding *The West Wing.* Christine Gardner interviewed people in her analysis of Christian LGBTQ+ individuals interacting with Christian and secular discourses.

Context: The Existing Discourse

When studying audience texts, a critic asks who the target audience of the existing discourse is. Answering this question often involves considering what the existing discourse reveals about its target audience. Here, the critic assesses the target audience's demographics and ideologies by analyzing the word choices, style, metaphors, complexity (or lack thereof), persuasive appeals, references or allusions, and broader environment of the existing discourse. Depending on whether that discourse has audiovisual components, whether it features a narrative, and what the medium is, the critic also considers what elements such as plotlines, characterization, cinematic techniques, and technological productions reveal about the target audience.

For example, imagine you are analyzing audience members' rhetoric regarding the cooperative board game, *Pandemic,* in which players work together (playing against the game rather than against each other) as medical experts to cure diseases. Considering what the game itself reveals about the target audience, you might note that the complicated nature of the game's rules and instructions, its lengthy playtime (over forty-five minutes), and the scholarly or highly educated nature of the game's characters (Scientist, Researcher, Quarantine Specialist, Archivist, Epidemiologist, and so on) suggest that *Pandemic* targets well-educated, experienced, strategy board-game players.

A critic also considers how an existing discourse is encoded, focusing on its culturally established codes and what those codes reveal about the target audience. For example, Janelle Monae's music video *Q.U.E.E.N.* uses widely accessible codes to convey a feeling of independence and resistance, as the artist sings about being shocked by how others want to judge her and wanting to be herself even if others are uncomfortable with who she is.[28] This music video also features more specific codes, however, as it features "historical Black iconography" and Black activist artists. (Eryka Badu features in the music video and the lyrics also reference Marvin Gaye.) Monae's closing lines refer to her earlier music when she addresses the audience as electric ladies.[29] Analyzing these codes, a critic would likely conclude that *Q.U.E.E.N.*'s encoding works at two levels for two different target audiences. Uninitiated audiences (those unfamiliar with Black iconography, Black activist artists, and Monae's science-fiction themed music) will generally decode Monae's spirit of resistance. Initiated audiences (those able to navigate the more specialized codes) have a much clearer understanding of Monae's specific concerns and can recognize and enjoy her cleverness, as she artfully brings so many coded references together to resist racism and homophobia. Essentially, *Q.U.E.E.N.* uses polyvocality and expects polysemy: the different codes speak to different audiences who derive different levels of understanding from the song.

Context: Official Paratexts

In addition to analyzing what an existing discourse reveals about its audience, a critic also assesses how official paratexts—those made by the rhetors of that discourse—encourage audiences to interact with the discourse. For example, a critic might consider how paratexts such as trailers, posters, campaign websites, and dust-jacket descriptions situate a discourse within a genre, feature celebrities, or refer to prior discourses.

The critic wants to get a sense of first, what type of audiences these paratexts target, and second, how the paratexts invite audiences to understand the discourse (for example, as a romantic comedy, a presidential candidate, or a feminist icon). Audience members' expectations regarding a discourse fundamentally shape how they interact with it. Consequently, these official paratexts play important roles in audience activity.

A critic studying how audiences interacted with the 2018 British royal wedding of Prince Harry and Ms. Meghan Markle could study the official web page and its official tweets, announcements, promotional interviews, photos, invitations, directions for watching the wedding, and directions for those planning to visit Windsor to celebrate the wedding.[30] These paratexts invite audiences to understand the wedding as a "true love" marriage, in which they can participate through a variety of respectful options such as hosting or attending a viewing party, planning a trip to Windsor, or donating to the seven charities Prince Harry and Ms. Markle chose as reflective of their values.[31]

Second, the critic considers paratexts designed by the rhetors (such as merchandise, DVD commentaries, documentary films, apps, games, and social media channels) that encourage ongoing audience interaction. For example, the Notorious R.B.G. Tumblr account advertises a book, *Notorious RBG: The Life and Times of Ruth Bader Ginsburg,* which is coauthored by Shana Knizhnik, the original creator of the account. Although the title suggests the book is a biography, it is an unusual one: full of cartoons, photos, lyrics, advice on how to "be like RBG," and even recipes. A critic might note that it invites audience members into even greater identification with the Tumblr account and with Ginsburg herself. By analyzing paratexts made by the rhetors of a discourse, critics can assess how audiences are intended to interact with that discourse.

Culturally Authoritative Audience Texts

When studying audience texts, a critic focuses on how audiences respond and relate to a discourse. Audience members are not all the same, however, so the critic ought to distinguish (at the very least) between audience members with cultural authority (such as film critics) and those without. The critic can begin by researching cultural reactions to the discourse, such as awards it won or was nominated for; reviews in mainstream, niche, and trade group publications; and other responses such as news reports, protests, rallies, commemorations, and republications. By studying cultural responses, the critic advances the analysis in three general ways.

First, the organizations that respond to a discourse can often indicate its audience. For example, *Q.U.E.E.N.* won BET's Soul Train Award for Video of the Year. *Pandemic* is mostly reviewed by critics at niche and trade publications such as *ArsTechnica* and *Board Game Quest.*[32] This information indicates that *Q.U.E.E.N.* is popular and acclaimed among audiences who listen to R&B, soul, and neo soul, whereas *Pandemic* is mostly of interest to established gamers.

Second, cultural reviews demonstrate how well-informed audience members interpreted the discourse. Although reviewers' reactions are not representative of general audience members' experiences with a discourse, they do demonstrate how experts in the culturally established codes decoded it. *Pandemic*'s reviewers in *ArsTechnica* and *Board Game Quest* are experts in strategy games and gamer culture, and well versed in the codes *Pandemic* uses to encode meaning. Reading their reviews provides a clear sense of how experts in this field interpret and interact with the game.

And third, because critics, pundits, and award judges hold cultural authority, their responses to a discourse can function as paratextual introductions to and commentary on a discourse. Their cultural reviews and awards can also shape how other audience members engage with a discourse. Analyzing how the reviews describe, praise, and criticize a discourse can provide a clear sense of the themes a critic can expect audience members to interact with as they make sense of and use the discourse.

Audience Members' Texts

Critics have many options when it comes to analyzing audience members' textual productions to assess how audiences decode a discourse, interact with it, and relate to it. A critic might analyze a Twitter thread, public comments on a policy proposal (such as the public comments regarding the FCC's revision of Net Neutrality or the Department of Education's 2018 Title IX proposal), the letters published in a local newspaper, the message board forums for online fan communities, or audience-made paratexts (such as fan fiction, videos, art, and merchandise). For a critic studying audience texts as the primary or sole mode of analysis, the assessment of audience members' rhetoric typically forms the heart and bulk of the critical essays. A critic can expect to spend the most time doing this part of the analysis. The critical essay largely showcases arguments and evidence based on audience members' discourse.

The critic then narrows the focus, choosing to study a specific segment of the audience, then analyzes that segment's decoding activity, interaction with and use of a discourse, or relationship with a discourse. For example, a critic might study audience responses to Harrison Wright's shocking death at the end of *Scandal*'s third season or how audiences interact with *Lost*'s puzzle-like plotlines. Studying "all audience members" and "all interactions" would bury the critic under far too many texts.

A critic starts by casting a wide net and becoming familiar with the breadth of audience rhetoric. Typically, the critic reviews fan communities, message boards, Twitter feeds, Etsy shops, and so on, then makes well-informed decisions, narrowing the focus to sites of audience rhetoric (such as fan sites, message boards, and public comments on policy proposals) that best address the research goals. The critic might select those sites that are representative, popular, or particularly important within a fan community. When a critic selects a narrow segment of audience rhetoric for analysis—such as specific message board threads or a hashtag—the critic must justify this choice, explaining the reason for this choice to readers. (See Appendix B.)

When analyzing audience members' rhetoric, critics look for trends and themes. For example, a critic might look for themes in how audience members describe a particular entertainment character, explain their overall impressions of a politician or policy proposal, or interact with a discourse. The critic then groups several audience statements into an overarching theme. For instance, reading comments on a discussion board in which audience members repeatedly describe a protagonist as "nice," "too nice," "sweet," "innocent," "well meaning," and "taken advantage of," the critic might group these comments, seeing a theme of decoding the protagonist as naïve. Reviewing other comments describing this protagonist as "dumb," "underprepared," "selfish," "irritating," and "shortsighted," the critic might group those comments, seeing a theme of decoding the protagonist as immature.

Critics need to spot similarities and differences—noting trends and themes—until they reach **saturation,** *the "point where little or no new information on the research topic emerges."*[33] Reaching saturation means that the critic has a full understanding of the trends and themes through which audiences interpret the discourse, interact with it, and/or relate to it. Once a critic reaches saturation, every new tweet, post, piece of fan art, message board response, merchandise item, and so on that emerges clearly belongs in one of the trends or themes the critic has already spotted. Ultimately, critics consider the themes and trends they have identified, then use them as evidence to support a claim about how a discourse functions in society.

RESEARCH EXAMPLES

Studying audience texts not only reveals how audiences decode a discourse, but also demonstrates how a discourse influences them and how they use and relate to a discourse—as the following two examples show. In the first example, Christine A. Wooley's analysis of fan responses to the series *The X-Files* focuses on the fans' discussion boards. Wooley argues persuasively that audiences used the series in ways cultural critics and theorists did not expect. In the second example, Rebecca Williams analyzes how audience members reacted to *The West Wing*'s series conclusion and used their relationships with the series to shape their life choices. The third example features Christine J. Gardner's analysis of how LGBTQ+ students at Christian colleges interact with both Christian and secular discourses.

Christine A. Wooley
"Visible Fandom: Reading *The X-Files* through X-Philes" (2002)*

Given today's fragmented and niche audiences for television and streaming entertainment, it is hard to describe the widespread popularity, appeal, and notoriety of *The X-Files* during the 1990s. The series featured a relatively empowered female lead (Gillian Anderson as Dana Scully) and a hunky male lead (David Duchovny as Fox Mulder) as FBI partners who solved weird cases every week. Throughout these "Monster of the Week" episodes, however, Scully and Mulder also worked cases involving a huge alien conspiracy.[34] The series was part crime drama, part science fiction, part conspiracy theory, and all magic. *The X-Files* and the widespread accessibility and popularity of the internet were born together during the 1990s. In addition to achieving widespread popularity, the show developed a large "cult phenomenon" of online communities in which fans self-identified as X-Philes (that is, lovers of *The X-Files*).[35]

By studying audience texts, Christine Wooley reveals a stark disconnect between how cultural critics explained the popularity of *The X-Files* and how fans actually engaged with the show. Cultural critics who wrote reviews for news outlets, even academic theorists such as Slavoj Žižek, focused on the show's conspiracy theories, claiming that the convoluted conspiracy plot comforted audience members by offering them human explanations for the seemingly uncontrollable (aliens, cancer, disasters, and so on). Even though the humans in control were a mostly evil cabal, cultural reviews—such as Johnathan Alter's writing in *Newsweek*—argued that audiences found it comforting to know that "someone's in control, even if he's evil."[36]

Wooley, however, rejects these reviewers' conclusions because they do not match the encoding of *The X-Files* or fans' responses. Analyzing the show, Wooley argues that far from comforting audiences, its encoding of the conspiracy plot invites audience members to make their own meanings. The conspiracy plot is notoriously inconsistent, often contradicting itself. Essentially, rather than offering audiences a puzzle to solve, *The X-Files* presents them with incomplete pieces from three different puzzles. Rather than finding solace and comfort in a completed puzzle that unambiguously features evil human agents, audiences who engage with the conspiracy plot are invited to enjoy the process of sorting through the pieces. Rather than inviting audiences to solve the puzzle, Wooley argues, *The X-Files* invites audiences to celebrate whenever they fit any two pieces together.

Analyzing audience rhetoric on two popular fan sites, Wooley found three clear themes. First, audience members accepted *The X-Files*'s invitation, creatively engaging with the show in a meaning-making process. Wooley cites evidence of how fans decoded *The X-Files* as they developed and discussed multiple theories and connections. Second, audience members felt jeopardized by the unresolved (and perhaps unresolvable) nature of the show. To explain this theme, Wooley cites online discussions in which people expressed a sense of anxiety that their intense commitment to the show—all the time and energy spent thinking about it, watching it, and discussing it with others—would not be honored by satisfying

*This essay may be found in *Journal of Film and Video* 53, no. 4 (2001–2): 29–53.

resolutions. And third, Wooley noted a clear trend in which audience members defined who they were in relation to the series.

In this third trend, audience members were not discussing plot points or characters, but rather the relationship between themselves as audience members and the series. They understood themselves as meaningful to the show: the creators and producers knew about the online fan communities, frequented their message boards, occasionally responded to their questions, and embedded special jokes and references into *X-Files* episodes that only audience members who were active in online fan communities would notice and enjoy.[37] Yet audience members acutely felt—and discussed online—their inferior standing compared to the creators and directors, who did what they wanted with the series while the fans often helplessly watched the series veer in a direction they did not want or expect.

Wooley noticed two different "styles of engagement" as audience members defined themselves in relation to *The X-Files.*[38] Some audience members were more optimistic, believing the series truly included them and valued their feedback. Others were more cynical and prepared for disappointment, feeling the series did not feel about them the way they felt about it. Fans were aware that their own style of engagement (optimistic or cynical) shaped their interpretations of the content and mechanics of the series.[39] The more optimistic fans commented that their interpretation of opaque and ambiguous events was likely naively trusting. The more cynical fans admitted that by preparing themselves for the worst, they were skewing their own interpretations, believing that the opaque evidence pointed toward what they considered unacceptable outcomes.

Ultimately, Wooley interprets these themes, arguing that when decoding the series (watching and making sense of each episode), fans essentially asked, "What does this episode mean for my relationship with *The X-Files?*" Their answers to this question guided their interpretations of how events in the episode connected to the overarching plot. A large part of making sense of any given episode was assessing how the episode shaped their relationship with *The X-Files*—whether the episode rewarded their fandom or ignored them. For these fans, the "question of their own inclusion" was part of their analysis of the series.[40] Wooley's analysis reveals that for fans of *The X-Files,* interpreting and relating to the show were fused experiences: how they interpreted it (optimistically or pessimistically) was determined by how they understood their relationship with *The X-Files*'s rhetors (as valued or not valued).

Rebecca Williams
"'This is the Night TV Died': Television Post-Object Fandom and the Demise of *The West Wing*" (2011)*

Have you ever felt sad when you finished reading a novel you really enjoyed? Or perhaps a little adrift when you finished streaming *The Office* or *The Mindy Project?* Rebecca Williams wanted to know more about such experiences—how fans missed a discourse and what happened in the fan/discourse relationship

---

*This essay may be found in *Popular Communication* 9, no. 4 (2011): 266–279.

after the discourse ended. Williams chose to analyze how audience members of *The West Wing* coped with the series conclusion. She narrowed her analysis to the discussion threads on forums for TelevisionWithoutPity.com that led up to the series finale and to posts made on those forums after the series ended. These discussion threads had so much content—over two thousand pages of audience texts—that Williams began by using a computer program called NVivo to sort the texts into themes. She found three central trends.

First, audience members used *The West Wing* in order to make sense of themselves and their experiences. Williams cites examples of how audience members used the characters to describe themselves. For example, one audience member claimed, "[I'm like] Josh, with a touch of Toby."[41] Similarly, audience members used the characters to explain themselves even when they did not identify with those characters. For example, one audience member wrote, "I am intensely organized at times, like to take care of my loved ones, and am proud of growing and taking on leadership in my own right. Does that make me Donna? . . . I'm not sure."[42]

Audience members were not simply decoding *The West Wing* or reflecting on its overarching meaning. Rather, they were using the series to decode their own experiences. Their experiences became meaningful (and mean specific things) on the basis of the show's values, plotlines, and characterizations. For example, audience members discussed how the series had made them more interested in politics, thus shaping their academic studies and ultimately their careers. (Some people recounted moving to Washington, DC, and taking government jobs because of *The West Wing*.) These audience members used the series to interpret the value and meaningfulness of real-world events (specifically, politics).

Second, audience members mourned the passing of *The West Wing*. Here, Williams sees audience members interacting with the series similarly to the way in which people mourn a healthy but failed relationship.[43] People often make sense of a breakup in a healthy relationship by processing how meaningful the relationship was, how much the relationship changed them, and whether the person they were dating will remain important to them. Fans processed the end of the series by recounting stories that proved how "close" they were to the series, explaining how the series impacted them, and articulating a kind of "enduring fandom" that promised the series would never be forgotten.[44] Williams argues that fans interact with television series in emotionally complex ways: although fans clearly know the difference between a television series and a significant other, they nonetheless interact with series they consider meaningful similarly to the ways they interact with people they consider meaningful.

Finally, Williams notes that although fans mourn the passing of a television series, the series does not actually die. Audience members persist and new audience members join the ranks long after the series disappears from the weekly lineup. For example, audience members discuss rewatching television series through DVDs, reruns, streaming, and so on; in addition, new people joined fan communities after watching the series on DVD, reruns, streaming, and so on.[45] Williams notes, however, that audience members describe using *The West Wing* as a source of comfort, and explicitly derive comfort from owning the DVDs (and thus having constant access to the episodes).[46] She suggests that after a television series concludes, fans' interactions with the series also shift; in this case, *The West Wing* shifted from a source of entertainment to a source of comfort.

Williams narrowed her focus to how audience members interact with a concluded television series and analyzed "how fans respond to the absence, rather than the presence" of a series.[47] Her findings (that fans use *The West Wing* to make sense of—decode—their own lives, they interact with the show in emotionally complex ways, and they derive comfort from watching the show even after it concluded) help us understand how television series function in society long after they conclude.

Christine J. Gardner
"'Created This Way': Liminality, Rhetorical Agency, and the Transformative Power of Constraint among Gay Christian College Students" (2017)*

It is fairly easy to imagine the audience for a concert, podcast, lecture, or television series. For other types of discourse, both the discourse and the audience can be harder to pin down. For example, consider all the individual messages from family members, guidance counselors, and politicians that coalesce into a discourse that teaches teenagers that a college education is an investment in their futures. The discourse is diffuse, consisting of many messages from many sources, expressed in many different ways, but all expressing the same principle. The audience is also diffuse. Rather than being gathered in a single movie theater or tracked through a social media algorithm, the audience is scattered in homes and high schools across the country.

Working to understand how people relate to and interact with such diffuse discourses, Christine Gardner used a field studies approach: she interviewed people and analyzed the rhetoric of their responses. She was specifically interested in how young adults who identify as LGBTQ+ and attend evangelical Christian colleges negotiate their sexual identities.[48] She identified two oppositional discourses, the first from some evangelical Christian denominations and the second from secular and scientific realms.

Christian denominations vary widely in their doctrines and practices; however, many denominations and churches maintain that same-sex sexual relationships and transgenderism are prohibited by biblical scripture. Although they consider themselves welcoming to all, these churches often teach that people experiencing same-sex attraction should remain celibate and that people experiencing transgender thoughts should act in gender accordance with their original biology. Additionally—in a complicated theological move—some churches then teach their congregants not to identify as LGBTQ+. They welcome celibate congregants who identify as "same-sex attracted" but teach them not to describe themselves as LGBTQ+.[49]

---

*This essay may be found in *Communication and Critical/Cultural Studies* 14, no. 1 (2017): 31–47.

These churches believe in an all-loving and all-powerful God who can transform same-sex desire into opposite-sex desire and transform transgenderism into cisgenderism so that all people can experience what these churches consider a thriving, biblically moral expression of sexuality. Within this discourse, it is wrong to identify as LGBTQ+ Christian, even if one is a celibate LGBTQ+ Christian, because—as pastor Kevin Miller stated—identifying oneself as LGBTQ+ "forecloses" the "possibility of change."[50] Within this framework, naming oneself as a "gay Christian" is seen as rejecting God's power to transform one's life.[51]

In contrast, a secular discourse drawing on scientific references describes LGBTQ+ identities as natural and naturally occurring. This discourse describes same-sex desire as an inherited trait and repeats the mantra "born this way." For example, although no one gene controls a person's sexuality, consider how scientists such as Benjamin Neale, a geneticist at the Broad Institute of M.I.T., draw on genetics to normalize same-sex sexuality.[52] Neale stated in a recent *New York Times* interview that same-sex behavior is "written into our genes and it's part of our environment. This is part of our species and it's part of who we are."[53]

Gardner's research works to understand how audience members relate to and interact with both these discourses. Gardner interviewed sixty-five students and recent alumni from nine evangelical Christian colleges and universities from across the United States.[54] She recruited her interviewees primarily through campus student groups. Interviews were typically between thirty minutes and three hours long. She then identified "key words, tropes, metaphors, and themes."[55]

In her analysis, Gardner recognized that audience members merge these two opposing discourses by responding that they are "created this way."[56] This phrase and accompanying assertions, such as "God made me gay," borrow from the secular/scientific discourse by normalizing LGBTQ+ identities as part of people's biology. By describing their LGBTQ+ identities as created by God, however, these students draw upon evangelical discourse that positions God as the all-loving and all-powerful creator of life.

Describing themselves as "created this way," these audience members respond to both discourses. To evangelical discourse that asks them to disavow their LGBTQ+ identities, they "appeal to a higher power" that "functions as an ultimate trump card: blame God, not me."[57] Essentially, LGBTQ+ Christians ask the people of the broader evangelical community to take up with God any problems they have with same-sex relationships and transgenderism, not with the individuals God has made. To secular/scientific discourses, these LGBTQ+ Christians assert that LGBTQ+ identities and Christianity are compatible—that God loves and rescues all people and that a "redeemed sexuality" is not synonymous with a "straight sexuality."[58]

Gardner's interviews reveal that navigating LGBTQ+ Christian identities is a complicated, multifaceted process, as people relate to, interact with, and respond to two oppositional discourses. Through her fieldwork, Gardner reveals how these audience members merge these oppositional discourses. She demonstrates that although discourses are powerful (it is difficult to think apart from the values and truths in which we are raised), audiences are also powerful: they can negotiate their relationship with a discourse and even alter the discourse itself.

STRENGTHS AND WEAKNESSES OF ANALYZING AUDIENCE TEXTS

Rhetorical criticism is fundamentally interested in symbolic action—what symbolic forms do, how they influence people, how people use them, and how people interact with and relate to them. The clear strength of the approach discussed in this chapter is that it takes the audience's rhetoric as its main focus. It is grounded in theories that take audiences seriously, understanding audiences as active. By focusing on active audiences, it directly studies how audience members describe their interpretation of, their interactions with, and their relationships to a discourse. By studying audience rhetoric, critics can observe audience members as they use and relate to a discourse in a variety of ways.

When used in combination with another method (or methods), analysis of audience texts can significantly increase a critic's understanding of a discourse and overall argument regarding its symbolic action. A critic could analyze audience texts in order to assess more robustly how audiences interact with campaign rhetoric, policy proposals, films, television series, and so on, rather than skimming the audience responses as mere context.

Studying audience texts as the primary or sole critical approach—as Christine Wooley and Rebecca Williams did in their analyses of *The X-Files* and *The West Wing*—is generally limited to discourses that have a significant number of recorded audience responses. Critics often use it to study online fandom surrounding entertainment, but it can also be used to study a wide variety of audience rhetoric. For example, a critic can analyze audience members' comments on news articles or blogs, product reviews on consumer websites (such as Amazon.com), a hashtag thread on Twitter, a viral photo (as Edwards and Esposito did in the research example in Chapter 8), public policy forums, social media platforms that people use to share information and coordinate protests in response to political speeches and policies, and many other scenarios.

When studying audience texts, however, critics are typically unable to study *all* the audience texts. Neither Christine Wooley nor Rebecca Williams analyzed the entirety of the audiences for *The X-Files* or *The West Wing*. Instead, they studied the rhetoric of very specific audiences, and it would be a mistake to generalize from their findings on these audience members to all audience members. For example, cultural reviewers found *The X-Files* reassuring as it established human control over seemingly uncontrollable events; online fans of this series, however, interacted with it much more intensely than the reviewers did. This intense interaction likely accounts for why fans did not experience reassurance but instead found the series disturbing, as the interaction constantly called into question the legitimacy of their relationships with the series.

CHOOSING THIS APPROACH

So how do you know whether you should analyze audience texts—whether as the primary approach or in coordination with other methods or modes of analysis—to interpret a particular piece of public discourse? To answer this question, you need to consider the audience's activity and the research question animating your analysis.

First, consider your audience's activity. Has the audience generated a significant number of publicly accessible, recorded responses? Are there online communities, cultural reviews, and paratexts? If you are contemplating using field methods and interviewing people, consider whether those people are engaged in activities or clubs that will help you find and approach them. For instance, Christine Gardner approached her respondents through their campus student groups. If the audience you want to study is not particularly active, this approach is unlikely to be a good fit for your analysis.

Second, consider your research motives. Do you have a specific question about how audiences act and interact with a discourse? Are you concerned with how discourses target and cultivate an audience? Are you curious about how an audience decodes, interacts with, and uses a specific discourse? About how a discourse and audience relate with one another? Studying audience texts is an excellent approach for answering the types of research questions that stem from these concerns.

Ultimately, analysis of audience rhetoric is like a telescoping lens: it brings you close to a specific part of the audience and shows you in great detail how those audience members responded to a symbolic form. This critical approach brings the critic close enough to the audience to see the audience activity and assess the audience rhetoric. As a result, the critic can see how symbolic forms (campaign rhetoric, films, policy proposals, television series, and so on) function in society, because the critic is looking at what the audience does in response to, with, and through their interpretations of a symbolic form. Ultimately, this approach helps critics understand audience texts as texts. In so doing, it welcomes a treasure trove of new texts into the realm of rhetorical criticism.

DISCUSSION QUESTIONS

1. Try to draw or diagram Stuart Hall's theory of encoding/decoding.
2. Explain a time when you decoded a discourse (such as a speech) using a dominant-hegemonic code, a negotiated code, or an oppositional code.
3. Have you and a friend or family member ever experienced polysemy as you decoded a discourse differently? Explain. Do you think your interpretations were different because you were using different culturally established codes to decode the discourse or because it was encoded polyvocally so it purposefully had multiple interpretations?
4. Name a discourse of which you are a fan. Describe your emotional, intellectual, and behavioral activity in relation to this discourse.
5. Describe a paratext that has shaped your interaction with a discourse.

NOTES

1. Erin Rand, "Fear the Frill: Ruth Bader Ginsburg and the Uncertain Futurity of Feminist Judicial Dissent," *Quarterly Journal of Speech* 101, no. 1 (2015): 80.
2. Dana Liebelson, "The 8 Best Lines from Ginsburg's Dissent on the Hobby Lobby Contraception Decision," *Mother Jones,* June 30, 2014, http://www.motherjones.com/politics/2014/06/best-lines-hobby-lobby-decision.

3. Jeremy Egner, "Season 8, Episode 5: 'The Bells,'" NYTimes.com, May 13, 2019, https://www.nytimes.com/2019/05/13/arts/television/game-of-thrones-season-8-episode-5-bells.html?searchResultPosition=3.
4. Rand, "Fear the Frill," 82.
5. Jonathan Gray and Amanda Lotz, *Television Studies* (Cambridge, UK: Polity, 2012), 60–63.
6. Stuart Hall, "Encoding, Decoding," in *The Cultural Studies Reader,* 2nd ed., ed. Simon During (New York: Routledge, 1993): 507–517.
7. Gray and Lotz, *Television Studies,* 6–7.
8. Evan Phifer, "Speeches in the White House," *The White House Historical Association,* November 1, 2016, https://www.whitehousehistory.org/speeches-in-the-white-house.
9. Hall, "Encoding, Decoding," 515.
10. Frank Abiocca, "Opposing Conceptions of the Audience: The Active and Passive Hemispheres of Mass Communication Theory," *Communication Yearbook* 11, no. 1 (1988): 51–80.
11. ". . . on the Dance Floor," YouTube.com, accessed May 25, 2018. https://www.youtube.com/watch?v=deQuFc3BP74.
12. David Buckingham, "Children and Media: A Cultural Studies Approach," in *The International Handbook of Children, Media and Culture,* ed. Kristen Drotner and Sonia Livingstone (Thousand Oaks, CA: Sage, 2008), 232.
13. Buckingham, "Children and Media," 232.
14. Sara Hayden, "Michelle Obama, Mom-in-Chief: The Racialized Rhetorical Contexts of Maternity," *Women's Studies in Communication* 40, no. 1 (2017): 14.
15. Tracy Gilchrist, "Elizabeth Banks: Gay Representation is 'Important' in *Charlie's Angels,*" TheAdvocate.com, November 13, 2019, https://www.advocate.com/film/2019/11/13/elizabeth-banks-gay-representation-important-charlies-angels.
16. See Lucy Wood, "Your First Glimpse of the Charlie's Angels Reboot Looks Suitably Awesome," MarieClare.com, April 12, 2019, https://www.marieclaire.com/celebrity/a27124523/first-glimpse-charlies-angels-reboot/.
17. Tracy Gilchrist, "Elizabeth Banks."
18. Quoted in Tracy Gilchrist, "Elizabeth Banks."
19. Lucy Wood, "Your First Glimpse."
20. Darren Franich, "*Charlie's Angels* Failed because the Franchise Era as We Know It Is Changing: Opinion," *Entertainment Weekly,* November 19, 2019, https://ew.com/movies/2019/11/19/charles-angels-box-office/.
21. Jonathan Gray, *Show Sold Separately: Promos, Spoilers, and Other Media Paratexts* (New York: New York University Press, 2010).
22. Gray, *Show Sold Separately.*
23. Gray, *Show Sold Separately.*
24. Christine Wooley, "Visible Fandom: Reading *The X-Files* through X-Philes," *Journal of Film and Video* 53, no. 4 (2001–2002): 29; Mark Andrejevic, "Watching Television without Pity: The Productivity of Online Fans," *Television and New Media* 9, no. 1 (2008): 25.
25. Andrejevic, "Watching Television without Pity," 24–46.

26. Quoted in Marshall Sella, "The Remote Controllers," *New York Times Magazine,* October 20, 2002, https://www.nytimes.com/2002/10/20/magazine/the-remote-controllers.html.
27. Sella, "The Remote Controllers."
28. Janelle Monae, *Q.U.E.E.N.,* music video, https://www.youtube.com/watch?v=tEddixS-UoU.
29. Sound Check, "Review: Janelle Monae Feat Erykah Badu Q.U.E.E.N.," AfroPunk.com, May 8, 2013, http://afropunk.com/2013/05/review-janelle-monae-feat-erykah-badu-q-u-e-e-n/; Janelle Monae, *Q.U.E.E.N.*
30. "The Royal Wedding 2018," Royal.uk, accessed December 31, 2018, https://www.royal.uk/royal-wedding-2018.
31. "Royal Wedding Charitable Donations," Royal.uk, accessed December 31, 2018, https://www.royal.uk/wedding-charity-donations.
32. Nate Anderson, "*Pandemic Legacy* Is the Best Board Game Ever—But Is It Fun?" *ArsTechnica,* March 12, 2016, https://arstechnica.com/gaming/2016/03/pandemic-legacy-is-the-best-board-game-ever-but-is-it-fun/; Tyler Nichols, "*Pandemic* Review," *Board Game Quest,* April 30, 2013, https://www.boardgamequest.com/pandemic-board-game-review/.
33. Emily Namey, Greg Guest, Kevin McKenna, and Mario Chen, "Evaluating Bang for the Buck: A Cost-Effectiveness Comparison between Individual Interviews and Focus Groups Based on Thematic Saturation Levels," *American Journal of Evaluation* 37, no. 3 (2016): 426.
34. Wooley, "Visible Fandom," 31.
35. Wooley, "Visible Fandom," 30–31.
36. Jonathan Alter, "The Weird World of Secrets and Lies," *Newsweek,* June 22, 1998: 76.
37. Wooley, "Visible Fandom," 37, 44.
38. Wooley, "Visible Fandom," 30.
39. Wooley, "Visible Fandom," 47
40. Wooley, "Visible Fandom," 47.
41. Rebecca Williams, "'This is the Night TV Died': Television Post-Object Fandom and the Demise of *The West Wing,*" *Popular Communication* 9, no. 4 (2011): 271.
42. Williams, "'This is the Night,'" 271.
43. Williams, "'This is the Night,'" 272–273.
44. Williams, "'This is the Night,'" 273.
45. Williams, "'This is the Night,'" 275–276.
46. Williams, "'This is the Night,'" 276
47. Williams, "'This is the Night,'" 278.
48. Christine Gardner, "'Created This Way': Liminality, Rhetorical Agency, and the Transformative Power of Constraint among Gay Christian College Students," *Communication and Critical Cultural Studies* 14, no. 1 (2017): 32.
49. Gardner, "'Created This Way,'" 41.
50. Quoted in Julie Roys, "Wheaton's 'Gay Celibate Christian,'" *World,* December 1, 2014, https://world.wng.org/2014/12/wheatons_gay_celibate_christian.

51. Gardner, "'Created This Way,'" 31–32.
52. Cited in Pam Belluck, "Many Genes Influence Same-Sex Sexuality, Not a Single 'Gay Gene,'" NYTimes.com, August 29, 2019, https://nyti.ms/2ZmHedC.
53. Quoted in Belluck, "Many Genes Influence."
54. Gardner, "'Created This Way,'" 32.
55. Gardner, "'Created This Way,'" 33.
56. Gardner, "'Created This Way,'" 36.
57. Gardner, "'Created This Way,'" 37.
58. Gardner, "'Created This Way,'" 42.

Chapter 10

Visual Rhetoric

In 2019, Nike won a Creative Arts Emmy for the best commercial.[1] The winning commercial features athletes such as Serena Williams, Lebron James, and the members of the US Women's Soccer Team. Colin Kaepernick appears on screen a full minute into the two-and-a-half-minute commercial, facing away from the camera. The camera circles him. As he slowly turns toward the camera, it becomes clear that Kaepernick is not only in this advertisement, he has been narrating it. Kaepernick is on screen for approximately thirteen seconds. Nike also created a grayscale poster advertisement featuring a close-up of Kaepernick's face, with some of the lines from the commercial and the Nike Swoosh logo superimposed upon it. Both the audiovisual commercial and the poster advertisement rely on visual symbols, visual aesthetics, and Kaepernick's visual recognizability to viewers.

We are so inundated by visual symbols that it can be hard to identify all the different pieces of what we have seen. For example, having seen both the poster and commercial, I was nevertheless uncertain at first whether the image on the poster was a freeze-frame from the commercial. The two visuals were fused together in my mind. Upon reviewing the commercial, I realized that the poster's imagery never appears in the commercial, yet I am still uncertain whether the poster is an entirely different visual from any used in the commercial or a zoomed-in, grayscale version of one of the commercial's frames featuring Kaepernick, with text superimposed upon it.

We are often overwhelmed by the volume of visual imagery we encounter and the speed at which we encounter it. Sometimes visual imagery can be hard to remember and distinguish. However, even young children can use visual symbols discerningly. For instance, by age three my sons could identify the Nike Swoosh, the logo of their favorite brand of orange juice, and a myriad of other visual imagery.

Commercials, advertising posters, and business logos are examples of visual rhetoric. **Visual rhetoric** is *the communicative, influential, and persuasive nature of visual imagery in logos, pictures, statues, movies, music videos, font styles, and so on.* It is often combined with words, sounds, or even three-dimensional objects. For example, a graphic novel combines visual images with verbal dialogue and narration; a music video combines moving visual imagery with lyrics and music; and a statue on a raised pedestal, although it is primarily seen, can also be touched and may be accompanied by words on a plaque.

Visual rhetoric functions symbolically. Just as words communicate meaning only because people agree that particular spellings and pronunciations correlate with particular meanings, so too with visual rhetoric. Consider, for example, a typical women's bathroom sign in the United States: a white, blocky silhouette of a person wearing a triangular dress on a blue, brown, or black background, or a black silhouette on a white background. The sign is well designed. It uses clean lines and high color contrast to increase its visibility. Yet nothing in this sign explicitly indicates that a toilet is nearby. Bathroom signs communicate effectively because people are trained to equate this visual symbol (the shapes, the colors, and the location high up on a wall) with toilets. Even though visual rhetoric often seems to have an automatic, obvious, or commonsense understanding, it relies on both the design of the imagery and its audience's interpretive skills.

When analyzing visual rhetoric, critics focus on analyzing (1) how people interpret and use visual rhetoric to communicate, (2) what meanings visual rhetoric is effective at communicating, and (3) how visual rhetoric functions in society. The discussion of critical approaches in previous chapters focused primarily on words and language use. When analyzing visual aspects of texts, critics focus on the imagery, not the words, yet critics maintain their focus on symbolic action. By analyzing visual rhetoric, critics are studying how symbols act in society.

By learning to analyze visual rhetoric, critics are able to study a variety of texts (such as photographs) that other methods are not well equipped to analyze. Critics can also combine this approach with other methods in order to create more robust analyses of texts that combine visual and other symbolic forms. To understand how to approach a visual text, we need a more precise understanding of visual rhetoric.

A THEORY OF VISUAL RHETORIC

Visual rhetoric seems like a fairly modern invention. After all, company logos, music videos, Tumblr, and Instagram are all fairly modern inventions. But within Western rhetorical theory, visual rhetoric is as old as Athens. Analyzing Aristotle's writings in *De Anima* and *Rhetoric,* Kathleen Lamp explains that in order to persuade an audience, Aristotle recommended speakers verbally depict a "vivid scene" so that the audience could see it in their "mind's eye."[2] Audience members who engage their imaginations and form a mental picture of what the speaker is talking about are more likely to be persuaded, for three central reasons.[3] First, they have committed more mental energy to the topic. Second, the speaker's emotions are aroused as s/he vividly describes a scene; the speaker's passion then influences the audience. And third, the audience members themselves experience strong emotions as a result of mentally visualizing the scene. Granted, Aristotle was offering advice on persuasion to speakers, not painters or sculptors, so it may seem like a leap to classify his advice within the realm of visual rhetoric. Nevertheless, he did connect the ideas of rhetorical persuasion to the visual—not necessarily the physically visual, but certainly to mental visualizations.

By the reign of Augustus, who ruled Rome from 27 BCE to 14 CE, visual rhetoric had a clearly established role in society. The historian Cassius Dio records Augustus as stating, "I found Rome built of clay and I leave it to you in marble."[4] Analyzing

Augustus's building projects, Kathleen Lamp concludes that they were explicitly rhetorical: the point of remaking the city in marble was to express the beauty, endurance, strength, and dignity of the empire.[5] The physical appearance of the city was rebuilt to display "Rome's place at the head" of the Roman empire.[6] The effect was meant to "elicit a reaction," especially from those who lived outside the city, implanting respect for Rome in its allies and striking "terror into [Rome's] enemies."[7]

Reflecting on the historic nature of visual rhetoric, rhetorical critics Lester Olson, Cara Finnegan, and Diane Hope suggest that all rhetoric can be understood as the ongoing intersection of images and texts in a related context.[8] Speakers are seen as well as heard. Statues have plaques. Murals incorporate words. Considered in this way, "the visual" is both an ancient, traditional aspect of rhetoric and a pressingly contemporary mode of rhetorical communication.

Much of this chapter will focus on more modern aspects of visual rhetoric, including mediated and digital aspects, but this Greek and Roman history lays the groundwork for three key understandings of visual rhetoric. First, Aristotle connected the visual to both emotions and persuasion. Second, he suggested that the verbal and visual intertwine (audiences mentally visualize speakers' words). And third, Roman history demonstrates how the powerful (such as the Roman Emperor Augustus) can mobilize whole structures (the state, tax monies, labor, and so on) in order to visually saturate a community in their preferred messages. Every marble surface in Rome reflected Augustus's power. These three concepts remain central in modern theories of visual rhetoric. The third concept, how the powerful saturate a community in their preferred visuals, links this critical approach with ideological criticism.

Seeing Is Knowing

Many cultures, especially Western cultures, rely on **sight-knowledge,** *knowledge or evidence derived from sight.*[9] For example, in 1965, Dolores Huerta led a grape workers' strike in California and then directed a national boycott of grapes. She famously chanted "*Sí se puede*," which is Spanish for "Yes, we can" and the inspiration for President Obama's campaign slogan. When National Public Radio (NPR) asked in an interview why she had organized the boycott, she replied by describing the farmworkers' conditions: "When I *saw* people in their homes—they had dirt floors and the furniture was orange crates and cardboard boxes. . . . I said, 'This is wrong,' because you *saw* how hard they were working, and yet they were not getting paid anything."[10] *Seeing* the farmworkers' houses convinced her that there was a crisis of injustice in the grape industry, and motivated her to action.

By relying on sight knowledge, Huerta continued a longstanding Western tradition. Rhetorical theorist Bruce Gronbeck tells us that both the Greek and Roman worlds grounded "knowing and believing" in "seeing and the visualized."[11] In ancient Western cultures and many modern cultures, to see is to know—indeed, the idiom "seeing is believing" emphasizes this close connection between sight and knowledge.

Not only is sight a common source of knowledge, knowledge derived from sight is especially valued. In ancient Western cultures and many modern cultures, eyewitness testimony is admissible in a court of law as well as a basis for everyday decisions. Gronbeck explains that the English word for *evidence* is derived from the Latin word *e-videre,* which means "out of or from seeing."[12] Seeing something is often considered the ultimate proof: sight is the bedrock of knowledge claims and typically functions as incontrovertible evidence in an argument. Consider again, Dolores Huerta's description of the farmworkers' houses. She offers eyewitness testimony of the farmworkers' conditions (dirt floors and furniture made out of orange crates and cardboard boxes); in so doing, she helps her audience mentally visualize the scene she saw. Huerta was persuaded through her sight knowledge and passes that sight knowledge on to her audience by describing the scene in a way that enables them to mentally picture it.

Visual Rhetoric in Context

Like other forms of rhetoric, visual rhetoric exists within a context. Traditionally, rhetorical theorists identify five basic elements for rhetoric and its context: the rhetor, the text (discussed in Chapter 1), and the three elements of what Lloyd Bitzer theorized as the rhetorical situation—exigence, audience, and constraints. (See Chapter 2.) For example, when a segregated political process in Mississippi sent an all-White delegation to vote at the 1964 Democratic National Convention, Mississippi's Fannie Lou Hamer (along with a racially integrated caucus) attended the convention to protest racist practices in the Democratic party and voting injustices more broadly.[13] Fannie Lou Hamer—who is famous for the line, "I'm sick and tired of being sick and tired"—delivered a powerful speech, vividly depicting the violence (insults, beatings, arrests, murders, and attempted murders) enacted upon Black Americans who were registering to vote.[14] In this example of verbal rhetoric, the rhetor is Fannie Lou Hamer. The text is the speech itself. The exigence is the racism in both the Democratic National Party and the broader political system. The constraints are elements such as time limits for her speech and the convention committee's racist mindsets. Finally, the audience is the Credentials Committee of the 1964 Democratic National Convention, along with those who watched the speech on television that evening, and those (including myself) who read or watched the speech in subsequent years.[15]

Visual rhetoric, however, rarely has such neat categories for its rhetor, text, exigence, constraints, and audience. For example, television series have executive directors (also known as showrunners). Each episode has a host of directors, writers, camerapersons, costume and makeup artists, actors, set managers, and so on. Here, the role of rhetor is diffused among many people.

Moreover, as design specialist Leslie Atzmon notes, for many visual entities the audience is not so much an audience as a user.[16] Consider a cereal box. The box is covered in visual imagery; the design, logo, and language-use hail shoppers in grocery store aisles. At home, family members sleepily gaze at the box—but they also pick it up, open it up, and pour cereal out of it. Similarly, although people look at buildings, we also go inside them, work and shop within them, open and close their windows, and interact with their infrastructures. Symbolic action arises as people interact with these visual entities by *using* them.[17]

In other instances, audience members become part of the diffusion of rhetors by recirculating the text. Communication critic Eric Jenkins notes that when someone "shares" a friend's meme, photo, or poster on social media, that "sharer" participates in the rhetor-ship of the text. As the rhetor-ship shifts, the audience, the exigence, the constraints, and even the form of the text itself shift as well.[18]

For example, on October 16, 2012, during the second presidential debate between Governor Mitt Romney and President Barack Obama, Romney shared an anecdote about hiring women. Infamously, he recounted that when presented with a predominantly male slate of job candidates he asked his staff, "Well, gosh, can't we—can't we find some—some women that are also qualified?" and then he continued to state in the debate, "I went to a number of women's groups and said, 'Can you help us find folks?' and I brought us whole binders full of—of women."[19] Although Romney can be understood as the original rhetor, new rhetors recirculated the phrase "binders full of women" in new forms for new audiences, creating a proliferation of new, negative, meanings. For instance, one meme featured a photo of Patrick Swayze from *Dirty Dancing* with superimposed text that read, "No one puts Baby in a binder."

Although Romney can be legitimately faulted for a statement that objectified women by claiming that he had "binders full of women" brought to him, as opposed to having binders full of women's resumés brought to him, this meme explicitly reframed Romney's statement as derogatory to women and radically politicized the visual image of Patrick Swayze. Here, we can see that visual rhetoric is malleable—especially in the digital realm. New rhetors can change existing visual rhetoric to create new visual rhetoric—with new meanings and new functions.

Cultural Practices of Seeing

Visual rhetoric involves both "visual stimuli" and "cultural practices of seeing."[20] In other words, when humans see things, there is something to see (visual stimuli); and the way in which we see is culturally shaped or constructed. Our **cultural practices of seeing** are *habits that inform what we pay attention to, how we see, and how we interpret what we see.* They train us to look at certain things while ignoring others, to process what we have seen in particular ways, and to interpret the meaning of different visual stimuli in culturally specific ways.

For example, consider the psychological experiment known as the Stroop effect. In its classic form, this experiment presents respondents with the names of colors (red, blue, green, yellow, black, pink, and so on) on a page or screen, but displays the words in a color that does not match the word. The word "yellow" might appear in pink, followed by the word "red" appearing in gray, and so on. The experiment asks respondents to ignore the meaning of the word and simply state the color. In so doing, it asks respondents to distinguish between two aspects of the visual stimuli: its color and its linguistic meaning. Respondents from high-literacy cultures find this experiment very hard: it is truly difficult to state the color rather than reading the word aloud. Psychologists generally agree that such respondents find the test difficult because they are taught from a young age to read automatically: to see a word is to read the word.[21] Broadly speaking, cultural practices of seeing (such as automatically reading words) shape and inform what types of visual stimuli capture our gaze, how we look at things, and how we interpret what we see.

Through cultural practices of seeing, cultures develop particular patterns of visual symbolism: within each culture, visual symbols come to represent particular meanings and function in specific ways. For example, consider the punk Riot Grrrl subculture that coalesced in the 1990s and 2000s around female punk bands such as *Bikini Kill*. Riot Grrrls circulated fanzines—homemade magazines—that celebrated female punk artists and featured short stories, poems, and photo collages. These fanzines were overtly political, often exploring issues related to "self-worth, the body, lesbianism, relationships and abuse."[22] In these fanzines, visual symbols took on complex meanings and functions. For instance, while "girl" and "grrrl" are often pronounced in identical ways, they have different visual features and different meanings within the Riot Grrrl subculture. "Girl" refers to a mainstream, nonfeminist young woman; "grrrl" refers to an independent, feminist, activist young woman who considers cuteness, youth, make-up, sexuality, and fun to be essential components of feminist activism.[23] Visually, "grrrl" implies a sort of growl since the repeating "r's" are visually reminiscent of how one might spell "grrr," conveying a sense of strength and activism. Essentially, Riot Grrrls celebrated girlhood as feminist activism.

Cultural theorist Clifford Geertz explains that visual imagery often communicates in such associative leaps. Visual imagery is implicated in a host of meanings, as viewers use their cultural practices of seeing to navigate the webs of associations and thus make sense of visual rhetoric.[24]

Cultural Imagery: Metaphors, Narratives, and Ideographs

Cultural practices fundamentally shape how people see, interpret, and use visual symbols. These practices create culturally specific visual metaphors, narratives, and ideographs. **Visual metaphors** are *metaphors (expressions of one idea or thing in terms of another idea or thing) that exist through visual imagery.* For example, drawing on the longstanding metaphors associating night/darkness with danger and daylight/light with safety, films often use light and darkness metaphorically to denote good and bad characters. Analyzing Peter Jackson's popular film version of *The Lord of the Rings* trilogy, media critics Charles Forceville and Thijus Renckens recount how good characters and geographies are bathed in light (for example, the good elves that live in Rivendell are "shown in excessively bright light"); evil characters and their geographies are filmed in dark environments and given dark names (for example, the primary villain, Sauron, is referred to as the "dark lord," and the last battle takes place at the "Black Gate").[25]

Visual texts can also participate in **visual narratives.** Design specialist Leslie Atzmon explains that, unlike verbal narratives, which rely on plot structures and chronology, visual narratives are *visual texts that achieve narrative structures through "layered and interconnected meanings" that coalesce into a story.*[26] Atzmon's explanation of visual narratives is not focused on films, silent films, television, graphic novels, or other visual texts that have clear plot structures, chronology, and verbal components; rather, she uses an example of a teacup to explain visual narratives.

Imagine a teacup with a delicate floral pattern, etched with gold trim, and set on its matching saucer. This teacup has no obvious plot or characters; however, the way its features look—its visuality—communicates how and when to use it, as well as the type of topics and word choices to be used in conversation as one drinks from it. Within US culture, this teacup's visuality communicates that it is precious, delicate, old-fashioned, refined, calm, special, and gentle; it is to be used in calm, refined environments to mark the specialness of the occasion. It is no common coffee mug. Its visuality clearly suggests that it should not be used while on the go.

A narrative arises from the "constellations of meanings embodied" in the teacup, constellations that are "assembled and reassembled by its users over time."[27] As we interpret the teacup's visuality and interact with it, we experience a narrative about what drinking tea means and who we are while we drink from the teacup.

We are rarely conscious of these visual narratives. Unless you stop to consider why you chose a specific mug or teacup, the choice feels fairly automatic. Visual theorists such as Atzmon, however, argue that "beneath the threshold of our conscious awareness," we rely on an "interpretive framework," meaning that when we look at visual texts (such as coffee mugs and teacups) we see meanings, messages, associations, and connotations in their visual features.[28] We do not need to pause and consciously puzzle through this interpretive process because the meanings, messages, associations and connotations of visual texts are "programmed" into us on "a deep level by various cultural beliefs and attitudes."[29] This interpretive process explains why people like particular cars or prefer Helvetica font to Times New Roman. The visual imagery is layered with meanings and messages that indicate how it should be used—how it functions in society—and what type of people should use it. As you interact with visual texts, you temporarily become the sort of person who drinks from a teacup, drives a Ferrari, or types in Helvetica. When interacting with visual texts, we enter into preexisting cultural narratives about what visual texts mean, how they are used, and who we are as we interact with them.

Finally, in addition to visual metaphors and visual narratives, cultural practices of seeing can culminate in visual ideographs. Ideographs are symbols that are commonplace within a culture, but that telegraph an ideology to the audience. (See Chapter 7.) For example, in the United States, the words <pro-choice> and <pro-life> function as ideographs: they quickly communicate a whole set of beliefs, values, attitudes, and assumptions. **Visual ideographs** are *ideographs that are images, instead of words or phrases.* For example, rhetorical critics Janis Edwards and Carol Winkler identified the image of five Marines and a Navy corpsman raising a US flag during the WWII battle of Iwo Jima as an ideograph.[30] When Americans view this image, it typically evokes patriotic ideology.

Visual ideographs are widely circulated and recirculated, and thus often appear in alternative forms, but they remain recognizable and retain at least some of their original connotations. The Iwo Jima photograph has been endlessly recreated in political cartoons, in which the Marines and Navy corpsman are depicted raising any number of politically loaded symbols instead of a flag. For instance, cartoonist Bill Schorr published a rendition of the Iwo Jima image in which the Marines lift and peer under a female recruit's skirt.[31] This image is clearly recognizable as an Iwo Jima image, but now the celebrated ideals of patriotism ring false or empty as the image juxtaposes patriotism against the reality of widespread sexual harassment in the military. Audience members are left to sort out the conflicting meanings, likely experiencing a sense of shame or frustration instead of the usual sense of pride and patriotic camaraderie the image usually evokes. Similarly, within US culture, images such as Mount Rushmore and the "I Want You" poster of Uncle Sam are routinely recirculated in ways that draw attention to current events while retaining their recognizability as Mount Rushmore or Uncle Sam.

From Aristotle forward, Western rhetorical theorists have recognized that imagery is particularly persuasive—whether that imagery is imagined by the audience, digitally portrayed, staged, or real. Cultural elites such as politicians, real estate moguls, and renowned artists, as well as film, television, music and advertising executives, have significant roles in the creation and dissemination of visual rhetoric, creating a close connection between popular visual rhetoric and hegemonic ideologies. (See Chapter 7.) Understanding visuality in these ways suggests that critics ought to analyze visual texts when attempting to understand (1) how visual rhetoric communicates meaning, (2) what visuality is particularly effective or ineffective at communicating, and (3) how visuality functions in society.

ANALYZING VISUAL TEXTS

Analyzing visual texts is an especially nonlinear process: the insights gained from one aspect of this approach inform and shape the insights gained from other aspects. Rather than progressing in a linear fashion, therefore, critics often cycle through the various aspects. Critics can also include this approach with other methods or modes of rhetorical analysis, in order to assess a text more robustly when it mixes visual and other symbolic communication.

Looking through Visual Rhetoric

Given that sight knowledge is culturally valued and that seeing often serves as evidence, critics need to slow down their own sight and interrogate their own assumptions in order to assess visual rhetoric. Visual theorists Kristie Fleckenstein, Scott Gage, and Katherine Bridgman recommend slowing down the gaze by **looking through,** *a process in which visual critics suspend belief, pausing between the "seeing" and the "believing" in order to understand what the visual entity asks viewers to know or believe and how it makes this invitation.*[32] The visual critic understands that the surface of the text is not factual evidence of full reality. For example, a photograph—even a candid one—is not the entire story; as a frozen snapshot in time, a photograph cannot capture how the events came to be or what happens next.

Moreover, our own cultural practices of seeing shape what we look at and how we look at it. One of the things critics can "see" when they look "through" the text is their own visual habits, thus seeing how they are culturally trained to see. Throughout the process, critics may find it helpful to focus their analyses with the following interpretive question: What argument is the visual entity making? Or to ask the question another way: What idea does this visual entity present as reality?[33]

To begin this practice of "looking through," I recommend that you make two columns of notes. In one column, list in detail the visual features of the text. In the other column, list your interpretations of those visual features. The idea is to carefully describe each aspect of your text, recording every detail of what you see with the correlating inferences and interpretations you are making from those details or groupings of details.[34] For some visual elements, you will note multiple interpretations; for others, you may have no inferences at all. By making such lists, a critic can begin to understand the argument in the visual text—the version of reality it presents to viewers.

For example, consider the portrait of Michelle Obama by Amy Sherald in the Smithsonian National Portrait Gallery. The portrait has famously evoked a sense

Figure 1

of royalty. People report being awestruck upon seeing it.[35] Engaging in this process of "looking through," a critic would note each feature of the portrait, such as the aura of light surrounding Obama; the predominant black and white color scheme; the bands of red, pink and yellow colors towards the bottom of her dress; her calm facial expression; the comfortable positioning of her arms and hands; the way she leans slightly forward; and the way she appears to be sitting but no chair is visible beneath her voluminous dress. Then, the critic would note assumptions about or interpretations of each of these items or groupings of items. For instance, the critic might interpret the aura of light as a sense of radiance, as if Obama were radiating light; Obama's arm positionings and slightly leaned forward pose as indicating that Obama is interested and engaged in what is happening; and the voluminous skirt as a throne in itself, making Obama appear to be a queen who needs no throne.

During this process, it is important that critics note not only the visual details they can see, but also what is invisible. In Obama's portrait, the fact that the chair is not visible is an important part of seeing and interpreting Obama's portrait—although the glow and voluminous dress implies a queenlike presence, it is the missing chair that seems to present Obama as a queen who needs no throne.

Particularly with still images, such as portraits, candid photographs, or staged photographs, critics need to consider what is outside the frame—what was left out of view. For example, in the aftermath of Hurricane Harvey, while rescue missions were still underway, conservative Christian blogger Matt Walsh tweeted a photo taken by Louis DeLuca for the *Dallas Morning News* of a woman holding a baby while being carried through the flood water by a male rescue worker.[36] (See Figure 1.) The picture Walsh recirculated on Twitter is gripping; there is a clear sense of heroism, solemnity, and danger in the photo. Matt Walsh added a caption to this photo in which he claimed the photo was evidence of universal gender roles in which women protect babies and men protect women and children—and that this evidence disproved gender studies professors' claims about gender.[37] Like all photos, however, this photo did not depict the entire story.

Another photo by DeLuca from a slightly different angle includes another person—a man carrying a bag with a red strap over one shoulder and bright red and pink sneakers in his other hand. (See Figure 2.) This photo has none of the first photo's gravitas. The pops of color are out of place with the otherwise depressing flood scene. Moreover, the familiarity of trying to keep a pair of shoes dry, along with the man's ability to navigate the flood waters, significantly lessens the sense of danger. Finally, the proximity of the figures suggests that the woman, the baby, and the man with the shoes are a family.

This second photo seems to include a father figure who is caring for his family—by keeping their things dry—while a physically more fit rescue worker assists the woman and baby. Leaving the man with the colorful shoes out of the image created a striking photo that Walsh interpreted to indicate a natural order of men caring for women and women caring for babies. By taking the photo from another angle and thus including a probable father figure, bags, and shoes, the second image is not only less gripping, it undermines Walsh's interpretation by picturing other ways that men can care for their families than through brute strength.

To assess what is invisible or left out of a visual text, critics typically engage in contextual research. When working with a photograph, a critic can review other photos of the scene or even visit the scene to understand its topography, architecture, surrounding decor, and so on. When studying artwork, such as a sculpture, a critic might review drafts and mock-ups of the artwork, then compare these preliminary renditions to the final version to see what was left out. When studying architecture such as memorials, monuments, or museums, a critic might consider the design proposals that were *not* selected—the ways in which other artists and architects imagined the project that were not chosen and therefore never came into visibility. By considering what is invisible—what was omitted from the visual—critics remind themselves that "seeing" is not "believing," that there is more to the story than visual rhetoric shows viewers. Indeed, knowing what would ruin the appeal—what had to be left out—helps the critic understand the nature of the visual appeal.

Throughout this "looking through" process, the critic remains "poised between the details of the image—visible and invisible," and their evocations and interpretations.[38] The critic can notice (1) which features of the text for which the critic has (or previously had) no conscious interpretations, (2) which features draw the critic's gaze and serve as the basis for interpretations of the text; and (3) which interpretations are precarious, resting on scant visual evidence. This process further encourages the critic to recognize how each act of perception (looking) is in fact "already a process of interpretation."[39] By relying on sight for knowledge and by focusing on some features rather than others, the critic has already begun interpreting the text, deciding that it matters and which features of it matter more than others. By mapping out each feature of the text and a corresponding interpretation

Figure 2

of it, the critic can slow down the process of looking, hovering between "seeing" and "knowing" and thus understanding how sight becomes knowledge.

Assessing Point of View

When analyzing visual rhetoric, critics consider the **point of view,** *the perspective through which audience members are invited to look at the visual text.* Essentially, critics ask the interpretive question, *with whom or what am I looking?* For example, most films and photographs encourage viewers to look through the camera lens from the perspective of the cameraperson.

When assessing the point of view, the critic assesses the visual text's features within the context of cultural practices of seeing. For example, rhetorical critic Anne Teresa Demo analyzed the Guerrilla Girls' 2012 poster "Do Women Have to be Naked to Get into the Met. Museum?" (See Figure 3, page 224.) The Guerrilla Girls, a collective of feminist activists who "use facts, humor and outrageous visuals to expose gender and ethnic bias as well as corruption in politics, art, film, and pop culture," rendered this image of a nude woman reclining in a way that is reminiscent of Jean Auguste Dominique Ingres's famous 1814 nude painting, the Grande Odalisque.[40] The nude woman in the poster, however, has a gorilla mask on her head. The background of the poster is banana yellow. Most of the text is black. In addition to the title question, the poster includes the following text: "Less than 4% of the artists in the Modern Art sections are women, but 76% of the nudes are female."[41] The percentages ("4%" and "76%") and the words "artists"

Figure 3

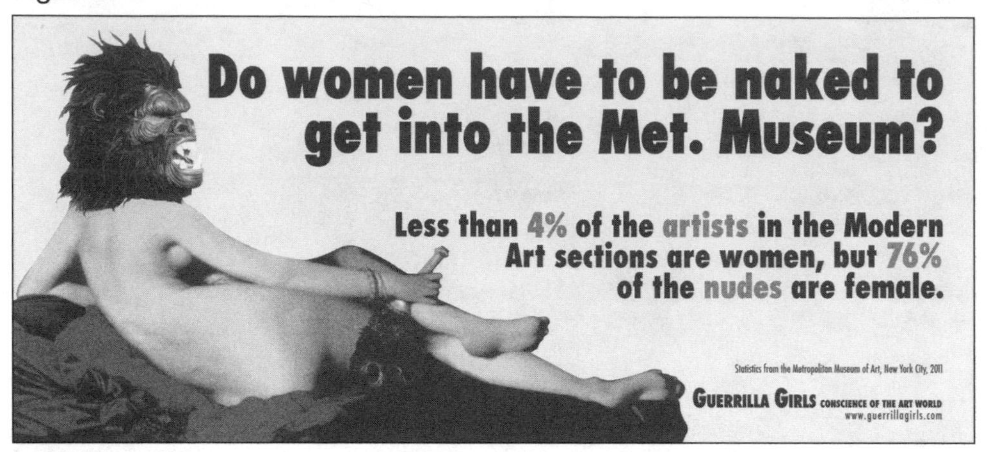

© 2012 Guerrilla Girls

and "nudes" are featured in hot pink. Analyzing the poster, Demo notes that the bright yellow background is eye-catching (drawing the gaze from a distance) and the bright pink font stands out, drawing the gaze specifically to the juxtaposition of the numbers of female artists and the numbers of female nudes on display in the museum.[42]

Through her analysis, Demo establishes how the poster invites the gaze and the point of view it offers to viewers. It is meant to surprise viewers and draw their attention to the juxtaposition of how few female artists have their work displayed in the museum and how many nude female bodies are on display in the museum. The poster works by drawing on and then inverting viewers' expectations about nude art. By juxtaposing the visual reference to the famous Grande Odalisque with the gorilla mask, the poster disrupts the normalcy of seeing objectified nude female bodies as art.

Visual entities can create the point of view in a wide variety of ways. Like the Guerrilla Girls example, posters tend to use shapes, visual allusions, and color to direct attention to specific visual elements. Statues on raised pedestals tend to force viewers to gaze up at the them: the point of view renders the statue prestigious and authoritative, and marks the person or event depicted as important within the intended audience's cultural practices of seeing. A video camera that zooms in on women's posteriors or pans up and down their bodies invites viewers to objectify women. A photograph limits the perspective to just that one frozen frame, inviting viewers to understand the image as reality—devoid of its surrounding context. Understanding how visual rhetoric invites viewers' gaze is an important step in making sense of how visual rhetoric functions in society.

Cultural Practices of Seeing and Ideology

Critics consider the cultural practices of seeing and the ideology at work in a visual text.[43] These can be apparent in the way the visual rhetoric is embedded in a larger text. Visual rhetorician Cara Finnegan reminds critics that when visual entities are embedded in larger texts (for example, photos in a magazine article), they cannot "be separated from the texts they accompany, nor should they be viewed as mere supplements to those texts."[44] When working with images that are combined with other modes of communication, a critic should attend to the whole rather than focusing on just one part—especially when considering cultural practices of seeing and ideology.

To focus on the cultural practices of seeing, critics can ask interpretive questions such as: How has culture trained viewers to "see" this visual rhetoric? Are there metaphors, narratives, and/or ideographs that viewers are expected to understand as they see the image? And are there additional aspects (such as a caption on a photo) that direct viewers to "see" the visual rhetoric in a specific way?

To focus on a visual text's ideology, critics can ask interpretive questions such as: What "common sense" meanings operate in this visual rhetoric? What does a viewer have to assume is true in order to make sense of this it? And who circulated this visual rhetoric and what is their ideology?

Let us return to conservative Christian blogger Matt Walsh's articulation of traditional gender roles in his recirculation of DeLuca's Hurricane Harvey photo. Walsh, who describes himself as "one of the religious Right's most influential young voices," has made his ideology of political conservatism and hierarchical gender roles quite clear.[45] His tweeted caption of the photo directed viewers' "practices of seeing" to attend specifically to the genders of the rescue worker and the person being rescued. Here, a visual metaphor and conservative political ideology intertwine as Walsh directs viewers to see the photo through larger US cultural practices of seeing. As theorist George Lakoff explains, conservative ideology in the United States imagines the nation as a family and the government as a strong father figure.[46] Walsh's caption invites viewers to see the photo through this conservative ideology—and, when seen through this ideology, the rescue worker (who wears military-style fatigues and a police SWAT cap) appears to represent the government. When seen through this cultural practice of seeing, the image visualizes the metaphor of the government as a father who protects and cares for the nation—pictured here as the woman and sleeping baby. The photo assures viewers that the government is stepping in to protect its vulnerable citizens while simultaneously drawing on and reinforcing the ideas that men ought to protect women and that women (and babies) need protection.

Assessing Context

Finally, to understand how a visual entity functions in society, the critic must assess the context or contexts that produced the image and circulate (or recirculate) it. Visual rhetorician Cara Finnegan recommends that critics ask the following interpretive question when considering context: Where, how, and why is this visual rhetoric circulated in society?[47]

By focusing on *where* a visual entity circulates in society, a critic can begin to understand its context. The critic should consider the medium, platform, and physical or digital location of the image. Then, the critic ought to consider the implications of where the text circulates by asking and answering questions such as: Who can put visual rhetoric in this location? Who can access this location to see its visual rhetorics? Who is likely to access this location? What does someone have to know to produce a text in this medium? What type of prestige or authority does this location/medium/platform have (if any)?

For example, a portrait gallery is a very different location from a Facebook photo album or magazine cover. Artists have to be invited to feature their work in the National Portrait Gallery or on a magazine cover, but almost anyone can make a Facebook album. Consequently, the Smithsonian National Portrait Gallery has far more prestige than a magazine cover, which, in turn, has more prestige than a Facebook album. Admission to the Smithsonian National Portrait Gallery is free, but for many people in the United States it is cost-prohibitive to travel to visit this museum; meanwhile, a magazine cover is accessible to anyone in a grocery store checkout aisle. A Facebook album can be limited to a select group of viewers. A critic needs to assess these multiple aspects of where a text circulates in order to understand how it functions in society.

By focusing on *how* a visual entity circulates in society, a critic works to understand the mechanisms and multiple avenues through which visual rhetoric becomes accessible to viewers. For example, when asking how a statue circulates in society, a critic might research its original creation—how the statue was commissioned or the original design prescriptions. Additionally, the critic would study how the statue is physically situated, its visibility, and the traffic flow surrounding it. The critic would also study how the image of the statue is circulated—for example, in pamphlets, tourist books, films, historical documentation, and websites—and how it is featured in magazines or online reviews.

By focusing on *why* visual rhetoric circulates in society, a critic attempts to make sense of how various rhetors use a visual image as they circulate it. For example, a music video might be released in conjunction with a film that features the song in its soundtrack. Correspondingly, the music video might feature clips from the film in its visual displays. Here, a critic might recognize the economic motivations: the music video and the film support each other's popularity and therefore economic profits. If the musician outgrows the success of the film, the music production house might recirculate the music video without the clips from the film. Here, a critic would again see economic motivations largely driving recirculation. But as the music video is shared on social media, turned into tweet-able, post-able, and text-able GIFs, and uploaded by fans to YouTube.com with subtitles in various languages, a critic might find a whole host of motivations as the text recirculates in society.

Since ancient times, the rich and powerful (such as a business CEO, an incumbent politician, or a celebrity) have had more access to visual media than others—whether the medium is city architecture, wartime propaganda, documentaries, magazine advertisements, or social media algorithms. Visual rhetoric is often expensive to produce and circulate; thus, cultural elites find it easier than others to blanket a society in their visual rhetoric. For example, it is nearly impossible for a middle-class citizen with a modest campaign budget to win a campaign for state governor when campaigning against an incumbent who blankets the state in television advertisements funded by Super PACs. The middle-class candidate makes advertisements, posters, and a website, but does not have the money to widely circulate this visual rhetoric. The middle-class candidate's visual rhetoric is buried beneath the richer candidate's means of production and circulation. Considering the ways in which visual rhetoric often favors the elite in a society, a critic ought to be particularly cognizant of these structural factors while studying the context of a text—where, how, and why it circulates in society.

Ultimately, visual critics focus on understanding how people interpret and use visual rhetoric to communicate, influence, and persuade one another. A critic can assess the interpretations that visual features evoke, the point of view through which viewers are invited to see the image, the cultural practices and ideology through which viewers see and interpret the text, and the context within which the text (re)circulates. This mode of analysis works to understand not just the features of a text, but the cultural gaze (how a society looks at the world) and how a society values and uses visuality.

RESEARCH EXAMPLES

The following three research examples provide excellent demonstrations of how a critic can approach the visual elements of a text. In the first study, Aisha Durham analyzes Beyoncé Knowles's 2005 hit music video, "Check on It." Her assessment focuses on the music video as a whole, while highlighting the meaning and function of the visual elements. The second example, Rachel E. Dubrofsky and Emily D. Ryalls's analysis of *The Hunger Games,* pays specific attention to the film medium and the ways in which current trends in cinematography focus visual attention on women's "authenticity." In the third example, Richard D. Pineda and Stacey K. Sowards analyze how flag waving operates as a visual argument. They specifically assess the ways in which foreign flags—when waved by US immigrants—operate as an ideograph that anti-immigration advocates understand as (at the very least) a failure to assimilate.

Aisha Durham
"'Check on It': Beyoncé, Southern Booty, and Black Femininities in Music Video" (2012)*

Beyoncé is a pop culture icon, a sensation who combines hit music with feminist and antiracist activism. Her 2016 album, *Lemonade,* not only topped the charts and won a Grammy Award for Best Music Video, but also received strident backlash and social controversy. During her Super Bowl performance of "Formation," one of *Lemonade*'s hit singles, performers wore costumes reminiscent of the Black Panthers. Some Americans responded with a #BoycottBeyoncé Twitter trend, while others countered with a #IStandWithBeyoncé hashtag.

Beyoncé, however, had a long career prior to *Lemonade.* This career had many phases, including her struggle to establish herself and control her image, her role in the female group Destiny's Child, her performances in major motion films, her solo career, her marriage to and collaborations with Jay-Z, her alter ego Sasha Fierce, her hit single, "Single Ladies," and her more recent visual albums featuring more personal and political themes.

---

*This essay may be found in *Feminist Media Studies* 12, no. 1 (2012): 35–49.

By analyzing Beyoncé's 2005 MTV award-winning music video, "Check on It," rhetorical critic Aisha Durham explores the visuality in one of Beyoncé's early hits, studying its depictions of "Black femininity" and "Black female sexuality."[48] In this video, Beyoncé performs many different versions of Black femininity as she sings in various pink settings about the pleasure derived from "watching her man watching her booty dance."[49] Interspersed in this music video are scenes of two Houston rappers, Slim Thug and Bun B, as well as clips from *The Pink Panther*—a film in which Beyoncé acted. The original music video opened with the Pink Panther cartoon figure inviting and transitioning viewers into the pink world in which Beyoncé sings "Check On It."[50]

Durham demonstrates how location functions visually within the video, arguing that the scene is simultaneously set in two different locations. First, the video is grounded in the spatial location of Houston. By including two prominent Houston rappers, "Check on It" ties into their "hip hop authenticity" and "street credibility," connecting Beyoncé's music with a Southern working-class aesthetic of Houston's Third Ward neighborhood.[51] Simultaneously, the music video takes place in a pink dreamworld. The Pink Panther ushers viewers into a dreamscape of "billowing pink satin fabric."[52] This dreamscape fantasy is created by film techniques (for example, the camera's insistent gaze at Beyoncé's backside as she dances) and narrative cues (such as understandings of Black female bodies that are based in cultural narratives of the nineteenth-century iconography of Saartjie Baartman, who was dubbed the "Hottentot Venus").[53] This dual location visually functions to position Beyoncé's body as authentically "urban" and yet transcendent in its sexual appeal.[54] In so doing, "Check on It" celebrates a particular performance of Black female sexuality ("bootylicious") as fantasy material for a wide range of heterosexual men.[55]

Durham also addresses the implications of the pink color scheme. Beyoncé performs various roles in "Check on It," appearing as a diva in a gown, as part of an all-women's dance troupe, as a girl gang member, as a "ghetto girl" at a subway stop, as a demure schoolgirl, and in many other roles.[56] Throughout, she wears pink and dances against pink backgrounds. Assessing the use of color, Durham argues that "Check on It" employs a pink continuum, where "pastel is pure and hot pink is well—hot."[57] For example, as a schoolgirl, Beyoncé wears a light pink angora sweater, and merely sways with the music as she kneels and bats her eyes at the camera. Here, "this scene conveys a passivity and prepubescent sexuality."[58] In contrast, when portraying the "ghetto girl," Beyoncé performs in front of shockingly hot pink subway tiles. In these scenes, the camera provides "long shots of her booty dance," emphasizing a sense of sexual proficiency.[59]

Ultimately, Durham argues that the visual locations, costuming, choreography, camera treatments, and color schemes combine to reproduce US cultural practices of seeing—directing a hypersexualized gaze at Black women's bodies. Moreover, "Check on It" relentlessly ties every version of Black femininity that it visualizes to the sexualization of the "booty." Here, Durham notes that the visuals are at odds with the lyrics, in which Beyoncé focuses on her own pleasure and establishes the parameters of these sexual interactions. In the lyrics, Beyoncé tells her partners that while she dances they can look but not grab; however, the point of view—the camera—visually objectifies her, by gazing at her backside rather than reflecting the lyrics by offering viewers Beyoncé's point of view.[60] That is, we gaze at her body rather than gazing through her eyes as we watch the video.

"Check on It" presents an image of Beyoncé that is rather different from her more recent albums. *Lemonade* presents Beyoncé as a subject—not an object. The recirculated version of "Check on It" removed the *Pink Panther* introduction and the interspersed scenes of the *Pink Panther*'s male actors gazing at Beyoncé's body. Essentially, as Beyoncé's fame outgrew the *Pink Panther*, the early music video's visuals were changed in a way that deemphasizes the "dreamworld" nature of the pink staging and the foregrounding of the heterosexual male gaze. These revisions help to re-center "Check on It" on Beyoncé's subjectivity, better reflecting her more recent visual performances.

Rachel E. Dubrofsky and Emily D. Ryalls "*The Hunger Games:* Performing Not-Performing to Authenticate Femininity and Whiteness" (2014)*

The Hunger Games was the "third highest grossing film" in 2012—outperforming the *Twilight* saga's last installment by over $100 million in domestic profits.[61] This film adaptation of Suzanne Collins's best-selling, postapocalyptic young adult trilogy tells the story of Katniss Everdeen as she is drawn into a reality-TV competition in which she battles other children to the death. Rachel Dubrofsky and Emily Ryalls focus on the ways in which surveillance operates within the film—especially as surveillance emphasizes sight as knowledge in its portrayal of Katniss. Specifically, Dubrofsky and Ryalls identify the connections of lighting and camera techniques with lines of dialogue, demonstrating how the whole comes together to present Katniss as "authentic."

For example, before the "games" begin, Katniss is featured on a talk show that is broadcast on the state-sponsored channel throughout the fictional nation of Panem. Katniss is explicitly told that she must perform well on this talk show in order to gain sponsors who will finance her experience in the games by providing her with useful items (such as medicine and information).[62] While the other competitors appear cocky and give clearly staged performances, Katniss appears to be her authentic self during the talk show interview. The camerawork specifically creates this impression by shakily following her out on to the stage and then alternating to show her perspective—looking out at the audience. The audio reinforces the sense of her nervousness by providing a muted audio track of the cheering crowd and the talk show host. The camera steadies and the audio returns as Katniss's body language visually calms. Throughout the interview—in which the host explicitly describes her as "nervous"—Katniss is depicted as "incapable of performing in front of an audience."[63] Even when facing life-and-death stakes, Katniss cannot put on a show to attract sponsors.

Here, surveillance is a necessary component of confirming Katniss's authenticity. In order to show that Katniss is true to herself (and incapable of pretense),

*This essay may be found in *Critical Studies in Media Communication* 31, no. 5 (2014): 395–409.

The Hunger Games has to show viewers what Katniss is like when she is not being watched as well as what she is like while she is being watched, in order to demonstrate that she is the same "self" in both instances. Dubrofsky and Ryalls note that this is a paradox: she must perform for viewers in order to prove that she is not performing—that she is authentic. They describe this visual "authenticity" as "performing not-performing."[64]

Dubrofsky and Ryalls specifically argue that Katniss's "authenticity" performs a very specific type of Whiteness. Notably, in the book version, Katniss is described as having "olive skin, gray eyes, and black hair," but the film version cast Jennifer Lawrence in the role, portraying Katniss as White.[65] Katniss has flawless skin, "naturally red and slightly bee-stung" lips, flushed cheeks, lustrous, shiny hair, and straight white teeth in every scene.[66] In contrast to her appearance, she is depicted as coming from an impoverished, food-scarce home and having no knowledge of makeup or grooming techniques, thus presenting her beauty as natural and effortless. Moreover, the lighting and camera techniques used throughout the film make Katniss's skin literally radiant. Connecting these visual depictions to US cultural ideologies and practices of seeing, Dubrofsky and Ryalls argue that her visuality is "associated with virtue and innocence" as her Whiteness, effortless beauty, and radiance combine in a way that "goodness can be read off her body."[67]

In contrast, the rich White character Effie and the rich White tributes—the other children competing in the games—appear inauthentic. Effie's skin is bumpy with "layers of stark white foundation" and her lips, cheeks, and eyes are unnaturally colored throughout.[68] The other White tributes (with the exception of Peeta, Katniss's love interest) are bloodthirsty characters who were raised to perform in these games. The comparison with these characters positions Katniss as an authentic or real White person, while the other characters become false representatives of the White race. Dubrofsky and Ryalls argue that although *The Hunger Games* presents a diverse cast, as well as both good and bad White characters, the decision to cast Katniss as White, combined with the "authenticity" of her goodness, reinforces and recirculates US cultural practices of seeing Whiteness as goodness.

Moreover, although Katniss verbally rejects romance and states that she does not want children in her future, she is relentlessly depicted as maternal. Once again, the film diverges from the books as it depicts Katniss in a maternal role with her younger sister, Prim, rather than featuring their mother as mothering Prim as she does in the books. Katniss wins the game by rejecting violence and instead acting loving and maternal. She cares for others, and through caring, wins the games. She kills only one other tribute, Cato, and only out of compassion, to spare him unnecessary suffering. Throughout, her "value, strength, and heroism" stem from her maternal instincts and "heterosexual femininity," creating a paradox in which "Katniss is uninterested in love and children yet presented as having the qualities to be the perfect wife and mother."[69] Moreover, these qualities are "so innate and instinctive, they emerge regardless of Katniss's stated desires."[70]

Ultimately, Dubrofsky and Ryalls demonstrate the ways in which the visual imagery, audio, and dialogue coalesce in *The Hunger Games* to present Katniss as authentic, while also premising her authenticity on preexisting ideology that connects Whiteness to goodness and female bodies to maternal instincts. Moreover, cultures of surveillance value authenticity—and Dubrofsky and Ryalls argue that the forces of social media and reality TV encourage such cultures. In surveillance cultures people must seek audiences before which they can perform, so they can perform not-performing and thus establish their authenticity. Dubrofsky and Ryalls are particularly concerned about the ways in which Whiteness and maternal instincts function as indicators of natural or authentic performances for female bodies.

Richard D. Pineda and Stacey K. Sowards "Flag Waving as Visual Argument: 2006 Immigration Demonstrations and Cultural Citizenship" (2007)*

People in the United States have long debated immigration, arguing about what it means to be American, who can be American, from which nations "new" Americans should come, and how many immigrants should become American at any given time. Historically, the arguments surrounding immigration engage in a rather paradoxical celebration of immigration (remembering the United States as a country of immigrants) and considerable fear of immigrants (concerns that the nation will be fundamentally changed by the admission of new immigrants). As a result, immigrants are lauded as fundamentally American and feared as irredeemably un-American throughout US political discourse. Richard Pineda and Stacey Sowards analyze how flag waving is visualized in US news media and how the image of waving flags operates as a "visual argument" about immigration—but one that is interpreted differently by different audiences.[71]

Immigrants and immigrant advocates regularly gather in large rallies across the United States to celebrate, protest, and organize future activism. For example, responding to the 2006 immigration debates in Congress and the media, between 350,000 and 500,000 immigration advocates rallied in Dallas; roughly 400,000 immigration advocates rallied in Chicago; between 300,000 and 400,000 rallied in Los Angeles; and approximately 75,000 rallied in Denver.[72] Smaller rallies were held in more than 70 cities around the country. The media coverage of these rallies featured images of people waving flags.

Pineda and Sowards note that the camera provides the sightlines, creating a point of view where the viewer (whether reading the story in a newspaper or watching it on the evening news) sees the story from the camera's perspective.[73] This perspective is not the perspective of someone participating in the rally, for whom most of the flags would have been waving above eye level. Instead, downward-angled shots of the whole rally provide a bird's eye view of all the waving flags. Moreover, rally participants would have engaged in call-and-response chants and listened to speakers who made verbal arguments regarding immigration. Those who viewed the rally through news discourse saw the imagery of the flags without the verbal arguments that were embedded in the rally; the visual imagery of flag waving was resituated within the verbal arguments of the news coverage itself.

---

*This essay may be found in *Argumentation and Advocacy* 43, no. 3-4 (2007): 164–174.

In the initial wave of pro-immigration rallies in 2006, those attending the rallies brought and waved the flag of the United States as well as the flags of other countries, such as Cuba, Honduras, Guatemala, El Salvador, Mexico, and the Philippines.[74] Pineda and Sowards argue that flag waving operates as a visual ideograph. That is, the visual image of waving flags operates as commonsense evidence of a particular ideological belief. However—unlike the image of Iwo Jima—flag waving functions as an ideograph that activates different ideologies in different US audiences. Pineda and Sowards argue that for immigrants and immigration advocates, waving both US flags and the flags of other countries activates a strong sense of pride in national diversity. Waving multiple flags celebrates the United States as a home for many, a place where difference is embraced, a place where all are free and all are equal. Pineda and Sowards demonstrate that just as people wave Irish flags on St. Patrick's Day as a sign of pride in participants' cultural heritage, without negating their pride in their US heritage, so too did these immigrant activists wave multiple flags as a sign of their pride in a dual identity.[75] For immigrants and immigrant advocates, the visual image of waving multiple flags represents an ideology, a belief that the United States is a home that welcomes the complexity and diversity of human experience and that values "freedom of expression."[76] It also activates a sense of unity among immigrants, a sense of solidarity and belief that all immigrants are united in their experience as immigrants.[77] In short, rather than representing loyalty to a foreign power, waving foreign flags represents unity with other immigrants.

Anti-immigration advocates, however, see the flag waving visuals quite differently. Pineda and Sowards argue that for anti-immigration advocates, foreign flags operate as a visual ideograph that represents three beliefs: First, that these immigrants have failed to assimilate. Second, that immigrants are "deviant" or not real Americans because they have "different cultural and class-related practices."[78] And third, that the United States has failed to "adequately control immigration."[79]

Two different ideologies of what it means to be a US citizen are at work in these two interpretations of these flag waving visuals. Anti-immigration advocates see the United States as a place that has only one culture and can have only one culture in the future if it wants to thrive. They see flying multiple flags as evidence that immigrants "aren't really interested in being Americans."[80] In contrast, immigration advocates see waving multiple flags as proof of the success of the American experiment—an experiment that creates a nation out of immigrants and welcomes cultural diversity.

Ultimately, Pineda and Sowards emphasize how different beliefs (ideologies) of what it means to be a US citizen undergird the way these visual ideographs were deployed and interpreted in news coverage. They demonstrate how visuals operate as an argument, and like all arguments have a back-and-forth interaction. In 2006, immigration advocates watched the news and, realizing that these visuals were operating in a different way than intended for this outside audience, urged rally participants to bring only US flags to the upcoming rallies. Instead of the "profusion of colors and emblems," subsequent rallies primarily featured the stars and stripes of the US flag.[81]

In this case, immigrants and immigration advocates changed their visuals in order to counter the argument that immigrants were uninterested in becoming

American. However, eliminating the visual ideograph of multiple waving flags also eliminates the circulation of the larger ideology—that the United States is a country of immigrants who are unified in the midst of diverse cultural heritages.

STRENGTHS AND WEAKNESSES OF ANALYZING VISUALITY

The key strength of this critical approach is that it takes visuality seriously. Visual analysis applies the longstanding insights of rhetorical theory to our current experiences with screen technologies, social media, advertising, and the internet, as well as the ubiquitous posters, cityscapes, architecture, fonts, company logos, and visual designs that seem to cover every inch of every surface in our lives. In so doing, this critical approach analyzes the proliferation of visual rhetoric and its influence on contemporary life.

Analyses of visual rhetoric tend to be fundamentally concerned with ideology, so it works well when combined with ideological criticism. Like ideological criticism, visual analyses are particularly well suited to revealing how underlying belief systems shape how people create and share meaning through symbolic action. As Pineda and Sowards demonstrate in their analysis of flag waving, the same visual image can serve as evidence in two very different arguments, depending on the ideology of the viewer.

One difficulty of visual analysis, however, is that a visual critic must be especially knowledgeable culturally. The critic must identify the visual allusions, narratives, metaphors, and ideographs in a visual text, requiring a broad understanding of visual images and cultural associations.

Finally, audience members for visual rhetoric are typically anonymous. For example, it is often impossible to identify who has seen a particular poster, who watched a television episode, who scrolled past a particular meme, and so on. As a result, visual critics typically make arguments about how sight functions in society or how visual texts act symbolically, but can find it difficult to demonstrate how audiences specifically responded to the visual rhetoric.

CHOOSING THIS APPROACH

A visual approach helps critics assess texts—or the visual portions of texts—that other methods are less adept at analyzing. Because almost every text has some visual component, this approach is particularly useful: a speaker is heard, but also usually seen; a blog is written, but its fonts and images are seen; a film can be distilled to its narrative, but that narrative is experienced through sight; and so on. As a result, a visual approach to criticism helps critics include texts or elements of texts that would otherwise be omitted. Moreover, a visual approach can be combined with other methods or modes of analysis to assess robustly how a text functions in society.

So how do you know whether you should focus on analyzing the visual aspects of a particular piece of public discourse? To answer this question, I recommend that you consider the quality or importance of the visuals of your text and your own animating research question.

First, does the text heavily rely on visuality for its communication, influence, or persuasion? Or does some aspect of its visuality significantly affect its action in society? For example, Aisha Durham's visual analysis of "Check on It" revealed not only that the music video relies on visuality to convey its meaning (for example, the pink continuum), but also that the camera's point of view specifically counters the lyrics' statements of Beyoncé's sexual empowerment. If Durham had not analyzed the visual rhetoric and relied only on the words, melody, and rhythm, her analysis would have missed the way the visuality of the text sexually objectifies Beyoncé. A critic needs to assess how prominent and meaningful the visuals are in order to know whether to focus on the visual imagery of a text.

Second, consider your own research motives. Are you concerned with how a culture is trained to see and to value sight knowledge? Are you interested in understanding how visual rhetoric interacts with hegemonic practices that saturate a culture in dominant ideology? Are you intrigued by what visuals are efficient at communicating? A visual approach to rhetorical criticism is particularly adept at answering the types of research questions that stem from these concerns.

Ultimately, this approach helps critics recognize how visual rhetoric conveys, creates, and shapes meaning in society. Simultaneously, however, it reveals how visuality functions in society—how people rely on sight, how they look at visual rhetoric, and how they value and use the knowledge derived from sight. This approach is like a hall of mirrors, where you look into a mirror and see not only your own reflection, but also the reflection of the reflection. When assessing visual rhetoric, critics not only look at their texts, but also assess the act of gazing, the ideologies through which viewers gaze, and the cultural uses for visuality.

DISCUSSION QUESTIONS

1. Describe an experience in which visual rhetoric persuaded you to do something.
2. Pick a film or television series that you enjoy. Now do some online research to find one meme or GIF that recirculates a part of that film or television series to support a political message. Explain the new context and how the new context affects the meaning of the visual entity.
3. In your own words, explain the idea of cultural practices of seeing. Now offer one example in which a cultural practice shaped how you saw a particular visual image.
4. Provide an example of a visual metaphor, a visual narrative, and a visual ideograph.

NOTES

1. Mary Papenfuss, "Nike's Controversial Colin Kaepernick Ad Wins Emmy for Best Commercial," *Huffington Post,* August 16, 2019, https://www.huffpost.com/entry/colin-kaepernick-donald-trump-nike-ad-creative-arts-emmy_n_5d7efe19e4b00d69059b023f.
2. Kathleen Lamp, "'A City of Brick': Visual Rhetoric in Roman Rhetorical Theory and Practice," *Philosophy and Rhetoric* 44, no. 2 (2011): 178.
3. Lamp, "'A City of Brick,'" 178–180.
4. Cassius Dio, *The Roman History: The Reign of Augustus,* trans. Ian Scott-Kilvert (London: Penguin, 1987), 56.30.

5. Lamp, "'A City of Brick,'" 171.
6. Lamp, "'A City of Brick,'" 171.
7. Lamp, "'A City of Brick,'" 171–172; Cassius Dio, *The Roman History: The Reign of Augustus,* 52.30.
8. Lester Olson, Cara Finnegan, and Diane Hope, "Visual Rhetoric in Communication: Continuing Questions and Contemporary Issues," in *Visual Rhetoric: A Reader in Communication and American Culture,* eds. Lester Olson, Cara Finnegan, and Diane Hope (Los Angeles: Sage, 2008), 2.
9. Cara Finnegan, *Picturing Poverty: Print Culture and FSA Photographs* (Washington: Smithsonian Books, 2003), x–xi.
10. Quoted in Maria Godoy, "Dolores Huerta: The Civil Rights Icon Who Showed Farmworkers 'Sí Se Puede,'" NPR.com, September 17, 2017, https://www.npr.org/sections/thesalt/2017/09/17/551490281/dolores-huerta-the-civil-rights-icon-who-showed-farmworkers-si-se-puede.
11. Bruce Gronbeck, "Visual Rhetorical Studies: Traces through Time and Space," in *Visual Rhetoric,* ed. Olson, Finnegan, and Hope, xxii.
12. Gronbeck, "Visual Rhetorical Studies," xxii.
13. Denise Graveline, "Famous Speech Friday: Fannie Lou Hamer's 1964 Convention Committee Testimony," *The Eloquent Woman,* last modified September 28, 2012, http://eloquentwoman.blogspot.com/2012/09/famous-speech-friday-fannie-lou-hamers.html.
14. "Testimony before the Credentials Committee, Democratic National Convention, Atlantic City, New Jersey, August 22, 1964," *Say It Plain: A Century of Great African American Speeches,* American Public Media, http://americanradioworks.publicradio.org/features/sayitplain/flhamer.html.
15. "Testimony before the Credentials Committee."
16. Leslie Atzmon, "Introduction: Visual Rhetoric and the Special Eloquence of Design Artifacts," in *Visual Rhetoric and the Eloquence of Design,* ed. Leslie Atzmon (Anderson, SC: Parlor Press, 2011), xxix.
17. Atzmon, "Introduction," xxix.
18. Eric Jenkins, "The Modes of Visual Rhetoric: Circulating Memes as Expressions," *Quarterly Journal of Speech* 100, no. 4 (2014): 445.
19. "Transcript and Audio: Second Presidential Debate," NPR.com, October 16, 2012, https://www.npr.org/2012/10/16/163050988/transcript-obama-romney-2nd-presidential-debate.
20. Jessy Ohl, "Nothing to See or Fear: Light War and the Boring Visual Rhetoric of U.S. Drone Imagery," *Quarterly Journal of Speech* 101, no. 4 (2015): 614; Olson, Finnegan, and Hope, "Visual Rhetoric in Communication," 3.
21. John Monahan, "Coloring Single Stroop Elements: Reducing Automaticity or Slowing Color Processing," *Journal of General Psychology* 128, no. 1 (2001): 98–112.
22. Teal Triggs, "Riot Grrrl Punk: A Case Study in the Personal Politics of British Riot Grrrl Fanzines," in *Visual Rhetoric,* ed. Leslie Atzmon (Anderson, SC: Parlor Press, 2011), 66.
23. Triggs, "Riot Grrrl Punk," 63–97.
24. Clifford Geertz, *The Interpretation of Culture* (New York: Basic Books, 1973), 5.
25. Charles Forceville and Thijs Renckens, "The Good is Light and Bad is Dark Metaphor in Feature Films," *Metaphor & The Social World* 3, no. 2 (2013): 166.

26. Atzmon, "Introduction," xiv.
27. Atzmon, "Introduction," xvii.
28. Atzmon, "Introduction," xv, xviii.
29. Atzmon, "Introduction," xvii.
30. Janis Edwards and Carol Winkler, "Representative Form and the Visual Ideograph: The Iwo Jima Image in Editorial Cartoons," *Quarterly Journal of Speech* 83, no. 3 (1997): 289–310.
31. Edwards and Winkler, "Representative Form and the Visual Ideograph," 302–303.
32. Kristie Fleckenstein, Scott Gage, and Katherine Bridgman, "A Pedagogy of Rhetorical Looking: Atrocity Images at the Intersection of Vision and Violence," *College English* 80, no. 1 (2017): 13.
33. Finnegan, *Picturing Poverty,* xv.
34. Fleckenstein, Gage, and Bridgman, "A Pedagogy of Rhetorical Looking," 24.
35. Amanda Arnold, "Little Girl Mesmerized by Michelle Obama Portrait Thinks She's 'A Queen,'" *The Cut,* March 3, 2018, https://www.thecut.com/2018/03/little-girl-at-museum-thinks-michelle-obama-is-a-queen.html.
36. Matt Walsh (@MattWalshBlog), "Woman cradles and protects child. Man carries and protects both. This is how it ought to be, despite what your gender studies professor says," *Twitter,* August 28, 2017, https://twitter.com/MattWalshBlog/status/902179828891353089.
37. Walsh, "Woman cradles and protects child."
38. Fleckenstein, Gage, and Bridgman, "Pedagogy of Rhetorical Looking," 25.
39. Fleckenstein, Gage, and Bridgman, "Pedagogy of Rhetorical Looking," 25.
40. *Guerrilla Girls,* "Our Story," accessed September 14, 2018, https://www.guerrillagirls.com/our-story/.
41. "Do Women Still Have To Be Naked to Get into the Met. Museum?" *Guerrilla Girls,* accessed September 13, 2018, https://www.guerrillagirls.com/naked-through-the-ages.
42. Anne Teresa Demo, "The Guerrilla Girls' Comic Politics of Subversion," *Women's Studies in Communication* 23, no. 2 (2000): 133–56.
43. Fleckenstein, Gage, and Bridgman, "Pedagogy of Rhetorical Looking," 25.
44. Finnegan, *Picturing Poverty,* xv.
45. Matt Walsh, "The Matt Walsh Blog," accessed September 13, 2018, https://themattwalshblog.com/.
46. George Lakoff, *Moral Politics: What Conservative Know that Liberals Don't* (Chicago: University of Chicago Press, 1996).
47. Finnegan, *Picturing Poverty,* 223.
48. Aisha Durham, "Check on It": Beyoncé, Southern Booty, and Black Femininities in Music Video," *Feminist Media Studies* 12, no. 1 (2012): 35.
49. Durham, "Check on It," 42.
50. Durham, "Check on It," 42.
51. Durham, "Check on It," 42–43.
52. Durham, "Check on It," 41.
53. Durham, "Check on It," 38.
54. Durham, "Check on It," 40–41.

55. Durham, "Check on It," 41.
56. Durham, "Check on It," 41.
57. Durham, "Check on It," 43.
58. Durham, "Check on It," 43.
59. Durham, "Check on It," 44.
60. Durham, "Check on It," 43. Beyoncé, "Check On It," YouTube.com, last modified October 2, 2009, https://www.youtube.com/watch?v=Q1dUDzBdnmI.
61. Rachel Dubrofsky and Emily Ryalls, "*The Hunger Games:* Performing Not-Performing to Authenticate Femininity and Whiteness," *Critical Studies in Media Communication* 31, no. 5 (2014): 395–396.
62. Dubrofsky and Ryalls, "*The Hunger Games,*" 399.
63. Dubrofsky and Ryalls, "*The Hunger Games,*" 399.
64. Dubrofsky and Ryalls, "*The Hunger Games,*" 398–399.
65. Dubrofsky and Ryalls, "*The Hunger Games,*" 400.
66. Dubrofsky and Ryalls, "*The Hunger Games,*" 400.
67. Dubrofsky and Ryalls, "*The Hunger Games,*" 401.
68. Dubrofsky and Ryalls, "*The Hunger Games,*" 402.
69. Dubrofsky and Ryalls, "*The Hunger Games,*" 407, 406.
70. Dubrofsky and Ryalls, "*The Hunger Games,*" 406.
71. Richard Pineda and Stacey Sowards, "Flag Waving as Visual Argument: 2006 Immigration Demonstrations and Cultural Citizenship," *Argumentation and Advocacy* 43, no. 3-4 (2007): 165.
72. Pineda and Sowards, "Flag Waving," 165.
73. Pineda and Sowards, "Flag Waving," 166.
74. Pineda and Sowards, "Flag Waving," 168.
75. Pineda and Sowards, "Flag Waving," 168.
76. Pineda and Sowards, "Flag Waving," 170.
77. Pineda and Sowards, "Flag Waving," 170.
78. Pineda and Sowards, "Flag Waving," 169.
79. Pineda and Sowards, "Flag Waving," 168.
80. M. King, "'Mexicans and Assimilation: The Challenge," *Atlanta Journal-Constitution,* April 6, 2006, 15A.
81. Pineda and Sowards, "Flag Waving," 172.

Chapter 11

Material Rhetoric

On a tour through a large university, my guide and I paused in a large plaza between buildings. It was beautiful but rather strangely configured. Rather than creating a wide-open lawn, as I am accustomed to on my campus, the university had terraced the plaza and built sidewalks surrounding raised, knee-level sections of lawn. This plan provided clear walking routes for students traveling to and from classes and created beautifully landscaped green areas so the plaza did not feel like a concrete slab. It also directly controlled where students walked (on the walkways, not the raised lawns), thereby protecting the landscaping.

Surveying this plaza, my guide—a senior professor—commented that the terracing serves two additional purposes. First, it keeps students from thinking of this plaza as a mass gathering place: no one would think of this plaza when planning a two-thousand-person rally, protest, or riot. Because the plaza is visually and physically broken up, it does not occur to the thousands of students who walk through it daily that the plaza is very large and might be an ideal place to gather *en masse.* Second, if several thousand people did gather in this plaza, the terracing would make it difficult for them to march, charge, retreat, or otherwise move. Normally, one can easily step onto and off the knee-high terraces. They would create a formidable challenge, however, if the plaza were crowded: the terraces would cause people to stumble and fall, generally slowing down any attempt at coordinated crowd movement. The plaza was designed to deter and resist student protests.

The terracing in this plaza is not only a physical, material thing, it is an example of **material rhetoric,** *the way material entities communicate to, communicate with, act upon, and interact with humans and other physical entities.* For instance, the sidewalks in this plaza clearly communicate to humans that this is where they should walk; the raised terraces act upon humans, deterring them from walking on the lawn; the sidewalks, buildings, and terraces interact with one another to act upon humans, preventing mass gatherings. Although the plaza communicates *to* humans, it does not interactively communicate *with* humans, but other material entities—such as computers and other bodies—do communicate with humans and one another. For example, when we shop for clothes online we regularly communicate with bots in an interactive process as they help us figure out clothing sizes.

Most of this book focuses on analyzing the symbolic world (words, images, and other symbols). This chapter focuses on analyzing the material world: including how material entities function symbolically, but also how material entities act through their materiality. For example, a bridge might symbolize connection, progress, or a transition—but bridges can also act materially. For instance, a new bridge changes traffic flow patterns; a one-lane bridge forces drivers to stop before crossing; a walking-only bridge in a large city affects small businesses as cafés pop up around the bridge to capitalize on the foot traffic.

Most rhetoric involves material entities and mixes together the material and symbolic.[1] For example, speeches are delivered by human bodies in physical places to audiences comprised of other human bodies; films have physical manifestations as DVDs and Blu-ray discs; and television is produced through material technologies (such as cameras in studios) and appears in our houses within material configurations (including television screens and living room furniture). Some rhetoric (such as an online newspaper editorial) is primarily symbolic: although it has a material entity (a web page manifested on a screen), it is primarily the symbols (words) contained within the web page that communicate. Other rhetoric (such as statues, memorials, landscapes, cityscapes, and architecture) is primarily material: the thing itself might be shaped in symbolic ways (for example, a statue of an angel), but it is primarily the thing that communicates, not symbols (such as words) contained within the thing.

Whether a text is primarily material or symbolic, for a critic, analyzing a text's materiality means analyzing how a text (1) intertwines symbolic and material communication, (2) materially communicates, and (3) materially acts in the world. By learning this critical approach, critics learn how to analyze texts (such as architecture) that might otherwise not be well suited to other methods and modes of criticism. Moreover, critics can combine this approach with other methods of rhetorical criticism in order to assess a text more robustly. Indeed, critics often assess a text's visuality and materiality, because the things we see are often also material things. To understand how to analyze a material text, we need more specific understandings of what material entities are and how they function rhetorically.

A THEORY OF MATERIAL RHETORIC

Rhetorical critics insist that rhetoric acts upon us. The chapters throughout this book have focused on tools that help critics figure out how rhetoric functions—how it acts, what it does in society. Rhetorical critics are fundamentally concerned with things that act upon us. In studying material rhetoric, critics focus on how bodies, spaces, places, and other material entities communicate to humans, communicate with humans, act upon humans and other entities, and interact with humans and other entities. By studying materiality, rhetorical critics maintain their focus on how meaning comes to be and acts within the world, and on the ways that objects activate meaning and communicate "not through language but through [other means]," such as "their spatial organization, mobility, mass, utility, orality, and tactility."[2] The idea here is that bodies and spaces—and the things within spaces—matter: their materiality acts upon us even as (or before) we cloak them in symbolism.

The Material Body

Rhetorical critics often focus on the symbolic and material entities that humans produce: we think about words, symbols, speeches, blog posts, news reports, art, music, sculptures, monuments, television series, and so on. Rhetorical critics consider these symbolic and material productions to be the unique products of the human *mind*—after all, beavers might produce dams, but they have yet to produce Mount Rushmore. By seriously considering materiality, however, rhetorical theorists such as Debra Hawhee and Cory Holding point out that the human mind is a material brain that is fundamentally integrated with the rest of the human body, and describe rhetorical persuasion as moving by and locating in "hands, skin, nerves, [and] veins."[3] That is, persuasive arguments are created in human brains (an organ and nerves), flow out of human mouths (nerves, muscles, respiratory systems, and so on), into human ears (cartilage, nerves, and so on), and manifest in changed attitudes (brain matter that contains our opinions, perspectives, and memories, as well as visceral "gut reactions") and changed actions (hands that help build a Habitat for Humanity house, feet that run a charity race).

Ultimately, the human body operates as a cohesive whole. Decisions made in the brain affect the body; simultaneously, bodily experiences affect the brain, because the brain and body are one entity. For example, when Hillary Clinton was on the campaign trail for the Democratic presidential nomination in 2008, she was asked this question: how can you remain so upbeat during the campaign? While answering, Clinton became choked up. Overcome with emotion, she replied that she passionately believed in America's future and in doing "the right thing" for "our country" and "our kids' futures."[4] Here—as rhetorical critic Joshua Gunn noted—Clinton experienced affect.[5]

In everyday use, the word "affect" typically means to create an effect. For example, one might say, "the sun's light affects plants' ability to grow." But within the field of communication, **affect** may also refer specifically to *the bodily manifestation of thought and emotion; the effect that thoughts and emotions have on your body.* Used in this sense, the word is pronounced 'a-fect (the "a" in "affect" sounds the same way it does in the word "apple" ['a-pel]), and the emphasis is on the first syllable).

As rhetors (speakers, artists, directors, artists, comedians, and so on) create and—when applicable—deliver their texts, they often experience passionate affects. For example, while drafting a paper you might let out a whoop or punch the air after writing a particularly striking sentence. Although these expressions are symbolic, they are also often involuntary: they are the physical manifestations of your passion. When delivering a speech, you might find yourself overcome with emotion—not just stage fright as you face the audience, but sadness, hurt, pain, despair, gratitude, joy, or delight as you express part of your planned speech. This affect fundamentally changes how you deliver your speech and how audience members understand and interact with it.

Theorizing how the materiality of our bodies shapes rhetoric, Debra Hawhee and Cory Holding draw on eighteenth-century researchers Joseph Priestley and Gilbert Austin, who conducted scientific experiments as part of their rhetorical study.[6] Although their experiments may seem outmoded now (especially as we now consider communication and chemistry to be different academic disciplines) their focus on "heat" and "impression" continue to matter. By "heat," Priestley and Austin meant the bodily manifestation of passion. Our bodies often become hotter when we passionately experience emotions. Priestley and Austin took this phenomenon as *material*, considering the ways in which heat expands, radiates, and can be conducted through other materials. They argued that the hotter a speaker, the more heat radiates to the audience, creating heat—passion—in the audience as well.

Priestley and Austin further reasoned that just as one can cut grooves into metal or create an impression in clay, so too can rhetoric create a material impression (affect) on the audience. For example, a poignant sermon might give you chills; a scary movie might make your heart race; a disturbing image or concept might make you gasp. They argued that just like scratching a metal table leaves grooves in its surface, rhetoric's material impressions change audience members—and the deeper the impression, the more lasting the change.[7]

The materiality of our bodies—our physical sensations, reactions, and movement—play a considerable role in rhetoric. Affect changes a speaker's delivery and shapes audience members' responses. Exploring the material nature of rhetoric, communication critic Stephanie Larson analyzed Chanel Miller's victim impact statement read during the 2016 trial of Brock Allen Turner and performance artist Emma Sulkowicz's widely publicized *Ceci N'est Pas un Viol* (*This Is Not a Rape*).[8]

Miller's and Sulkowicz's rhetoric brought national attention to rape and sexual assault, especially on college and university campuses. Both women faced legal systems that define rape and sexual assault in terms of what the perpetrator does rather than what the victim experiences. Many state laws, such as California Penal Code 261, legally define rape in terms of penile violation while other forms of penetration (fingers, foreign objects) fall under the category of "sexual assault" and receive lesser charges.[9] In other words, the legal definition hinges on the perpetrator's body and actions while disregarding the physical violence enacted on the victim's body.

The legal distinctions between rape and sexual assault significantly differ from legal definitions of murder and attempted murder—which are based on the victim's experience, not the perpetrator's. Moreover, victims are often met with suspicion, and female victims are often dismissed because US culture has long treated women as if they were categorically unreliable witnesses.[10] Responding to these legal and cultural situations, and to their experiences of assault, Chanel Miller and Emma Sulkowicz did not attempt to argue rationally that they had been raped; rather, they created texts that enable audiences to "sense what rape feels like."[11] Their rhetoric foregrounds the material: they put their own bodies at the center of their rhetoric and experienced affect in their rhetorical delivery. Their texts primarily work to invoke visceral reactions—affect—in their audience members.

Theorizing how our corporeal bodies interact with rhetoric, Debra Hawhee describes the **rhetorical sensorium,** *the interconnected senses (both internal and external) through which animals (such as humans) discern the world.* The sensorium includes *external senses,* such as hearing (sound), sight (light), touch (temperature and pressure), taste (sweet, sour, bitter, bland, and so on), and smell (such as aromatic perfumes and "attention to ventilation").[12] These external senses can be extended or expanded through technology. For example, hearing aids and contact lenses enable us to hear and see beyond our corporeal capabilities. The sensorium also involves *internal senses* such as pain, hunger, arousal, fatigue, and "visceral organ senses," such as butterflies in your stomach or heartbreak.[13] These internal senses can also be extended or expanded through technology. For example, by wearing insulin pumps with glucose monitors, a person with diabetes can use technology to internally sense their blood glucose levels.

The rhetorical sensorium is the *interconnectedness* of these external and internal senses. The concept urges critics to consider how our senses interconnect and work in concert, rather than thinking about one sense at a time. For example, analyzing the experimental documentary *Leviathan,* film critic Michael Unger documents how its disorienting GoPro footage and the "unrelenting" din of its soundtrack creates a sensorial experience for audience members.[14] By placing the GoPro cameras on a fishing boat, on poles that extended above the decks and below the water, *Leviathan* captures multiple disorienting perspectives that do not belong to the sailors, the fish, or the filmmakers.[15] The footage and audio combine to create an interconnected sensorial experience. Audience members visually and audibly experience the "choppy, dangerous waters"—and so do their stomachs.[16] Viewers report that the film often renders them physically nauseated.[17] Moreover, *Leviathan* features footage "shot at night," creating a "pervasive nocturnal atmosphere" that is clearly visual and yet also internally sensed—audience members experience night while watching it.[18] Ultimately, the nearly dialogue-free documentary creates a sensory experience in which audience members live out the "deadly industry" of fishing in all of its "blood, salt and sweat."[19] In so doing, it brings seafood lovers and ethics-oriented or environmentally oriented pescatarians (vegetarians who also eat fish) to a sensory understanding of the violence of this industry.

Hawhee describes the rhetorical sensorium as prior to knowledge or meaning.[20] That is, sensation happens first, and then we (or technology) interpret those sensations to make meaning. The material (our rhetorical sensorium and its technological extensions) acts upon us. It prefilters our experiences with the world, determining what we can be aware of. Then, our minds and meaning-making systems further filter our experiences of reality by selecting some sensations to focus on while ignoring others.

Spaces, Places, and the Things within Them

In addition to considering the material capacities of human bodies for communication, theorists also focus on the communicativeness of space and place. **Space** refers to *abstract conceptualizations of geography, architecture, and locations, or the distance or expanse between objects.* **Place** refers to *a specific location.*[21] For example, town halls, monuments, and public parks, are public *spaces*, but the Capitol Building, the Lincoln Memorial, and New York City's Central Park are all public *places*. Places exist "in the interrelationship with spaces," which means that particular locations—shopping malls or parks—are designed, built, and used according to how a culture imagines commercial spaces and green spaces.[22] Thus, a culture's abstract conceptualizations of spaces informs the design and use of places: our imagination of what libraries are like (space) shapes how we build and interact with specific libraries (places). In turn, our interactions with those places inform how we understand that type of space: our experiences in specific libraries (places) shapes what we imagine when we imagine libraries more generally (spaces). Analyzing space and place, communication theorists demonstrate how both can function rhetorically and act upon humans and other material entities.

Analyzing space, Kenneth Zagacki and Victoria Gallagher assess the ways in which we encounter **spaces of attention,** *aspects of a place that are designed to direct humans' attention to particular features of that place, or to the nature of the place itself, through multimodal (sight, sound, smell, taste, touch) or mixed-modal interactions.*[23] Spaces, places, and their material entities interact with our bodies (sight, sound, smell, taste, and touch), directing our attention through our existing value and symbol systems to particular locations, features, or entities within that place.

Often, humans create spaces of attention as we spatially configure material entities in ways that direct other humans' attention.[24] For example, when students enter classrooms, their attention is drawn toward the "front" of the classroom and its projector screen, white/blackboard, podium, and/or audio speakers. Classrooms are configured in a way that directs students' attention toward where the instructors will position themselves. The multiplicity and orientation of the desks, as well as the singularity of the projection screen and the instructor's podium or desk, clearly communicate that students should fix their attention on the screen and podium rather than on one of the many identical student desks. Students encounter classrooms in multimodal or mixed-modal ways: they see the classroom layout, they touch it as they sit in desks, and they aurally experience the classroom—whether the instructor uses a technological sound system or not. The material configurations of classrooms create spaces of attention—they act upon students and direct their attention in a particular direction.

Rhetorical critics Danielle Endres and Samantha Senda-Cook further explain how people can use the materiality of a place to construct material rhetoric. A rhetor might stage a speech or protest at a location that has a historic or cultural meaning for the audience. For example, in 1886 a large gathering of laborers met in Chicago, protesting for an eight-hour workday. They were met with police brutality. Next, they gathered in Haymarket Square to protest police brutality. As police disrupted the gathering, demanding that the protesters disperse, an unknown person detonated a bomb, killing and wounding protesters and police officers. Shortly thereafter, the police arrested eight protesters on charges of conspiracy. Although there was no evidence linking them to the bomb, seven of the men were sentenced to death. The eighth was sentenced to fifteen years in prison.[25] Subsequently, four were executed; a fifth died in his jail cell. The remaining three were pardoned and set free seven years later.

At the gravesite of the four executed men stands a large monument known as the Haymarket Martyrs' Monument, surrounded by the graves of many prominent members of the labor movement—some of whom died as recently as 1985. The monument offers a preexisting meaning that labor activists tap into as they stage their rallies, parades, speeches, and other gatherings in this graveyard.[26] The monument itself and its surrounding burial sites "speak" to those who know the Haymarket history. By staging protests here, labor activists add their voices to the symbolic and material communication that the monument already offers.

Rhetors can also create material rhetoric by temporarily reconfiguring a place in unconventional ways.[27] For example, Take Back the Night protests on US college campuses often engage in a temporary reconstruction of place. At these protests, students, staff, faculty, and community members often march throughout campus while chanting, singing, and waving signs and banners, then pause in particular campus locations (such as a classroom or a dorm lounge), where they hold vigils for sexual assault survivors, share information on "sexual assault, domestic violence, dating violence, [and] sexual abuse," and share survivors' stories.[28]

These protests radically—but temporarily—reconstruct the meaning of the campus locations. For instance, a classroom that typically carries a fairly neutral meaning of learning is suddenly reinterpreted as a place of sexual violence and a place of responsive protest. Through the strategic placement of their campus rallies, Take Back the Night protesters ask college communities to reinterpret classrooms and dorm lounges as crime scenes—and then further ask college communities to commit themselves to supporting survivors and ending sexual violence, thus transforming those classrooms/crime scenes into activist spaces.

When rhetors repeatedly reconfigure a place as they create material rhetoric, they can permanently change its meaning.[29] For example, at my alma mater, there is an outdoor, picturesque place known as the Senior Bench. It is a normal stone bench, one of many on campus; however, for decades thc junior and senior classes have routinely attempted to steal this bench and taunt each other over which class has possession of it. Within this tradition, the bench must remain within fifteen miles of its original site, so classes rarely manage to keep the bench for long. Moreover, a wide variety of students paint the bench as part of protests, pranks, jokes, and publicity stunts. The original meaning of this place (of idyllic rest and picturesque repose) has been reconstructed through the repeated protests, shenanigans, and rivalries played out upon this place, the bench. Indeed, this place is now a site of rebellion—both playful and serious.

The material and symbolic combine and intertwine. We can see that the symbolism of the Haymarket Martyrs' Monument intertwines with the materiality of the graveyard: the labor protests that take place here must contend with gravestones even as the protesters draw upon the historic symbolism of the monument. Protesters encounter physical grave markers that affect where they can walk and stand. This physical interaction emphatically reminds labor activists that they risk their lives when they challenge corporate strongholds.

The theories of material rhetoric direct critics' attention to the ways in which materials and symbols intertwine, as well as the ways in which the material (bodies, spaces, places, and entities) communicates and acts in the world. These theories suggest that a critic should focus on analyzing the materiality of a text when (1) the text is primarily material, (2) the critic is interested in rhetoric's "real consequences for bodies and environments," and (3) the critic is interested in the ways that the material and symbolic intertwine.[30]

ANALYZING MATERIAL TEXTS

When analyzing material texts, some critics focus on specific places, such as a museum, neighborhood, park, landfill, or conservation area. Other critics focus on a type of space (such as a public space) and analyze several places (such as a town hall, a library, and a police station) that represent that type of space. These critics pick **representative places** to analyze—*places that are widely recognized as examples of that type of space*—and then generalize from those places to make claims about how that type of space functions in society. Still other critics focus on a particular sense (sound, sight, taste, touch, smell), analyzing the corporeal body's capacity for that sense (for example, how we hear or see something) or the corporeal body's emission of that sense (such as the sounds our bodies make). Still other critics analyze particular material entities, such as statues, perhaps assessing how their materiality acts upon human corporeality—that is, how we sense the material entity as it interacts with us.

To use this approach to rhetorical criticism, a critic might ask a sequence of interpretive questions. This process is not strictly linear; a critic may revisit any of these questions, allowing insights from one aspect of the analysis to inform other aspects. The critic can include this material approach with other methods or modes of analysis in order to assess the intertwining symbolic and material rhetoric of a text more robustly.

Material Action

To begin using this approach, critics often take stock of the material elements of their texts. For example, a critic might make a list of all the material elements that comprise a statue (granite, iron, concrete, and so on), or all of the material entities within a place (chairs, desks, a whiteboard, and so on), or the related corporeal and material elements connected to the sense of smell (noses, breezes as they waft airborne odorants, olfactory receptors in the nasal cavity, and so on). Analyzing Chris Drury's *Cloud Chamber for the Trees and Sky* (an exhibition in the Museum Park at the North Carolina Museum of Art), material critics Kenneth Zagacki and Victoria Gallagher identified the material elements of their text. Materially, the cloud chamber is a small hut made out of stone and thatch—natural materials typically found in forests such as the one in which this exhibition is positioned.[31] The cloud chamber is dark inside with a small pinhole opening in the roof that creates a *camera obscura,* projecting an inverted image of the sky and leafy canopy onto the dark interior of the hut.

Once a critic has a thorough understanding of a text's material elements, the critic is ready to ask the first interpretive question: how does the material act?

Material critics consider first what the material elements do "with or against" other material elements, and second, how the material acts on people.[32] For example, Zagacki and Gallagher note that the stone and wood interact, creating the cloud chamber's physical smallness, which in turn acts by limiting how many people can experience the exhibit at a given time. Ultimately, the materiality of the cloud chamber acts by creating an intimacy and privacy not typically found in museums.[33]

It is important to consider the multiplicity or mixed nature of the text's materials, which are filtered through the rhetorical sensorium and thus interact with our interconnected senses. For example, entering the cloud chamber affects a person's sight (it is dark inside), hearing (it is quiet inside), touch (the temperature is different inside and the stone and wood feel different on the skin), and potentially smell (depending on the day it may smell "earthier" inside; depending on who else is in the hut, it may smell of human sweat in the enclosed area). The cloud chamber acts upon humans by causing sensations that are different inside the exhibit from those experienced outside.

When considering how the material acts on people, critics further consider how the material (including a speaker's body) might act on people by producing affect in those people. For example, the material conditions of the cloud chamber—its dark, quiet, earthy-smelling stillness—might produce a peaceful affect in visitors by slowing their heart rates and lengthening and deepening their breaths.

Symbolic Elements

The critic must also consider the symbolism of the text, noting, perhaps, its symbolic shape and the words on its plaque, the preexisting meanings of the place, the predominant ways in which a type of space is culturally interpreted, or the cultural values associated with the text. For example, the *Cloud Chamber* exhibition features an informational plaque that names the artist (Chris Drury), briefly describes the exhibition, briefly lists its material elements (stone, wood, turf), and then goes on at length to describe the camera obscura and the ways in which it inverts the view of the trees and sky.[34]

After taking stock of the symbolic elements, the critic is ready to ask the second interpretive question: what is symbolically communicated by this text? To answer this question, critics should first consider the symbolic elements of the text. For example, a critic might note that the material elements of the cloud chamber are merely listed ("stone, wood, turf") on the informational plaque, but its camera obscura is described at length. The critic would conclude that the symbolic elements communicate an emphasis on the camera obscura as the most important feature.

In addition to the overtly symbolic elements of a text, the material elements can also function symbolically. Materials, places, and spaces can come to function symbolically through cultural repetition, and thus communicate various meanings (for example, bridges symbolically represent unity, connection, or transition). Consequently, a critic ought to consider whether and how the text communicates spaces of attention, whether the text has a preexisting meaning, or whether the meaning of the text is being reconstructed, either temporarily or permanently.

For example, Zagacki and Gallagher note that the shape, size, and construction materials of the cloud chamber symbolically communicate with museum visitors by reminding them of "ancient huts constructed out of natural materials."[35] Although this place does not have a preexisting meaning in the way that the Lincoln Memorial does, its shape, size, and construction materials communicate by reminding visitors of the huts they have seen in other museums, in National Geographic photos, and in history classes.

The Intertwining of the Material and Symbolic

Having identified and begun interpreting both the material and the symbolic elements, the critic can now move to the third interpretive question: how do the material and symbolic elements of the text intertwine to create meaning and act in the world? To answer this question, the critics must determine various elements of the text and how those elements interact. Here, the critic will do well to keep the context and surroundings in mind.

For instance, Zagacki and Gallagher argue that the small, enclosed, material nature of the hut in *Cloud Chamber* creates an "intensely private" area in the middle of a public, well-populated museum area.[36] Moreover, although the hut is made of natural materials, it is clearly human-made and positioned within nature. The exhibit is outdoors, situated under trees. Simultaneously, however, through the camera obscura—which is emphasized symbolically on the exhibit's plaque—nature infiltrates the human-made hut, reflecting trees and sky upon its floor and interior walls. Analyzing the ways in which this exhibit's material and symbolic elements intertwine to create meaning and act in the world, Zagacki and Gallagher argue that far from dividing private and public, inside and outside, or human-made and nature, the exhibit joins these dichotomies together, creating an experience in which "nature's solitude is possible even within the confines of urban space."[37] They situate their argument through contextual considerations as they discuss this museum's stated goals and objectives for designing exhibits as a response to environmental issues, and assess how well the rhetoric of *Cloud Chamber* embodies the museum's goals.

Human Movement

Finally, material critics consider how human movement—the movement of our corporeal bodies—functions within surrounding material entities, is acted upon by those material entities, and interacts with the entwinement of material and symbolic communication. To analyze this aspect of material rhetoric, critics ask a fourth interpretive question: what role does human movement play in the meaning making experience?

To answer this question, a critic considers how human bodies move through, in, and around the materiality of the text. To some extent, the critic may have already considered this question when considering how the material acts. For example, the material may act upon the human body by directing or controlling its "vector, speed, or possibilities of physical movement."[38] Indeed, when labor-rights activists host rallies at the Haymarket Martyrs' Monument, the gravestones act upon the activists' vectors, speed, and possible movements as they rally together. Even as the material may direct or control some aspects of human movement, however, our movement itself often generates meaning—to others and ourselves.

As we move within a place, interacting with its materiality, our movement can play a meaning-making role. Zagacki and Gallagher note that by entering and then emerging from the cloud chamber, humans perform a "particular experience" that "animates a new perspective."[39] They must double over to enter the small hut and relinquish their ability to see their surroundings, accepting a view of nature as it is darkly reflected through the camera obscura. Emerging from "the womb-like enclosure," humans move from darkness into the daylight and from confinement into openness.[40] This movement is mediated through, and directed or acted upon by, the material rhetoric. Yet the corporeal movements of bending over to enter and exit the exhibit, as well as the dilation of the eyes as they first adjust to the darkness and then the daylight, play a significant role in the meaning-making experience.

By analyzing the materiality of a text, a critic can work to understand how meaning comes to be and acts within the world. Although most critical methods focus on how language and symbols act within the world, this approach recognizes that not all action is rooted in language use and symbols. It allows the critic to explore how materiality (including corporeality) acts and communicates.

RESEARCH EXAMPLES

The following three research examples provide excellent demonstrations of how critics analyze the materiality of texts. In the first example, Adam J. Gaffey and Jennifer L. Jones Barbour analyze the Bonfire Memorial on the campus of Texas A&M University. In 1999, the "famed Aggie Bonfire collapsed, killing twelve students and injuring twenty-seven others."[41] Gaffey and Jones Barbour study how the materiality of the memorial shapes visitors' understandings of the tragedy. In the second example, Alyssa A. Samek analyzes the 1977 International Women's Year Torch Relay, demonstrating how bodies in motion created a strong persuasive argument that US women are citizens and thus ought to have full access to the rights, opportunities, and responsibilities of US citizens. Finally, the third example merges a material and visual approach by analyzing how space functions within television series. Here, David R. Coon focuses on how space is designed in television sets, how space is portrayed on television screens, and how actors corporeally navigate that space.

Adam J. Gaffey and Jennifer L. Jones Barbour "'A Spirit That Can Never Be Told': Commemorative Agency and the Texas A&M University Bonfire Memorial" (2018)*

Texas A&M University is known for its spirit. Aggies (as the students are known) experience great pride, loyalty, and enthusiasm for Aggieland (as the campus is known). I completed my Masters at Texas A&M University. While I was at Aggieland, I was often baffled by the complex rituals and traditions undergraduate

---

*This essay may be found in *Rhetoric & Public Affairs* 21, no. 1 (2018): 75–116.

Aggies enjoyed, but their zeal was real. Driving into campus each day, I passed the Bonfire Memorial—a large, prominent monument commemorating both the deaths of twelve students and the Bonfire tradition, even though the Bonfire killed those students.

The Aggie Bonfire was an annual campus tradition that started in 1909 and lasted ninety years. Students would build an enormous bonfire out of felled trees (Texas A&M restricted the bonfire's height of stacked lumber to fifty-five feet in 1969, but this restriction had limited effect) and then set it ablaze.[42] The bonfire took months to organize and build, and the tradition was rife with hazing, alcohol abuse, and "occasional public displays of racism."[43] At 2:42 AM on November 18, 1999, the stack of over five thousand logs collapsed, killing twelve students who were constructing the bonfire structure and injuring twenty-seven others. Despite the clearly dangerous conditions involved in constructing the Bonfire—it had claimed lives thrice before—after the collapse an injured Aggie student interviewed by news crews vocalized a full exoneration of Aggieland and its "spirit," saying that this was "a tragedy that no amount of foresight, or no amount of prevention, or no amount of anything could have stopped, prevented, or even told us it was coming."[44]

Texas A&M University never apologized for the school-sanctioned conditions that led to these students' deaths on its campus. Instead, five years after the tragedy, the university unveiled a memorial that was designed to "honor the victims, as well as the tradition's legacy."[45] Adam Gaffey and Jennifer Jones Barbour assess how the material of the memorial acts, particularly noting how it intertwines with symbolism and directs corporeal movement. Ultimately, they argue that this memorial functions to absolve Texas A&M University (and the problematic student culture surrounding the bonfire) of any role in the students' deaths and thus limits visitors' abilities to productively reconsider Aggie spirit.

There are three distinct parts to the Bonfire Memorial. The first is the entry point known as Traditions Plaza, where a large square stone features a line from the school song, "There's a spirit that can ne'er be told." Around this entry point, still within Traditions Plaza, stands a large stone wall etched with the poem "The Last Corps Trip," which was traditionally recited before lighting the bonfire. This poem narrates Judgment Day for the Aggie football team, the Aggie marching band, and Aggie students: they stand before Saint Peter and he grants them entry to heaven based on their school spirit, loyalty, and "unrelenting determination."[46]

The second part is a long, straight, narrowing walkway made of crushed rock, known as History Walk, that leads due north from Traditions Plaza to the third section—Spirit Ring. This History Walk is lined with granite stone markers, one for each annual bonfire, each of which is etched with a symbolic representation of the bonfire it represents. The markers for 1955, 1982, and 1996 are additionally etched with the names of the students who died constructing those bonfires.

The third part is the focal point of the memorial. Spirit Ring is a large, circular structure with twelve rectangular portals that each memorialize one of the twelve students who died in 1999. Each portal contains a portrait of the student, their signature, and reflections from friends and family members. The portals are positioned around the Spirit Ring circle to spatially indicate the direction of each victim's hometown. Visitors can walk through the twelve portals into a "spacious green" area with a central marker indicating where the center pole of the bonfire once stood.[47] Visually, the Spirit Ring—with its circular and rectangular configurations—is reminiscent of Stonehenge.

Gaffey and Jones Barbour examine the meaning-making capacities of these intertwining material and symbolic elements. They argue that the memorial communicates two conceptualizations of time: linear time and time eternal. The History Walk communicates linear time through its materials and symbolism. The first stone marker is etched with the date 1909, indicating the beginning of the bonfire tradition. Although the subsequent stone slabs do not have dates etched on them, each one clearly symbolizes a year. The path is straight, but narrows as visitors progress along it, creating an arrow-like sight path and funneling visitors closer together as they near the Spirit Ring. Thus, visitors experience a linear progression of time from 1909 to 1999 as they walk down History Walk.

Gaffey and Jones Barbour argue that the Spirit Ring enacts time eternal: a circle without beginning or end. With its visual and geometric similarity to Stonehenge, the Spirit Ring ties into a preexisting meaning of place—evoking the enduring, ahistorical connotations of Stonehenge. In addition, the Spirit Ring symbolically establishes a sense of time eternal: the time of the bonfire's collapse is etched in the center of the ring, and the portal reflections memorizing the students are all phrased in past tense. In the Spirit Ring, it is eternally 2:42 AM on November 19, 1999. Here, we can see that the material (the straight, narrowing walkway leading to the circular configuration with its Stonehenge allusions) communicates linear time and time eternal, yet clearly does so in combination with the symbolic elements. Moreover, the material directs corporeal movement, as visitors must linearly progress through history and then pass through a portal of death into the eternal.

Focusing on corporeal movement, however, Gaffey and Jones Barbour note that visitors also regress through linear time, back through history into Traditions Plaza as they leave the memorial. There is no other exit. The memorial directs corporeal movement, creating an out-and-back-again route for visitors that begins and ends in the "traditions" of Aggie Spirit. The memorial is then an open-and-shut experience rather than a path toward the future: it functions to make sense of something that happened, while grounding the whole meaning-making experience in the ongoing traditions, spirit, administration, and student culture of Texas A&M University.

Gaffey and Jones Barbour demonstrate how the material and symbolic combine and intertwine to create meaning and act upon human visitors. Their analysis draws attention to the complex ways in which materiality and symbolism interact and the impact on corporeal movement. Ultimately, they argue that as visitors interact with the memorial, they undergo a meaning-making experience in which the Aggie Bonfire is sealed off into an eternal history. They note that Texas A&M University missed the opportunity to create a monument that could have instead guided visitors (who are mostly students and alumni) into a process of learning from past mistakes. That is, with different material configurations and symbolic representations, university could have invited visitors to pass through the Bonfire

Memorial into the future of Aggie Spirit, rather than eternally historicizing the Bonfire's memory.

Alyssa A. Samek
"Mobility, Citizenship, and 'American Women on the Move' in the 1977 International Women's Year Torch Relay" (2017)*

My spouse and I usually run an annual 5K race that benefits a local summer camp for teens and adults with moderate cognitive impairments. This race raises funds, making the summer camp affordable, but also raises awareness as our running bodies disrupt local traffic. As we run, each step further commits us—to finishing the race and to supporting the cause. Our movement represents and enacts our commitment. Perhaps you too have participated in a 5K race, raising funds and awareness for (and commitment to) a local or national nonprofit organization.

Analyzing this type of mobility, Alyssa Samek considers how running can function as a form of public address. She likens organized, public running to a political speech or a protest march, arguing that bodies in motion not only enact political commitments but persuasively communicate those commitments. To demonstrate, Samek analyzed the 1977 International Women's Year Torch Relay from Seneca Falls, New York, to Houston, Texas. In this all-woman relay, over two thousand women ran day and night to carry a torch over twenty-five hundred miles, crossing through fourteen states, and arriving in Houston in time for the annual National Women's Conference. Among the runners were Kathy Switzer, the first female to run the Boston Marathon; Millicent Brady Moore, a direct descendent of one of the signers of the 1848 Declaration of Sentiments (a document created in Seneca Falls that petitioned the US government for women's suffrage, in addition to other rights); and Judy Carter, former president Jimmy Carter's daughter-in-law.

Samek notes how the relay draws together "space/place, movement, and citizenship."[48] That is, the relay traversed a large expanse of space, yet each runner moved through particular places. By moving through space/place, the runners performed and argued for their rights as citizens—clearly demonstrating the success of Title IX (enacted in 1972) and attempting to propel the ratification of the Equal Rights Amendment (ERA).

Title IX mandates that public educational institutions cannot discriminate based on sex. As a result of this law, educational institutions changed many of their admissions policies to be more equitable. More famously, the law increased athletic opportunities for women and instituted some administrative offices that respond to sexual assaults, harassment, and discrimination.

Congress also passed the ERA in 1972. If this constitutional amendment had been ratified by the requisite thirty-eight states, it would have mandated equal rights for men and women in the eyes of the federal government. In 1977, thirty-five of the required thirty-eight states had ratified the ERA. The relay was designed, in part, to raise awareness for the ERA, especially as it traversed through states such as Alabama, which had not ratified it. Ultimately, however, the ERA remained three states short and was not ratified.

---

*This essay may be found in *Quarterly Journal of Speech* 103, no. 3 (2017): 207–229.

Focusing on the relay runners' velocity—the speed at which something moves—Samek identifies how running creates a unique persuasive appeal. Human velocity matters: the velocity of someone who is walking determines whether the walk can be construed as a march or a romantic stroll. Similarly, as mobility scholars Tim Cresswell and Peter Merriman explain, the velocity of a person who is running determines whether the run can be construed as "efficient, powerful, or exhausting."[49]

In general, running is faster than walking. The increased velocity has material effects: runners cover more space than walking. Moreover, as Samek notes, running also "tames an unruly body" and "requires more endurance and stamina" than walking.[50] Given the material effects on the body, running culturally symbolizes a "body in control," "able-bodiness," "athleticism," and "intense physical effort."[51] In the United States, running has historically been culturally linked to ideas of masculinity, as male-ness is tied to ideas of physical prowess, stamina, athletics, and the occupation and control of geographic territories. For example, men often run at dusk because they are considered in control of physical space and thus safe, while women are often dissuaded from running in darkening conditions. By running, then, women embodied, performed, and persuasively proclaimed women's status as equals: women as physically fit athletes who are in control of their geographic surroundings. The women's relay celebrated Title IX, proclaiming women's athleticism and sexual agency. (These women were not afraid of the dark.)

During the relay, women often ran together. Even when they ran alone, they still did so as part of a relay, thus featuring running as a "collective, shared, and coordinated activity" in which bodies traverse space in a coordinated effort; the whole is greater than the sum of its parts.[52] The structure and material elements of the relay mattered. Different runners had to gather at different times in different places. A torch was passed from one body to the next, to the next, to the next. During this relay, the runners embodied, enacted, and communicated the collective nature of feminism. Whether running together or alone, the runners ran in coordination with one another, expressing the joint, shared, and collective nature of feminist activism.

Samek's analysis focuses on embodied movement (running) through space, and the ways in which this movement taps into existing symbolic connotations related to citizenry and personhood. Although the relay did not convince enough state legislatures to ratify the ERA, it was a resounding testament to female athleticism and coordination. As such, it was a much-needed response to the massive "STOP ERA" movements led by antifeminists such as Phyllis Schlafly, who argued that equal rights—and athleticism—would turn women into men.[53]

David R. Coon
"Putting Women in Their Place: Gender, Space, and Power in *24* and *Alias*" (2011)*

In my mind, I can picture the layout of the office space in *The Office* (2005–2013) and Leonard and Sheldon's apartment in *The Big Bang Theory* (2007–2019). I

*This essay may be found in *Feminist Media Studies* 11, no. 2 (2011): 231–244.

imagine that you too can picture the set layout for one or more of your favorite television series. Many fictional texts (films, television series, and books) feature space in ways that are essential or at least important to their meanings. For example, *La La Land* (2016) is meaningfully set in Los Angeles; the city (its traffic, neighborhoods, buildings, and cityscape) feature prominently in the film.

Analyzing both visual and material rhetoric, David Coon focuses on the spatial design within two television programs, the long-running spy series *24* (2001–2010, 2014) and the fan favorite *Alias* (2001–2006). Both *24* and *Alias* established headquarters for their spies. On *24,* Jack Bauer (Kiefer Sutherland) reported to the Counter Terrorist Unit. On *Alias,* Sydney Bristow (Jennifer Garner) reported to SD-6. The headquarters in both series were sets in which the series were repeatedly filmed; they had established layouts and their materiality mattered.

Connecting these series to their generic predecessors, Coon demonstrates that the spy genre, which blossomed during World War II and the subsequent Cold War, predominantly features male protagonists: for example, James Bond in the *James Bond* franchise, Napoleon Solo and Illya Kuryakin in *The Man from U.N.C.L.E.,* Kelly Robinson and Alexander "Scotty" Scott in *I Spy,* Maxwell Smart in *Get Smart,* and Dan Briggs and Ethan Hawk in *Mission Impossible.* (Dan Briggs was the starring character in the 1966–1973 TV series. Ethan Hunt was the star character in the 1996, 2000, 2006, 2011, 2015, and 2018 films).

Following the generic conventions of a spy drama, *24* stars a male operative, but *Alias* diverges from this convention and stars a woman. Coon focuses on the ways in which gender and space intersect in these series. He demonstrates how these two action/spy series dealt with space in very different ways.

Geographer Doreen Massey notes that space itself is socially determined and the social is, correspondingly, "spatially constructed."[54] Explaining this concept, Coon says that if a low income family moves into subsidized housing, they will soon find that they have a "harder time gaining access to jobs and opportunities that only exist in other parts of town," because a family's "socioeconomic position is determined by their geographic location, which was itself originally determined by their socioeconomic situation."[55] Space and social hierarchies intersect.

Focusing on the TV series' headquarters, Coon demonstrates how they spatially enact gender hierarchies. On *24,* the Counter Terrorist Unit (CTU) building has an open floor plan where most agents have their desks, then an isolated, elevated office for the Director of CTU. The director's office has a door and a mixture of frosted and transparent windows, providing the director with privacy. No one can see what the director does in the office, but the director can see the other agents as they work; and in the espionage business, information is power. Coon likens CTU's office layout to the panopticon, which theorist Michel Foucault famously wrote about—a structure originally intended for prisons or hospitals, allowing the guards or doctors to see out from a central location into the prisoners' cells or patients' rooms, allowing the supervisors to watch without being watched.

In *24*'s CTU, men primarily occupy the panopticon office. Although they are occasionally in conflict with the series protagonist, Jack Bauer, these men are "portrayed as good men and heroes."[56] When women occupy this office, they are cast as villains or incompetent, and are swiftly removed from the office. As a slight exception, the fifth-season character Karen Hayes brings the prior director (a man) back to the office to codirect CTU with her, then moves most of her activities out of the office and down onto the main floor of CTU, leaving a man in the panopticon office.

Unlike the director's office, CTU's main floor has very few men but plenty of female characters. Coon notes that with the exception of one "mama's boy" character, the men who work on the main floor are only "bit players and extras."[57] Analyzing how space and gender intersect, Coon notes that the women on *24* cannot control any information because they have no private space: they cannot keep secrets because they have no privacy. CTU's layout—with its panopticon office—shifts the "balance of power in favor of men" because they can literally close the office doors during private conversations and thus control secrets, even as they observe the other agents.[58]

On *Alias,* the spy headquarters SD-6 has a technological panopticon. The protagonist, Sydney Bristow, works in an open floor plan. Her boss, Arvin Sloane, occupies a spacious office. Sloane's office does not directly observe the open floor area as CTU's layout did, but Sloane has rigged his headquarters with audiovisual recording devices that he uses to spy on his agents. At SD-6, all the open-floor agents believe they work for the CIA; however, their agency is actually villainous and Sloane is evil. When Sydney Bristow discovers this, she joins the real CIA and becomes a double agent, spying on Sloane and SD-6 from within. She knowingly navigates SD-6's panoptic gaze and attempts to "pry information and power" from Sloane and his closed-door office.[59]

Coon argues that although both series feature "closed door/open floor" areas and panoptic surveillance, they handle space in very different ways.[60] Viewers experience CTU through "the point of view of a man with access to the 'closed door' office and the panoptic gaze."[61] Indeed, in *24*'s pilot episode, Jack Bauer shoots another character with a tranquilizer and leaves him immobilized in the office. He not only has access to the office and its privacy, he also uses this private place to keep his own activities secret. In contrast, on *Alias,* viewers experience SD-6 through the point of view of a woman "who is relegated to an 'open floor' job and is the object of the panoptic gaze."[62] While *24* presents the panoptic office as a positive area in which Bauer controls secrets, *Alias* presents the panoptic office as a negative area that Bristow overcomes. Coon concludes that how space is portrayed, how characters navigate space, and whose perspective on space is featured fundamentally shape the meanings of the television series.

STRENGTHS AND WEAKNESSES OF ANALYZING MATERIALITY

A material approach to rhetorical criticism is particularly adept at analyzing how the material acts, communicates, and intertwines with the symbolic to make meaning in the world. Its first strength is that it seriously considers the material nature of our world and the complex ways in which material entities function rhetorically. Most rhetorical methods assess symbols and sometimes consider how material entities function symbolically, but this approach moves beyond symbolism as it explores action and meaning-making in material entities (including corporeality).

Second, a material approach welcomes a new host of "texts" into the realm of rhetorical criticism. It considers relay races, monuments, buildings, architecture, memorials, neighborhood configurations, road networks, sonograms, and so on as acceptable texts to study rhetorically, thus moving the field of rhetorical criticism beyond traditional texts such as speeches, newspaper editorials, films, and television series.

A third strength is that even as this approach moves some critics beyond traditional texts to explore other avenues of meaning-making, it also adds a layer of analysis into how rhetorical critics study traditional texts. By considering the material aspects of speeches, films, and television series, a critic can explore how bodies, movement, spaces, places, technology, and other material entities contribute to the symbolic action of a text. Analyzing the materiality of a text can bring to light aspects that go unnoticed when critics focus exclusively on symbols.

For example, upon reviewing rhetorical criticism of public speeches, rhetorical theorist Karma Chávez notes that critics tend to work from transcripts of the speech and ignore the speaker's body—unless that body is female, of color, or physically disabled.[63] She notes that when a body is White, able, and male, rhetorical critics act as if that body has no meaning—as if it is the default—and thus its materiality is irrelevant to the nature of its symbolic communication (that is, the speech). Rhetorical critics are much more likely to pay attention to speakers' bodies that are female, of color, or physically disabled—thus marking them as bodies that matter as different, abnormal, and thus inherently contributing to the nature of their symbolic communication. Chávez challenges us to consider the social and political impact of treating White, able, male bodies as so normal we forget that they too are bodies, while fixating on the bodies of women, people of color, and people with disabilities—and thus treating women, people of color, and people with disabilities as if they were bodies first and people second.

Chávez offers the analysis of materiality as a corrective. Because this approach considers the bodily elements of texts, it can help critics who are analyzing speeches see and make sense of the White, able, male bodies that are delivering those speeches. The hope is that by recognizing the embodiment of all people, we might stop considering only some people to be people and other people to be bodies.

One key difficulty of studying the materiality of a text is that the terminology is still elusive. For example, material theorist Carole Blair noted in 1999 that this mode of criticism still calls the object of study a "text," but material entities routinely do not have any text in, on, or around them.[64] Generally speaking, rhetorical criticism focuses on the symbolic; thus the terminology rhetorical critics use is largely designed to describe, analyze, and make sense of symbols. Although the rhetorical analysis of materiality has advanced since 1999, this critical approach still struggles with terms, such as "text," that are not well suited to helping critics make sense of the material entities they study.

CHOOSING THIS APPROACH

A material approach helps critics assess texts—or the material portions of texts—that other methods are less adept at analyzing. Almost every text has some material component, so this approach helps critics include texts (or elements of texts) that would otherwise be omitted. This approach can also be used with other methods or modes of analysis to assess robustly how a text functions in society.

So how do you know whether you should focus on the materiality of a text? To answer this question, I recommend that you consider the text itself, its context, the text/audience interaction, and your animating research question.

First, does the text have prominent material aspects? If you are working with a text that is a place or a material entity (such as a statue, memorial, museum, body, or landscape), then this approach is likely to be the best fit for your text. If you are working with a text that seems more symbolic in nature (such as a speech, film, or television series), consider using this approach or combining it with another method to see what role the material plays in the text. For example, David Coon combined an analysis of the visual and material to assess the sets for *24* and *Alias,* as well as the ways in which the characters navigated those spaces on screen. By incorporating materiality into his analysis of what is often considered to be primarily a visual text, Coon discovered how influential space was in the symbolic action of these series. Carole Blair notes that "rhetoric is not rhetoric until it is uttered, written, or otherwise manifested or given presence": in other words, all rhetoric has a material element.[65] This critical approach can help critics identify that element and how it acts upon other material entities, the symbolic, the audience, and the world.

Second, consider the context of the text. Most methods of rhetorical criticism focus on the text and use the context to shed light on the text. Like the analysis of audience texts, however, the analysis of material texts can take this text/context relationship and turn it on its head by focusing on the "context" (such as the place, the body, or the surrounding material elements) rather than the "text." A critic ought to ask whether the context might strongly influence the nature of the text or the way the audience interacts with the text. If it does, analyzing the material aspects could help the critic focus on the influential role that context plays in the meaning-making, influence, and action that takes place in the rhetoric they are analyzing.

Third, consider the text/audience interaction. How does the text (or its context) act upon audience members' bodies? Does the audience physically interact with the text, and if so, how? Does the text involve corporeal movement? How does the audience sense the text? Or to put it another way, how does the text act upon an audience member's rhetorical sensorium? Thinking through these questions can help a critic assess how materiality rhetorically functions in a text and whether this critical approach would help identify how the text acts in the world.

Finally, consider your own research motives. Are you concerned with how symbols and materials intertwine? How materiality communicates? How materiality acts in the world or acts upon humans? Analyzing the materiality of a text is an excellent approach for answering the types of research questions that stem from these concerns.

Ultimately, this approach offers critics X-ray vision, helping them see through the symbolic to the material. Depending on the text and the research question, a critic can use this material approach alone or with other methods. All rhetoric has some material elements. This approach can help a critic make sense of them.[66]

DISCUSSION QUESTIONS

1. Draw the layout of a place where you lived when you were a child. Reflecting on the layout, consider and explain how the materiality of that home might have influenced family dynamics and behaviors.
2. Think about a place you call home and make a list of all the statues, art (including graffiti), parks, fountains, monuments, memorials, and public buildings (libraries, town halls, museums, and so on) that you regularly encounter while walking, driving, or riding on the bus, train, or metro in that place. Looking at this list, consider what this material communicates about this place.
3. Describe a time when you experienced affect. What thoughts/emotions were you experiencing? How did those thoughts/emotions physically manifest? How did you respond in the moment (what did you do, say, or think) while you were experiencing affect?
4. Describe how your rhetorical sensorium (both external and internal senses) operates while you (1) listen to a speech or lecture, (2) watch a movie in the theater, and (3) watch a television series in your dwelling place. That is, note what your rhetorical sensorium senses in those different experiences, and keep track of the different—but interconnected—ways that it senses. Then, consider how the rhetorical sensorium shapes or influences how you learn, remember, enjoy and/or are persuaded during those experiences.
5. Name a type of space and then list three places that represent that type of space.
6. Visit a park or public library near you and analyze its spaces of attention. While visiting, note where your attention is directed and how your attention was directed to that space of attention. Draw the park or public library and indicate in your drawing where the space of attention is and what entities, spaces, and/or symbols direct your attention to that space.

NOTES

1. Carole Blair, "Contemporary U.S. Memorial Sites as Exemplars of Rhetoric's Materiality," in *Rhetorical Bodies,* eds. Jack Selzer and Sharon Crowley (Madison: University of Wisconsin Press, 1999), 16–57.
2. Barbara Dickson, "Reading Maternity Materially: The Case of Demi Moore," in *Rhetorical Bodies,* ed. Jack Selzer and Sharon Crowley, 297.
3. Debra Hawhee and Cory Holding, "Case Studies in Material Rhetoric: Joseph Priestley and Gilbert Austin," *Rhetorica: A Journal of the History of Rhetoric* 28, no. 3 (2010): 264.
4. In Associated Press, "Hillary Clinton Gets Emotional in N.H.," January 7, 2008, https://www.nydailynews.com/news/politics/hillary-clinton-emotional-n-h-article-1.344579.
5. Joshua Gunn, "On Speech and Public Release," *Rhetoric & Public Affairs* 13, no. 2 (2010): 26.
6. Hawhee and Holding, "Case Studies," 261–289.

7. Hawhee and Holding, "Case Studies," 278–280.
8. Stephanie Larson, "'Everything inside Me Was Silenced': (Re)defining Rape through Visceral Counterpublicity," *Quarterly Journal of Speech* 104, no. 2 (2018): 123–144.
9. Larson, "'Everything inside Me,'" 129.
10. Rebecca Solnit, *Men Explain Things to Me* (Chicago: Haymarket, 2014), 108.
11. Larson, "'Everything inside Me,'" 125.
12. Debra Hawhee, "Rhetoric's Sensorium," *Quarterly Journal of Speech* 101, no. 1 (2015): 2–3.
13. Hawhee, "Rhetoric's Sensorium," 2–3.
14. Michael Unger, "Castaing-Taylor and Paravel's GoPro Sensorium: *Leviathan* (2012) Experimental Documentary, and Subjective Sounds," *Journal of Film and Video* 69, no. 3 (2017): 5.
15. Unger, "Castaing-Taylor and Paravel's," 8.
16. Unger, "Castaing-Taylor and Paravel's," 9.
17. Unger, "Castaing-Taylor and Paravel's," 9.
18. Unger, "Castaing-Taylor and Paravel's," 9.
19. Philip Hoare, "*Leviathan:* The Film That Lays Bare the Apocalyptic World of Fishing," TheGuardian.com, November 18, 2013, https://www.theguardian.com/film/2013/nov/18/leviathan-fishing-film-moby-dick.
20. Hawhee, "Rhetoric's Sensorium," 4–5.
21. Danielle Endres and Samantha Senda-Cook, "Location Matters: The Rhetoric of Place in Protest," *Quarterly Journal of Speech* 97, no. 3 (2011): 259–260; David Coon, "Putting Women in Their Place: Gender, Space, and Power in *24* and *Alias,*" *Feminist Media Studies* 11, no. 2 (2011): 232.
22. Endres and Senda-Cook, "Location Matters," 260.
23. Kenneth Zagacki and Victoria Gallagher, "Rhetoric and Materiality in the Museum Park at the North Carolina Museum of Art," *Quarterly Journal of Speech* 95, no. 2 (2009): 172, 186–188.
24. Zagacki and Gallagher, "Rhetoric and Materiality," 172, 186–188.
25. Thai Jones, "Relitigating the Haymarket Trial," *Dissent,* September 7, 2012, https://www.dissentmagazine.org/online_articles/relitigating-the-haymarket-trial; "Haymarket Riot," History.com, accessed August 13, 2018, https://www.history.com/topics/haymarket-riot.
26. "The Haymarket Martyrs' Monument as a Labor Icon," *Illinois Labor History Society,* accessed August 13, 2018, http://www.illinoislaborhistory.org/labor-history-articles/the-haymarket-martyrs-monument-as-a-labor-icon.
27. Endres and Senda-Cook, "Location Matters," 268.
28. "Take Back the Night," TakeBacktheNight.com, accessed August, 13, 2018, https://takebackthenight.org/.
29. Endres and Senda-Cook, "Location Matters," 270.
30. Edgar, Amanda Nell, "The Rhetoric of Auscultation: Corporeal Sounds, Mediated Bodies, and Abortion Rights," *Quarterly Journal of Speech* 103, no. 4 (2017): 351.
31. Zagacki and Gallagher, "Rhetoric and Materiality," 180.
32. Zagacki and Gallagher, "Rhetoric and Materiality," 172; see also Blair, "Contemporary U.S. Memorial Sites," 16–57.

33. Zagacki and Gallagher, "Rhetoric and Materiality," 180.
34. Kris Montgomery, "Hobbit House & More at NCMA Museum," RaleighParks.org, July 31, 2014, https://raleighparks.org/2014/07/31/hobbit-house-more-at-ncma-museum-park/.
35. Zagacki and Gallagher, "Rhetoric and Materiality," 183.
36. Zagacki and Gallagher, "Rhetoric and Materiality," 180.
37. Zagacki and Gallagher, "Rhetoric and Materiality," 180.
38. Blair, "Contemporary U.S. Memorial Sites," 46.
39. Zagacki and Gallagher, "Rhetoric and Materiality," 186.
40. Zagacki and Gallagher, "Rhetoric and Materiality," 186.
41. Adam Gaffey and Jennifer Jones Barbour, "'A Spirit That Can Never Be Told': Commemorative Agency and the Texas A&M University Bonfire Memorial," *Rhetoric & Public Affairs* 21, no. 1 (2018): 75.
42. Henry Petroski, "Vanities of the Bonfire," *American Scientist* 88, no. 6 (2000): 486.
43. Gaffey and Jones Barbour, "'A Spirit That Can Never Be Told,'" 76–77.
44. "Bonfire Tragedy at Texas A&M University," *WFAA-TV-Channel 8 News-Dallas* November 18, 1999, https://www.youtube.com/watch?v=aFPgUl5XzSA.
45. Gaffey and Jones Barbour, "'A Spirit That Can Never Be Told,'" 77, 80–81.
46. Gaffey and Jones Barbour, "'A Spirit That Can Never Be Told,'" 90–91.
47. Gaffey and Jones Barbour, "'A Spirit That Can Never Be Told,'" 85.
48. Alyssa Samek, "Mobility, Citizenship, and 'American Women On the Move,' in the 1977 International Women's Year Torch Relay," *Quarterly Journal of Speech* 103, no. 3 (2017): 207.
49. Tim Cresswell and Peter Merriman, eds., *Geographies of Mobilities: Practices, Spaces, and Subjects* (Farnham, UK: Ashgate, 2012), 6.
50. Samek, "Mobility, Citizenship,'" 214.
51. Samek, "Mobility, Citizenship'" 214.
52. Samek, "Mobility, Citizenship,'" 216.
53. Samek, "Mobility, Citizenship,'" 217.
54. Doreen Massey, "Introduction: Geography Matters," in *Geography Matters!,* eds. Doreen Massey and J. Allen (Cambridge, UK: Cambridge University Press, 1984), 6.
55. Coon, "Putting Women in Their Place," 234.
56. Coon, "Putting Women in Their Place," 236.
57. Coon, "Putting Women in Their Place," 237.
58. Coon, "Putting Women in Their Place," 237.
59. Coon, "Putting Women in Their Place," 238.
60. Coon, "Putting Women in Their Place," 238.
61. Coon, "Putting Women in Their Place," 242.
62. Coon, "Putting Women in Their Place," 242.
63. Karma Chavez, "The Body: An Abstract and Actual Rhetorical Concept," *Rhetoric Society Quarterly* 48, no. 3 (2018): 242–250.
64. Blair, "Contemporary U.S. Memorial Sites," 18.
65. Blair, "Contemporary U.S. Memorial Sites," 18.
66. Blair, "Contemporary U.S. Memorial Sites," 18.

Appendices

Appendix A

Writing a Critical Essay

Critical essays are their own genre of academic writing. Just as a scientific lab report is expected to record specific types of data, a critical essay is expected to present particular types of evidence and argumentation. Learning to write a critical essay helps critics develop strong, persuasive arguments as they demonstrate how texts function in society. This appendix offers advice for how to write that essay. It begins with the heart of a critical essay—the interpretation of textual evidence presented in the analysis section. Then, it offers specific advice for how to craft a thesis statement and a preview statement, cite other scholars in a literature review, and use citations.

INTERPRETING TEXTUAL EVIDENCE

Throughout an essay, a critic typically presents an argument for *what* a text accomplishes in society, *how* it accomplishes that symbolic action, and ultimately, *why* this information matters. This argument must be substantiated with evidence from the text itself in order to persuade readers. Rhetorical critics cannot make large claims about what a text does in society and how it does it—much less show the importance of that argument—without being able to clearly prove that the text accomplishes that symbolic action.

For example, in her analysis of *Beauty and the Beast* (discussed in Chapter 8), Kathryn M. Olson argues that this animated children's film teaches viewers to see relational violence as normal, even romantic behavior. This effect, she argues, is *what* the film accomplishes in society.[1] She points to the epideictic rhetoric throughout the film (the instances in which the adult characters explain and describe Beast's behavior, especially to the child character, Chip), arguing that this rhetoric is *how* the film accomplishes the symbolic action of normalizing and romanticizing relational violence. Finally, she demonstrates *why* this effect matters by pointing to two cultural trends: first, the widespread nature of relational violence ("almost half of US adults have experienced psychological aggression from a romantic partner" and a third have experienced physical violence from a romantic partner); and second, US adults' inability to recognize relational violence *as* violence—even when that violence includes "slapping, hitting, threats, [and] verbal abuse" and plays out right in front of them.[2]

Olson presents her analysis of *Beauty and the Beast,* arguing that this film and others like it act detrimentally in society, resulting in adults who cannot recognize relational violence, cannot teach their children how to recognize relational violence, and ultimately cannot stop relational violence from terrorizing our society. Olson's argument, however, would not be persuasive if she could not point to evidence from the film in order to substantiate, first, that relational violence occurs between Beast and Belle, and second, that the other characters (the castle staff) normalize and even romanticize that violence in order to keep Belle in the relationship.

Essentially, critics rest their argument on **textual evidence,** *evidence from the text itself that the critic presents to readers.* In order to make a strong argument, a critic presents the evidence alongside the interpretation of the evidence. Essentially, the critic shows readers what the text is and provides an interpretation of what the text does.

Showing Readers Your Textual Evidence

Because texts and their symbolic action can be quite complex, rhetorical critics often make multipart arguments concerning their texts. In order to substantiate or prove an argument, then, a critic must present textual evidence that supports each part of a multipart argument. A critic presents textual evidence primarily through description and quotation: the critic describes the text or portions of the text, and quotes directly from it.

For example, Olson's analysis of *Beauty and the Beast* presented multiple claims in support of her overarching argument that the film acts in society to make it harder for people to recognize relational violence. Olson argues that (1) *Beauty and the Beast* portrays the real-world relational violence of expressive aggression (threats, physical violence, and so on); (2) the film portrays the real-world relational violence of coercive control (isolating victims from family and friends, controlling their whereabouts, and so on); (3) this behavior is normalized and even romanticized in the way the castle staff interacts with Belle; and (4) this behavior is normalized and even romanticized in the way the castle staff explain Beast's behavior to the child character, Chip. Olson has at least four key claims to her overarching argument—and she must present textual evidence for all four of them.

She presents this evidence by describing scenes and quoting lines of dialogue from the film. For instance, she presents evidence of Beast's expressive violence by describing scenes in which Beast breaks, throws, and smashes objects, and yells threats at Belle. Similarly, she presents evidence of Beast's coercive control by quoting lines of dialogue in which Beast expels Belle's father, Maurice, from the castle—never to see his daughter again—and extracts promises from Belle that she will never leave him. She presents further evidence of this coercive control by describing the scene and quoting the dialogue between Beast, Belle, and the castle staff in which Beast first invites Belle to dinner, but ultimately decides to control her access to food by proclaiming that Belle can only eat if she eats with him.

Olson presents even further evidence of Beast's coercive control by recounting the various scenes in which Beast spies on Belle through his magic mirror.

Moreover, she presents evidence of the ways in which the staff—who are clearly terrified of Beast—normalize and romanticize his violence in their conversations with Belle. Here, she describes the scene and quotes the lines of dialogue in which Wardrobe attempts to convince Belle to go down to dinner by claiming that Beast is not so bad and that Belle ought to get to know him better. Olson quotes the lines of dialogue in which Lumiere and Cogsworth (the candlestick and clock) attempt to convince Belle to stay in the castle—and in a relationship with Beast—after Beast violently destroyed his lair upon finding Belle in his private chambers.

Finally, Olson presents evidence of how the characters explain Beast's actions to Chip. She reminds readers that Chip is present throughout the film—bearing witness to Beast's violence—and that the household staff (including Chip) are afraid of Beast. She describes multiple scenes in which the staff flinches away from Beast, cowers in front of him, and hides from him. She then describes the scenes and quotes lines of dialogue in which Lumiere, Cogsworth, and Mrs. Potts teach Chip about romance through Beast and Belle's relationship; for example, when the staff prompts Beast to show Belle the library as a romantic present.

In order to substantiate their (multipart) arguments, critics must present textual evidence, primarily through description and quotation. The idea is to show the text—the evidence for your argument—to your readers. Indeed, the persuasiveness of your argument rests on your ability to show your readers enough evidence or strikingly compelling evidence from your text. A critic typically needs both quantity and quality when it comes to textual evidence. You will have to show your readers a substantial portion of the text (quantity) and your evidence will have to be compelling (quality) for readers to accept your argument.

Interpreting Your Textual Evidence

Textual evidence, however, cannot stand alone. A critic cannot simply describe and quote from the text and consider the job done. After all, millions of people have watched *Beauty and the Beast* without seeing relational violence or considering that this film symbolically acted in ways that made audiences less likely to recognize real-world relational violence. If Olson simply described the film and quoted lines of dialogue from it, it would be no different for us than if we simply watched the film a second time: we would be unlikely to see what the text does in society, how it accomplishes that symbolic action, or why it matters.

In order to substantiate their arguments, critics must do more than show readers their texts. A critic must simultaneously interpret the text and explain how each piece of textual evidence serves as evidence in a larger argument. Often, the critic accomplishes this throughout the analysis section of the critical essay by (1) introducing the topic of each paragraph in a way that shows how it links back to the multipart argument, (2) presenting textual evidence intermixed with the interpretation of that evidence, and then (3) concluding the paragraph by linking from the interpreted evidence back to the multipart argument.

For example, below is a paragraph from Olson's analysis of *Beauty and the Beast.* Watch how she introduces the topic of coercive control in her analysis, provides textual evidence intermingled with her interpretation of it, and then concludes her paragraph by directly linking the evidence to its relevance within her larger argument.

> In a display of coercive control common with intimate partner abusers, the first moves Beast makes are to exact Belle's promise never to leave him, to imprison her at home, and to separate her from her family. Belle's father Maurice begs Beast "please spare my daughter" to which Beast responds: "She's no longer your concern." As Beast sends Maurice unceremoniously and permanently on his way, Belle sobs: "You didn't even let me say good bye. I'll never see him again. I didn't get to say good-bye." In the same scene, Beast makes his love interest swear that she will never leave him, no matter what—and the situational context in which the promise is extracted (i.e., an exchange of Maurice's life for hers) suggests that there will be severe consequences for Belle, and possibly also her father, if she breaks that vow. "BEAST: . . . you must promise to stay here forever. BELLE: You have my word." Victims in abusive romantic relationships often report that the abuser systematically cuts them off from communication with and the support of the family and friends who most care about their well-being and might threaten harm to those people to keep the victim compliant.[3]

Looking at the first sentence in that paragraph, we can see that this paragraph will be about the topic of coercive control in *Beauty and the Beast.* Yet we can also see that Olson is reminding readers of how this topic fits within her broader argument. By stipulating that what Beast does to Belle is "common with intimate partner abusers," Olson reminds readers that part of her larger argument is that the film portrays real-world relational violence.[4] In the sentences that follow, she presents textual evidence as she describes and quotes from the film.

Notice, however, that Olson is not exclusively presenting textual evidence; she also intermingles her interpretation with these scenes. In the middle of the paragraph, she states, "the situational context in which the promise is extracted (i.e., an exchange of Maurice's life for hers) suggests that there will be severe consequences for Belle, and possibly also her father, if she breaks that vow." Olson then returns to quoting from the dialogue.[5] Here, Olson interprets the scene, pointing out how the threat of violence hangs over these lines of dialogue. Finally, her concluding sentence in the paragraph directly reminds readers of how this interpreted evidence substantiates her argument, explaining that real-world victims report their abusers engaged in the same behaviors that Olson just proved Beast enacts. Olson has soundly argued that *Beauty and the Beast* portrays real-world relational violence.

If critics fail to show their texts to their readers, they fail to present evidence for their arguments. If they fail to intermix an interpretation of that evidence, they fail to explain what the evidence is evidence of, and thus their readers may not understand its significance. If critics fail to show how their interpreted evidence links to their larger points, they fail to offer their readers a clear sense of how their evidence functions as support in their multipart arguments. Ultimately, critics work throughout their critical essays to show readers their textual evidence, to interpret that evidence for readers, and to show readers how the interpreted evidence supports their larger claims. Through such argumentation, critics attempt to persuade readers that their analyses are correct: that they have correctly identified what their texts do in society, how they accomplish those symbolic actions, and ultimately, why it matters.

THESIS STATEMENTS

A thesis statement is a clear and succinct presentation of the critic's argument. Typically, a rhetorical critic's thesis statement makes an argument regarding what a text does in society and how it accomplishes that action. The thesis statement is typically placed in the latter half of the introduction of the critical essay. A critic often gestures toward why this argument matters in the introduction and then strongly revisits why it matters in the conclusion of the essay. The critic will also link back to this thesis statement throughout the analysis section, rephrasing and repeating portions of it. For instance, when presenting evidence, a critic should clearly state how that evidence relates to the thesis statement.

Most critical essays avoid using first-person pronouns (I, me, mine, and so on). However, some critics make an exception to this general rule in their thesis statements, using phrases such as, "I argue . . . ." or "I demonstrate . . . ." Other critics prefer not to use first-person pronouns at all. Instead, they might present their theses by using phrases such as "This essay argues . . ." or "This essay demonstrates . . . ."

Many thesis statements have two parts, with one part focusing on the communicative techniques in the text (how the text operates) and another part focusing on what those communicative techniques enact in society. Sometimes, a critic uses two sentences for the thesis statement—one for each part of the argument. For example, Leroy G. Dorsey and Rachel M. Harlow presented the following thesis statement in their analysis of Theodore Roosevelt's writings, *The Winning of the West*. (See Chapter 3.)

> We argue that Theodore Roosevelt's *The Winning of the West* attempted to popularize simultaneously the idea of immigration and the assimilation of American culture through a mythic narrative that grounded both the origins of American society and the future strength of its people in immigration and in martial struggle. Specifically, in his version of the Frontier Myth, Roosevelt portrayed the immigrant as the archetypal hero of American history.[6]

Dorsey and Harlow begin their thesis statement by stipulating what their text accomplished in society: it popularized assimilationist immigration in US culture. Then they explain how this symbolic action was achieved: through the mythic narrative and especially the portrayal of an immigrant as the archetypal hero.

Theon E. Hill, in his analysis of Barack Obama's 2007 address in Selma, Alabama (see Chapter 6), presented the following concise thesis:

> By reframing the past, [Obama] restricted its rhetorical force to speak to pressing social inequalities in the present.[7]

Prior to this thesis statement, Hill had briefly outlined how Obama had reframed the memory of the Civil Rights movement—most notably, by reframing the past through his Joshua generation metaphor. This thesis statement begins with how the text accomplishes its symbolic action (by reframing the past). Then it explains what was symbolically accomplished: a limitation or restriction on how the memory of the civil rights movement can inform or shape our decisions about the present and the future.

When writing a thesis statement, there are four basic pitfalls that critics ought to avoid. The first pitfall to avoid is announcing a topic instead of making an argument in your thesis statement that can be proven through evidence and argumentation. For example, a critic who writes, "This essay is about the theme of fashion in Taylor Swift's song, 'Style'" or, "In this essay, I examine how Taylor Swift discusses teenage romance in her song, 'Style,'" has fallen in to the mistake of simply announcing a topic rather than presenting an argument.

The second pitfall to avoid is presenting a subjective opinion in your thesis statement. This type of thesis statement does indeed make a claim, but the claim cannot be proven or disproven through evidence and argumentation because it is entirely a matter of taste. Such problematic thesis statements often use words such as "best/worst" or make moral claims that are culturally relative. For example, a critic who writes, "'Style' is Taylor Swift's best song" or "Listening to Taylor Swift's songs, especially 'Style' is bad for you," has fallen into the pitfall of presenting a subjective opinion instead of presenting a claim that can be proven through evidence and argumentation.

The third pitfall to avoid is announcing an empirical observation as your thesis statement. Empirical observations do not need substantive evidence or argumentation to support them because they are obvious to anyone who looks at the text. For example, a critic who writes, "In 'Style,' Taylor Swift sings about fashion and teenage romance," has fallen into the pitfall of simply making an observation rather than an argument.

The fourth pitfall to avoid is combining a subjective opinion with an empirical observation in your thesis statement. Such a thesis statement fails to demonstrate how a text functions in society. Instead, it uses evidence (empirical observations) to support a subjective claim—which, again, is a matter of taste that cannot be proven. For example, a critic who writes, "'Style' is a beautiful song" (subjective opinion) "because it uses major chord structures and has good vocals" (empirical observation), has fallen into the pitfall of combining a subjective opinion and an empirical observation rather than crafting a thesis statement that explains *what* the text does in society and *how* it accomplishes this symbolic action.

PREVIEW STATEMENTS

A preview statement briefly lists the organization of a critical essay, providing a "preview" of the topics and arguments so readers know what to expect. A preview statement is typically provided as a courtesy. It helps readers understand how the essay is laid out, so they can be on the lookout for key ideas and understand how the different parts of the argumentation connect to one another.

A preview statement is typically positioned at the very end of the introduction of a critical essay. It may even be the final paragraph of the introduction, if the critic provides a sentence (or two) to describe each section of the critical essay. The preview statement reflects the organization of the essay, and may use listing words such as "first," "next," and "finally."

For example, David R. Coon presented the following preview statement in his critical essay examining the material aspects of *Alias* and *24*. (See Chapter 11.)

> I begin my analysis with the primary sets used in *24* and *Alias*, paying particular attention to the ways that these sets establish the series within the genre of espionage dramas, and to the ways that they establish a particular set of gendered relationships. I then move to an examination of broader special concepts, showing how the two series negotiated the boundaries between the domestic sphere and the professional sphere. I argue that the ideologies of gender and work in both *24* and *Alias* are clearly expressed through the design and use of physical and conceptual spaces.[8]

Coon begins his preview statement very directly, announcing that the body of his essay will begin by analyzing his texts in light of the literature on espionage dramas. Next, he says, he will focus on the gendered aspects of the material sets of his texts. The next sentence indicates that he will have another section in the body of his essay (and indeed, he does) that focuses on the way these sets differentiate between domestic and professional space. The last sentence in his preview statement is a restatement of his thesis. Because the preview statement is typically the last paragraph in the introduction, a critic might end the preview statement with a restatement of the thesis, to remind readers of the main point as they transition into the body of the essay.

Richard D. Pineda and Stacey K. Sowards's analysis of how flag waving functions as a visual argument (see Chapter 10), presents a more compact preview statement:

> In what follows, we explore the literature relating to visual argument and then explain how flag waving functions as visual argument for two audiences: immigrant rights advocates and anti-immigration advocates. We conclude with some observations about what flag waving means for cultural citizenship and the study of visual arguments.[9]

Pineda and Sowards begin their preview statement by signaling that the first section of their essay will be a literature review. Then, in the same sentence, they signal that their analysis will have two parts: one part focused on immigration rights advocates and the other on anti-immigration advocates. The second sentence previews the conclusion of their critical essay.

LITERATURE REVIEW

A literature review is a part of a critical essay in which the critic succinctly outlines the scholarship regarding the concepts and arguments with which the research engages. (See Chapter 2.) Although critics often analyze texts that no other rhetorical critics have ever analyzed, they do so by building on concepts, theories, and arguments that other critics and theorists developed. Consequently, each newly developed critical essay builds upon the groundwork laid by prior scholars. Metaphorically speaking, then, rather than reinvent the wheel, the critic cites the scholars who invented wheels and then builds a Ferrari on top of those wheels. The purpose of a literature review is to (1) define for your readers the important concepts your analysis is going to use; (2) catch your readers up on the relevant scholarly arguments that have already been established so you do not have to re-prove those arguments in your own critical essay; and (3) join a scholarly conversation.

In many critical essays, the critic dedicates a whole section to this review of the literature. This section is typically placed after the introduction but before the analysis. In my own critical essay comparing and contrasting different commencement addresses given by famously feminist women, I used a heading titled "Feminist Commencement Addresses" to mark the beginning of a literature review section in which I reviewed how other scholars had conceptualized commencement addresses as well as feminism.[10] This section was directly after the introduction, but before the analysis.

Not all critical essays have stand-alone literature review sections. Occasionally, a critic will sprinkle some review of scholarly concepts and arguments in the introduction and some more review of scholarly concepts and arguments throughout the analysis section. Alternatively, a critic might build two different literature review sections, and so on. If you are writing a critical essay as a course assignment, review the syllabus and assignment description/rubric to see whether your instructor has clearly stipulated that your essay should have a stand-alone literature review section. If the course documentation does not clearly answer this question, ask your instructor. If you are writing this critical essay for submission to a scholarly journal, scan through the articles in the most recent two issues from that journal to see whether recently published critical essays featured stand-alone literature review sections. If essays in this journal are typically organized this way, I recommend you organize yours that way, too.

A good literature review avoids summarizing other scholars' entire critical essays and avoids multiple or lengthy block quotes. Instead, the literature review maintains the critic's authorial voice. That is, you are the author of your critical essay. The whole essay—including the literature review section—should be geared toward your argument.

For example, consider how critics Suzanne M. Enck and Blake A. McDaniel cited other scholars in their analysis of Eminem and Rhianna's music video, *Love the Way You Lie:*

> The importance of studying the genre of hip-hop has been well-rehearsed by a wide array of cultural critics (see, e.g., Dyson, 2007; Kitwana, 2003; Rose, 1994, 2008). As Alan Light (2004) contends, "rap is unarguably the most culturally significant style in pop, the genre that speaks most directly to and for its audience, full of complications, contradictions, and confusion" (p. 138) . . . . For a generation of younger adults who often lack voice in the dominant political spheres, rap becomes one venue for negotiating some of life's most significant tensions, especially with regard to issues of identity, ideology, and agency.[11*]

In the first two sentences, Enck and McDaniel have cited five different scholarly publications. Notably, they did not need to quote directly in their first sentence.

---

*Reprinted from Suzanne Marie Enck and Blake A. McDaniel, "Playing with Fire: Cycles of Domestic Violence in Eminem and Rihanna's 'Love the Way You Lie,'" *Communication, Culture & Critique* 5, no. 4 (2012) by permission of Oxford University Press on behalf of the International Communication Association.

They read the scholarship by Dyson, Kitwana, and Rose, then offered their readers a summary statement: all these scholars agree that hip-hop is important. Then, using a direct quotation from Alan Light, Enck and McDaniel specified why hip-hop/rap is important to our culture. Light's quotation emphasizes that rap speaks to and for the audience, voicing our cultural conflicts.

For the sake of brevity, I omitted part of this paragraph; however, throughout the paragraph, Enck and McDaniel maintain their authorial voice. That is, they are making their argument and summarizing others' scholarship in order to substantiate their own argument. They avoid spending a paragraph explaining Dyson's research and then another paragraph explaining Kitwana's, and then two more paragraphs for Rose's research projects. Instead, they group four citations together in the first sentence of the paragraph. If their readers want to know the details of these other scholars' research projects, they can use the bibliographic entries at the end of the essay to locate and read those works. As a result, Enck and McDaniel do not need to provide full summaries of these scholars' critical essays; they can simply provide an accurate summary statement (all these scholars agree hip-hop is important) and then move on to their own argument.

Enck and McDaniel conclude this paragraph by summarizing the prior scholarship in a way that directly links it to their own argument regarding *Love the Way You Lie.* The final sentence in the paragraph emphasizes how young adults use rap to negotiate difficult life situations and conceptualize their own identities. Using this sentence as a transition, Enck and McDaniel then begin a new paragraph regarding how *Love the Way You Lie* portrays the difficult tensions of love, violence, abuse, and identity.

Ultimately, Enck and McDaniel build on the scholarship they cite. The concepts and arguments they present in the literature review are directly relevant to their argument, and they make that link explicit in their transition sentence. They do not let the prior scholarship upstage their argument even during the literature review. Instead, they cite prior research in order to build their own argument, but keep the focus on their own analysis. In so doing, they accomplish three specific things. First, they substantiate the relevance of studying the music video *Love the Way You Lie.* Second, by citing these scholars, they build upon their arguments rather than having to reinvent them. They don't have to prove to readers that hip-hop matters; they can just point to these other scholars' proof. And third, they have joined the scholarly conversation about hip-hop/rap.

As you draft your literature review section(s), keep these ideas in mind:

1. Other scholars' ideas, concepts, terminology, and so on must be represented accurately.
2. Most paragraphs in your literature review section(s) should begin and end with a sentence that contains only (or almost only) your own words. The idea is to begin and end each paragraph with your ideas, your argument.
3. Rather than quoting lengthy sentences, whole sentences, or entire passages from your sources, consider how to summarize and paraphrase your sources, as Enck and McDaniel did in their first sentence. Aim to quote only an important word or short phrase from a source and weave it seamlessly into your own sentence.

4. After drafting your literature review section(s), read through your own writing and make sure your paragraphs are not dedicated to explaining other scholars' work. The idea is to explain and build on their salient ideas, not summarize their entire research.
5. Ultimately, your literature review section(s) should summarize the key concepts that others have developed in service of your argument.

CITATIONS

Throughout your critical essay, you will use information, concepts, and ideas that you have gleaned from other scholars' writings, as well as from popular culture sources such as news reports and websites. You will also provide evidence from your text itself. When you do these things, you must use citations in order give credit where credit is due (and thus avoid plagiarizing), as well as to let your readers know where to locate your source material so they can further explore the information, concepts, ideas, or evidence to which you refer.

When you directly quote from someone else's work, you need to put the quoted material inside quotation marks (or longer quotations in block quotes, indented but omitting quotation marks) and then use parenthetical citations or endnote citations, according to the citation style you are using. Similarly, any time you use information, concepts, ideas, or evidence that you paraphrase from someone else's work, you need to parenthetically cite that work. There are many citation styles, but rhetorical criticism typically uses one of the following three: the Modern Language Association's citation style (known as MLA), the American Psychological Association's citation format (known as APA), and the *Chicago Manual of Style* (known as *Chicago* or *CMOS*). The MLA and APA styles both use parenthetical citations combined with a list of "works cited." *Chicago* style uses endnotes for writing in the humanities. These citations allow readers to know where you got the words you quote and enables readers to look up the original authors' work.

After the conclusion of your critical essay, if you are using MLA or APA, you should place the full bibliographic entries in an alphabetized list that includes all the sources you have directly quoted or paraphrased, or from which you have otherwise used information. If you are using *Chicago* style, the full bibliographic entry is placed in the first note for that source; subsequent notes referring to that source use abbreviated bibliographic entries.

If you are writing a critical essay as a course assignment, review the syllabus and assignment description/rubric to see whether your instructor has stipulated which citation style your essay should use. If the course documentation does not clearly answer this question, ask your instructor. If you are writing this critical essay for submission to a scholarly journal, review the website for that journal—especially the "instructions for authors" page—to learn which citation style that journal prefers.

To learn how to cite your sources correctly, I recommend you use Purdue University's citation resource. Simply type "Purdue OWL" into an Internet search bar. The search results will link you to a website where you will be able to access what is known as the Purdue Online Writing Lab (OWL). Here, you will find detailed instructions for how to cite your sources using MLA, APA, or *Chicago* style. The librarians at your institution and your institution's library website will likely also be able to help you learn to cite your sources correctly.

NOTES

1. Kathryn M. Olson, "Violence in Disney's *Beauty and the Beast:* Inter-Generational Lessons in Romanticizing and Tolerating Intimate Partner Violence," *Quarterly Journal of Speech* 99, no. 4 (2013): 448–480.
2. Olson, "Violence," 450.
3. Olson, "Violence," 465–466.
4. Olson, "Violence," 465–466.
5. Olson, "Violence," 466.
6. Leroy G. Dorsey and Rachel M. Harlow, "'We Want Americans Pure and Simple': Theodore Roosevelt and the Myth of Americanism," *Rhetoric & Public Affairs* 6, no. 1 (2003): 55–78
7. Theon E. Hill, "Sanitizing the Struggle: Barack Obama, Selma, and Civil Rights Memory," *Communication Quarterly* 65, no. 3 (2017): 354–376.
8. David R. Coon, "Putting Women in Their Place: Gender, Space, and Power in *24* and *Alias,*" *Feminist Media Studies* 11, no. 2 (2011): 232.
9. Richard D. Pineda and Stacey K. Sowards, "Flag Waving as Visual Argument: 2006 Immigration Demonstrations and Cultural Citizenship," *Argumentation and Advocacy* 43, no. 3–4 (2007): 164–174.
10. Sarah Kornfield, "Speaking in the Language of White Women: Second- and Third-Wave Metaphors," *Women & Language* 41, no. 2 (2018): 123–128.
11. Suzanne Marie Enck and Blake A. McDaniel, "Playing with Fire: Cycles of Domestic Violence in Eminem and Rihanna's 'Love the Way You Lie,'" *Communication, Culture & Critique* 5, no. 4 (2012): 621.

Appendix B

Analyzing a Single Text or Multiple Texts

Some texts—such as films or speeches—seem like single, discrete entities. These texts seem to have clear boundaries: A speech starts when a speaker steps up to the podium and ends on the final word. A film starts when the title sequence begins and ends when the credits roll.

To some extent, however, the "singularity" or "discreteness" of such a text is a figment of the imagination. After all, the speech might have been presented by the speaker but written by a team of speechwriters; it might quote from prior speeches, films, novels, or scriptures; it might be the "speech" version of an idea the rhetor has also written a book about; it might be an autobiography of the speaker's life. Similarly, a film might be based on a novel; it might be a sequel—or spawn any number of sequels; it might be produced by a director who is famous for a particular approach to filmography; it might star an actor so famous for a different role, audiences cannot shake the memory while watching this film; it might participate in a larger genre.

Moreover, some texts seem like single entities (such as a television series, a story arc within a television series, or an ad campaign), but are also clearly diffused into multiple entities (a sequence of episodes, a number of advertisements, and so on). Critics exercise their own authority and artistry as they analyze such texts. The critic decides where the text starts and stops, what counts as part of a single text, and what lies outside of it.

Other texts are clearly multiple texts, such as policy speeches on a given topic, a genre of films, a metaphor that recurs across popular culture, an array of campaign paraphernalia, or a comparison of narratives in two different television series. When analyzing multiple texts, critics exercise their own authority and artistry as they group disparate texts together, arguing that specific symbolic actions become visible in the simultaneous analysis of the texts. Whether analyzing one text or multiple texts for analysis, a critic must justify the textual selection and demonstrate that the evidence was not cherry-picked.

JUSTIFYING A TEXT SELECTION

At the most general level, rhetorical critics typically make arguments about *what* a text does, *how* it accomplishes that, and ultimately, *why* it matters. Certainly plenty of texts do not merit rhetorical analysis. Some texts do not have enough of an audience: what they do and how they do it generally does not matter because their audiences are so small. Other texts typically do not warrant rhetorical analysis because the action they seek to accomplish in society—what they invite their audiences to think, feel, believe, and ultimately do—is so minor or ubiquitous that there is no point in studying them. Still other texts do not typically warrant rhetorical analysis because they are so obvious in their symbolic action: they do not need rhetorical analysis because anyone who experiences the text understands its desired symbolic action and the ways in which it seeks to accomplish that action.

When making an argument about what a text does, how it does that, and why it matters, a critic must first substantiate that the text is worth studying. Typically, the critic does this in the introduction of the critical analysis. (See Chapter 2.) There are many ways to justify the selection of a text, but the strategies for justifying a single text versus those for justifying the selection of multiple texts are somewhat different.

Justifying the Selection of a Single Text

When justifying the selection of what a critic presents as a single text, a critic will often argue that the text is influential, popular, or uniquely adroit in its arts of address, or a representative example of a specific type of rhetoric. For instance, rhetorical critic Stephen Howard Browne justified his choice to analyze George Washington's first inaugural address—the first inaugural address in US history—by noting that Article II, Section 1, of the United States Constitution provides very little explanation of the role of the president. Browne notes that the founders were deeply divided over the question of how to balance the "competing claims of" infusing the presidency with enough power to get things done, yet simultaneously safeguarding American liberty so as not to recreate a monarchy or dictatorship.[1] Given the fledgling country's deep concerns over what the presidency should be, and given the lack of clarification in the Constitution, Browne argues that it fell to George Washington to create the role of the presidency—which he did in his inaugural address, as he told the US citizenry (and the surrounding nations) what his role as president would be—and, more broadly, what our federal government would be. Essentially, Browne justifies his selection of this text by claiming that it is *influential* because it created the role of the presidency, a role with which every subsequent president has had to contend. In addition, Browne's larger argument is that Washington's words made the presidency what we know it to be: that rhetoric makes things—real things like governments, that words act in society, that deeds are done in words.

When analyzing texts of national impact, such as presidential speeches, it can be fairly straightforward to argue that their influence justifies their selection. Such texts quite clearly act in society. Many texts, however, are not so influential, requiring critics to justify their selections much more rigorously. For example, I selected an episode from *I Dream of Jeannie* as my text for a critical analysis. One of my goals was to study how 1960s entertainment media portrayed feminism (known then as the women's liberation movement). I justified my textual section of a single episode in the following way:

> I selected "The Americanization of Jeannie" on the basis of four criteria. The first two criteria, (1) that the episode was popularly received when originally aired in the 1960s and (2) that the episode has continued cultural significance in the U.S., limited the selection to classic Americana television series. Not wanting to isolate an episode that deals with themes its larger series rarely invokes, the third criterion was that the series, as a whole, deal with gender issues. This criterion essentially limited the possibilities to *Bewitched* or *I Dream of Jeannie*. Finally, the fourth criterion was that the episode directly represents the women's liberation movement. This requires that the episode goes beyond staging a gendered conflict (where, for example, a housewife decides to start a job outside the home), to create a plotline in which the characters directly talk about and participate in women's liberation. As such, I selected "The Americanization of Jeannie" because it directly represents the feminist movement as Jeannie reads a feminist "how to" article in a magazine, sets about becoming an emancipated, modern, American woman—and comedy ensues.[2]

Ultimately, I justified my selection of this episode of *I Dream of Jeannie* by arguing that it was a particularly robust example of how entertainment media portrayed feminism during the 1960s. I argued that this episode *represented* the 1960s approach to portraying feminism in media entertainment.

Justifying the Selection of Multiple Texts

When critics analyze multiple texts, they are less likely to have chosen shockingly popular texts, prestigiously influential texts, or texts that are unique in their rhetorical approaches. Indeed, a critic who was working with such texts would likely do a single-text analysis in order to devote the entirety of the research to that one text. A critic rarely justifies analyzing multiple texts by claiming that the popularity, influence, or unique strategies of the texts warrant analysis; however, the critic might claim the texts are representative of a certain type of rhetoric or that the ubiquity of the texts justifies analysis.

For example, in my analysis of Ursula Le Guin's 1983 and Sheryl Sandburg's 2011 commencement addresses to all-women's colleges, I justified my selection of these speeches by positioning them as representative of how popular White feminists—in their respective decades—spoke about feminism to audiences they assumed would be mostly women and mostly White.[3] I had tried for some time to publish an analysis of only Ursula Le Guin's commencement speech, justifying my selection of this text based on its uniquely adroit rhetoric. The speech is strangely moving. I was unable, however, to persuade reviewers that the speech warranted our scholarly attention; reviewers pointed out that although the speech was uniquely adroit in its rhetoric, I had failed to demonstrate the relevance of those unique rhetorical techniques for contemporary readers. Essentially, reviewers told me that I had yet to explain why the text and its action mattered. To rectify this problem, I put Le Guin's speech into comparison with Sheryl Sandburg's 2011 commencement address, and was thus able to compare and contrast the metaphors surrounding feminism in these speeches. Then, positioning the speeches as representative of their decades, I argued that they mattered to contemporary readers because studying them allowed us to understand changes in White feminist metaphors over time.

Alternatively, when analyzing multiple texts, critics can often demonstrate why those texts matter—and thus justify their textual selections—by pointing to the ubiquitous nature of those texts. Here, critics make the opposite argument than one would use to justify working with a single text. Instead of claiming a text is singularly influential, outrageously popular, or unique in its rhetorical techniques, critics claim that their texts are everywhere, permeating and saturating our society. The idea is that although any one of the texts may be irrelevant, the aggregate of them matters. For instance, although any given episode of crime TV is fairly irrelevant in contemporary society, the continued persistence of this genre in the US entertainment landscape matters.

Emily Martin justified her textual selection in this way when analyzing the metaphors surrounding eggs and sperm in biology textbooks and scientific research publications.[4] (See Chapter 6.) No particular textbook mattered; no singular metaphor mattered. What mattered was the aggregate—the accumulation—of particular (sexist) metaphors and their proliferation across the whole of biological textbooks and scientific discourse regarding reproduction.

Rhetorical critic Karrin Vasby Anderson made a similar argument when analyzing the campaign discourse surrounding the female candidates—Sarah Palin and Hillary Clinton—in the 2008 presidential campaign.[5] She collected a wide variety of texts from a wide variety of sources, from campaign T-shirts to political cartoons, *Saturday Night Live* skits, photoshopped memes, toy action figures, Super PAC names, and a variety of other texts. Had she sought to study just one of these texts, she likely could not have demonstrated that it mattered. Many of her texts would have had only small audiences. Many were incredibly obvious in their symbolic action: one need not work too hard to understand the patriotic sex appeal of a meme in which a picture of Palin's head was photoshopped onto the picture of a woman "clad in a U.S. flag bikini" and holding a rifle.[6] By collecting these texts and analyzing them *en masse*, however, Vasby Anderson was able to reveal how sexist discourse (both linguistic and visual) has permeated our presidential campaigns—on both the Right and the Left.

Ultimately, when studying a single text or multiple texts, critics must be able to substantiate what their texts do in society, how they do it, and why that matters. When studying only one text (or what a critic presents to readers as a discrete entity), a critic typically relies on arguments that foreground the influence, popularity, uniquely adroit arts of address, or representativeness of the text for a specific type of rhetoric. When studying multiple texts, a critic might argue that the texts are representative of a specific type (or era) of rhetoric, or that the ubiquity of the texts—their very commonplaceness—renders them relevant.

AVOIDING CHERRY-PICKING YOUR EVIDENCE

Cherry-picking is selecting only the evidence that fits your claim and ignoring all the evidence that would contradict your claim. For instance, a cherry-picking critic might argue that *Game of Thrones* presents a feminist narrative by focusing on textual evidence in which the female characters are portrayed as powerful rulers and mighty warriors—and ignoring the scenes and story arcs in which women are sexually objectified, sexually abused, and enslaved. Another cherry-picking critic could argue the exact opposite (that *Game of Thrones* presents a sexist narrative) by focusing on the sexual objectification, sexual abuse, and enslavement of women while ignoring the portrayals of women as powerful rulers and mighty warriors. Both arguments would be unpersuasive to anyone who had even passing familiarity with *Game of Thrones,* because both critics ignored important aspects of the text.

Whether analyzing a single text or multiple texts, critics ought to work with the supposition that half their readers are familiar with their texts. This supposition keeps critics from ignoring relevant aspects of their texts, because they know half their readers will say, "but what about . . . ?" On the other hand, critics must provide sufficient summaries and overarching descriptions of their texts so that the other half of their readers—those who have never experienced the texts—will still understand their arguments.

Many texts have contrasting aspects. For example, *Game of Thrones* has characters that seem fairly feminist and narrative arcs that seem fairly sexist. When analyzing a conflicted text, a critic must address the conflicting elements—especially if the argument pertains to a conflicted aspect within the text. Failing to mention that the text offers conflicting elements that lead toward different symbolic actions is the very essence of cherry-picking. This does not mean that critics should just throw up their hands and say "well, it's complicated!" without rendering judgment on conflicted texts. If a critic has the textual evidence to support an argument that the text ultimately endorses one side of the conflict over the other, the critic should make that argument—but show both aspects of the text and demonstrate how one aspect is more prominent than the other.

Cherry-Picking and the Single Text

To make persuasive arguments, critics must not only avoid cherry-picking their evidence but also present their textual evidence in such a way that it is clear they did not cherry-pick. When working with a single text—or what the critic presents as a discrete entity—a critic typically offers a summary description of the text early in the essay and then presents so much evidence from the text in the analysis section that readers are generally satisfied the argument does not rest on cherry-picked evidence.

Returning to Stephen Howard Browne's analysis of George Washington's first inaugural speech, for example, we can see how Browne offers a summary description of his text. He informs readers that "the speech is fairly brief, at a little less than 1,500 words" and that it is "arranged into six paragraphs."[7] The speech, he continues, was cowritten by George Washington and James Madison, and is "clear, direct, and formal" in its language use.[8] Browne then summarizes the content of the speech. First, he notes that the whole speech is concerned with the topic of virtue—specifically the type of virtue the role of the presidency requires.[9] Then, he walks readers through the content of the speech's six paragraphs, noting that the speech starts by explaining Washington's virtue, then invokes God as an aid to virtue, then turns to an interpretation of the Constitution, then to a description of the audience's virtue, and finally, ties all of these elements (Washington, God, the Constitution, and citizens) together to present a rationale for republican government and the president's role within it.[10]

In his summary, Browne offers a full description of the text: its length, organization, rhetorship, style, and content. Such a description helps readers understand the nature of the text before they start seeing glimpses of it in the analysis sections. It also gives readers a "bird's eye" view of the text so they can know the textual evidence presented in the following analysis sections is reflective of the whole text.

Then, in the analysis section, Browne presents lengthy block quotes from Washington's speech. Readers see almost the entirety of this short speech as they read the analysis: clearly, Browne does not cherry-pick. The choice to present block quotes is well suited to this text: a short, old speech. Readers need to feel the rhythms of what (to our modern ears) sound like unusual sentences in order to fully understand their symbolic action. And because the speech is short, Browne can show most of it by using block quotes. Although I would not universally recommend critics present block quotes of textual evidence, it can be an effective approach with some texts.

Regardless of how they present their textual evidence, a critic who analyzes a single text ought to show readers a considerable portion of the text in the analysis. For small-sized texts (short speeches, one TV episode, an advertisement, a poster, a music video, a statue, and so on), a critic may be able to describe and directly quote from most of the text. Indeed, when analyzing a small text, a critic usually assesses the entirety of the text in the analysis section.

For a larger single text (a lengthy speech, a film, a video game, a novel, a museum, and so on), a critic will likely have to choose which parts of the text to summarize and which parts to fully analyze. For instance, the critic might describe a film early in the essay, acknowledging that a subplot occurs within the main plot but then explaining why the analysis section will focus on the main plot. The analysis would then focus on presenting textual evidence from the main plot while basically ignoring the subplot. The critic avoids cherry-picking by acknowledging that other parts of the text exist, summarizing them, and in the process demonstrating that they have no bearing on the argument.

For example, Rachel E. Dubrofsky and Emily D. Ryalls open their critical essay on *The Hunger Games* (Chapter 10) by explaining the popularity of the film, then explore the idea of "authenticity" and how the characters, constantly under surveillance, perform for the cameras. Next, they present their thesis statement—that Katniss's seeming "authenticity" (the way she "performs not-performing") renders her "heroic" in the eyes of the surveillance cameras.[11] This equation of her performances with "authenticity" and thus "heroism" is, however, grounded in cultural assumptions about femininity and Whiteness.[12]

Following the introduction, Dubrofsky and Ryalls offer a section (titled "The Hunger Games") in which they present three paragraphs that summarize the narrative of the film. They then move into a literature review on authenticity and surveillance, followed by their analysis section, which they present in two subsections: one focused on femininity and the other on Whiteness. The analysis need not address the full film because they have already faithfully summarized it; their argument is specifically about authenticity/surveillance and White femininity in *The Hunger Games.*

Cherry-Picking and Multiple Texts

When analyzing multiple texts, it is simply impossible to provide an individual summary of every text and also present textual evidence from most of each text. For instance, I have published several articles in which I contrast multiple crime series.[13] In these articles, not only am I analyzing multiple episodes, I am analyzing multiple episodes from multiple series. I cannot summarize each series individually and present textual evidence from each scene of each episode from each series without radically overshooting my publication page limit and boring my readers to tears.

Critics must demonstrate, however, that they are not cherry-picking their evidence when they are analyzing multiple texts. To do so, they typically build on the justification of the textual selections. Typically, a critic argues that the cohort of texts is representative of or demonstrates the ubiquity of a type of rhetoric. Thus, critics can summarize the texts *en masse* by demonstrating what they have in common—their type of rhetoric—rather than presenting a separate summary for each text. For instance, I can summarize hundreds of crime series episodes by explaining that they each open with a corpse, proceed with an investigation, and conclude with a conviction. With this foundational summary in place, I can focus the analysis section on the aspects of these crime dramas that pertain to my specific argument. When analyzing a set of speeches, films, television series, novels, music videos, advertisements, and so on, a critic can offer an overarching summary that presents readers with the basic structure of the type of rhetoric that the selected texts represent.

Not all analyses focus on just one type of text, however. Karrin Vasby Anderson's analysis of the 2008 campaign discourse surrounding Sarah Palin and Hillary Clinton, for example, provides a clear demonstration of how to work with texts from a wide variety of sources. Vasby Anderson studied political cartoons, *Saturday Night Live* skits, campaign T-shirts, and other types of texts. She could not simply summarize what political cartoons are like, or the key features of *Saturday Night Live* skits, yet her texts were still examples demonstrating the ubiquity of a certain type of text: sexist political discourse. She summarizes what sexist political discourse is like in the opening pages of her article, specifically focusing on what she describes as "pornified" discourse—sexist discourse that uses sexualized imagery, vocabulary, and narratives drawn from the genre of pornography. Then, in her analysis, she demonstrates how each text features this "pornified" imagery, vocabulary, or narrative structure.

Whether working with a singular text or with multiple texts, the critic must offer readers a summary of the text (or type of texts), and present compelling textual evidence from the text or texts. How much is summarized and how much is presented as textual evidence will vary from analysis to analysis. Yet critics must faithfully offer their texts to their readers, providing them with enough text to satisfy them that the argument is not supported merely by cherry-picked evidence.

NOTES

1. Stephen Howard Browne, "'Sacred Fire of Liberty': The Constitutional Origins of Washington's First Inaugural Address," *Rhetoric & Public Affairs* 19, no. 3 (2016): 399.
2. Sarah Kornfield, "The E-man-ci-pation of Jeannie: Feminist Doppelgangers on U.S. Television," *Communication, Culture & Critique* 5, no. 3 (2012): 446–447.
3. Sarah Kornfield, "Speaking in the Language of White Women: Second-and Third-Wave Metaphors," *Women & Language* 41, no. 2 (2018): 123–128.
4. Emily Martin, "The Egg and the Sperm: How Science has Constructed a Romance Based on Stereotypical Male-Female Roles," *Signs* 16, no. 3 (1991): 485–501.
5. Karrin Vasby Anderson, "'Rhymes with Blunt': Pornification and U.S. Political Culture," *Rhetoric & Public Affairs* 14, no. 2 (2011): 327–368.
6. Vasby Anderson, "Rhymes with Blunt," 338.
7. Browne, "'Sacred Fire of Liberty,'" 407.
8. Browne, "'Sacred Fire of Liberty,'" 407–408.
9. Browne, "'Sacred Fire of Liberty,'" 407
10. Browne, "'Sacred Fire of Liberty,'" 409.
11. Rachel E. Dubrofsky and Emily D. Ryalls, "The Hunger Games: Performing Not-performing to Authenticate Femininity and Whiteness," *Critical Studies in Media Communication* 31, no. 5 (2014): 398.
12. Dubrofsky and Ryalls, "The Hunger Games," 398.
13. Sarah Kornfield, "Re-solving Crimes: A Cycle of TV Detective Partnerships," in *Multiplicities: Cycles, Sequels, Remakes and Reboots in Film & Television,* eds. Amanda Klein and R. Barton Palmer (Austin: University of Texas Press, 2016), 202–221; Sarah Kornfield, "Detecting Fatherhood: The 'New' Masculinity in Primetime Crime Dramas," in *Deconstructing Dads: Changing Images of Fathers in Popular Culture,* eds. Laura Tropp and Janice Kelly (New York: Lexington, 2016), 117–142; Sarah Kornfield, "Pregnant Discourse: 'Having It All' while Domestic and Potentially Disabled," *Women's Studies in Communication* 37, no. 2 (2014): 181–201; Sarah Kornfield, "Televisual Pregnancy Beauty," *Feminist Media Studies* 19, no. 2 (2019): 163–178.

Credits and Acknowledgments

Pages 283 and 284 are an extension of the copyright page.

Grateful acknowledgment is made for permission to use the following:

Excerpts on pages 29–31 and 34 from Thomas Benson, "The Rhetorical Structure of Frederick Wiseman's *High School*," *Communication Monographs* 47, no. 4 (1980), copyright © National Communication Association, reprinted by permission of Informa UK Limited, trading as Taylor & Francis Group, www.tandfonline.com on behalf of The National Communication Association.

Excerpts on pages 141 and142 from Edwin Black, "The Second Persona," *The Quarterly Journal of Speech* 56, no. 2 (1970), copyright © National Communication Association, reprinted by permission of Informa UK Limited, trading as Taylor & Francis Group, www.tandfonline.com on behalf of The National Communication Association.

Excerpts on pages 31–33 from Karlyn Kohrs Campbell, "Stanton's 'The Solitude of Self': A Rationale for Feminism," *Quarterly Journal of Speech* 66, no. 3 (1980), copyright © National Communication Association, reprinted by permission of Informa UK Limited, trading as Taylor & Francis Group, www.tandfonline.com on behalf of National Communication Association.

Excerpts on pages 254, 255, and 269 from David R. Coon, "Putting Women in Their Place: Gender, Space, and Power in *24* and *Alias*," *Feminist Media Studies* 11, no. 2 (2011), reprinted by permission of Taylor & Francis Ltd, http://www.tandfonline.com.

Excerpts from Emily Dickinson, "The Lightning is a yellow Fork" (1140) on page 109 and "I dwell in Possibility—" (466) on page 115, are reprinted by permission from THE POEMS OF EMILY DICKINSON: READING EDITION, edited by Ralph W. Franklin, Cambridge, Mass.: The Belknap Press of Harvard University Press, Copyright © 1998, 1999 by the President and Fellows of Harvard College. Copyright © 1951, 1955 by the President and Fellows of Harvard College. Copyright © renewed 1979, 1983 by the President and Fellows of Harvard College. Copyright © 1914, 1918, 1919, 1924, 1929, 1930, 1932, 1935, 1937, 1942 by Martha Dickinson Bianchi. Copyright © 1952, 1957, 1958, 1963, 1965 by Mary L. Hampson.

Excerpts on pages 229, 230, and 280 from Rachel E. Dubrofsky and Emily D. Ryalls, "*The Hunger Games:* Performing Not-Performing to Authenticate Femininity and Whiteness," *Critical Studies in Media Communication* 31, no. 5 (2014), copyright © National Communication Association, reprinted by permission of Informa UK Limited, trading as Taylor & Francis Group, www.tandfonline.com on behalf of The National Communication Association.

Excerpts on pages 121–123 and 267 from Theon E. Hill, "Sanitizing the Struggle: Barack Obama, Selma, and Civil Rights Memory," *Communication Quarterly* 65, no. 3 (2017), reprinted by permission of Eastern Communication Association, www.ecasite.org and Taylor & Francis Ltd, http://www.tandfonline.com.

Excerpt on page 277 from Sarah Kornfield, "The E-man-ci-pation of Jeannie: Feminist Doppelgangers on U.S. Television," *Communication, Culture & Critique* (2012) 5, no. 3, 445–462, by permission of Oxford University Press on behalf of the International Communication Association.

Excerpts on pages 73–76 from Mollie Murphy and Tina M. Harris, "White Innocence and Black Subservience: The Rhetoric of White Heroism in *The Help*," *Howard Journal of Communications* 29, no. 1 (2018), reprinted by permission of Taylor & Francis Ltd, http://www.tandfonline.com.

Excerpts on pages 177, 178, 263, 264, and 266 from Kathryn M. Olson, "An Epideictic Dimension of Symbolic Violence in Disney's *Beauty and the Beast:* Inter-Generational Lessons in Romanticizing and Tolerating Intimate Partner Violence," *Quarterly Journal of Speech* 99, no. 4 (2013), copyright © National Communication Association, reprinted by permission of Informa UK Limited, trading as Taylor & Francis Group, www.tandfonline.com on behalf of The National Communication Association.

"Statement on the Death of John Allen Chau," Oral Roberts University, http://www.oru.edu/news/oru_news/20181121-john-chau-statement.php, reprinted by permission of Oral Roberts University.

Photo credits appear below the photos.

Index

About the Author

Sarah J. Kornfield is an associate professor of communication and an affiliated professor of women's and gender studies at Hope College, where she teaches courses in rhetorical criticism, rhetorical theory, gender communication, and television culture. She received her BA from Wheaton College (Illinois), her MA from Texas A&M University, and her PhD from the Pennsylvania State University.

Professor Kornfield's research has been published in *Rhetoric & Public Affairs; Critical Studies in Media Communication; Feminist Media Studies; Women's Studies in Communication; Women & Language; Communication, Culture & Critique; the Journal of Communication & Religion; the Journal of Broadcasting & Electronic Media;* and the *Journal of International and Intercultural Communication.*